Targeting Employment Services

Targeting Employment Services

Randall W. Eberts
Christopher J. O'Leary
Stephen A. Wandner
Editors

2002

W.E..Upjohn Institute for Employment Research
Kalamazoo, Michigan

Library of Congress Cataloging-in-Publication Data

Targeting employment services / Randall W. Eberts, Christopher
    J. O'Leary, Stephen A. Wandner, editors.
        p. cm.
    Proceedings from a conference held on April 29 to May 1,
    1999 in Kalamazoo, Michigan.
    Includes bibliographical references and index.
    ISBN 0-88099-244-1 (cloth : alk. paper) — ISBN 0-88099-243-3
    (pbk. : alk. paper)
        1. Unemployed—Services for—Government policy—United
    States—Congresses. 2. Employment agencies—United States
    —Management—Congresses. 3. Manpower policy—United States
    —Congresses.   I. Eberts, Randall W. II. O'Leary, Christopher
    J. III. Wandner, Stephen A.
HD5875.T37 2002
362.85′84′0973—dc21

                                                    2002024572

Cover design by Jan Underhill.
Index prepared by Nancy Humphreys.
Printed in the United States of America.

To our parents:

Dorothy and Harry Eberts

Rita and George O'Leary

Hilda and Irving Wandner

Contents

Preface

This volume includes the papers and proceedings of a conference on the topic of "Targeting Employment Services," which was held in Kalamazoo, Michigan, from April 29 to May 1, 1999. The conference was jointly sponsored by the W.E. Upjohn Institute for Employment Research and the U.S. Department of Labor. The aim of the conference was to review recent developments in targeting of employment services and to consider the possible application of targeting to other areas of employment policy. The conference comprised the presentation and discussion of research papers as well as panel discussions. Presenters, panelists, discussants, and attendees at the conference included a rich mix of scholars, practitioners, and policymakers. As editors of this conference volume, we have tried to ensure that the material is presented in a way that is accessible to a broad audience.

During the early 1990s in the United States, rising long-term unemployment and tight budgets for employment services combined to yield an interest in targeting employment policy expenditure to clients for whom the added benefit would be greatest. Field experiments sponsored by the U.S. Department of Labor suggested that early and intensive provision of job search assistance could reduce the risk of long-term joblessness, with the beneficial side effect of conserving unemployment insurance (UI) reserves. This led to a federal requirement in 1993 that states establish and operate Worker Profiling and Reemployment Services (WPRS) systems. WPRS requires UI beneficiaries who are not expecting recall to their prior job, and who are identified as potentially long-term unemployed, to receive job search assistance or risk losing their UI entitlement.

Worker "profiling" in WPRS was the first U.S. application of formal statistical models for targeting resources to employment policy. In most cases, the chapters in this book use the term "targeting" rather than the more familiar "profiling" for two main reasons. First, targeting is a more generic term that suggests both formal and informal approaches; that is, procedures that use either statistical or nonstatistical methods. Second, targeting is a more inclusive concept that covers both the selection and resource allocation process. Profiling, however, is popularly understood as only being part of a selection process.

This volume presents a comprehensive view of current knowledge on targeting employment services. Such a task would have been impossible by ourselves. We gratefully acknowledge the contributions of our talented group of chapter authors. A brief biographical statement about each author is provided at the back of this book. Following the conference, the chapters of this book were revised based on the comments of conference discussants. The text of discussants' comments are included after the chapters. We thank the discussants and other conference attendees for their constructive guidance for the authors. A complete list of conference attendees can be found at the back of this book.

The remarks of our panelists enlivened the conference and greatly add to the relevance of this book for our intended broad audience. As state and national policymakers, they presented diverse perspectives and helped to shape our understanding of the practicality of targeting employment services. We thank them for their contributions.

The conference was successful because of the generous contributions of many. In particular, we thank our speakers John Beverly and Jim Vollman, and our conference session chairs David Balducchi and Eric Johnson. We also thank the conference planning and event staff at the W.E. Upjohn Institute for Employment Research: Claire Black, Nancy Mack, and Phyllis Molhoek. Finally, for help in producing this book we thank Allison Hewitt Colosky, Kevin Hollenbeck, and David Nadziejka of the W.E. Upjohn Institute for Employment Research publications staff.

Views expressed are opinions of the chapter authors and do not necessarily reflect the positions or policy of the U.S. Department of Labor, the W.E. Upjohn Institute for Employment Research, or the trustees of the W.E. Upjohn Unemployment Trustee Corporation.

1

Targeting Employment Services under the Workforce Investment Act

Stephen A. Wandner
U.S. Department of Labor

The Workforce Investment Act (WIA) of 1998 changed the employment policy landscape in America. It reduced eligibility requirements for program participants, changed administrative relations among service delivery agencies, and refocused systems for performance accountability. Taken together, these features are expected to increase the volume of customers at local employment centers, require frontline service delivery staff to perform a multitude of new functions, and induce management to place an even greater emphasis on operational efficiency and program effectiveness. Since the resources of the workforce development system are limited, service referral must be judicious to achieve the greatest social return.

Under WIA, a premium is placed on serving customers effectively and efficiently. Consequently, frontline staff could benefit greatly from tools that help to quickly identify customers who would benefit the most from particular services. The administrative process by which individuals are selected to participate in programs may be referred to as "targeting."

Targeting can be thought of as a selection and allocation process in which a limited number of participants are selected from a broader pool of eligible customers. This selection process takes place in an environment where receipt of services is not an entitlement, and where the number of potential program participants greatly exceeds the resource capacity. Employment services targeting can be done in either a formal or an informal way. Targeting is either explicit or implicit. Whenever selection and allocation decisions are made, targeting is being done.

Traditionally, the process of selecting clients for program participation has been done informally; that is, without the aid of structured statistical models. Informal targeting can take many forms. Procedures followed at the local level depend on budget and administrative conditions, as well as on the information and assessment tools available to frontline workers in the workforce development system. The result may be a first come, first served approach. It may be done by purchasing blocks of services, and then finding customers to fill the available slots. It may also be done by an active outreach process, such as the use of rapid response teams that serve future dislocated workers before layoffs occur for large publicly known enterprises. In most cases, informal targeting is not systematic and uses little or no objective data to make program referral decisions. Informal targeting is frequently time-sensitive, seasonal, and driven by funding cycles.

Formal targeting involves having frontline staff in employment centers use targeting tools that are based on previously analyzed patterns of service receipt and reemployment success. Such statistics-based tools can provide frontline workers a guide to help make service referral decisions lead to better labor market outcomes. Targeting, using statistical profiling methods, has been recognized by the Organisation for Economic Co-operation and Development (OECD 1998) as an approach with broad application to the workforce development programs of industrial nations.

> Evidence on the effectiveness of active labor market policies . . . suggests that they should be well targeted to the needs of individual job seekers and the labor market, and that treatment should start as early as possible in the unemployment spell. But offering individual treatment along with early intervention would be very costly. There is thus a premium on accurately identifying job seekers at risk.
>
> The early identification of job seekers at risk of becoming long-term unemployed is a longstanding and basic endeavor of the public employment services (PES). Indeed, good judgment in this area forms part of the professional competence and work experience of PES staff. However, a few countries have gone further by introducing more formal methods of identifying at-risk job seek-

ers and laying out procedures on what to do with them. This is usually referred to as profiling and is used in this paper to cover the approach of i) the identification of individuals at risk of long-term unemployment; ii) the referral to various active labor market programs.

Such programs have been implemented on a nationwide basis in the United States and Australia and have received considerable developmental attention in Canada (Eberts and O'Leary 1997).

Under WIA, the need for targeting is greater than under its predecessor, the Job Training Partnership Act (JTPA). WIA service referral principles are summarized relative to those of JTPA in Table 1.1; specific citations from the acts are provided. WIA has established a hierarchy of services from core, to intensive, to training. Targeting could be useful to help determine which users of core services also may benefit from intensive services. A refined targeting tool could also help select which among the intensive services could most help the client, or whether training is appropriate.

Core services include eligibility determination, outreach, intake and orientation, initial assessment, job search assistance and placement assistance, and provision of information relating to labor market conditions, program performance, supportive and follow-up services, as well as the availability of unemployment insurance (UI) and welfare-to-work (WTW) programs. These services are available on a self-serve basis but frequently require staff assistance. Intensive reemployment services universally require staff assistance and include individual and group counseling, expanded job search workshops, service coordination assistance, and development of customer service plans. Training services may be either in occupational job skills, job search skills, remedial reading and mathematics, or on-the-job training.

When thinking about targeting under WIA, it is important to remember that current economic conditions do not remain stable forever. Although the United States experienced an unprecedented period of prosperity with low inflation in the 1990s, the business cycle has proven not to be dead. In periods of recession, statistical targeting methods are particularly useful.

While these methods are useful at all times for a selection process of choosing the right services for the right people, the resource allocation issue becomes more severe during recessions. As resources be-

Table 1.1 WIA Service Principles Relative to JTPA

Increased Reemployment Services Emphasis: The emphasis under WIA is promoting return to work. Relative to its predecessor, JTPA, the focus is less on training and more on searching for work first. Under JTPA, at least 50 percent of program funds had to be spent on training (JTPA, section 108(b)(4)(B)); WIA has no such requirement. The emphasis in WIA is using core services to get a job and moving to intensive services or training only if necessary to get a job.

Universal Access to Core Services: Section 134(d)(2) of WIA states that core services "shall be available to adults or dislocated workers, through the one-stop delivery system . . ." While there is universal access under WIA, eligibility was restricted under JTPA to participation of adults and dislocated workers found eligible under section 202(d)(1)(A) as economically disadvantaged adults or under section 301 as dislocated workers.

Targeting of Intensive Services: Receipt of intensive services under WIA depends upon the flow of customers from core services, as well as decisions by one-stop operators. Intensive services are open to adults and dislocated workers who are either "unemployed and are unable to obtain employment through core services" and "determined . . . to be in need of more intensive services . . . to obtain employment" or employed but are "determined by a one-stop operator to be in need of such intensive services . . ." (See WIA section 134(d)(3)(i) and (ii).)

Targeting of Training: Training is more broadly available, subject to one-stop operator decision making, under WIA for both adults and dislocated workers (section 134(d)(4)) than under JTPA. This broad availability of training must be coupled with the priority issue raised in WIA section 134(d)(4)(E): "In the event that funds . . . for adult employment and training activities . . . are limited, priority shall be given to recipients of public assistance and other low-income individuals for intensive services and training . . ."

Core Performance Measures: Although the core standards in JTPA section 106 and WIA section 136(b)(2)(A) appear fairly similar, WIA section 136 is far more developed and sophisticated. For example, there is a distinction under section 136(d)(2) about additional information that a state must include, such as retention and earnings received in unsubsidized employment 12 months after entry into employment (section 136(d)(2)(D)) and entry into unsubsidized employment related to training received (section 136(d)(2)(A)).

---

come relatively more limited in recessions and choices must be made among a much larger pool of potential customers, these statistical tools can be adjusted in their application over the business cycle.

The chapters of this book review U.S. experience with targeting reemployment services and self-employment assistance to UI beneficiaries most likely to exhaust benefits, suggest other employment programs that might benefit from targeting, examine Canadian efforts toward targeting reemployment services, and consider prospects for a new Frontline Decision Support System (FDSS) for one-stop centers. The remainder of this introductory chapter considers each of these in a bit more detail.

WORKER PROFILING AND REEMPLOYMENT SERVICES

In November 1993, the U.S. Congress enacted legislation that included provisions requiring each state to implement its own permanent Worker Profiling and Reemployment Services (WPRS) system. These systems identify likely dislocated UI claimants using statistical models and provide them with job search assistance during the early weeks of their unemployment. By law, a WPRS system must identify which claimants are likely to exhaust their regular UI entitlement and will need job search assistance services to make a successful transition to new employment. WPRS was operational in all states by early 1995. There is now more than five full years of experience with the operation of a national program.

The WPRS initiative was based on a large body of experimental research conducted by the states and the federal government (U.S. Department of Labor 1995; Meyer 1995; Corson and Decker 1996). That research suggested WPRS systems could be an effective and efficient way to speed dislocated workers back to productive employment. The U.S. Department of Labor (DOL) worked with a number of states to conduct a nationwide evaluation of WPRS with the goal of suggesting ways to improve the system (Dickinson, Kreutzer, and Decker 1997).

Implementation of WPRS systems in every state represented a large effort by the U.S. workforce development community, especially the UI, Wagner-Peyser, and Economic Dislocation and Worker Adjustment Assistance (EDWAA) programs.[1] Implementation has required the establishment of operational linkages between employment and training programs at the state and local levels of government. It also has required cooperation between local, state, and federal government entities. The WPRS initiative is making referrals to reemployment services at an annual rate of about 800,000 workers per year nationwide (Messenger, Schwartz, and Wandner 1999). This referral level represents about one-third of the more than two million workers who become dislocated each year.[2]

WPRS profiling is a two-step process to identify permanently separated workers with reemployment difficulty. First, permanently separated workers are identified by screening out two groups of workers: those subject to recall and/or those subject to union hiring hall agreements.[3] These workers must also be UI-eligible as demonstrated by the requirement that they receive a UI first benefit payment. Second, the likelihood of UI benefit exhaustion is predicted using a statistical model (Wandner 1997, 1998).

For most states the profiling referral model was developed using logit regression analysis applied to historical data from various state administrative records. The dependent variable in the model is usually a binary variable (i.e., a zero or a 1, depicting whether or not the worker exhausted all entitlement to UI benefits).[4] The profiling model estimates a probability of UI benefit exhaustion for individuals based on their individual characteristics and current labor market conditions. The variables in this model include education, job tenure, change in employment in previous industry, change in employment in previous occupation, and local unemployment rate.

Because of federal civil rights legislation, the states were prohibited from using certain variables as part of their profiling mechanisms, such as age, race/ethnic group, and gender. An analysis comparing results when including and omitting these variables indicated that the effect of this omission on the predictive power of the profiling model is generally very small.[5]

A few states profile based on characteristic screens alone. The process involves a small number of characteristics, each of which has a preset cutoff value or criterion. Individuals are selected if they meet the criteria for each screen used. A number of states that initially used characteristic screening have decided to convert to statistical models because statistical models have proven to be a more flexible and accurate targeting device for making referrals to reemployment services.

For each local workforce development office, UI claimants are ranked by their exhaustion probabilities—from high to low—to form the basis for referral to reemployment service providers. Staff members from the service providers work with referred customers to develop an individual service plan. There is a wide variation among states regarding the extent of services and the degree of individualization of each plan.

The WPRS evaluation (Dickinson, Kreutzer, and Decker 1997; Hawkins et al. 1996) found that states were successful in implementing their statistical profiling models, and the models successfully identified those UI claimants most likely to exhaust their UI benefits. States appear to be successfully determining service capacity for providing reemployment services.

The Department of Labor (DOL) has recommended that the states provide a comprehensive and intensive set of reemployment services, although all participants do not need and probably should not receive the same set of services. Rather, the focus should be on the development of an individual service plan for each referred worker—to meet the needs of the individual customer and to avoid an approach that would be "one size fits all" (U.S. Department of Labor 1994a, Field Memorandum 35-94).

Reemployment services can be provided by a number of different organizations, but the usual provider in most states is the Wagner-Peyser agency, the employment service. This choice is related to the history of workforce development programs. The employment service and UI were created as two interdependent programs in the 1930s and have been closely associated at state and local levels ever since. Nine out of 10 workforce development local offices around the country house both Wagner-Peyser and UI units.

In early 1998, DOL established a WPRS policy workgroup consisting of state and federal representatives. Based on the first three years of WPRS operation, the workgroup made seven recommendations in its final report (Messenger, Schwartz, and Wandner 1999).

1)   states should update their profiling models regularly,
2)   states should profile all claimants who file an initial claim,

3) states should accelerate their profiling and referral process to ensure early intervention,

4) states should improve reemployment services provided to profiled and referred claimants,

5) program linkages should be improved between Wagner-Peyser Act, JTPA Title III, and UI programs,

6) adequate funding should be devoted to providing more and better reemployment services through state WPRS systems, and

7) WPRS feedback and reporting systems should be improved.

An important consideration is that the state and federal governments need to devote more resources to reemployment services, because profiling, no matter how well implemented and targeted, cannot be effective unless substantial and effective reemployment services are provided to WPRS participants. The federal government responded in FY 1999 by providing $5.2 million in funding for innovative approaches to providing reemployment services to dislocated workers collecting UI and served by the WPRS system. More recently, Congress provided $35 million in both the FY 2001 and FY 2002 budgets to provide reemployment services to workers identified as in need by WPRS.

Part I of the book presents two chapters and a panel discussion that examine the WPRS system in some detail. Chapter 2, by Rob Olson, Marisa Kelso, Paul Decker, and Daniel Klepinger, considers the statistical modeling challenge of predicting who among UI recipients is most likely to exhaust their benefits. Chapter 3, by Katherine Dickinson, Paul Decker, and Suzanne Kreutzer, summarizes an evaluation of WPRS effects in a select group of states. Chapter 4 reports the panel discussion involving Pete Fleming, Al Jaloviar, Helen Parker, and Marc Perrett on the experience of federal and state policymakers with WPRS.

APPLICATIONS OF TARGETING METHODS

Part II of the book examines employment policy applications of targeting in the United States beyond the WPRS system. These include experience with targeting self-employment assistance, the possibility of targeting reemployment bonuses, optimal training choices for displaced workers, targeting welfare to work services, and possibilities for targeting job retention services for welfare recipients who have gained employment. Some background on these chapters follows.

Self-Employment

Outside of the WPRS system, targeting participants with a formal statistical model is now being done for only one other U.S. employment program: self-employment assistance (SEA). Indeed, states that have implemented SEA use exactly the same logit-based targeting model as is used for WPRS.

From 1990 to 1993, DOL ran SEA experiments in two states, Massachusetts and Washington. The experiment conducted in Massachusetts used a form of profiling to target participation. The profiling model for the experiment was different from the WPRS model, but it used similar variables to predict likely exhaustion of UI benefits. Profiling was also intended to assuage employer concerns that workers who were not permanently laid off by employers might otherwise be eligible for SEA.

Based on preliminary impact analysis results from the two SEA experiments available in mid 1993, a provision allowing states to establish SEA programs as part of their UI programs was enacted into federal law as part of Title V (transitional adjustment assistance) of the North American Free Trade Agreement (NAFTA) implementation act (Public Law 103-182, U.S. Department of Labor 1994b). Signed into law December 8, 1993, this provision allowed states the option of offering self-employment assistance to profiled UI claimants as an additional means of helping assist dislocated workers obtain new employment. However, SEA authorization was temporary and set to expire in December 1998 (Orr et al. 1994). The legislation was enacted because profiling was believed to target the program to appropriate participants, and because it was expected to have a neutral impact on the federal budget. Cost neutrality resulted from targeting offers to individuals who likely would have exhausted their UI benefit entitlements in the absence of the program.

After the temporary authorization for SEA under NAFTA, the final evaluation report on the SEA experiments in Massachusetts and Washington was completed and published by DOL in June 1995. Based on a three-year follow-up, offers in the Massachusetts SEA experiment increased participants' total time employed by nearly 1.9 months and increased net annual earnings by $5,940 over the three-year follow-up period. As a result, the final evaluation report recommended that ". . . SEA should be permanently incorporated into the U.S. employment security and economic development system" (Benus et al. 1995).

In accordance with the 1993 legislation, DOL conducted a review of the SEA program through 1996. All state programs used a WPRS model to target participation offers. Just as in the Massachusetts experiment, SEA is administered through UI and amounts to a work search waiver so that weekly UI payments continue while self-employment activity begins. Slightly more than 2,600 individuals participated in SEA programs during 1996 in the five states that had operational programs at that time (New York, Maine, Oregon, Delaware, and New Jersey). In addition, based on annual program outcome data submitted by New York, Oregon, Maine, and Delaware, over two-thirds of SEA program participants started their own businesses, and between 18 percent and 50 percent also worked in wage and salary employment (Vroman 1998).

The states with SEA programs wished to continue them beyond the sunset date in December 1998. New York, with the oldest and largest program, led the effort together with Pennsylvania, which had the newest program. Congress authorized a permanent SEA program in September 1998, and the bill was signed into law on October 28, 1998.

By 2001, eight states had developed and implemented SEA programs: New York, Maine, Oregon, Delaware, New Jersey, California, Maryland, and Pennsylvania (in order of program implementation). Most SEA programs remain small. Less than 1 percent of all UI recipients participate. All states require demonstration of the interest and ability to start and run a small business before granting SEA participation. The SEA programs have removed a barrier to self-employment in the UI law, and instead have actively supported eligible workers in making the transition from unemployment to self-employment.

Under the new legislation, DOL issued amended federal guidelines to inform the participating states that they may continue their existing programs and encourage other states to consider implementing their own programs. SEA remains the same program it was during the five-year trial period, retaining the requirement that states select participants using a profiling mechanism. Profiling relating to potential exhaustion of UI benefits continues to be a requirement under the new program, but states are no longer required to submit SEA program plans to DOL in advance of implementing their programs.[6]

Chapter 5, by Jon Messenger, Carolyn Peterson-Vaccaro, and Wayne Vroman, reports on the experience with targeting self-employment assistance. This is the only other currently operating statistical targeting application in U.S. employment policy. The remaining chapters of Part II suggest further opportunities for formal targeting of employment services.

Reemployment Bonuses

Between 1984 and 1989, reemployment bonus experiments were conducted in the states of Illinois, New Jersey, Pennsylvania, and Washington. Each experiment involved random assignment of UI claimants to treatment and control groups. The experiments each offered different levels of lump sum payments to workers who took new, full-time jobs within 6 to 12 weeks and stayed employed for at least three to four months. These experiments were conducted to learn more about the behavioral response of UI recipients to UI program parameters. In particular they were tested as a positive incentive for speedy return to work. The idea of reemployment bonuses originated in Japan, where unemployed workers can receive a cash bonus for accepting a new job. In Japan, unemployed workers can receive a bonus once every three years.

UI claimants would improve their economic situation if they went back to work sooner at similar or better paying jobs than they would have taken in the absence of bonus offer. The government sector would be better off if the cost of the bonus were offset by a decrease in UI payments to unemployed workers and by an increase in tax receipts during their longer period of employment. The Reemployment Act of 1994 proposed to permit states to provide reemployment bonus programs, but the legislation was not enacted.

All four reemployment bonus experiments had similar eligibility requirements for inclusion in treatment or control groups. The re-

quirements were set to assure that workers filed for or drew UI benefits, to simplify administrative details, and to select workers who had
experienced some degree of work displacement. Program designs set
the bonus amount, the time period during which workers could qualify for the bonus, and the conditions under which they could receive the
bonus.

A number of lessons have been learned from the bonus experiments. As predicted by job search theory, cash bonuses have a significant impact on job search behavior and lead to reduction in the average
duration of unemployment, resulting in a desirable expedition of reemployment. Larger bonuses also had the largest impact on unemployment durations. As expected from the empirical literature on UI work
disincentives, the bonuses had no effect on wages, indicating no decline in the quality of jobs taken in response to the offer of reemployment bonuses. There is also no evidence that the bonuses had any effect on worker attachment to their previous employer, as they had no
effect on workers subject to recall (Woodbury and Spiegelman 1987;
Decker and O'Leary 1995).

On the other hand, because unemployment durations did not directly relate to the dollar level of the bonus offer, there was not a continuously increasing response. The initial findings left uncertainty about
the design of an optimum bonus offer. None of the options tested were
found to be cost-effective for either the general UI claimant population,
or for claimants similar to dislocated workers.

O'Leary, Decker, and Wandner (1997) reexamined evidence from
the bonus experiments to determine whether a reemployment bonus
targeted to those UI claimants most likely to exhaust benefits would be
more cost-effective. They found that profiling models similar to those
used by states as part of their WPRS system can be effectively used in
this targeting. Using these models can increase the cost-effectiveness
of bonus offers by generating larger average reductions in UI benefit
payments than a nontargeted bonus offer.

The single treatment design that emerged as the best candidate for
a targeted reemployment bonus is a low bonus amount, with a long
qualification period, targeted to the half of claimants most likely to exhaust their UI benefit entitlement. Such a targeted bonus offer emerged
as a realistic prospect for a cost-effective early intervention strategy to
promote reemployment. It was estimated to yield appreciable net ben-

efits to the UI trust fund if implemented as a permanent national program.

Chapter 6, by Christopher O'Leary, Paul Decker, and Stephen Wandner, summarizes the authors' research on targeting reemployment bonuses offered to UI beneficiaries in the states of Pennsylvania and Washington using WPRS models.

Choice of Training

Improved targeting of training could be a powerful tool to guide dislocated workers to the type of training proven to be most cost-effective. Based on their labor market and personal characteristics, dislocated workers could be referred to different types of training such that their employment and earnings outcomes could be improved over a simple random assignment process.

Jacobson, LaLonde, and Sullivan (1999) studied the training decisions of displaced workers in the state of Washington during the early 1990s, examining the community college courses taken by these workers. Data on dislocated workers enrolled in 25 Washington community colleges included the types of courses they took, their grades, and the period of time in which they were enrolled. Dislocated worker status and reemployment earnings history were identified using UI wage records.

The study divided training into nine categories. It found that, averaging across all kinds of training, displaced workers who received training through community colleges experienced small earnings gains. However, these overall mean effects masked the fact that high earning gains accrued to those taking quantitative or technical courses; specifically, courses in three categories: health services, technical skills, and science and mathematics. The study also examined how the labor market and personal characteristics of dislocated workers affected their enrollment and participation in community college. Rates of enrollment, training, and training completion were found to be related to educational level, industry, prior wages, urbanization, job tenure, age at separation, gender, and minority status.

The impact of participation by dislocated workers in community college training on earnings was an increase in quarterly earnings of about $6 for each credit earned. The distribution of earnings gains varied by minority status, age, tenure at displacement, industry, region of the state, and prior education. The highest return to community college schooling accrued to workers with high tenure, more prior schooling, and those in the state's largest labor market (Seattle). The study concluded that training for dislocated workers was most cost-effective when provided in three (health services, technical skills, and math and science) of nine types of training studied, and that the effectiveness of providing this training can be increased by targeting to those workers who can achieve the greatest earnings gains from this training.

Chapter 7, by Louis Jacobson, Robert Lalonde, and Daniel Sullivan, summarizes the authors' research on returns to different types of community college training in Washington for dislocated workers.

Welfare-to-Work

In August 1996, federal welfare reform legislation was enacted in the form of the Personal Responsibility and Work Opportunities Reconciliation Act. The new program, called Temporary Assistance to Needy Families (TANF), replaced Aid to Families with Dependent Children (AFDC). In August 1997, to support the employment emphasis of TANF, the DOL-administered welfare-to-work (WTW) program was enacted. It provided $3 billion to states and localities to assist welfare recipients in obtaining and retaining employment. Under welfare reform, the WTW program provides employment assistance to welfare recipients using a "work first" approach, such that recipients receive assistance in finding jobs first before being referred, as needed, for additional services, such as education and training. They can receive training as well as other postemployment services, such as child care and transportation assistance, but generally only after they become employed.

States have both TANF and WTW federal funding to assist welfare recipients in their employment efforts. TANF provides for block grant funding to states, with funding fixed at the 1994 level. Welfare rolls have fallen sharply, however, leaving a substantial budget for assisting TANF recipients in achieving initial employment, as well as helping former welfare recipients retain their jobs and advance their careers.

WTW and similar programs initiated by the states are particularly amenable to targeting. Welfare recipients vary a great deal in their prior labor force attachments, which makes their abilities to become employed very different. Welfare recipients with strong work histories need relatively less assistance, while those with no work experience have very great needs. Further, while many welfare recipients can get a job, other barriers to steady employment and career growth exist, including having reliable child care and transportation.

Similar to dislocated workers who provide data used for statistical targeting when they file for UI benefits, welfare applicants provide welfare and work-first agencies similar data that could be used to benefit their career development choices.

Welfare targeting can be used by the WTW agency whether it is the local workforce development agency or the local welfare agency. Regardless of the location, service to clients can be improved by making use of client data to more effectively target employment services. The existence of targeting mechanisms may also make it easier to encourage cooperation between the workforce development and welfare agencies when the functions are separated.

The Department of Labor is interested in helping local WTW agencies make more informed choices about the provision of employment services to welfare recipients. To that end, DOL decided to test whether a statistical targeting mechanism could be developed to determine which welfare recipients should receive particular types of WTW services. DOL funded the W.E. Upjohn Institute for Employment Research to develop and test the use of WTW profiling to help welfare recipients find their initial jobs. The model was developed during 1997. During 1998 and 1999, the Upjohn Institute tested this model in Michigan in the Kalamazoo-St. Joseph county service delivery area. The WTW service targeting model reversed the concept of WPRS profiling to instead estimate the probability of becoming employed. The variables used to explain the propensity for employment reflect labor market experience and characteristics of the welfare population (Eberts 1997). They are

1) age at time of enrollment,
2) parental status,
3) educational attainment,

4) AFDC/TANF history,
5) target group (long-term welfare recipient, older children, little
    or no work experience or education),
6) prior employment, and
7) compliance history in previous WTW enrollment.

Chapter 8, by Randall Eberts, reports on a field experiment for targeting WTW services, which was done in Kalamazoo and St. Joseph counties in Michigan. WTW profiling models were also developed by
Broward County, Florida, with a number of other states interested in
trying the approach.

Job Retention and Advancement by Former Welfare Recipients

As more welfare recipients become employed, it has become clear
that finding a job is just the first step toward becoming a stable working
member of the labor force. In recognition of this reality, states have
been spending increasing portions of their TANF and WTW funds on
job retention and advancement. As part of this effort, the U.S. Department of Health and Human Services (HHS) has sponsored a number of
research projects dealing with job retention. Included in these projects
is an analysis of what postemployment services are needed and how to
target these services to those most in need of them. HHS was interested to see if such analysis would allow the design of programs that encourage job retention and advancement or, in the case of job loss, rapid
reemployment.

Rangarajan, Schochet, and Chu (1998) examined the feasibility of
targeting welfare recipients who initially find jobs for job retention services based on their personal and labor market characteristics. As with
dislocated worker profiling, the goal of the study was to try to improve
the efficiency of resource use, targeting postemployment services to
clients most in need, as measured by those welfare recipients who are
most likely to have long periods without employment.

Using the National Longitudinal Survey of Youth data, the study
constructed a nationally representative sample of welfare recipients
who found jobs during the panel period and analyzed their employment
experiences over the five-year period after they entered the labor force.
Similar to other profiling methods, Rangarajan, Schochet, and Chu de-

veloped regression models for predicting which sample members might have negative employment outcomes, using individual and labor market characteristics available in welfare administrative data. They were able to determine the weighted effect of each factor on employment. Their models were sufficient to target job retention services by identifying individuals who initially find jobs but have the greatest risk of subsequent periods without employment.

The variables used to predict long periods without employment are

1) age younger than 20 years when first applied for welfare,
2) employed less than half the time in year prior to job start,
3) no high school diploma/GED,
4) presence of preschool child,
5) wage less than $8.00 per hour,
6) no fringe benefits,
7) no valid driver's license, and
8) has health limitations.

The study found that the characteristics most strongly related to spells without employment were working without fringe benefits and having a health limitation. The result of this analysis again shows that a series of personal and labor market characteristics can be used to identify who could benefit most by referral to services—in this case, postemployment services.

Chapter 9, by Anu Rangarajan, Peter Schochet, and Dexter Chu, reviews possibilities for targeting job retention services for welfare recipients who have gained employment.

CANADIAN APPROACHES FOR TARGETING EMPLOYMENT SERVICES

Part III of the book presents two chapters that report on the Canadian perspective for targeting employment services. Chapter 10, by Terry Colpitts, discusses the Service and Outcome Measurement System (SOMS) developed by Human Resources Development Canada to be a tool for promoting employment. SOMS was intended to help frontline staff in local public employment service offices counsel job seekers about the best strategies for gaining employment and to assist analysts and managers in determining the best employment and/or training strategies for specific client groups. A microcomputer-based prototype of SOMS was built in 1994.

SOMS has not been adopted in Canada; however, many useful lessons were learned in the course of its development and pilot testing. Chapter 10 describes the most important lessons and tells the story of SOMS. The policy context, technical structure, and intended use of SOMS by frontline staff and management are all discussed. The chapter concludes by reviewing some recent events in SOMS development and reflecting on SOMS prospects for the future.

To date, Canada has not developed a policy for targeting services to the long-term unemployed. It has not been a pressing concern, because until recently the incidence of long-term unemployment in Canada has been low. Public concern about long-term unemployment surfaced in the 1990s as the ratio of unemployment compensation beneficiaries to all unemployed (B/U) fell dramatically from 0.83 in 1989 to 0.42 in 1997. Research revealed that about half of this drop was due to tightening of the unemployment compensation system, but the other half was due to changes in the nature of the labor market. In particular, B/U dropped because the share of unemployed Canadians who have not worked for the last 12 months has nearly doubled, from 20.8 percent in 1989 to 38.4 percent in 1997.[7]

Chapter 11, by Ging Wong, Harold Henson, and Arun Roy, documents the rise in Canadian long-term unemployment and the related trends in exhaustion of unemployment compensation entitlement. The chapter then reports on an empirical exercise using Canadian data, which attempts early identification of individuals who are at risk of remaining jobless for 52 weeks or more. Such a model, however, is useful only if linked to effective employment measures. Consequently, the chapter then reports which services are most likely to promote reemployment for those at risk of long-term joblessness. For Canadian unemployment compensation recipients, estimates are provided on how net benefits of interventions vary depending upon the timing of the intervention. Summary and concluding remarks are also provided.

NEW DIRECTIONS FOR TARGETING
EMPLOYMENT SERVICES

The Department of Labor is working with the Upjohn Institute to pilot test a frontline decision support system (FDSS) for workforce development staff in one-stop centers. The goal of FDSS is to assist staff in quickly assessing and properly targeting services to customers. FDSS tools are being tested in new WIA operating systems in Georgia and Washington.

Chapter 12, by Randall Eberts, and Christopher O'Leary, and Kelly DeRango, reports on efforts to develop an FDSS for targeting reemployment services in a one-stop environment. FDSS is comprised of two main modules: systematic job search and service referral.

The systematic job search module is a means for structured searching of vacancy listings. The module informs job seekers about their prospects for returning to a job like their prior one, provides a realistic assessment of likely reemployment earnings, and identifies occupations related to the prior one. The first component is called the industry transition component. It provides an estimate of the likelihood that a customer can find a job in his or her prior industry. The second component provides a realistic assessment of likely reemployment compensation levels. This feature relies on an earnings algorithm which is a statistical model based on personal characteristics, work history, prior earnings, and educational attainment to predict earnings upon reemployment. The third component is the related-occupations algorithm. The algorithm offers individuals who have exhausted job prospects within their prior occupation a list of other occupations that are similar to their prior occupation.

The second module of FDSS is the service referral component. The primary purpose is to identify the sequence of activities that most often lead to successful employment. The service referral module uses information about the characteristics and outcomes of individuals who have recently participated in and completed core, intensive, and training services. This information is used to estimate the statistical relationships between personal attributes and outcomes. This algorithm has two basic components. The first is an estimate of a person's employability, or likelihood of finding a job. The second component is a delineation of the paths, or sequential combinations of services, that lead to successful outcomes. By conditioning these paths on the employability of a specific customer, the algorithm can offer estimates of the effectiveness of various programs for individuals with specific measurable characteristics.

An FDSS pilot is in process in Georgia. The data requirements and system design of FDSS have been completed, and it is expected to be implemented in the Athens and Cobb-Cherokee career centers in mid 2002. A decision will then be made whether to implement the system statewide. Based on input from Georgia users, a second, revised system will then be completed. Pilot implementation efforts in Washington are expected to start after the Washington one-stop computer system is operational. Operational system documentation and a technical assistance guide will be developed for use in other states. Training will then be provided for implementation in other states.

Chapter 13 concludes the book, with a panel discussion involving Rich Hobbie, Jim Finch, Chuck Middlebrooks, and Jack Weidenbach on the experience with and future plans of the states for targeting employment services.

ADDITIONAL OPTIONS FOR TARGETING

Statistical targeting methods can be applied to a wide number of workforce development programs. The only requirement is that they have an appropriate set of historical administrative data that can be applied to developing accurate statistical targeting methods. Below are some examples of possible additional applications that are not discussed elsewhere in this book but could be developed.

Training Targeting for Welfare Recipients and Low-Wage Workers

An extension of the training targeting approach for dislocated workers (as in Jacobson, LaLonde, and Sullivan 1999) might be an application to other adult workers, particularly low-wage workers and current and former welfare recipients. Such models would be valuable in determining whom to train among a large number of low-wage workers who may be coming to one-stop centers. developing such models for former welfare recipients would need to take into consideration the work-first environment of welfare reform.

Underemployed Workers (Skills Mismatch)

Under WIA, many more employed workers are likely to visit/access the one-stop centers in search of career advancement, labor market information, and education and training opportunities. One group of employed workers for whom mediated services may be particularly effective is underemployed workers, especially those with skills that greatly exceed the skill set needed for their current jobs. A particularly cost-effective approach may be to target, identify, and assist these workers in finding jobs that better match their skills. The result should be a substantial increase in earnings for workers and productivity for society.

Targeting UI Non-Filers among Dislocated Workers

About two-thirds of all dislocated workers apply for UI, and a much larger portion of those dislocated workers who remain unemployed for five or more weeks claim UI. However, a significant minority of dislocated workers never apply for UI. The one-stop centers can provide information about UI benefits that may result in increased application rates for the program. These workers will be able to apply for UI benefits in the center, either in person or by telephone. In addition, the availability of wage data as part of FDSS could be used to calculate the monetary eligibility for UI benefits. Supplying such information also could increase filing for UI benefits, and the net effect of the one-stop center may be to increase recipiency rates for UI benefits.

For those dislocated workers who choose not to apply for UI, however, profiling would be useful—using the state WPRS model—to make a determination of the need for reemployment services similar to that done under the WPRS system. It should be noted, however, that profiling within the one-stop center and the resulting identification of workers in need of services and their referral to services would not result in mandatory participation in those services.

Job Corps Selection and Retention

Another possible application of targeting to a national DOL program would be as a guide for selection of Job Corps participants. Using data on past participants, individuals could be profiled to assist in the selection of participants based on whether they have characteristics similar to successful Job Corps graduates.

For newly enrolled Job Corps participants, profiling could also be used to determine which individuals are most likely to drop out of the Job Corps prior to graduation. This information could be used to target the provision of remedial assistance that could increase the Job Corps retention rate.

The effect of targeting efforts, combined with improved selection processes and provision of remedial assistance, could increase the cost-effectiveness of the Job Corps by reducing the program's drop-out rate. Dynarski and Gleason (forthcoming) conducted an analysis for predicting which students are most likely to drop out of school, indicating that the development of such methods could yield positive results.

Notes

1. The EDWAA program was the principal JTPA dislocated worker program in the United States. It traditionally recruited participants through either 1) early outreach ("rapid response") to workers experiencing mass layoffs or plant shutdowns, or 2) walk-ins to their local intake centers. The employment service serves all employed and unemployed workers, including dislocated workers. Both programs have supplemented recruitment of program participants with WPRS referral and been active participants in the overall WPRS system. For the EDWAA program, most but not necessarily all WPRS-referred workers are eligible for EDWAA services.

2. The term *dislocated worker* refers to workers who are permanently laid off from long-tenured jobs. These workers tend to suffer extended periods of joblessness and earn lower incomes when they become reemployed. For the EDWAA program, section 301(a) of Title III of JTPA in part, defined *eligible dislocated workers* as "individuals who: 1) have been terminated or laid off or who have received a notice of termination or layoff from employment, are eligible for or have exhausted their entitlement to unemployment compensation, and are unlikely to re-

turn to their previous industry or occupation, and 2) have been terminated or have received a notice of termination of employment, as a result of any permanent or any substantial layoff at a plant, facility or enterprise . . ." The Bureau of Labor Statistics (BLS), on the other hand, collects data about displaced workers in its bi-ennial survey. It defines *displaced workers* as workers who permanently lost their jobs because their plant or company closed or moved, there was insufficient work for them to do, or their positions or shifts were abolished. BLS distinguishes be-tween long-tenured workers who lost jobs they had held for three years or more, and displaced workers regardless of tenure. This chapter does not distinguish be-tween the terms "dislocated" and "displaced" workers; it uses the former term in all cases.

3. The WPRS system is designed to provide reemployment services to permanently separated workers who are likely to be unemployed for long periods in their search for new jobs. Workers who find their jobs exclusively through union hiring halls, e.g., longshoremen, are considered to be job attached and not searching for new jobs; they are waiting to return to their old jobs. They are not eligible to participate in WPRS reemployment services.

4. Benefit exhaustion takes place when claimants draw their potential duration of reg-ular benefits. Potential duration usually depends on prior earnings. The maximum potential duration is 26 weeks in all states except Massachusetts and Washington, where it is 30 weeks.

5. Prohibited variables and the effect of their omission are discussed in U.S. Depart-ment of Labor (1994a), pp. 63 and 151–152.

6. UI Program Letter 11-98, Permanent Authorization of the Self-Employment Assis-tance Program, issued on December 17, 1998.

7. See OECD (1998, pp. 41 and 43). Note that the number used in the analysis is not the long-term unemployed, but those not employed for a year, which includes both unemployed and out of the labor force.

References

Benus, J.M., T.R. Johnson, M. Wood, N. Grover, and T. Shen. 1995. *Self-Employment Programs: A New Reemployment Strategy, Final Report on the UI Self-Employment Demonstration.* UI Occasional Paper 95-4, Washington D.C.: U.S. Department of Labor.

Corson, Walter, and Paul T. Decker. 1996. "Using the UI System to Target Services to Dislocated Workers." In *Background Papers*, Volume III, Advisory Council on Unemployment Compensation. Washington, D.C.: U.S. Department of Labor.

Decker, Paul T., and Christopher J. O'Leary. 1995. "Evaluating Pooled Evidence from the Reemployment Bonus Experiments." *Journal of Human Resources* 30(3): 534–550.

Dickinson, Katherine P., Suzanne D. Kreutzer, and Paul T. Decker. 1997. *Evaluation of Worker Profiling and Reemployment Services Systems: Report to Congress*. Washington, D.C.: U.S. Department of Labor, Employment and Training Administration, Office of Policy Research.

Dynarski, Mark, and Philip Gleason. Forthcoming. "Do We Know Whom to Serve? Issues in Using Risk Factors to Identify Dropouts." *Journal of Education for Students Placed at Risk*.

Eberts, Randall W. 1997. "The Use of Profiling to Target Services in State Welfare-to-Work Programs: An Example of Process and Implementation." Staff working paper no. 98-52, W.E. Upjohn Institute for Employment Research, Kalamazoo, Michigan.

Eberts, Randall W., and Christopher J. O'Leary. 1997. "Profiling and Referral to Services of the Long-Term Unemployed: Experiences and Lessons from Several Countries." *Employment Observatory: Policies (inforMISEP)*, 60 (Winter): 32–39.

Hawkins, Evelyn K., Suzanne D. Kreutzer, Katherine P. Dickinson, Paul T. Decker, and Walter S. Corson. 1996. *Evaluation of Worker Profiling and Reemployment Services Systems*. UI Occasional Paper no. 96-1, Washington, D.C.: U.S. Department of Labor,

Jacobson, Louis, Robert LaLonde, and Daniel Sullivan. 1999. "Participation in the Effects of Community College Schooling for Displaced Workers: A Study of Displaced Workers from Washington State." Report to the U.S. Department of Labor.

Messenger, Jon, Suzanne Schwartz, and Stephen A. Wandner. 1999. *The Worker Profiling and Reemployment Services Policy Workgroup: Policy Analysis and Recommendations*. Washington, D.C.: U.S. Department of Labor, Office of Policy and Research.

Meyer, Bruce D. 1995. "Lessons from the U.S. Unemployment Insurance Experiments." *Journal of Economic Literature* 33(1): 91–131.

O'Leary, Christopher J., Paul T. Decker, and Stephen A. Wandner. 1997. "Reemployment Bonuses and Profiling." Staff working paper no. 98-51, W.E. Upjohn Institute for Employment Research, Kalamazoo, Michigan.

OECD. 1998. *Early Identification of Jobseekers at Risk of Long-Term Unemployment: The Role of Profiling*. Paris: Organisation for Economic Co-operation and Development.

Orr, Larry, Stephen A. Wandner, David Lah, and Jacob M. Benus. 1994. "The Use of Evaluation Results in Employment and Training Policy: Two Case Studies." Paper presented at the annual research conference of the Association for Public Policy Analysis and Management, held in Chicago, Illinois, October 26–29.

Rangarajan, Anu, Peter Z. Schochet, and Dexter Chu. 1998. *Employment Ex-*

periences of Welfare Recipients Who Find Jobs: Is Targeting Possible? Princeton, New Jersey: Mathematica Policy Research.

U.S. Department of Labor. 1994a. *The Worker Profiling and Reemployment Services System: Legislation, Implementation and Research Findings.* Washington, D.C.: U.S. Department of Labor, UI Occasional Paper no. 94-4.

———. 1994b. *Self-Employment as a Reemployment Option: Demonstration Results and National Legislation.* Washington, D.C.: U.S. Department of Labor, UI Occasional Paper no. 94-3.

———. 1995. *What's Working (and What's Not): A Summary of Research on the Economic Impacts of Employment and Training Programs.* Washington, D.C.: U.S. Department of Labor, Office of the Chief Economist.

Vroman, Wayne. 1998. "Self-Employment Assistance (SEA) Program: Report to Congress." Unpublished paper, Department of Labor, Washington, D.C.

Wandner, Stephen A. 1997. "Early Reemployment for Dislocated Workers in the United States." *International Social Security Review* 50(4): 95–112.

———. 1998. "Worker Profiling and Reemployment Services in the United States." In *Early Identification of Jobseekers at Risk of Long-Term Unemployment: The Role of Profiling.* Paris: Organisation for Economic Co-operation and Development, pp. 99–117.

Woodbury, Stephen A., and Robert G. Spiegelman. 1987. "Bonuses to Workers and Employers to Reduce Unemployment: Randomized Trials in Illinois." *American Economic Review* 77(4): 513–530.

Part I

Worker Profiling and Reemployment Services

2

Predicting the Exhaustion of Unemployment Compensation

Robert B. Olsen
Mathematica Policy Research

Marisa Kelso
U.S. Department of Labor

Paul T. Decker
Mathematica Policy Research

Daniel H. Klepinger
Battelle Human Affairs Research Center

It has been seven years since the Unemployment Compensation Amendments of 1993 (Public Law 103-152) spawned the Worker Profiling and Reemployment Services (WPRS) system. In that time, the U.S. Department of Labor (DOL) and the states have designed and implemented the WPRS system, which uses the unemployment insurance (UI) system to target reemployment services to permanently displaced workers early in their unemployment spells. The method of targeting used in most states is a two-step process called the worker profiling model. The model is intended to identify permanently separated workers who are likely to exhaust their UI benefits. The likelihood of benefit exhaustion is determined based on a statistical model of the relationship between worker characteristics, which are referred to as the explanatory variables in the model, and benefit exhaustion, which is the dependent variable in the model. As new claimants enter the UI system, they are assigned a probability of exhaustion based on their characteristics. Those claimants with the highest probabilities of exhaustion are referred to mandatory services under WPRS.

In this chapter, we examine the profiling models that states have constructed under WPRS, and we consider the efficacy of these models in targeting services to UI claimants who are most in need of services. In the first section of this chapter, we describe the details of the profiling models used in a sample of states. We focus particularly on the ways in which states have extended their profiling models beyond the prototype model that was developed by DOL. In the second section, we assess the predictive ability of the type of statistical model of benefit exhaustion that many states use. Our assessment is based on comparing the benefit exhaustion rates between claimants who are targeted for WPRS services and claimants who are not. In the third section, we consider whether states can update their statistical models without losing the capacity to identify claimants with high exhaustion probabilities.

WORKER PROFILING MODELS IN THE WPRS SYSTEM

WPRS attempts to identify UI claimants with a high potential for exhausting their benefits and provide them with reemployment services. Prior to WPRS, no objective or equitable mechanism existed for allocating reemployment services to those who needed them most. WPRS is a tool that facilitates both the identification of needy claimants and the allocation of services, such that those claimants most likely to exhaust their benefits receive highest priority in receiving available reemployment services.

In identifying likely exhaustees, states may use either characteristic screens or statistical models. Each method identifies characteristics common to recent exhaustees and targets current claimants who share these characteristics. Although neither method can target exhaustees with complete accuracy, both screens and models have been found to be more accurate than less systematic processes, such as random selection. Most states have chosen to implement statistical models since they offer greater accuracy and procedural flexibility than characteristic screens, and DOL has recommended that states adopt a statistical approach. A few states without sufficient historical data to develop a statistical model have chosen to implement screening methodologies and have taken steps to collect data necessary to develop models in the future.

With either method, the target population specified in the WPRS legislation is claimants who are "likely to exhaust." While the specific make-up of this population differs among states, the ultimate goal is to identify claimants whose job search skills are no longer sufficient to obtain suitable employment in their most recent line of work. Identifying these potential exhaustees is complicated for a number of reasons. First, the availability and integrity of historical data is poor in many states. Data from separate intake systems must often be merged, and these merges face logistical obstacles. Second, some readily available data on personal characteristics (such as ethnicity) have been determined to be discriminatory under federal equal opportunity legislation and thus cannot be used in profiling. Third, and perhaps most importantly, some key influences on benefit exhaustion, such as motivation and networking skills, are not quantifiable. These influences affect whether or not a claimant exhausts his/her benefits but cannot be measured and factored into a profiling model. Given these problems, it is difficult to develop a profiling model that accurately predicts exhaustion.

Although predicting exhaustion is an inexact science, states have been able to develop models that considerably reduce prediction errors relative to less rigorous methods. Most have either directly adopted the model initially developed by DOL in 1993 or have used it as a benchmark in developing state-specific models for identifying likely exhaustees. The DOL model consists of two initial screens, recall status and union hiring hall; a set of variables capturing the claimant's education, job tenure, industry, occupation, and the local unemployment rate. Originally developed from national data, the DOL model was first applied to state-level data in the test state of Maryland.

The national analysis demonstrated that education, job tenure, industry, occupation, and the local unemployment are all statistically related to UI benefit exhaustion. The Maryland test state project showed further that an operational state system could be readily developed from the national model. A number of states followed Maryland's lead in developing their own profiling models using very similar sets of variables. Such models, when applied to out-of-sample historical data (i.e., data not used to develop the model), are able to identify a higher percentage of exhaustees than the alternatives of random selection and characteristic screening. We further examine the predictive power of the profiling model in the section "Accuracy in Identifying Likely Exhaustees."

Since considerable diversity exists among states, it is not surprising that several states have found that alternative specifications are needed to effectively model their populations. Because state data systems often retain a great deal more information than just these five variables from the national model, several states have expanded upon that model by testing additional variables in an effort to increase predictive ability. These states retained the variables from the national model and added those additional variables found helpful in identifying exhaustees.

The Dependent Variable in Worker Profiling Models

Since the inception of WPRS, benefit exhaustion has been the focal point in targeting those who are eligible. Public Law 103-152 requires states to "identify which claimants will be likely to exhaust regular compensation." Therefore, the law focuses on a binary outcome: a claimant either exhausts regular unemployment insurance compensation or (s)he does not. The dependent variable in the national model was coded as "1" for exhaustees and as "0" for non-exhaustees. The output of the model is the predicted probability that each claimant will exhaust benefits. Both the national and Maryland versions of the DOL model use logistic regression to model benefit exhaustion. A few states have correctly noted that this approach discards information; a claimant who almost exhausted is not distinguished from a claimant who came nowhere near exhausting, although the near-exhaustee may experience a greater need for reemployment assistance. Also, since benefits in most states are subject to variable potential duration, referrals of likely exhaustees may include some claimants with very low potential duration among those referred to reemployment services.

As a result, some states have experimented with alternatives to a binary dependent variable representing exhaustion of unemployment compensation. Some states have tested different dependent variables, such as UI duration and the ratio of benefits drawn to benefit entitlement, and estimated these profiling models via ordinary least squares (OLS). While these states typically found that these models targeted exhaustees no more accurately than the logistic model predicting the binary exhaustion variable, the OLS estimation used to test these models ignores the fact that the alternative dependent variables are "censored." UI duration cannot exceed some maximum (usually 26 weeks), and the benefit ratio must be between zero and 1. Maximum likelihood techniques exist to accommodate censored dependent variables, and evidence suggests that combining these techniques with dependent variables that use differences between short-term claimants and near-exhaustees can improve the targeting of profiling models (Berger et al. 1997).

Modeling the binary exhaustion variable still allows several options for defining what constitutes "exhaustion." In the DOL model, claimants are coded as exhaustees if they draw 100 percent of their entitlement and are otherwise coded as non-exhaustees. Some states have expanded the scope of the exhaustion variable by using a more general definition. For example, some states code claimants who depleted at least 90 percent of benefits as exhaustees. A related variation is to code claimants who exhaust a high percentage of benefits within a given time frame as exhaustees (e.g., 80 percent within six months of their benefit year begin [BYB] date). This variation would also expand the definition to include both exhaustees and near-exhaustees, and it would also shorten the lag time for discerning exhaustion outcomes. Finally, exhaustion has also been redefined to automatically include claimants collecting extended unemployment compensation, since they had, by definition, exhausted regular benefits.

Other states have narrowed the scope of the exhaustion variable. For example, some states have determined that claimants who take a full calendar year to exhaust 26 weeks of benefits are not truly in need of reemployment services; they may simply be collecting UI benefits between intervening spells of employment. To compensate, a time limit has been set (for example, eight months from BYB date) after which historic claimants would not be coded as exhaustees. Weeks of potential duration have also been used as a criterion for narrowing the scope of the dependent variable. Variable duration complicates the use of exhaustion as the dependent variable because, *ceteris paribus*, claimants with shorter potential durations have higher likelihoods of exhaustion but may not need reemployment assistance. To compensate, some states have set a minimum potential duration below which historical claimants cannot be coded as exhaustees. Narrowing the definition of exhaustion using potential duration has been most useful for states that find that many short-duration—and perhaps seasonal—exhaustees pass all of the initial screens (e.g., recall, union hiring hall) yet are not truly in need of reemployment services.

Explanatory Variables in Worker Profiling Models

While a few alternative definitions of the dependent variable have been tested, most experimentation has involved the explanatory variables. The national model includes the following five variables: education, occupation, industry, tenure, and unemployment rate. Some states, such as Maryland, adopted only these five variables into their own models and estimated state-specific parameters. Others included additional variables in their models. Most states collect education, occupation, and tenure through their job service registration. Industry information (as well as other, noncore variables) typically come through information gathered during the qualification process for unemployment benefits. The unemployment rate and information on declining industries and occupations often come from a labor market information unit.

Education

Education is often measured as the number of years completed and is then categorized into intervals for inclusion in the model. When education data are accurate and variation exists within the population, profiling models often identify a strong inverse relationship between education and exhaustion. However, in areas where skill levels and educational backgrounds are fairly homogenous, education is not a very effective predictor of exhaustion.

Job tenure

Like education, job tenure is measured in years and categorized into intervals, which are included in the profiling model. There are reasons to believe that job tenure and exhaustion should be positively related. Claimants with long pre-unemployment job tenure are likely to have outdated skills or be unfamiliar with current job search strategies. The evidence suggests that exhaustion is positively associated with years of job tenure.

Occupation

The occupation of a claimant's pre-unemployment job may contain valuable information about the likelihood that the claimant will exhaust UI benefits. Unfortunately, occupational coding is a significant obstacle to including occupations in profiling models. In general, most problems with occupational coding involve either incomplete data or multiple coding schemes. Few states have been able to incorporate meaningful occupational effects into their WPRS systems. Because occupational information would likely be valuable in predicting long-term unemployment, the development of reliable methods for coding claimants' occupations could be very helpful to state WPRS systems.

Industry

Because states are legally required to use either industry or occupation in their WPRS systems, and because creating reliable occupation variables is difficult, most states have included industry variables in their profiling models. Data on industries tend to be fairly reliable because they are typically captured from UI wage records. Industry information is included in some profiling models as a categorical variable indicating employment in a particular industry, and in other models as a measure of the employment change in the industry. Regardless of how industry information is captured, almost all states have partially collapsed the Standard Industrial Classification codes from the four-digit levels in which they are typically recorded because four-digit industries are typically too small to reflect the labor markets faced by claimants.

Unemployment rate

In their profiling models, most states account for regional differences that may affect UI exhaustion. Even the smallest states exhibit a great deal of regional diversity. Therefore, it should not be surprising that regional indicators are usually strong predictors of exhaustion. Because exhaustion is likely higher in areas with high unemployment, most states include unemployment rates from the Local Area Unemployment Statistics program in their models. In states where unemployment and exhaustion are not closely correlated, regional indicator variables are used to control for regional differences in exhaustion. Although these regional variables do not vary across claimants within particular regions, the inclusion of regional information may produce a more accurate profiling model.

Other variables

While some states have used only the five variables from the national model, others have used them as a benchmark for building a model with a more extensive list of explanatory variables. Development and testing of additional variables is encouraged by DOL, provided either industry or occupation is included and all discriminatory variables are excluded. Several states have done a considerable amount of research, yielding the additional variables described in the remainder of this section.

The variable "pre-unemployment earnings" contains information about the claimant's job skills and reservation wage, i.e., the lowest wage offer that the claimant would accept. Job skills are difficult to measure directly, but to the extent that workers are paid according to their productivity, higher wages are associated with higher skills. Furthermore, because claimants will not work for wages below their reservation wages, pre-unemployment earnings provides information about the minimum earnings that would be required for them to leave unemployment for work. Therefore, some states include pre-unemployment earnings in their profiling models. Other states use it to compute the UI replacement rate and then include the replacement rate in their models.

A claimant's weekly benefit amount (WBA) may contain information about his or her likelihood of exhausting benefits. WBA can be used to compute UI's "wage replacement rate," which equals WBA divided by pre-unemployment weekly earnings. Because this rate is inversely related to the financial hardship from remaining unemployed, we would expect a positive relationship between the wage replacement rate and exhaustion. This expectation is confirmed by the estimates from state profiling models. However, at least one state found that the replacement rate primarily identifies exhaustees with low potential duration because they worked less during the base period.

Some states have included the potential duration of UI benefits as an explanatory variable in their profiling models. Claimants with a short potential duration are much more likely to exhaust their benefits but are unlikely to be "dislocated workers," i.e., the target population for WPRS services. Therefore, we may want to think of two different groups of variables that help to explain exhaustion: those that explain exhaustion because they indicate "dislocation" (such as job tenure) versus those that explain exhaustion for programmatic and other reasons (such as potential duration). To target WPRS services toward dislocated workers, it may be reasonable to use all of these variables in estimating the profiling model, but to use only those that signal worker dislocation to assign claimants to mandatory WPRS services.

A measure of the delay in filing for unemployment compensation has also been included by some states as a predictor of exhaustion.[1] This delay is captured by either a single variable measuring number of days, or by several variables indicating different ranges for the number of days. Claimants who do not expect to have reemployment difficulty may not immediately file for UI benefits. Four states (of the 13 sampled) were impressed enough with the ability of delay variables to predict exhaustion that they included them in their profiling models. The delay variable appears to be more effective at predicting exhaustion in urban areas than in rural areas. Among rural workers, difficulty in accessing a UI (field) local office may be the primary reason for delays in filing for benefits.

The ratio of highest quarterly earnings to the earnings in the base year is also used as an explanatory variable in their profiling models. Large values of this ratio may identify intermittent workers, workers with difficulties in holding a steady job, or perhaps workers in seasonal industries. While states have found a strong positive relationship between this ratio and exhaustion, the type of workers identified by high ratios are probably not the dislocated workers targeted by WPRS. Therefore, it may be sensible to include this variable in the profiling model but to exclude it in selecting workers for mandatory WPRS services.

A claimant with many employers in the base year may have either worked multiple jobs at the same time, suggesting a strong preference for or need to work, or switched employers, suggesting recent experience with the process of searching for a job. Either scenario suggests a low exhaustion probability. Estimates of state profiling models support this prediction: controlling for the other explanatory variables, exhaustion is negatively correlated with the number of employers in the base year. However, because it is unclear whether this variable helps to identify displaced workers, the use of this variable in worker profiling deserves further consideration.[2]

Whether or not states include certain explanatory variables in the statistical model may depend on their philosophy with respect to WPRS targeting as well as the predictive power of the variable. Claimants may be likely to exhaust their benefits either because they face barriers to reemployment or because they are reluctant to return to work quickly. Variables that help predict exhaustion may be related to either of these factors. Most of the variables in the DOL prototype profiling model were intended to identify claimants who were likely to exhaust their benefits because they faced barriers to reemployment. Some variables that states have considered adding to the model are more closely related to the incentives claimants face to return to work quickly. For example, higher WBAs are probably positively related to exhaustion because the financial incentive to return to work quickly is lower for claimants with higher WBAs, other things being equal. In deciding whether to include WBA in the profiling model, states need to decide whether they want to target reemployment services to such claimants. Although these claimants do not necessarily face barriers to reemployment, the mandatory nature of WPRS may still bring about a significant reduction in their UI spells.

ACCURACY IN IDENTIFYING LIKELY EXHAUSTEES

The two-step profiling model is designed to identify UI claimants likely to exhaust their benefits and refer them to services. If the approach is at least partially successful, we would expect that in the absence of services, the claimants targeted for services would collect more benefits and exhaust their benefits at a higher rate than claimants not targeted. To investigate the success of the profiling model, we compare claimants targeted for services to other claimants on the basis of exhaustion and benefits collected. However, simply comparing claimants referred to services with claimants not referred will not provide a valid comparison if services have an impact on outcomes. If, for example, services substantially reduce UI receipt, the claimants referred to services may exhaust benefits at a lower rate than nonreferred claimants, even though services were targeted to claimants with high expected probabilities of exhaustion.

Ideally, to conduct a test of the profiling model, we would like data on a group of nonreferred claimants and a group of referred claimants who were not actually offered services. Fortunately, data from two recent UI experiments sponsored by the U.S. Department of Labor provide just such a group. In the Job Search Assistance Demonstration, which was conducted in Washington, D.C., and Florida from 1995 to 1996 (prior to implementation of WPRS), claimants were profiled using the two-step profiling model, and those claimants identified as likely to exhaust their benefits were randomly assigned to one of three treatment groups or a control group. Claimants assigned to a treatment group were offered special, mandatory reemployment services, while those assigned to the control group were offered only the existing services offered to all UI claimants (pre-WPRS) and were not offered the mandatory services.[3] The control group therefore provided a representative group of claimants targeted for extra services based on the profiling model who were not actually offered extra services—therefore, they were on a "level playing field" with nonreferred claimants in terms of available services. Hence, Decker, Freeman, and Klepinger (1999) were able to make comparisons between the control group and the nonreferred claimants that are attributable to profiling and not to the services linked to profiling.

Another recent UI experiment, the New Jersey UI Reemployment Demonstration Project, also offered an opportunity to test the profiling model. In their long-run follow-up study of the data from the New Jersey project, Corson and Haimson (1996) used the control group and the ineligible claimants to construct and estimate a two-step profiling model. They then applied the model to the same group, simulating the selection of a group to be referred to services and a group not referred to services. Since none of the claimants used in the exercise were offered services, the differences in outcomes for the simulated groups can be attributed to the profiling model.[4]

In this section we present findings from the Job Search Assistance (JSA) and New Jersey demonstrations on the effectiveness of the profiling model in targeting claimants who are likely to experience long spells of UI receipt and exhaust their benefits. Our analysis is based on three conceptual groups of profiled claimants, which are shown in Figure 2.1. The first group (group A) consists of claimants who did not pass the initial eligibility screens. The claimants who passed the screens are divided into two groups. One group (group B) consists of claimants who passed the initial screening criteria but whose predicted probabilities of benefit exhaustion were below the threshold used to identify claimants to be referred to services. The other group (group C) consists of control group members who passed the screens and whose predicted exhaustion probabilities were above the threshold. This group is representative of all claimants who were referred to demonstration services based on having high exhaustion probabilities.

We examine the effects of both steps in the profiling model by comparing mean outcomes among the three groups defined above. Our comparisons are conducted in two stages in order to examine separately the effect of each step in the profiling model. In the first stage, we compare outcomes for claimants who were excluded by the initial screens (group A) with outcomes for claimants who passed the screens (groups B and C combined). Outcomes for these claimants are shown in Table 2.1. In the second stage, we focus just on claimants who

Figure 2.1 Profiled UI Claimants: Three Conceptual Outcomes

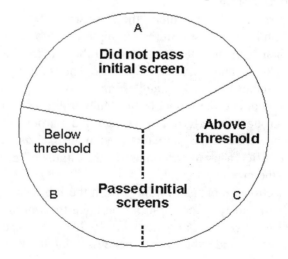

Table 2.1 Mean UI and Employment Outcomes by Initial Screening Status

Outcome	Washington, D.C.		Florida		New Jersey[a]	
	Did not pass initial screens	Passed initial screens	Did not pass initial screens	Passed initial screens	Did not pass initial screens	Passed initial screens
Exhausted UI benefits (%)	43.9	54.6[b]	37.7	43.3[b]	29.7	44.1
Weeks of UI benefits	18.5	19.6	13.6	15.2	ND[c]	ND
Earnings in first quarter[d] ($)	1,819	1,543[b]	2,370	1,933[b]	ND	ND
Earnings in fourth quarter[d] ($)	1,837	1,785	2,658	2,953[b]	ND	ND
Employed with same employer (%)	61.2	50.6[b]	44.4	29.1[b]	ND	ND

[a] Significance tests were not run on the New Jersey outcomes.
[b] Mean outcome for group that passed initial screens is significantly different than the mean outcome for group that did not pass at the 95% confidence level.
[c] ND = no data available.
[d] The first and fourth calendar quarters after the benefit year begin date.

passed the initial screens. For this group, we compare outcomes of claimants above the probability threshold (group C) with those below the threshold (group B). Outcomes for these claimants are shown in Table 2.2.

The primary outcome of interest is the rate of benefit exhaustion, because the second stage of the profiling model assigns a predicted probability of exhaustion to each claimant. We expected the targeted group—the group above the threshold—to have a higher rate of benefit exhaustion than the group below the threshold or the group not passing the initial screens.[5] We also expected claimants above the threshold to have longer UI spells, higher earnings, and to return to their previous employers at a lower rate, since the initial screens are related to employer attachment.

Our findings confirm that the profiling model identified claimants who were likely to spend a long time on UI, and each step of the model appears to contribute to this identification. Although the initial screens used in the first step of the profiling model were not designed specifically to exclude claimants with short spells, they appear to have done so. Claimants who passed the initial screens had higher exhaustion rates and longer UI spells than those who did not pass, as shown in Table 2.3. In Washington, D.C., the claimants who passed the screens had a benefit exhaustion rate of 54.6 percent, compared with 43.9 percent for those who did not pass the screens. Similar differences were found for Florida and New Jersey, although the differences between the groups are somewhat smaller in Florida than in either of the other two states.

Comparisons of the average UI spells yield similar findings. In Washington, D.C., the claimants who passed the screens had average UI spells that were about a week longer than the average for claimants excluded by the screens: 19.6 for those passing compared with 18.5 for those not passing. In Florida, the difference between the groups is a bit greater than one week: 15.2 for those passing compared with 13.6 for those not passing.

Not surprisingly, given the findings on UI benefits, the use of the initial screens also tended to target claimants with low earnings early in their benefit year. In both Washington, D.C. and Florida, claimants passing the screens had substantially lower earnings in the first quarter after their BYB date than those not passing. However, this difference

Table 2.2 Mean UI and Employment Outcomes by Probability Threshold Status

Outcome	Washington, D.C.		Florida		New Jersey[a]	
	Below threshold	Above threshold	Below threshold	Above threshold	Below threshold	Above threshold
Exhausted UI benefits (%)	47.9	58.8[b]	40.0	45.0[b]	40.5	52.5
Weeks of UI benefits	18.6	20.1[b]	14.1	15.8[b]	ND[c]	ND
Earnings in first quarter[d] ($)	1,739	1,422[b]	2,232	1,772[b]	ND	ND
Earnings in fourth quarter[d] ($)	2,118	1,580[b]	3,462	2,679[b]	ND	ND
Employed with same employer (%)	49.1	51.4	27.6	29.9	ND	ND

[a] Significance tests were not run on the New Jersey outcomes.
[b] Mean outcome for group that passed initial screens is significantly different than the mean outcome for group that did not pass at the 95% confidence level.
[c] ND = no data available.
[d] The first and fourth calendar quarters after the benefit year begin date.

Table 2.3 Contamination in Worker Profiling

	Uncontaminated profiling model[a]	
Contaminated profiling model[b]	Below threshold	Above threshold
25% Threshold for eligibility		
Below threshold	66.2	8.8
Above threshold	8.8	16.2
50% Threshold for eligibility		
Below threshold	36.5	13.5
Above threshold	13.5	36.6

[a] The workers used to estimate the uncontaminated profiling model include ineligibles and workers who were assigned to the control group. Explicitly excluded are workers assigned to Structured Job Search Assistance, IJSA, or IJSA+.

[b] The workers used to estimate the contaminated profiling model include ineligibles and workers who were assigned either to Individualized Job Search Assistance (IJSA) or to Individualized Job Search Assistance Plus Training (IJSA+).

disappeared or reversed late in the benefit year. In the fourth quarter after the BYB date, earnings were similar for the two groups in Washington, D.C., and in Florida the claimants who passed the screens had higher earnings than those not passing. The findings suggest that the initial screens tended to exclude claimants who quickly returned to work but who also did not have high earnings once back on the job.

As expected, the initial screens excluded claimants who were more likely to return to their previous employer. Of the claimants in Washington, D.C., who were excluded by the screens and reemployed in the first quarter, 61.2 percent returned to their previous employer. This exceeds the 50.6 percent of Washington, D.C., claimants who passed the screens and returned to their previous employer. The difference between these groups is probably attributable to the screen that excluded claimants who reported that they expected to be recalled by their previous employer on a particular date.

The second step in the profiling model—the application of the exhaustion probability threshold—further directed services to a group of claimants with high exhaustion probabilities and long UI spells. Table 2.1 shows that in Washington, D.C., 58.8 percent of claimants above the threshold ultimately exhausted their benefits compared with 47.9

percent of those below the threshold. The difference between the groups was somewhat smaller in Florida, where there was a 45.0 percent exhaustion rate for those above the threshold compared with 40.0 percent for those below. The pattern of these differences also holds for New Jersey, where claimants above the threshold had an exhaustion rate of 52.5 percent compared with 40.5 percent for those below.

The findings for the other outcomes are consistent with those for exhaustion. Claimants above the threshold in Washington, D.C., and Florida had longer UI spells and lower earnings throughout the benefit year. It is interesting to note that claimants above and below the threshold did not differ greatly in their likelihood of being recalled to their previous employer. In each state, the recall rate is slightly higher for the group above the threshold, but the difference is not statistically significant. Since the probability threshold (unlike the initial screens) is not directly tied to the date of recall, these findings are not surprising.

Overall, our findings demonstrate that the profiling model achieves the objective of targeting claimants who are likely to have long UI spells and exhaust their benefits, and both steps of the model contribute to this achievement. However, the targeting effect of the profiling model is limited. The models do not separate claimants into one group in which nearly everybody exhausts and another group in which practically nobody exhausts. Our estimates for Florida demonstrate this clearly. The claimants who were targeted for services because they were above the probability threshold had a benefit exhaustion rate that was a relatively modest 5 percentage points higher than those below the threshold (45 percent compared with 40 percent). The differences were somewhat larger in the other two states, but never greater than 12 percentage points. This is a reflection of the difficulty in predicting UI outcomes, especially a binary outcome like whether benefits are exhausted, based on the characteristics and work experience of individual claimants at the time they filed their initial claim. Even after accounting for the characteristics included in the statistical model, a substantial part of the variation in exhaustion and UI spells remains unexplained by the models.

The analysis in this section has provided only a first step in evaluating the efficacy of the profiling model. Our findings suggest that the model targets services to workers who appear to be most in need of services. But we may also be interested in whether the profiling model targets services to claimants who will benefit most from the services. To answer this question, we would need to be able to estimate and compare the impacts of services for referred and nonreferred claimants. Although we do not have the data necessary to address this question directly, we can at least use the data from our evaluation of the JSA demonstration to evaluate how service impacts vary as the probability threshold is increased. Findings on this point have been presented in the final report on the JSA demonstration.

CONTAMINATION IN ESTIMATING THE WPRS MODEL

The worker profiling model used to determine eligibility among UI claimants in Florida was estimated from data collected in the JSA demonstration in 1995–1996. However, as the economic environment changes, the effectiveness of this profiling model in identifying UI claimants likely to exhaust their benefits is likely to decline. Therefore, Florida and other states should consider updating their profiling models as economic conditions change.

Given the implementation of the WPRS system, new estimates of these profiling models will be "contaminated" because eligible UI claimants are required to participate in WPRS. Worker profiling is designed to identify UI claimants who would likely exhaust their benefits if they were not required to participate in WPRS. However, those identified as likely exhaustees are required to participate in WPRS, and whether they subsequently exhaust their benefits is influenced by WPRS participation if the program is effective. Therefore, profiling models estimated from UI data that are collected after the implementation of WPRS and used in WPRS models will provide biased estimates of the exhaustion probabilities if targeted workers were not required to participate in WPRS.

Fortunately, data from the JSA demonstration in Florida can be used to measure the size of this contamination. This demonstration included a control group of UI claimants who passed the state screens (and were thereby deemed eligible by the state), who exceeded the threshold probability of exhaustion, but who were *not* assigned to a mandatory treatment group with requirements similar to those in

WPRS. We can combine the control group with the claimants determined to be ineligible for the demonstration to construct a claimant sample that is representative of the claimant population. Since none of these claimants were required to participate in demonstration services, this sample can be used to estimate and test an "uncontaminated" profiling model.[6]

Because the current WPRS system is very similar to two of the three treatments in the JSA demonstration—Individualized Job Search Assistance (IJSA) and Individualized Job Search Assistance with Training (IJSA+)—we can use claimants assigned to these two treatments, along with demonstration-ineligible claimants, to represent the UI population under WPRS. Only those claimants deemed likely to exhaust their benefits were required to participate in either IJSA or IJSA+. From this sample of participants and ineligible nonparticipants, we estimate and test a "contaminated" profiling model.[7]

In this section, profiling results from the contaminated model are compared to profiling results from the uncontaminated model in Florida. Each model is used to predict exhaustion and to select claimants to be referred to services on the basis of two different eligibility criteria (described later). To measure the impact of contamination, we address the following three questions:

1) Does the contaminated profiling model target services to a different group of claimants than the uncontaminated model? (And to what extent?)

2) Does the contaminated profiling model target services to claimants who are less likely to exhaust their benefits than the uncontaminated model? (i.e., does contamination lead to less effective targeting of services to claimants likely to exhaust their UI benefits? And to what extent?)

3) Does the contaminated profiling model target services to claimants whose characteristics are different from the characteristics of claimants targeted by the uncontaminated model? (And to what extent?)

To address the first question, we measure the degree of overlap between the claimants targeted for services by the uncontaminated profiling model and the claimants targeted for services by the contaminated model under two possible targeting rules. Under the first targeting rule, claimants in the top 25 percent of all profiling scores are referred to services; the 75th percentile in the profiling score distribution defines the profiling score threshold above which claimants are assigned to services. Under the second targeting rule, claimants in the top 50 percent of all profiling scores are referred to services. Because the contaminated and uncontaminated models produce different profiling scores, the group of claimants referred to services under any targeting rule might depend on which model was used to compute profiling scores. For the two targeting rules, Table 2.3 presents the percent of claimants who would be referred to services based on 1) both the uncontaminated model and the contaminated model; 2) the uncontaminated model only; 3) the contaminated model only; and 4) neither model. If both models targeted the same group of claimants for services, we would expect those percents to be 25 percent, 0 percent, 0 percent, and 75 percent, respectively, for the first targeting rule, and 50 percent, 0 percent, 0 percent, and 50 percent, respectively, for the second targeting rule.

Table 2.3 shows that there is a high degree of consistency between the claimants who would be referred to services based on the two profiling models. For the 25 percent threshold, 16.2 percent of claimants are targeted by both models, versus the 25 percent that we would expect if the two models were perfectly consistent. For the 50 percent threshold, 36.6 percent of claimants are targeted for services by both models, versus the 50 percent that we would expect if the two models were perfectly consistent. The two models are highly if not perfectly consistent because they predict high exhaustion probabilities for many of the same UI claimants.

However, contamination may still be a serious issue if the claimants targeted by the contaminated model have much lower exhaustion rates (in the absence of IJSA and IJSA+) than the claimants deemed eligible by the uncontaminated model (question 2). To answer this question, we compare the two models with respect to exhaustion rates. The sample for this comparison excludes those used in estimating the two models and excludes those assigned to one of the demonstration treatments, which may influence exhaustion. Table 2.4 provides exhaustion rates separately for those targeted for services according to each of the two models.

Table 2.4 UI Exhaustion Rate by Profiling Status (%)

Threshold/model	Below threshold	Above threshold
25% Threshold for eligibility		
Uncontaminated profiling model[a]	41.3	48.9
Contaminated profiling model[b]	41.7	47.7
50% Threshold for eligibility		
Uncontaminated profiling model[a]	40.2	46.2
Contaminated profiling model[b]	39.8	46.6

[a] The workers used to estimate the uncontaminated profiling model include PTS ineligibles and workers who were assigned to the control group. Explicitly excluded are workers assigned to Structured Job Search Assistance, IJSA, or IJSA+.

[b] The workers used to estimate the contaminated profiling model include PTS ineligibles and workers who were assigned either to Individualized Job Search Assistance (IJSA) or to Individualized Job Search Assistance Plus Training (IJSA+).

Before addressing the implications of Table 2.4 for contamination, consider the targeting effectiveness of the uncontaminated model. A perfect model deems only those claimants who would subsequently exhaust their benefits in the absence of mandatory services as eligible. Those predicted by a perfect model to be above the threshold should exhaust at a rate of 100 percent, versus 0 percent for those below the threshold. While the model falls far short of this ideal, it performs better than a process that selects eligibles randomly. Random selection would lead to exhaustion rates that are nearly identical for those above and those below the threshold. However, Table 2.4 indicates that those above the 25 percent threshold exhaust at a rate of 48.9 percent, versus 41.3 percent for those below the 25 percent threshold. Therefore, the uncontaminated model helps to target mandatory services to those more likely to exhaust their benefits.

Does the contaminated model target those with high exhaustion probabilities as effectively as the uncontaminated model? The answer appears to be yes. For both eligibility thresholds, the difference between the exhaustion rates of those above and those below the threshold—a measure of targeting effectiveness—is nearly the same for the contaminated model as for the uncontaminated model. Therefore, contamination from IJSA and IJSA+ does not appear to reduce the targeting effectiveness of Florida's profiling model.

Lastly, we may want to know whether the characteristics of eligibles selected by the contaminated model differ from the characteristics of eligibles selected by the uncontaminated model (question 3). Table 2.5 contains the mean characteristics for the following four groups from the sample:

1)   All of those above the 25 percent threshold (i.e., deemed eligible) according to the uncontaminated model.
2)   All of those above the 25 percent threshold according to the contaminated model.
3)   All of those above the 25 percent threshold according to the uncontaminated model, but below the threshold according to the contaminated model.
4)   All of those above the 25 percent threshold according to the contaminated model, but below the threshold according to the uncontaminated model.

The difference in the mean characteristics between those deemed eligible by the uncontaminated and contaminated models (group 1 vs. 2) is driven by two factors. First, as shown in Table 2.2, the two models do not select exactly the same set of eligibles. Second, those selected only by the uncontaminated model may differ from those selected only by the contaminated model (3 vs. 4). Therefore, the differences between groups 3 and 4 will be larger than and partially responsible for the differences between groups 1 and 2. Table 2.5 provides the means needed to make these comparisons for a subset of the variables used in profiling: the unemployment rate, job tenure, and education.

Table 2.5 reveals that the mean characteristics differ considerably between those deemed eligible by the contaminated model and those deemed eligible by the uncontaminated model. These differences result from differences in the estimated logit coefficients between the contaminated and uncontaminated models. However, because both profiling models are imprecisely estimated (perhaps because of small sample sizes), the differences in the estimated coefficients and there-

Table 2.5 Mean Characteristics of Workers above the 25% Threshold by the Profiling Model (Uncontaminated or Contaminated)

Variable	All uncontaminated	All contaminated	Only uncontaminated	Only contaminated
Predicted exhaustion (PTS)	0.520	0.512	0.528	0.505
Unemployment rate	7.962	7.501	7.733	6.419
Job tenure (yr.)				
0–3	0.556	0.615	0.533	0.702
3–6	0.162	0.075	0.272	0.025
6–10	0.142	0.105	0.150	0.043
10+	0.140	0.205	0.044	0.230
Education				
High school dropout	0.446	0.477	0.261	0.350
High school graduate	0.364	0.429	0.374	0.561
Associate's degree	0.104	0.038	0.206	0.017
Bachelor's degree	0.073	0.043	0.135	0.048
Master's/doctoral degree	0.013	0.013	0.024	0.023
N (unweighted)	2,658	2,629	950	921
N (weighted)	22,734	22,724	7,979	7,969

fore in the characteristics of the eligibles selected may largely be attributable to sampling error. We believe that additional studies are required to determine whether the differences revealed in this table are robust. Furthermore, despite the differences in mean characteristics, the difference in the mean exhaustion probabilities used to determine eligibility in the JSA demonstration is very small. This suggests that the mean differences in characteristics used to predict exhaustion are off-setting. Both the actual exhaustion rates (Table 2.4) and those predicted by the JSA demonstration (Table 2.5) are comparable between those deemed eligible by the contaminated model and those deemed eligible by the uncontaminated model.

Tables 2.3, 2.4, and 2.5 suggest that the degree of contamination in estimating exhaustion probabilities from data that include workers required to participate in Florida's JSA demonstration is very small. If these results are proven robust across states and years, states planning to reestimate their worker profiling models should not be concerned about contamination from mandatory service provision through WPRS. This conclusion is consistent with previous research that measures fairly modest effects of WPRS on UI receipt, because the contaminating effect of WPRS on exhaustion should only be large if WPRS generates large reductions in UI receipt.

However, results not shown here suggest that states with more intensive programs may face greater contamination from the effect of WPRS on exhaustion rates. Florida's JSA demonstration included a program, Structured Job Search Assistance (SJSA), that provided more intensive services than the existing WPRS program in Florida. Therefore, workers randomly assigned to SJSA can be used to estimate the amount of contamination that might occur in states with more intensive WPRS programs than Florida's. Results from an analysis of this group suggest that the contamination of Florida's profiling model by mandatory SJSA services reduces our measure of targeting efficiency—the difference between the exhaustion rates of those above and those below the threshold—by 35 percent (if half of the claimants are eligible). Therefore, more intensive services with a greater impact on exhaustion rates may diminish the effectiveness of updated profiling models in predicting which UI claimants would exhaust their benefits without these services.

CONCLUDING REMARKS

The goal of the WPRS system is to provide reemployment services to displaced workers, and different states take different approaches to selecting claimants for these services. However, most states use some form of statistical model to predict whether or not claimants will exhaust their benefits in the absence of mandatory WPRS services. Furthermore, most states using statistical models use those variables selected for the national model—education, occupation, industry, job tenure, and the unemployment rate—and perhaps include some additional variables described in the first section of this chapter.

The evidence suggests that the states' efforts in developing profiling models that target likely exhaustees have not been in vain. The profiling models appear to perform better at such targeting than random selection. Both the benefit exhaustion rate and the duration of UI benefits were higher for targeted claimants (who were not assigned to mandatory treatment services) than for other claimants.

However, the targeting power of the profiling models is modest. While the gain in targeting may well produce benefits that exceed the costs of the program (an issue not addressed in this chapter), profiling models fall far short of perfect targeting. In Washington, D.C., for example, even those not targeted for reemployment services had an exhaustion rate of 47.9 percent (versus 58.8 percent for targeted claimants). Exhaustion seems to be very difficult to predict accurately with available demographic and labor market data.

Perhaps more interesting than how well profiling models targeted exhaustees in the past is how well they will target exhaustees in the future. Changes in the economy suggest the need for states to update their profiling models. However, given the legal requirements of WPRS, it is no longer possible to observe whether claimants would have exhausted their benefits in the absence of WPRS because the most likely exhaustees are required to participate in the system. Furthermore, if the program is effective in decreasing unemployment duration, the effect of the program contaminates the exhaustion data and the profiling models estimated from these data.

However, our results suggest that contamination from assignment to WPRS is very small, at least in Florida. This result is consistent with the evidence suggesting modest effects of mandatory reemployment services. WPRS systems that are modestly effective in reducing exhaustion rates can probably update their profiling models with minimal concern about the contamination issue addressed in this chapter.

Notes

1. This variable is calculated as the difference between the "separation" and "claim filed" dates.
2. It is worth noting that one contribution of this variable is to lower the predicted exhaustion probability of claimants without demonstrated capacity to maintain long-term jobs.
3. Three different packages of services were tested. These packages look broadly similar to services currently provided by states through the WPRS systems.
4. The findings from Washington, D.C., and Florida are generated by a process that is much closer to the way that WPRS actually operates than the findings from New Jersey. However, the findings among all states are similar enough to lead us to the same conclusions.
5. The initial screens used in the first step of the profiling model, specifically permanent layoff and union hiring hall attachment, were not designed to target claimants with long UI spells. Rather, these were intended to exclude claimants for whom WPRS services are inappropriate because they may still be employer attached. Regardless, some of these screens may contribute to the identification of claimants likely to exhaust their benefits.
6. Half of the sample is used in estimating the model. The other half is reserved for comparing it to the "contaminated" model described in the next paragraph.
7. Half of the sample is used in estimating the model. The other half is reserved for comparing it to the "uncontaminated" model.

References

Berger, Mark C., Dan A. Black, Amitabh Chandra, and Steven N. Allen. 1997. "Kentucky's Statistical Model of Worker Profiling for Unemployment Insurance." *The Kentucky Journal of Economics and Business* 16:1–18.

Corson, Walter, and Joshua Haimson. 1996. *The New Jersey Unemployment Insurance Reemployment Demonstration Project: Six-Year Follow-Up and*

Summary Report (revised edition). UI Occasional Paper no. 96-2, U.S. Department of Labor, Employment and Training Administration, Washington, D.C.

Decker, Paul T., Lance Freeman, and Daniel H. Klepinger. 1999. "Assisting Unemployment Insurance Claimants: The One-Year Impacts of the Job Search Assistance Demonstration." Report prepared for the U.S. Department of Labor, Employment and Training Administration.

Comments on Chapter 2

Mark C. Berger
University of Kentucky

The chapter "Predicting the Exhaustion of Unemployment Compensation" has two distinct purposes: to provide an overview of profiling models among states and to report reestimation results using demonstration projects from Washington, D.C., Florida, and New Jersey. The summary among states is important, both to provide information on what other states have done and what might be successful in other programs. The reestimation work is also important, especially if the results on contamination bias are similar in other settings. Overall, this chapter may become an important reference for policymakers and technical specialists as states update their profiling models and as profiling is extended into other policy areas.

OVERVIEW OF PROFILING MODELS

In reviewing models used in other states, the authors discuss the dependent variables used, the estimation methods, and the set of explanatory variables included in the model. The authors point out that both the national and Maryland versions of the Department of Labor model use a binary dependent variable indicating exhaustion and a logistic estimation technique. They state that alternative dependent variables such as number of weeks or fraction of benefits exhausted have been tested in some states.

At the Center for Business and Economic Research at the University of Kentucky, we do the modeling, estimation, and operation for the Kentucky Profiling Model.[1] We use the fraction of benefits exhausted as our dependent variable. There is a fair amount of variation in the distribution of completed spells that cannot be exploited using a simple binary exhaustion variable, but that can be picked up by a variable such as the fraction of benefits exhausted.

We have considered a series of estimation techniques and dependent variables. We tested the predictive power of each (probit, logit, ordinary least squares, Cox model, and double limit tobit) along with random assignment of claimants for profiling services using 10 percent of our sample that was held out from the original estimation. The double limit tobit model consistently came out on top in these exercises.

In discussing explanatory variables, the authors make the point that some states use only the five variables included in the original national model: education, occupation, industry, tenure, and the unemployment rate. In Kentucky, we found that there were many more accessible variables that significantly affected exhaustion and were included in the profiling model. While these variables add to the data collection exercise, they also enhance the model and help insure that the "right" individuals are selected for services. The collection of these additional variables has not been overly burdensome. The key is setting up a system for collection and sticking with it.

The authors also discuss substate indicators, either local unemployment rates or local categorical variables. Regional variables can be used to separate regions and to allow for different effects of personal characteristics across regions. In Kentucky, we defined eight regions across the state based on similar economic circumstances. Thus, region indicators are in essence interacted with other characteristics to produce unique effects of the various characteristics by region.

REESTIMATION RESULTS USING
DEMONSTRATION PROJECTS

The authors have embarked on an extensive reestimation exercise in order to assess the effects of "contamination" of the program itself on the estimation process. The idea is that we should not necessarily use the experiences of those receiving services to predict the exhaustion of new claimants in the absence of extra services. They use demonstration project data from Florida to estimate "contaminated" and "uncontaminated" models.

The "uncontaminated" model uses the control group and those who passed the threshold but did not receive extra services in a Job Search Assistance 1995–1996 demonstration. The "contaminated" model uses those assigned to treatment and program ineligibles from the same demonstration. One-half of each sample was held out for comparisons using the two sets of estimates. The authors find that there is significant overlap in those chosen for services in the two models. Thus, contamination bias may not be a big problem. They also find that the two models are similarly effective at targeting exhaustees. This again points to the possibility that contamination is not a large issue. The result of small contamination effects is consistent with what we have been finding in our reestimation efforts in Kentucky.

This reestimation work is important, although much more work should be done on the robustness of the contamination findings and appropriate estimation techniques. More work needs to be done on how the contaminated observations should be appropriately incorporated into the estimation process. Should we just ignore the treatment or somehow model it? The latter seems preferable.

In the end, perhaps we should not be surprised that contamination bias is not a big problem. The treatments that claimants receive are not extensive, and the effects of profiling on labor market outcomes appear modest.[2] The net effect may be that estimates of profiling models and, more importantly, the predicted rank ordering of claimants by profiling scores are not influenced to any great extent by the use of contaminated data. If this reasoning is correct and if the Florida results are robust, it would be good news to states confronted with the task of reestimating their profiling models.

Notes

1. For a description of the Kentucky model, see Berger et al. (1997).
2. For experimental evidence on the effects of profiling on labor market outcomes in Kentucky, see Black et al. (2002).

References

Berger, Mark C., Dan A. Black, Amitabh Chandra, and Steven N. Allen. 1997. "Profiling Workers for Unemployment Insurance in Kentucky." *The Kentucky Journal of Economics and Business* 16: 1–18.

Black, Dan A., Jeffrey A. Smith, Mark C. Berger, and Brett J. Noel. 2001. "Is the Threat of Reemployment Services More Effective than the Services Themselves? Experimental Evidence from the UI System." National Bureau of Economic Research Working paper no. W8825, March.

3
Evaluation of WPRS Systems

Katherine P. Dickinson
Social Policy Research Associates

Paul T. Decker
Mathematica Policy Research

Suzanne D. Kreutzer
Social Policy Research Associates

In 1993, Congress enacted Public Law 103-152, which amended the Social Security Act by requiring states to establish a system of profiling new unemployment insurance (UI) claimants that

- identifies which claimants are likely to exhaust UI benefits and, therefore, need job search assistance to successfully transition to new employment,
- refers such claimants to reemployment services in a timely manner, and
- collects follow-up information relating to reemployment services received by such claimants and the employment outcomes subsequent to receiving such services.

The law also requires claimants referred to reemployment services to participate in those or similar services as a condition of eligibility for UI unless the claimant has already completed services or has "justifiable cause" for not participating.

The U.S. Department of Labor (DOL) funded Social Policy Research Associates and Mathematica Policy Research to evaluate the implementation and impact of this Worker Profiling and Reemployment Services (WPRS) Systems initiative. The goals of the evaluation were to

1) Describe the ways that states are operating WPRS systems. Aspects of WPRS implementation include
   - developing coordination among partnering agencies,
   - identifying and selecting claimants at risk of benefit exhaustion,
   - providing reemployment services,
   - obtaining feedback about the extent that profiled and referred claimants meet their participation requirements, and
   - identifying different strategies for implementing and operating WPRS systems that may influence the effectiveness of WPRS systems.
2) Determine the effectiveness of WPRS systems. Specifically, we evaluated the effectiveness of WPRS in
   - increasing receipt of reemployment services among those likely to exhaust their UI benefits,
   - reducing receipt of UI and the extent that UI benefits are exhausted, and
   - increasing subsequent employment and earnings of UI claimants.
3) Provide recommendations to enhance the ability of WPRS systems to meet the goals of the WPRS legislation.

This chapter highlights the results of this four-year evaluation.[1]

The results presented in this chapter are based on data from two primary sources. First, in both 1996 and 1997, we surveyed administrators in all states about the implementation and operations of their WPRS systems. Because WPRS requires coordination among several agencies, we surveyed four respondents in each state: administrators of the UI, the employment service (ES), and Economic Dislocation and Worker Adjustment Assistance Act (EDWAA) programs, and the administrator responsible for coordinating WPRS operations.

Second, we obtained claimant-level data from a sample of eight states, which were chosen to represent variation in the intensity of reemployment services provided under WPRS. We obtained UI and labor market outcome data for all claimants who filed an initial claim in the last two quarters of 1995 or any time in 1996 and who were subject to referral to mandatory reemployment services through WPRS (that is, not screened out because of a definite recall date, union hall membership, or other characteristics). Those who were referred to WPRS services constitute the "treatment group" and those who were not referred constitute the "comparison group."

IMPLEMENTATION AND OPERATION OF WPRS SYSTEM

Developing effective WPRS systems involves many complex tasks. States need to develop methods to identify claimants who are at risk of exhausting their benefits, refer such claimants to local offices for services, provide services appropriate to those claimants, track claimants' progress in services, establish policies about determinations and denials for those who do not participate satisfactorily, and track the subsequent outcomes of WPRS claimants. To accomplish these tasks, states need to develop effective coordination and communication linkages among the participating agencies—usually UI, ES, and ED-WAA—that may not have worked closely together in the past.

The results of both the 1996 and 1997 state administrator surveys indicate that, by and large, states have carried out these complex tasks, meeting the legislated requirements as well as following DOL guidance for implementing WPRS systems. Below we describe the implementation of each of the WPRS requirements.

Identification and Selection of UI Claimants

All states have implemented a two-step profiling process to identify claimants at risk of exhausting their benefits. First, all states screened out claimants on recall status and those attached to union hiring halls, as required in DOL guidance. States also frequently screened out claimants working in seasonal industries, who may also be expected to be recalled, and interstate claimants.

Second, all states then used a further profiling method to identify claimants who had high probabilities of exhausting their benefits. DOL encouraged states to use a statistical model to identify such claimants. To facilitate this, DOL developed a national model as an example and provided technical assistance to states in developing their own models.

By 1997, about 85 percent of the states were using a statistical model to identify claimants at risk of exhausting their benefits. Among those states using a model, 85 percent developed state-specific models to predict which claimants were likely to exhaust UI benefits in their specific state. Most of these used a single model statewide, although a few states, such as Kentucky and Washington, developed multiple models that were fine-tuned to the specific circumstances of separate regions within their states.

In contrast, 15 percent of the states that used a statistical model simply adopted the entire national model, including its coefficients. Although the national model identified key variables that affected UI exhaustion nationally, we found that state-specific models varied widely both in the characteristics that affected UI exhaustion and in the direction of the impacts of those characteristics. For example, some states found that lower-wage workers were more likely to exhaust benefits, while other states found that higher-wage workers were more likely to do so. States that use the coefficients from the national model, therefore, probably are not targeting WPRS services as accurately as states that developed their own model.

The 15 percent of states that did not use a statistical model relied instead on a characteristics screen. Under this approach, the state identifies a few characteristics associated with exhaustion, creates a pool of claimants with those characteristics, and then randomly selects claimants among the pool to refer to WPRS services. This approach is also less accurate than a state model because it accounts for relatively few characteristics and makes no distinction among individuals within the pool.

States used a variety of characteristics in their profiling model or characteristics screens in 1997. Virtually all states included a measure of the claimant's previous industry or occupation. Over 90 percent of the states included some claimant characteristics in their statistical model or characteristics screen, most commonly education and job tenure. Three-quarters of states included some indicator of the local economy in the area where a claimant lived. Less frequently, states included a claimant's previous wage in their profiling methodology (30 percent) or measures of potential UI benefits, such as weekly benefit amount or total entitlement (45 percent).

Although all states intended to refer claimants with the highest probability of UI exhaustion to services, this did not always occur because of errors in implementing profiling and selection at both the state and local levels. In our impact analyses in this phase and an earlier phase of the project, we collected claimant-level data from 12 states. Two of these 12 states made errors in implementing their profiling procedures. One inadvertently matched the wrong profiling score to individual claimants' records; the other incorrectly identified which claimants had the highest scores. Further, in three additional states, we found that a substantial number of local offices did not systematically refer claimants with the highest scores to services. None of these states were aware of their implementation problems.

Given the problems that we uncovered, we strongly recommend that states or DOL establish quality control measures to ensure that states are carrying out profiling as intended and that local offices are selecting claimants as intended. We recommend that states review on an ongoing basis the information used for profiling and selecting claimants for WPRS services, the resulting calculated scores, and the relationship between those scores and referral to services in each local office.

The percentage of profiled claimants (i.e., those not initially

Table 3.1 Percentage of States Referring Profiled Claimants to Services

Percentage of profiled claimants referred to services	FY 96–97	FY 97–98
<5	24	31
5–9	33	29
10–19	25	22
20–29	6	7
30 or more	12	11

SOURCE: Employment and Training Administration Form 9048.

screened out) who were referred to services varied widely across states, from a low of 1 percent to a high of 100 percent, with an average of 13 percent. Further, the percentage of states that referred fewer than 5 percent of their claimants to WPRS services increased from 24 percent in FY 96–97 to 31 percent in FY 97–98, as shown in Table 3.1.

One reason for this trend may be that states increasingly deferred to local offices in determining the number of claimants referred in each office. Although this policy helped states and local areas match the capacity for service to the number of claimants who are referred (as required by DOL guidance), it resulted in states having less control over the number of claimants receiving reemployment services.

We found that the WPRS goal of referring selected claimants early in their unemployment spell was being met. Most states profiled claimants within two weeks of their initial claim, notified claimants promptly, and required them to report to services soon after notification. As states have gained experience in conducting these tasks, the timeliness of WPRS referrals has increased.

Reemployment Services

The legislation authorizing WPRS allows a wide range of reemployment services within WPRS. An increasing number of states established specific requirements for a core set of mandatory services to be provided to all WPRS claimants, although the content of those services was most often left to local discretion. Virtually all states required an orientation—typically an hour or less—to explain WPRS services and claimants' responsibilities.

More than half of the states then required claimants to attend a group workshop. Typically these workshops provided labor market information, training in job search methods, guidance in preparing resumes, and help in exploring career alternatives. In two-thirds of these states, required workshops also provided claimants with referrals to job openings. About half of these workshops culminated in the development of individual service plans. Most of these required workshops were brief, the majority lasting four hours or less. About three-quarters of the states required all profiled and referred claimants to meet one-on-one with an employment counselor, usually for one hour, to assess claimants' interests and abilities and develop a service plan.

Although one of DOL's "basic operational concepts" for WPRS calls for customized services that are based on each claimant's needs, the extent that states conformed to this principle varied. In about one-third of the states, almost no claimants were required to participate in any services beyond the mandatory core services required of all WPRS claimants. In contrast, in 30 percent of the states, more than half of WPRS claimants were required to participate in varying types of additional services, as specified in their individual service plans.

As shown in Table 3.2, the length and number of services required of WPRS claimants varied widely among states.[2] Several states required substantial WPRS participation, whether measured as the number of required services or the length of required participation in services. About 26 percent of states required a large number of services (i.e., seven or more), while 27 percent required relatively long participation (i.e., more than 10 hours). At the other end of the spectrum, 23 percent of states required no more than three services, and 16 percent of states required no more than four hours of participation.

In states that provide less extensive services, customers are likely to be less satisfied with WPRS services. In an earlier phase of this

Table 3.2 Length and Number of Required Services

Services	Percentage of states in 1997
Length (hr.)	
1–4	16
5–9	29
10–19	18
20 or more	9
Claimants required to participate until UI benefits stop	22
Number	
3 or fewer	23
4–6	51
7–9	17
10 or more	9

SOURCE: Employment and Training Administration Form 9048.

study, we conducted a customer satisfaction survey of 2,000 claimants who were referred to services in six states that implemented WPRS early. We found that customers were far more satisfied with WPRS services when they received more services and services of longer duration. For example, among WPRS claimants who received two or fewer services, only 15 percent rated the services as very or extremely helpful. In contrast, among those who received seven or more services, nearly 55 percent rated WPRS services highly. Similarly, among claimants who participated in services lasting five or fewer hours, only 25 percent rated services extremely or very helpful compared to 60 percent of those who participated in services lasting 20 hours or more.

In selecting providers of WPRS services, states generally followed two strategies. About two-thirds of the states referred most of their WPRS claimants to ES for reemployment services and generally referred claimants to EDWAA only for education or training services. In these states, ES provided services to 75 percent or more of the WPRS claimants.

The remaining states referred the most job-ready to ES for job referral services and referred to EDWAA those who needed more services, including more extensive reemployment services as well as occupational or educational skills training.

Tracking WPRS Claimants' Progress in Services

The WPRS legislation requires referred claimants to participate in services as a condition of UI receipt. To ensure that profiled and referred claimants report to services and participate satisfactorily, WPRS service providers must provide UI with accurate and timely feedback.

Virtually all states developed an automated data system to track WPRS claimants' progress in services. The information contained in the automated systems, however, varied widely. Only half of the states automated WPRS claimants' service plans so that the progress of the claimants could be automatically tracked. In the remainder of the states, staff needed to manually check that claimants were participating satisfactorily in the services called for in their service plans.

About one-half of the states developed new data systems specifically for WPRS, although the sophistication of the resulting data systems varied. In many cases, the WPRS systems were not linked electronically to the UI or service provider systems. As a result, data often had to be entered twice, and paper reports were needed to communicate about WPRS participants.

Most of the remaining states modified their existing systems—predominately their ES systems—to track WPRS claimants' progress. Again, many of these systems lacked linkages with UI data systems so that data needed to be entered twice.

UI administrators reported that developing a system to track the progress of claimants was one of the most difficult WPRS-related tasks. It is clear that further automation of claimant tracking processes, especially automated service plans, could make these processes more efficient.

Determinations and Denials

Because participation in WPRS services is a condition of continued UI eligibility, states needed to develop policies about how and when WPRS claimants would be denied benefits for failure to cooperate with the WPRS requirements.[3] The process of denying UI benefits because of failure to comply with WPRS requirements varied among states. About 25 percent of the states initiated the benefit-denial process when a claimant missed a scheduled meeting, while the other 75 percent of the states gave claimants a warning and a chance to reschedule. When claimants were denied benefits, about half the states continued to deny benefits until the problem had been corrected, while the other states denied benefits for only one week.

The most common reason that WPRS claimants were denied benefits was failure to report to orientation. Denials for claimants failing to make satisfactory progress in the required services were far less common. Increasingly, states assumed that claimants were participating satisfactorily unless notified to the contrary by providers. This is not surprising given the difficulty in automatically tracking claimants' progress in most states' management information systems.

Tracking Outcomes

Legislation requires that states track the outcomes achieved by WPRS claimants, and DOL has established a required outcome report. In 1997, only 58 percent of the states collected information on outcomes for WPRS claimants. It is likely, however, that the number of states tracking outcomes has increased since the DOL reporting requirements took effect last year. Among states collecting information on outcomes, states commonly tracked initial placements and/or entered employments, earnings for specific periods after initial claims, and reemployment industry. Over 40 percent of UI administrators reported that identifying appropriate outcomes or developing a system to track outcomes for WPRS was a very or extremely difficult task.

Coordination among Agencies

In many states, the UI, ES, and EDWAA programs coordinated extensively in WPRS-related activities. To summarize the extent of cooperation, we grouped WPRS activities into three major tasks: tasks related to developing services, tasks related to developing data systems, and tasks related to developing a profiling method.[4] We found the following three modes of cooperation between UI and ES, the agencies most involved in WPRS activities:

- Dominant agency: In about 25 percent of the states, a single agency was either very or extremely involved in developing WPRS policies in all areas, while the other agency was at most somewhat involved. In a large majority of the cases it was ES that was the dominant agency.
- Division of labor: In another 20 percent of the states, ES and UI divided responsibility for WPRS tasks. Most commonly, ES led the tasks related to services and the data system, while UI led the development of the profiling model.
- Shared leadership: In the remaining 55 percent of the states, UI and ES shared the leadership of at least one of the three major tasks. Most commonly, these two agencies shared the tasks related to data systems and the development of the profiling model, while ES led the service-related tasks.

In about half of the states, EDWAA was not substantially involved in any of the three groups of tasks. When EDWAA was involved, it was almost always in cooperation with ES. Not surprisingly, EDWAA was most involved in service-related tasks, although in about one-quarter of the states EDWAA was also involved in developing data systems.

Even though WPRS requires extensive coordination among agencies, the administrators reported that getting the state agencies to work together was not difficult. States also reported that it was not difficult to get the local offices to work together on WPRS tasks.

FUNDING OF WPRS

UI funds accounted for 40 percent of total funding earmarked for WPRS. Most UI funding came from grants that DOL awarded to help states cover the costs of implementing WPRS systems—such as developing profiling models and tracking systems.

EDWAA funding of WPRS activities equaled UI funding in 1997. Most of the EDWAA funds came from Governor's Reserve funds, although supplemental EDWAA grants for WPRS implementation accounted for about 10 percent of WPRS funding. Because UI implementation grants were one-time grants, funds for dislocated workers will likely be a primary source of WPRS funding in the future.

ES funding specifically earmarked for WPRS accounted for less than 15 percent of total WPRS funding, despite the fact that ES was the major provider of WPRS services and many local offices have dedicated specific staff to WPRS activities. Over one-third of ES administrators reported that arranging for adequate funding for WPRS was a very or extremely difficult task.

OPINIONS ABOUT WPRS SYSTEMS

Overall, state administrators were very supportive of the WPRS approach. About two-thirds of all administrators felt that WPRS met its goal of reducing the length of UI receipt among profiled and referred claimants. Most felt that the mandatory nature of services was justified.

Administrators indicated that WPRS had other benefits as well, including improving overall coordination among their agencies. Most also felt that WPRS improved services for all job seekers, not just WPRS claimants.

OUTCOMES OF WPRS

The second component of this study is an analysis of the impacts of WPRS on UI and labor market outcomes of referred claimants. To determine the effectiveness of the WPRS systems on claimants' outcomes, we needed a method to determine what the outcomes for the referred claimants would have been in the absence of WPRS. To do this, we selected a "comparison group" of similar claimants who were not referred to WPRS. The ideal way to develop such a comparison group would be to conduct a classical experiment by randomly assigning claimants to two groups: one group that is referred to WPRS and another that is not. Because WPRS was implemented as an ongoing statewide program, however, we were unable to conduct such an experiment to evaluate it.

We therefore chose an alternative comparison group—claimants who passed the initial WPRS screens but were not referred to services. Although nonreferred claimants, by design, differ from referred claimants in that they have lower predicted probabilities of UI exhaustion, two factors enhance the validity of this design.

First, because claimants were referred to WPRS on the basis of known criteria, we can control for these criteria using regression methods. This situation is unlike that in other quasi-experimental evaluations where individuals choose to participate in a program. In those cases, the participation in services is determined partly by unmeasurable factors, such as individual motivation, which cannot be included in a regression model. Our ability to know and control for the factors that determine referral to WPRS should enhance the validity of our comparison group methodology and, therefore, the results of our analysis.

Second, the validity of our design is enhanced because the predicted probabilities of UI exhaustion for referred and nonreferred claimants overlap considerably. This overlap usually came about because of local capacity constraints. In the eight states in our study, each local office was responsible for selecting the number of claimants to refer to services, based on its capacity to serve new claimants each week. Because these capacity constraints varied by office and by week, the predicted probabilities of claimants referred to services statewide overlapped considerably with the probabilities of those not referred to services. As a result, we can compare outcomes for claimants referred to services with those for claimants with similar scores but who were not referred to services.

Impacts on Services

Comparison of referred and nonreferred claimants in our sample of states indicates that WPRS is meeting the goals of providing reemployment services at a greater rate and earlier in claimants' unemployment experience. Referred claimants were up to 50 percentage points more likely to receive at least one service (beyond WPRS orientation), and they received significantly more types of services than nonreferred claimants. WPRS had the largest impacts on receipt of job search workshops and job clubs. Referred claimants were also more likely to be enrolled in EDWAA, although usually for basic readjustment services rather than training. Finally, in most states, referred claimants received services earlier in their unemployment spells than did nonreferred claimants.

Impacts on UI Benefits, Employment, and Earnings

WPRS services were expected to reduce UI benefit receipt among claimants targeted for services by assisting them in finding a new job quickly. Previous studies found that the general service approach used in WPRS can reduce UI receipt. For example, a mandatory job search assistance package offered to UI claimants in the New Jersey UI Reemployment Demonstration in 1986–1987 reduced average UI receipt by about half a week (Corson et al. 1989). More recently, similar mandatory job search assistance services provided to claimants in Florida and in Washington, D.C., in 1995–1996 reduced UI receipt by about half a week in Florida and about one week in Washington, D.C. (Decker et al. 2000). Experiments in job search assistance in other states have generated similarly moderate reductions in UI receipt (Meyer 1995).

To determine the impact of WPRS on claimants' UI receipt, we used two measures as dependent variables in our regressions: weeks of UI benefits paid and dollars of UI benefits paid. The estimated impacts of WPRS are shown in Table 3.3.

Table 3.3 Estimated Impacts of WPRS on UI Outcomes

Benefit receipt	Connecticut	Illinois	Kentucky	Maine	New Jersey	South Carolina
Weeks	-0.25**	-0.41***	-0.21*	-0.98***	-0.29***	0.02
	(0.12)	(0.07)	(0.12)	(0.32)	(0.05)	(0.12)
Dollars	-55.53*	-64.28***	-20.92	-135.03***	-139.99***	2.50
	(28.42)	(14.11)	(22.53)	(41.18)	(13.22)	(21.27)

NOTE: Standard errors are in parentheses. *** = Statistically significant at the 99 percent confidence level in a two-tailed test; ** = statistically significant at the 95 percent confidence level in a two-tailed test; * = statistically significant at the 90 percent confidence level in a two-tailed test.

WPRS generally reduced UI benefits received by the claimants in the states we examined. In five of the six states for which we were able to generate estimates—Connecticut, Illinois, Kentucky, Maine, and New Jersey—WPRS significantly reduced average weeks of UI benefits per claimant.[5] As shown in Table 3.3, the estimated UI reductions ranged from 0.21 weeks in Kentucky to nearly a full week in Maine.[6] In all five states except Kentucky, WPRS also significantly reduced dollars of benefits received, with reductions of up to about $140 per claimant in New Jersey. In the sixth state, South Carolina, WPRS appears to have had no impact on UI receipt—claimants referred to WPRS services had approximately the same UI outcomes as did similar claimants not referred to services.

WPRS was also expected to help claimants return to work sooner, thereby increasing employment and earnings in the short run. Furthermore, to the extent that WPRS claimants learned about better paying, more stable jobs through WPRS than they would have found on their own, it was possible that WPRS would increase employment and earnings in the long run as well.

Earlier studies of the WPRS approach have generated inconsistent findings about the impact on employment and earnings. In the New Jersey UI Reemployment Demonstration, mandatory job search assistance was found to have significant impacts on employment in the first two quarters after the initial benefit claim and significant impacts on earnings in the first quarter (Corson et al. 1989). More recently, the Job Search Assistance Demonstration was found to have uneven impacts on employment and earnings of claimants, improving earnings in one demonstration state (Washington, D.C.) but not in the other (Florida).

Our estimates provide little evidence that WPRS increased the employment or earnings of referred claimants. Most of the estimated impacts on employment and earnings, which are presented in Table 3.4, are not statistically different than zero, and the statistically significant estimated impacts are as likely to be negative as they are to be positive. The only significantly positive impacts on earnings occurred in Maine (in the first, third, and fourth quarters) and New Jersey (in the third quarter), both states where WPRS significantly reduced UI receipt. However, our estimates also suggest that WPRS reduced the rate of employment in New Jersey.

Table 3.4 Estimated Effects of WRPS on Employment and Earnings

Effect	Connecticut	Illinois	Kentucky	Maine	New Jersey	South Carolina
Probability of employment (%)						
Quarter 1	0.61	−0.69*	0.02	1.39	−1.61***	−1.05
	(0.62)	(0.41)	(0.67)	(1.41)	(0.31)	(0.69)
Quarter 2	−0.54	−1.10**	−0.49	−0.16	−0.75**	−0.67
	(0.60)	(0.44)	(0.68)	(1.35)	(0.31)	(0.66)
Quarter 3	−0.59	−0.03	−1.34*	0.54	−1.84***	−0.88
	(0.62)	(0.47)	(0.77)	(1.53)	(0.32)	(0.68)
Quarter 4	0.42	0.70	0.45	1.52	−1.90***	−2.31***
	(0.69)	(0.53)	(1.00)	(1.86)	(0.35)	(0.75)
Earnings ($)						
Quarter 1	37.25	−29.72	30.52	128.87**	19.71	41.78
	(43.33)	(29.82)	(38.43)	(57.57)	(24.64)	(44.64)
Quarter 2	−5.42	−64.40	40.85	98.23	126.91***	13.10
	(44.92)	(34.38)	(39.90)	(69.23)	(24.24)	(40.50)
Quarter 3	−67.27	67.33*	−94.35*	158.81*	41.55	−69.05
	(50.00)	(38.04)	(48.36)	(83.23)	(26.28)	(43.68)
Quarter 4	8.83	−48.93	3.01	176.51*	37.61	−116.35**
	(57.46)	(44.94)	(64.08)	(101.28)	(28.71)	(48.85)

NOTE: Quarters 1, 2, 3, and 4 are the first, second, third, and fourth full calendar quarters following the first payment. Standard errors are in parentheses. *** = Statistically significant at the 99 percent confidence level in a two-tailed test; ** = statistically significant at the 95 percent confidence level in a two-tailed test; * = statistically significant at the 90 percent confidence level in a two-tailed test.

CONCLUSIONS AND RECOMMENDATIONS

On the basis of the results of this study, we make the following recommendations to improve the implementation and impact of WPRS services.

Improving Profiling and Referral to Services

- States should provide greater ongoing monitoring of state and local profiling and referral practices to ensure that they are being carried out as intended.

Profiling, selection, and referral processes are complex and involve many levels of staff: statistical analysts who develop the profiling procedures, programming and data processing staff who implement profiling procedures and calculate probability scores for claimants each week, and state and/or local program staff who select and refer specific claimants based on those probability scores. We found several states where staff were not carrying out these processes as intended, either because of errors or lack of understanding of the intent of WPRS. We strongly recommend, therefore, that states routinely monitor the ways that both state and local staff are implementing WPRS procedures.

- States should periodically update their models to reflect changes in the factors that affect UI exhaustion.

Many states have not modified their profiling models since they first implemented WPRS. In our discussions with state and local staff, several respondents indicated that they felt their models had become out of date, especially because industries and occupations in decline in their states have changed over time. We recommend, therefore, that states reestimate their models with current data.

Improving WPRS Services

- States and local areas should provide more extensive, in-depth services that are customized to the needs of individual claimants.

We found that a substantial number of states are neither requiring nor making available extensive services for claimants. Our customer satisfaction survey found that customers highly valued more extensive services, and those who received such services found WPRS much more helpful than did other claimants. Further, our impact results suggest that the states in which WPRS reduced UI receipt were also states with large impacts on claimants' receipt of services. Improving WPRS services, therefore, is likely to both increase customer satisfaction and result in greater UI savings.

The administration recently announced a Universal Reemployment initiative, which has a five-year goal of ensuring that every dislocated worker can receive the training and reemployment services that they want and need. To support this initiative, DOL has requested funding for Reemployment Services Grants to the ES, which are to be used for providing increased reemployment services to UI claimants. These grants, therefore, are a potentially important funding source for more extensive WPRS services.

- To facilitate improving services, DOL should provide guidance to states and local areas about Workforce Investment Act services appropriate for WPRS claimants.

The recently enacted Workforce Investment Act (WIA) revamps the workforce delivery system, replacing the existing EDWAA program with new dislocated worker services that must be delivered, along with ES services, through one-stop centers. The legislation calls for universal access to one-stop core services but limits access to WIA intensive services to individuals who have been determined in need of such services to obtain employment. Many WPRS claimants will likely need more than the core services, which are often self-access services that provide labor market information and information about job openings. To encourage states to provide WPRS claimants with intensive services when needed, we recommend that DOL provide guidance that claimants referred to WPRS services automatically qualify for WIA intensive services.

Increasing the Number of Claimants Referred to WPRS

- States that currently refer few claimants through WPRS should increase the number of UI claimants who receive reemployment services.

In 30 percent of the states, fewer than 5 percent of claimants are referred to WPRS services. These states should increase the percentage of claimants referred. Further, trends within the UI system imply that other states should consider increasing the referral rates as well. As more states shift to taking initial claims by telephone and eliminate the requirement for mandatory ES registration, WPRS is increasingly the only means through which claimants are systematically linked to reemployment services. The proposed Reemployment Services grants could also be used to provide services to more WPRS claimants.

Enforcing Participation Requirements

- States should enforce the requirement that referred claimants participate in the services required in their service plans.

Most states appear to enforce the requirement that WPRS claimants report for an orientation but are more lax in enforcing requirements for satisfactory progress in required services. Our outcome evaluation suggests that strict enforcement is important to WPRS achieving its goal of reducing UI receipt. We recommend, therefore, that states more strictly enforce participation requirements.

Improving Data Systems to Track Progress in Services and Outcomes

- States should improve their WPRS tracking process to make it more efficient and more accurate.

One reason that states do not more vigorously enforce participation requirements may be that their data systems are not fully automated and do not link the UI and the service providers' information about claimants. Although DOL provided implementation grants to help fund more coordinated data systems, it appears more assistance is needed. As part of WIA implementation, states may be developing new data systems to better coordinate the management information systems of partners in their one-stop systems. If so, we strongly recommend that states explicitly design those systems to support WPRS.

- States should develop outcome reporting systems so that states can comply with the reporting requirements.

Although the WPRS legislation requires that states collect follow-up information about claimants' employment outcomes subsequent to receiving WPRS services, over 40 percent of the states have not developed a follow-up reporting system. Many UI administrators indicated that developing such a system was a very difficult task. We recommend, therefore, that DOL provide more assistance to states in developing such reporting systems. The implementation of WIA, which also requires states to track subsequent employment and earnings of customers, provides an opportunity to incorporate WPRS tracking requirements into states' one-stop reporting systems.

Notes

1. Reports available from this study include U.S. Department of Labor (1996, 1997, 1999).
2. WPRS administrators were asked directly about the length of required services. We calculated the number of required services by summing the services provided in any required workshops, one-on-one services, and supervised job search.
3. When claimants are denied benefits in UI, they do not receive benefits for a specific period but their total entitlement is not changed. Thus, for claimants who receive their full entitlement, the effect of denial is to postpone their benefits, not to reduce them.
4. We grouped the tasks using factor analysis of the extent of involvement of the three agencies in individual WPRS activities.
5. We collected data from two other states, Mississippi and Texas, but we chose not to present estimates based on these two states because of problems with the reliability of these data for evaluation purposes.
6. A recent paper (Black et al. 1998) examined the impact of WPRS in Kentucky over approximately the same period used in our study. The authors of that paper found considerably larger impacts in Kentucky than we found. According to their estimates, WPRS reduced UI receipt by more than two weeks among their sample members, compared with the 0.21-week reduction for our sample. Black et al. used a random assignment design that focuses on claimants whose benefit exhaustion probabilities were near the probability threshold used to identify claimants to be referred to WPRS services. Since this approach focused on a relatively small subgroup of claimants, the findings it yielded apply only to that subgroup.

References

Black, Dan A., Jeffrey A. Smith, Mark C. Berger, and Brett J. Noel. 1998. "Is the Threat of Training More Effective Than Training Itself? Experimental

Evidence from the UI System." Unpublished manuscript, University of Kentucky.

Corson, Walter, Paul Decker, Shari Dunstan, and Anne Gordon. 1989. *The New Jersey Unemployment Insurance Reemployment Demonstration Project: Final Evaluation Report.* Occasional Paper no. 89-3, U.S. Department of Labor, Employment and Training Administration, Washington, D.C.

Corson, Walter, and Joshua Haimson. 1996. *The New Jersey Unemployment Insurance Reemployment Demonstration Project: Six-Year Follow-Up and Summary Report* (revised edition). UI Occasional Paper no. 96-2, U.S. Department of Labor, Employment and Training Administration, Washington, D.C.

Decker, Paul T., Robert B. Olsen, Lance Freeman, and Daniel H. Klepinger. 2000. *Assisting Unemployment Insurance Claimants: The Long-Term Impacts of the Job Search Assistance Demonstration.* Office of Workforce Security Occasional Paper no. 2000-02, U.S. Department of Labor, Employment and Training Administration, Washington, D.C.

Meyer, Bruce D. 1995. "Lessons from the U.S. Unemployment Insurance Experiments." *Journal of Economic Literature* 33(1): 91–131.

U.S. Department of Labor, Employment and Training Administration. 1996. *Evaluation of Worker Profiling and Reemployment Services Systems: Interim Report.* Occasional Paper no. 96-1, U.S. Department of Labor, Washington, D.C.

———. 1997. *Evaluation of Worker Profiling and Reemployment Services Systems: Report to Congress.* Occasional Paper, U.S. Department of Labor, Washington, D.C.

———. 1999. *Evaluation of Worker Profiling and Reemployment Services Systems: Final Report.* Research and Evaluation Report Series 99-D, U.S. Department of Labor, Washington, D.C.

Comments on Chapter 3

John Heinberg
U.S. Department of Labor

My biggest challenge in trying to comment on Worker Profiling and Remployment Services (WPRS) systems is what to call it. It's really a mouthful, so in my comments I am mainly going to use the word "system." Although they reflect my own views, my comments come from the perspective of my office, the Unemployment Insurance Service (UIS) in the U.S. Department of Labor. It has been the primary responsibility of UIS to oversee development of the state WPRS systems from the federal perspective. I think it's fortunate that we have a panel of state policymakers immediately following my comments, because I can't possibly summarize state views on these systems.

My comments are directed to what I believe the chapter, and the larger evaluation on which the chapter is based, tells our office and the Labor Department more generally about the implementation and impact of this system for targeting services. The chapter really demonstrates the wisdom of beginning an evaluation at the time an initiative is launched. Most often that is not done, so we have a great deal of information on the system at what is still a very early point in its operation. This system has been a very complex undertaking for the states. The authors have done an excellent job of pointing out the many challenges and problems with system implementation. These include the profiling selection and referral practices, provision of reemployment services, enforcing participation requirements, and tracking progress, services, and outcomes.

My strongest impression from the chapter, however, is that the state systems have had a variable but limited impact on the intended outcomes such as reducing UI payments, benefit duration, and the rate of benefit exhaustion. Even though the impact estimates are preliminary, it seems to me unlikely that the final version will turn out very differently. So I think the key question, which we cannot yet answer, is whether the lack of impact, particularly in some states, stems from faulty logic or from incomplete implementation of an inherently sound idea.

If we try to look for reasons for the lack of impact, I think they have to be teased out indirectly. The authors provide some clues, but one strong limitation of the evaluation is that it had a relatively minor field component. A point that was not brought up in the chapter itself concerns what is actually happening in the system as it was implemented at state and local levels. Nevertheless, here are what appear to be some of the factors. It is important in the context of this meeting, and as the chapter states early on, that developing effective systems involves many complex tasks.

The system that we are talking about here goes much beyond simply targeting services. It involves the whole range of how referrals are done, services are provided, outcomes are observed, and then what people do with that information. So, as designed, the system requires very sophisticated methods for identifying and prioritizing clients and referring them, developing individual service plans, providing the intensity and range of reemployment services, then tracking progress, establishing and enforcing policies about denial of benefits, and measuring and reporting the outcomes. I think the chapter does not get into this as much as I might emphasize. The system, I believe, requires strong management oversight of the total process so that all of the elements fit together.

The chapter implies that there are various points in the process where the logic can and does break down in full scale real world implementation. It points most clearly to two areas: 1) providing an adequate range of reemployment services to referred claimants, and 2) procedures on denial of benefits for failure to comply with requirements. One comment I want to make about Dickinson's presentation this morning concerns a point that was not made in the chapter. She hypothesized that states aren't requiring services in which clients are unlikely to participate, since states would then be forced to deny benefits. However, the evidence is that states don't deny benefits to people for failing to participate in services. I also want to note that because of the limited field component, the chapter does not provide a lot of information on effective practice for reemployment services provision—not enough to provide a basis for system improvement.

Here are some other factors that go beyond the two that the chapter emphasized. Dickinson did emphasize these quite a bit in her presentation. The state-specific profiling models have not been fully implemented or consistently updated. As the chapter says, the states did not consistently refer to services claimants with highest probability of exhaustion. In her presentation, Dickinson reviewed the evidence on this.

Even though the authorizing legislation requires that states track outcomes, the chapter indicates that only about three-fifths of states were doing so in 1997. I looked at some of the more recent federal reporting data that have come in to us, and those numbers have edged up only slightly. Maybe two-thirds of the states recently reported that information. Reporting has been hampered to a large extent, I understand, by Y2K concerns. Furthermore, WPRS system reporting has not been fully automated. The WPRS report is not in the regular group of periodic reports which we receive from the states. Unless the outcome information is consistently tracked, validated, and reported, the vital feedback information is not available for oversight and corrective action. Finally, it's not clear exactly who is in charge of the system at either the federal or state level.

To summarize, the chapter shows us where in this complex process the train can run off the track, and it gives strong evidence of the number of places where it in fact has. I want to stress the following point: at this relatively early stage in the implementation of this complex initiative, in trying to do something with all of the elements that we have here, it is really soon to deduce much about what's going on. Furthermore, the evaluation is still incomplete, but I think the limited findings call for increased attention from both federal and state overseers to ensure adherence to principles of WPRS implementation.

I want to talk now about some of the next steps at the federal level that we are either doing, or in some cases should be doing more intensively. But before I do that, I again want to mention two points that Dickinson talked about somewhat in her presentation and in the chapter, they are: the issue of referral to employment service registration for people who are not in profiling, and the effect of telephone claims.

My understanding is that telephone claims don't change the process. They may change practices, but there is no relaxation of requirements for referring profiled claimants to outside services simply because the claim is taken by telephone. I also think it goes too far to say that profiling is the only way UI claimants can get referred to services.

We are currently making funds available to states for significant improvement grants that are intended to increase the effectiveness of reemployment services. We are really hoping for creative proposals from states to address one or more of the implementation concerns mentioned above. One of the conclusions we've come to is that the most important thing to do right now is to go directly to continuous improvements and not overprescribe. Instead, we plan to make money available to the states to work on whatever they think will help make this complicated system work better. We need to ensure that there are complete and valid data reported to the federal government for use by the states on services provided and outcomes. The Labor Department should analyze that data and use the findings for oversight of the WPRS system.

Finally, and this reiterates some of the points that Dickinson made in her remarks, we should give more attention to providing oversight and management of profiling and reemployment services. This should be considered a key part of ETA's (Employment and Training Administration, U.S. Department of Labor) implementation of the Workforce Investment Act. Only when we can say that this initiative is fully in place will we really be in a position to validly assess the system's impacts on outcomes, and conclude whether it is cost-effective.

Comments on Chapter 3

Walter Nicholson
Amherst College

This chapter provides a summary of the ongoing research on the Worker Profiling and Reemployment Services (WPRS) Systems initiative. That initiative and the research on it are interesting from a variety of perspectives. On a conceptual level, WPRS represents one of the first attempts to use statistical modeling to target social services to clients. There is an obvious interest in determining how well this works and the circumstances under which it can be more or less successful. Evaluating the success of the process also raises some unique statistical issues that deserve detailed analysis. On a more practical level, the WPRS initiative raises questions about interagency coordination, the construction of appropriate information systems, and the actual selection of reemployment services. In these comments I focus primarily on Dickinson, Decker, and Kreutzer's treatment of the conceptual issues, concluding with only a few words about their analysis of the WPRS process.

PROFILING

The unique aspect of the WPRS initiative is, of course, the use of statistical models to predict unemployment insurance (UI) claimants' probabilities of exhaustion of benefits and the use of those probabilities to target reemployment services. Dickinson, Decker, and Kreutzer report the interesting fact that most states have developed their own profiling models and that some states even disaggregate these models by substate region. As someone who has run many, many regressions on unemployment insurance (UI) benefit exhaustions, I would have liked somewhat more detail about differences among the state models and why those differences arise. Are state models importantly constrained by the availability of certain variables on their administrative data files? How well do these models seem to fit the data, and do some states manage to achieve much higher explanatory powers than others? Are the models employed in a "pure" way to calculate an index of service needs? Or is there some tinkering with the model results to achieve what service deliverers believe to be "more reasonable" results? I believe more detailed answers to these questions would be interesting to researchers who wish to learn something about labor markets from the states' experiences in seeking to model exhaustion. It would also be quite interesting to state UI staff charged with trying to develop as good a model as possible with existing data. Finally, the development of a more detailed typology of profiling models might be of help to the authors in their ultimate goals of evaluating whether profiling actually improves the delivery of reemployment services, the focus of my next set of comments.

EVALUATING PROFILING

Although research on the effectiveness of the WPRS system is only in its initial stages, the Dickinson, Decker, and Kreutzer chapter gives a roadmap of how they intend to proceed. Because implementation of a random assignment experiment was infeasible in the current context, the authors have instead opted for methodology that uses as a comparison group claimants who passed the initial WPRS screens but who were not referred to services. In general, of course, those not referred to services will have lower profiling "scores" than will those referred, so a simple comparison between these two groups would undoubtedly yield biased results. Assuming that the profiling model can, at least with large errors, identify claimants who will experience substantial problems in finding new jobs, this bias would tend to understate the impact of reemployment services, possibly even to the extent of yielding the result that these services apparently harm claimants' prospects. Dickinson, Decker, and Kreutzer assure us that their procedure is more promising than most other comparison group analyses because they "control for these criteria (i.e., the profiling scores) in regression models." They also point out, optimistically, that the variation in capacity constraints over both time and region will help to break up what would otherwise be an exact relationship between scores and service referral, thereby improving the independent explanatory power of the profiling score. This procedure and the arguments that the authors make in support of it remind me of the "design dispute" that took place nearly 30 years ago in connection with the New Jersey Income Maintenance Experiment. In that case also, the researchers argued that a nonrandom assignment could in principle be accommodated in a regression framework if the variables used to assign experimental cells were used as additional independent variables in the analysis of experimental results. The need to use such variables together with the inherent uncertainty about the correct regression specification raised many concerns about the validity of the New Jersey results, especially among practitioners outside the community of research economists. I fear the same result may occur here. At the very least, I hope Dickinson, Decker, and Kreutzer will investigate the assumptions that must be made both to assure that unbiased estimates can be obtained by including profiling scores and to assess the importance of varying capacity constraint effects across their samples.

THE PROFILING PROCESS

The attention that Dickinson, Decker, and Kreutzer give to describing the profiling process and the data collection efforts that accompany it is, in my mind, one of the real strengths of the research. Two aspects of their discussion seem to me to be especially interesting: their attempts to measure the extent of reemployment services received, and their discussion of state tracking systems. With regard to the former, I would have liked to see even more on the actual content of reemployment services offered to claimants. Research on the effectiveness of such services continues to suffer from a "black box" approach that offers little insight about what clients actually get. Without such detail I fear we will never be in a position to determine what works. Dickinson, Decker, and Kreutzer have made a good start on trying to look into the box—I hope they will push that part of the project further.

I hope that the authors' discussion of the limitations of some state data systems will provide a spur for improvements, perhaps directed from the national level. In their research they have managed to learn quite a bit about how these data systems work in practice. One very valuable outcome of the project could be the development of a general blueprint for "best practices" that might be adopted more widely.

In all, this is an interesting progress report on one of the most important current initiatives in reemployment policy. The authors have done a good job of touching on both the practical and the analytical aspects of their project, and I look forward to seeing their final results.

4

A Panel Discussion on the WPRS System

Panel Chair: Pete Fleming
U.S. Labor Department, Atlanta Region

Panelists: Al Jaloviar
Wisconsin Unemployment Insurance Division

Helen Parker
Georgia Department of Labor

Marc Perrett
Oregon Employment Department

Pete Fleming

I am not a state practitioner, although I have worked for states in the past. The purpose of our panel today is to bring you the perspective of the state practitioners on profiling. My role in the U.S. Department of Labor regional office, in fact, is one of overseeing state programs. That means focusing attention and priorities on details, and that's not easy to do, especially in this constantly evolving and changing world we live in.

I am reminded of the invasion of Normandy, one of the greatest planned events in human history, which, when soldiers got on the beach, erupted into utter chaos. That's kind of what happens in local offices sometimes. One thing we must always remember is that this system really has not been recession-tested. We should keep that as a backdrop. However, in one sense Worker Profiling and Reemployment Services (WPRS) gives us a way to do intensive planning in advance.

WPRS is only as effective as we maintain it and keep it up to date. That's where we usually fall down, and I confess we have done that in

91

the Atlanta regional office by not maintaining the intensive oversight and priority setting that we need to do. We need to do a better job of that.

In the Southeast, statistical profiling models are now used in all eight states. In 1998, we profiled a million claimants of whom one-third were put in a selection pool and 45 percent of those received some service. What I don't know from the statistics is what happened to that 45 percent? I do know from other data that among all claimants in the United States who were placed in a job, the Southeast placed 32 percent, or about 200,000 people.

I believe that three essential factors make profiling work: augmenting all Wagner-Peyser funds with either Title III or other state funds, maintaining and updating the model, and close coordination between the employment service and unemployment insurance (UI) operations at both the state and local levels.

Our panelists today are Al Jaloviar, who is Director of Benefit Operations for the UI Division in Wisconsin. He will speak first. He has 38 years of service in this business—37 or 38, we couldn't decide exactly last night. Second is Dr. Helen Parker, who is the Employment Service Director in the Georgia Department of Labor. She has 25 years of experience beginning as an employment counselor or interviewer in North Carolina. She has worked in almost all phases of ES and JTPA operations. Finally, Marc Perrett is a 22-year veteran of the Oregon Employment Department and is now the Field Services Supervisor. Without further ado we will get to the panel.

Al Jaloviar

I am going to talk about how we profile in Wisconsin, what services we provide, what fund sources we use for those services, and observations and experiences about profiling.

How we profile

We use a mathematical model with the standard ingredients: a four-digit industry code, occupation, education, and total unemployment rate for the county of residence of the claimant. Our profiling system is a mainframe program, and we gather the data regarding the individual claimant in a variety of ways. We take all of our initial UI claims via telephone through an IVR (interactive voice response) system whereby claimants provide data using their telephone Touch-Tone key pad. Therefore, claimants enter our UI data system via the IVR. Later in the telephone call, a claims specialist will access data in our mainframe database using graphical user interface screens that don't allow specialists to complete the claim unless certain required fields have been completed. Among required data are any needed for profiling.

Once each week, a mainframe program is run to assign a profiling score to each individual claimant. The system then delivers these results to 36 different sites in Wisconsin that provide services for profiled claimants. The data are sent electronically to each site, listing residents in that geographic area in order of their profiling score. The local service provider simply addresses the screen when they have slots available to provide service, and the system tells them who will be scheduled in the available slots.

Local staff enter the number of available slots, and the system tells the staff person which people are scheduled for services. The computer, which is centrally located in Madison, automatically mails out invitations to come in for services. The letters make the claimant aware that failure to attend will result in a disqualification from UI benefits. The local service provider then enters information on a mainframe screen after the end of the session to indicate who has or has not attended, and the system automatically notifies UI of any individual who failed to attend. We put a suspension on their claim and schedule them for an interview to determine whether or not there is going to be a disqualification of benefits.

What we do

We provide pretty much the basic ingredients: an orientation to our system, guidance on how to use the system, general labor market information, and an individualized reemployment plan, which is entered into our system and tracked electronically. We have in-depth assessment for those whom the initial reemployment plan indicates need further assessment and help. We offer job search workshops, guidance in resume writing, labor market counseling, job placement, and training programs. The fund sources that we use are Wagner-Peyser and JTPA-EDWAA (Job Training Partnership Act–Economic Dislocation and Worker Adjustment Assistance). We use $500,000 a year from our UI penalty and interest fund, and in fact I just attended the first meeting for negotiating to use $250,000 from the UI program to finance some workshops for ES services to UI claimants for fiscal year 2000, which starts July 1 in Wisconsin.

Our observations

Profiling has served to be a mechanism that has resulted in a cohesive service delivery system between UI and our EDWAA, JTPA, and Wagner-Peyser partners. In particular, this has shown itself in the field offices, where the services are provided. In the past there has been distance and competition among programs as opposed to cooperation and coordination, but with profiling, we all act as a team in getting these services delivered.

Another thing we hadn't anticipated is that profiling is providing added services to our many smaller communities in Wisconsin. The WARN (Worker Adjustment and Retraining Notification) system, which in Wisconsin is a 60-day notice of a plant closing or a substantial layoff, has some limits in terms of the size of the company that is covered. Through the plant closing notice or the substantial layoff notice, we find that profiling characteristics help us identify many clients who would not have come to our attention before. We are now finding those people through profiling and are able to provide services to them.

We keep track of our profiling results by service delivery site as opposed to statewide, but we ultimately compile statewide figures. Some locations were showing wage replacement rates in excess of 100 percent, so we examined the reasons they were doing so well. It turned out that such areas usually had a large plant closing that was either nonskilled or nonunion, and that low wage rates were being paid. The labor market in general was paying a higher wage.

On the other side of that, we've seen a location with excellent performance show a high exhaustion rate of profiled claimants and a placement rate lower than the state average. The reason appears to be the result of a plant closing or layoff of a highly unionized business with high pay rates and workers whose skills cannot command similar rates in the market, or because there are no other jobs requiring those particular skills. Such individuals often participate in training because they're covered by Trade Adjustment Assistance. So we find that highly unionized and highly skilled jobs often result in a lower than average replacement rate and a greater than average participation in skills training.

Our statewide wage replacement rate is 85 percent for individuals who go through profiling. Three-quarters of all people profiled return to work within four quarters of their entering profiling. Sixty percent of those are employed in a new industry, and the average duration of unemployment claims for the individuals profiled is 14 weeks. That compares with a statewide average of 11 weeks, and a statewide average of 21 weeks for individuals who exhaust benefits. So these profiled individuals are identified as most likely to exhaust, yet the average claim is only 14 weeks long. Our statewide average for all claimants, which includes those who are screened out because of job or industry attachment, is eight weeks.

Helen Parker

Georgia had a little bit of a leg up when WPRS came into being, because we were already using state dollars to operate a claimant assistance program (CAP), which was an intensive 14-week service strategy for claimants with Georgia wages only. WPRS gave us an opportunity to expand that and use it as a core for WPRS. Not creating from scratch turned out to be a huge advantage for us. I want to walk through some of the characteristics of our process. It is very different from Wisconsin, and I was taking notes because we are going where they're going in terms of telephone claims, and I haven't yet figured out how that's going to work.

As a response to WPRS, we established reemployment units in all of our offices, which include the staffing that had been our claimant assistance staff (our state-funded staff), our Wagner-Peyser staff, and 80–90 equivalent positions from Title III dislocated worker state funding. When we first set up the reemployment units, each individual participating in the unit carried his or her funding sources. So when we lobbied for cross-training and cross-functioning, the theory did not translate easily to practice. In reality, any time a dislocated worker walked into the room, everyone pointed to the Title III staff person. Some people were still operating in their silos even though they were now in a unit. In order to fix that, we split-funded all of the positions so there are no more Title III–funded positions that can be pointed to.

There are no more claimant assistance positions, and in that unit there are no distinct Wagner-Peyser positions. Everybody is funded by all three, and it's amazing what removing that label has done to get people to really work together and to see services as a whole and not as silos.

Another benefit of CAP is that it had an automated tracking system that we could enhance and use for WPRS. This system provides tracking through the 17th week of the structured staff intervention program, and it also links to unemployment insurance. So there is a running record of the services that are delivered, and automatic reporting to the UI system if someone fails to report for a service or fails to follow through on a job referral. Naturally, we don't have too many of those negatives.

One of the most unique features of our program is that we profile at intake. When someone comes in to file a claim and register for the employment service, which is done in a single act with a single employment specialist, the profiling model is run at that point while the claimant is there. If the profiling score is such that the individual does need to be referred to reemployment services, or if the individual seems otherwise in need of reemployment services, then the individual is literally physically walked to the reemployment unit. That was something our local offices insisted on because it was the "bread and butter" key that we learned through the CAP; they didn't want folks getting out the door before they got a shot at them. We have followed through on that with WPRS and with the reemployment services strategy.

We now have an operation where the same service strategy and the same scheduling is used for our CAP customers, for our Title III customers, and for our WPRS-referred customers, and it is transparent to the customers. They don't know which program they are actually in, and they don't need to know. We insist, both at the local level and in our state monitoring, on same-day services; being able to profile at intake allows us to do that. Each individual who is referred to the reemployment unit on the day they file their claim gets the assessment and an orientation. There is a customized service plan developed, and in most (but not all) cases there is a fairly thorough effort at job referral and job development for that individual.

During that initial visit, customers are also introduced to our self-help resources. Each of our local offices has a resource area to which each client is introduced during the first visit to the office. That has proved to be extremely successful, but it is a very labor-intensive process. It requires a good deal of staff intervention to provide these services. I am very interested in some of the electronic tools that are in production to be able to assist with that.

Just to give a few numbers to put things into perspective, last year more than 60,000 people were referred to the reemployment units across the state, and about two-thirds of those were a result of profiling. There were nearly 6,000 workshops conducted across the state for individuals going through the system and nearly 119,000 counseling sessions with individuals who went through the reemployment units. So it is labor-intensive, and it is much more of a high-touch strategy than a high-tech strategy, although we are getting better at the high-tech. Our employment rate has remained pretty consistent over the last two or three years at around 60 percent, and that's more or less the same for all claimant groups.

One of the commitments we made to the legislature when we initiated CAP is that we would try to track and report back on UI trust-fund savings resulting from placing claimants in jobs more quickly. Our guarantee was that we would return at least as much as was given to us for CAP. The first year they gave us 10 million and we gave them back 14 million. Last year we gave them back just over 31 million in trust-fund savings. So the legislature's happy, and when the legislature is happy, so are we.

This year we are still on track. The entered employment rate for the first part of program year 1998 is running about 60 percent, and trust-fund savings are a little over $20 million. We feel good about what we are doing, and it's got to get better. The Workforce Investment Act does change the scenario, so we'll soon have to step back again and assess what else needs changing.

Marc Perrett

I am going to talk from a bit more general perspective; that is, from reemployment services for the claimant, rather than how profiling gets done. Oregon was one of the first five or six states to start worker profiling back in 1994. From the start we had a fair degree of success. The unemployment insurance (UI) and employment service (ES) units, which work for the employment security agency in Oregon, and the

JTPA partners, which are independent, cooperated to set up a system to identify and refer claimants to reemployment services and obtain good outcomes based upon individual needs.

The intervening years have witnessed several changes, one of which was, quite honestly, a drop in interest from our JTPA partners. It ended up that all the systems in Oregon for worker profiling were done by ES, and that was at a time when ES had limited resources and the capacity to serve clients was being stretched in directions other than UI claimants most likely to exhaust benefits. About the same time, the Wagner-Peyser funding was pretty flat. Fortunately, the state of Oregon decided that we needed to do more for both our employer and claimant customers, so we, like my panel colleagues from other states, received more state funding for our activities.

Oregon established a "Supplemental Employment Department Administrative Fund," and in 1996 we started using some of that money in close relationship with worker profiling. We are still using the list of profiling scores, as we always have, to identify those most likely to exhaust UI and bring them in for reemployment services.

We also work the WPRS model results from a slightly different angle. We identify those less likely to exhaust UI as prime candidates for job matching and refer them to existing job orders. This seems to work relatively well, however, this strategy proved to be very staff intensive, as Helen has alluded to. In the past year or two, we have backed off from aggressively serving both ends of the profiling list. Instead of each client looking at the job orders, we found ourselves individually matching one claimant at a time to the job orders, and it just took too much time.

Worker profiling in Oregon has expanded slowly over the last four to five years. As state managers we can encourage or mandate how much emphasis is put on it, but its degree of fit in the package of all ES services has fluctuated. Currently, profiling has again moved further up the list of priorities, and as state managers we are encouraging, and expecting, offices to do more and more.

We welcome the Wagner-Peyser recognition that claimant reemployment is an important aspect of what we have to offer. We talked about the supplementary state money. In Oregon it makes up 60 percent of our ES budget, but it is also a potential curse. It means that we can do a lot of things that other states can't. Many of our achievements are probably largely a result of this extra money, but it does make us very responsive to the state governor and state legislature. We have a legislative session once every two years, and we're very, very reactive to their needs. At any point in time, or at least every two years, we see the potential of this money being diverted. So state funding is not nearly as stable as Wagner-Peyser funding.

In July of 1997, Oregon had 37,000 claimants who entered employment, which is not bad for a state the size of Oregon. This was as many entered employments as Illinois, Indiana, and Iowa combined. That's pretty fantastic, and I think our entered employment rate is not what Georgia's is, but it is well above the national average. We still admire the success of states such as Georgia, North Carolina, and Alabama. We can't imagine what's causing their success. Is it something in the drinking water down there? Also Missouri, Wisconsin, and Texas are other states that are doing outstanding work on claimant reemployment efforts. All of these numbers come from the annual report of the U.S. Employment Service, which is a great resource from an overview perspective. I thank David Balducchi for providing such concrete evidence of program success.

One of the things we do in Oregon is establish annual goals for each office. The expectations are formalized in specific numbers that we set as targets for each office on two outcomes: claimants placed and claimants who have entered employment. Currently we have an output-based system, and we count the actual number of claimants placed and entering employment. We have not adopted relative measures of outcomes such as entered employment rate or claimant placement rate. Our hesitation to do that comes from the concern that such measures would push us toward those clients who are easiest to serve, rather than serving as many as we can serve. However, we do want to study reemployment success by local office over time and against other offices. Such comparisons are increasingly important as we move closer to Workforce Investment Act (WIA) implementation.

Again, let me mention that our supplementary state funding is one of the major reasons we have been able to accomplish what we have. Another reason is the labor exchange. We still feel that our primary function is to be an employment office. Whether it is in the form of a job and career center, a one-stop system, or an Internet service, our key function is matching job seekers with jobs. About 30 percent of our referrals and 50 percent of our placements come from job matching.

In addition to our staff working with employers and job seekers, we also have a self-referral system. We have a Web site with job vacancy listings and job seeker listings, and both types of listings may be either self-entered or staff-entered to the Web-based data system. For referrals to job interviews, we have not moved as far as some states have toward a reliance upon self-service. It doesn't get the outcomes that we want for our customers. We have also somewhat rejected the concept of case management. It takes too much time for what we get out of it. We sometimes do case management for some special contracted groups, especially vocational rehabilitation clients and disabled veterans, but we do not use that approach for our UI claimant and ES client populations.

Two other things that contribute to our output are our job and career centers. Our resource rooms have been a big hit in Oregon, especially with many of the folks that never thought they'd be coming into an employment office or accessing our services, especially those searching for jobs in an occupation with a nationwide job market and those in high-tech industries. The most popular services are labor market information, job finding classes, PC resume preparation, access to America's Job Bank, and, of course, regular job listings. When we have a little bit of tracking and friendly, effective staff assistance, we get both customer satisfaction and a high level of measured program outcome performance.

We believe in accountability within the state, and we are disappointed with some of the proposed WIA performance indicators. In particular, the plan to not count many of the services that are provided by the system is perplexing to us. We feel a need to focus on customers but also to be accountable for what we do through reporting to both the federal and state levels. There is some concern that the proposed performance measures within WIA could actually jeopardize the success of the system rather than contribute to success. To some extent, that also ties in with profiling.

When I was a local office manager, I welcomed profiling. It enabled me to take a triage approach to serving a broad population with a limited number of resources. But as we move toward performance accountability, I think it is going to boil down to more of an outcome-based or result-based system, which looks at the results rather than the process. I welcome this approach wholeheartedly. However, I see a danger that some offices, especially one-stops, may be looking to get the biggest bang for the buck, and profiling may not be one of those things. I say this while realizing that duration is a performance indicator that gets discussed at the national and state levels but seldom gets adopted in a formal manner. I believe worker profiling is valuable. It has been a successful tool in our claimant reemployment efforts in Oregon.

Comments on Part I

The Changing Role of the Public Employment Service

U.S. Department of Labor

During the 1990s, state employment service (ES) agencies, authorized by the Wagner-Peyser Act, delivered reemployment services to an increased share of unemployment insurance (UI) claimants. To expand this growth, the U.S. Department of Labor's (DOL) FY 2000 congressional appropriation contained new, special grants to state ES agencies totaling $35 million to deliver reemployment services to an estimated 156,000 additional UI claimants.

The term *reemployment* is not new to the ES system. In the summer of 1933, DOL advanced the reemployment services concept by establishing a temporary placement division within the U.S. Employment Service called the National Reemployment Service (NRS). By November 1933, NRS had established 2,000 federal reemployment offices to match millions of Great Depression-era unemployed workers with agencies hiring workers for a multitude of public works projects (U.S. Department of Labor 1933, p. 1). Once a state established a public ES system, federal reemployment offices were turned over to the state ES agency. The NRS proved to be a successful incubator for the federal/state ES system. By 1939, a national ES system operating under the Wagner-Peyser Act was in place, and the NRS was abolished (Haber and Kruger 1964, p. 28). Through the ensuing decades, as the nation's economic circumstances changed, so did the application of ES policy.

In the mid 20th century, labor exchange services became intertwined with manpower policy, and a larger share of workforce development funds was directed to skills training (Haber and Murray 1966,

p. 431). In the late 1970s, economic restructuring and resultant unemployment enkindled a dialogue about the effectiveness of public employment and training programs that led to a series of reemployment demonstration studies conducted by DOL in the 1980s. Evidence emerged that early identification and referral to reemployment services of claimants likely to exhaust UI benefits was a cost-effective public intervention.

In November 1993, new federal legislation required states wishing to maintain eligibility for receipt of UI administrative grants to establish Worker Profiling and Reemployment Services (WPRS) systems. The law required UI claimants who were identified by state WPRS systems to be at risk of UI benefits exhaustion to participate in reemployment services or risk losing UI benefits (Balducchi, Johnson, and Gritz 1997, p. 473).

In January 1994, the Clinton Administration pressed for an expansion of the reemployment concept. In the President's State of the Union address, Clinton pledged to "transform America's outdated unemployment system into a reemployment system" (Clinton 1995). The administration introduced an employment and training reform bill in March 1994 called the Reemployment Act.[1] While the bill was never enacted, the reemployment concept became wedded to the emerging one-stop concept being designed to consolidate the delivery of federal and state employment and training services. These concepts were embodied in the Workforce Investment Act (WIA) of 1998.

TRENDS IN LABOR EXCHANGE SERVICES

States collect data on UI claimants who have registered for work during the program year (PY) (i.e., July 1 to June 30), and send quarterly statistical reports to DOL summarizing labor exchange services activity.[2] Noteworthy labor exchange services trends can be seen through data reported in Table 1 on three activities: 1) received some reportable service, 2) job search activities, and 3) entered employment.

- *Received some reportable service* is defined as having received interviewing, counseling, testing, referral to jobs or training, job

Table 1 Labor Exchange Activities of Eligible UI Claimants Registered for Work

Activity	Program year 1993	1994	1995	1996	1997
Received some	4,270,711	4,012,523	4,004,707	3,985,194	3,599,511
reportable service	46.2%	52.4%	54.0%	54.9%	54.0%
Participated in a job	1,588,223	1,740,209	2,149,171	2,306,738	2,262,883
search activity	37.2%	43.4%	53.7%	57.9%	62.9%
Number who entered	890,504	885,721	879,562	924,322	918,294
employment	20.9%	22.1%	22.0%	23.2%	25.5%
Total UI claimants	9,235,977	7,662,050	7,413,036	7,254,009	6,663,475

SOURCE: U.S. Department of Labor (1996, 1999).

search activities, or other similar services. It is the closest proxy to "reemployment services" tracked in state ES agency activity reports (U.S. Department of Labor 1993, p. III-11).

- *Job search activities* is a subset of *received some reportable service.* It includes "resume preparation assistance, job search workshops, job finding clubs, provision of specific labor market information, and development of a job search plan" (U.S. Department of Labor 1993, p. III-11).
- *Entered employment* is defined as the number of UI claimants who enter employment after having received a reportable service (U.S. Department of Labor 1993, p. II-12).

In PY 1997, 6.6 million UI claimants registered for work, and 3.6 million received a reportable reemployment service. Between PY 1993 (the year preceding WPRS implementation) and PY 1996, the percent of UI claimants who received reemployment services increased by 8.7 percentage points despite steadily improving economic conditions. The biggest uptick in activity occurred in PY 1994. Since that year, the share of UI claimants receiving reemployment services has stabilized at approximately 54 percent.

The period PYs 1993–1997 witnessed a significant increase in the use of job search activities by UI claimants. In PY 1993, only 37.2 percent of UI claimants who received a reemployment service received it in the category of job search activities. In PY 1997 this percentage was 62.9, an increase of 25.7 percentage points.

The entered employment rate for UI claimants who received a reportable service increased from 20.9 percent in PY 1993 to 25.5 percent in PY 1997.[3] So despite decreases in the volume of claimants and the number of services delivered, the effectiveness of services steadily improved over the period.

REASONS FOR GROWTH IN RECEIPT OF SERVICES

The growth in the share of UI claimants who received reemployment services may be due to four interrelated events.

- Federal/state implementation of WPRS. During 1993–1996, state and local implementation of WPRS systems necessitated establishing new services (e.g., job search workshops). In a WPRS report to Congress, the U.S. Department of Labor (1997a) observed that state ES agencies were the dominant providers of reemployment services to UI claimants.
- Employment and Training Administration policy leadership. Since 1993, the Employment and Training Administration of DOL has issued numerous WPRS policy and technical guides, hosted national conferences to promote effective practices, and required states to establish individual reemployment services plans that "increase the number of UI claimants that enter employment, reduce UI benefit duration, and speed the referral of those UI claimants who need additional help to training providers or other support services" (U.S. Department of Labor 1997b, p. 4). In response, most state ES agencies delivered services to an increased share of UI claimants.
- One-stop grants. Between PYs 1994 and 2000, the Employment and Training Administration distributed to the states $826.5 million in one-stop grants, under Wagner-Peyser Act authority, to replace their fragmented employment and training program structures with one-stop delivery systems. States used these grants to make infrastructure improvements and to introduce

electronic labor exchange services. Many states selected their state ES system as the platform for erecting their one-stop delivery system. Under WIA, the nation's nearly 2,400 local ES offices were either designated as one-stop centers or affiliated sites.

- Sustained economic growth. According to the Bureau of Labor Statistics, during PYs 1993–1997, the nation's total unemployment rate averaged 5.5 percent. During the same period, the number of UI claimants who registered for work fell by 2,572,502, a 27.8 percent decrease. A bustling U.S. economy with a strong demand for workers has reduced UI claimant workloads, and may have enabled states to deliver additional reemployment services to UI claimants who face greater job-finding challenges.[4]

CONCLUSION

The delivery of reemployment services is a long tradition of state ES agencies. Despite a bustling U.S. economy, the gait of technological change has influenced the rate and duration of unemployment (Baumol and Wolff 1998, p. 1). According to findings by International Survey Research, there remains a persistent anxiety among workers about job security. No wonder "[d]own sizing has become a permanent feature of the corporate American landscape" (Belton 1999, p. 2). As a result, workers may likely experience periodic job changes requiring transitional reemployment services and retraining to obtain new jobs. To better administer new workforce development services, the Employment and Training Administration, state ES agencies and other workforce development agencies should consider systematic screening of job seekers to effectively identify their needs and to efficiently ration public funds.

Notes

1. H.R. 4040, 103rd U.S. Congress.
2. Labor exchange services data are reported on DOL's Employment and Training Administration Form 9002. This form reports on the activity of UI eligible claimants who have registered for work with the state ES agency and who, during the PY, are or have been determined to be monetarily eligible for UI benefits under federal or state UI laws. Wagner-Peyser Act reporting requirements are contained in *ET Handbook No. 406*.
3. This entered employment rate is different from the measure described in Department of Labor (1996, 1999). The rate reported in Table 1 is conditional upon receipt of a reportable service, and therefore may be a more meaningful measure of service effectiveness. In 2001, DOL used this methodology to calculate the PY 1999 entered employment rate for each state.
4. In PY 1997, the civilian labor force averaged 137 million workers and the total unemployment rate was 4.6 percent.

References

Balducchi, David E., Terry R. Johnson, and R. Mark Gritz. 1997. "The Role of the Employment Service." In *Unemployment Insurance in the United States: An Analysis of Policy Issues*, Christopher J. O'Leary and Stephen A. Wandner, eds. Kalamazoo, Michigan: W.E. Upjohn Institute for Employment Research.

Baumol, William J., and Edward N. Wolff. 1998. "Side Effects of Progress." Public Policy Brief no. 41A, Annandale on Hudson, New York: The Jerome Levy Economics Institute of Bard College (July).

Belton, Beth. 1999. "Despite Humming Economy, Workers Sweat Job Security." *USA Today*, March 2.

Clinton, William J. 1995. *Public Paper of the Presidents of the USA*. Book 1—January 1 to July 31, 1994 (January 25).

Haber, William, and Daniel H. Kruger. 1964. *The Role of the United States Employment Service in a Changing Economy*. Kalamazoo, Michigan: W.E. Upjohn Institute for Employment Research.

Haber, William, and Merrill G. Murray. 1966. *Unemployment Insurance in the American Economy: An Historical Review and Analysis*. Homewood, Illinois: Richard D. Irwin.

U.S. Department of Labor. 1933. *Bulletin to the Members of Committees of Reemployment Offices*. National Reemployment Service, Washington, D.C.: U.S. Employment Service.

———. 1993. *ET Handbook No. 406: ETA 9002, Data Preparation.* Washington, D.C.: Employment and Training Administration.

———. 1996. *Annual Report, U.S. Employment Service; Program Report Data, Program Year 1995.* Washington, D.C.: Employment and Training Administration.

———. 1997a. *Evaluation of Worker Profiling and Reemployment Services Systems.* A report to Congress, Washington, D.C.: Employment and Training Administration.

———. 1997b. *Reemployment Services for Unemployment Insurance (UI) Claimants through State Worker Profiling and Reemployment Services (WPRS) Systems.* Employment Service Program Letter no. 1-98. Washington, D.C.: Employment and Training Administration.

———. 1999. *Annual Report, U.S. Employment Service; Program Report Data, Program Year 1997.* Washington, D.C.: Employment and Training Administration.

Part II

Applications of Targeting Methods

5
Profiling in Self-Employment Assistance Programs

Jon C. Messenger
U.S. Department of Labor

Carolyn Peterson-Vaccaro
New York State Department of Labor

Wayne Vroman
Urban Institute

The nature of unemployment has changed dramatically in the last two decades. As global competition and rapidly evolving technologies have resulted in the dislocation of millions of workers from their jobs—even as new jobs are being created—layoffs have become permanent in nature, rather than simply a temporary experience during fluctuations in the business cycle. These "dislocated workers" who have been permanently laid off from a long-term job face substantial earnings losses and often have difficulty finding a new job (U.S. Department of Labor 1995, p. 47). In 1984, the Bureau of Labor Statistics (BLS) initiated a biennial series of special dislocated worker surveys. These surveys have revealed that, on average, over two million individuals are dislocated in the United States each year.[1] The new reality is that a large portion of those who lose their jobs never get them back; thus, affected workers often have to make a transition to a new job.

The U.S. Department of Labor (DOL) conducted a series of national demonstration projects over a 10-year period (1986–1996) that explored innovative alternative ways of using unemployment insurance (UI)—the first stop for most of these dislocated workers—to assist these workers in making the transition to new jobs. Beginning in 1987, DOL sponsored two UI Self-Employment Demonstration Projects, in the states of Washington and Massachusetts, that rigorously tested the viability and cost-effectiveness of self-employment as a reemployment option for permanently laid-off, or dislocated, workers. Both of these demonstrations were run as field experiments which granted individuals monetary self-employment assistance in lieu of unemployment insurance and provided participants with entrepreneurial training, business planning, counseling advice, and technical assistance. The final evaluation found that self-employment assistance (SEA)—using the Massachusetts demonstration program model, which is the basis for current federal law—is highly cost-effective to program participants, the federal government, and society as a whole (U.S. Department of Labor 1995). The report recommended that the SEA program be made a permanent option for the unemployed.

The establishment of the SEA program was one of the infrequent instances when rigorous policy research led to legislative action. At the time when the UI SEA experiments were undertaken, the field of microenterprise development was just forming, and there was a great deal of skepticism about the utility of self-employment assistance as an employment strategy. The positive results from experimental self-employment demonstration projects conducted by DOL, in collaboration with state employment security agencies, was instrumental in spurring Congress to pass federal legislation in 1993 that authorized self-employment assistance as an alternative use of unemployment insurance.

This 1993 SEA legislation authorized the states to provide unemployed individuals periodic self-employment payments instead of regular unemployment insurance payments. The legislation allows states to use unemployment insurance funds to provide income support to those unemployed individuals who want work full time on starting their own businesses. The program was initially authorized for five years and was made permanent by Public Law 105-306 in October 1998.

The early identification tool commonly known as "profiling" played a key role in one of the two self-employment demonstrations, the Massachusetts project, which became the model for the SEA national legislation. Profiling is based on a set of criteria—a "profile"—that can be used to identify and select those UI claimants who are likely to be dislocated workers out of the broad population of UI claimants. By providing a mechanism for targeting the SEA provided by the demonstration on claimants who are dislocated workers, profiling enabled the project to be both cost-effective to the government and politically viable to several key constituency groups, particularly employers. Thus, profiling made a large contribution to the establishment of the SEA program.

This section has provided a brief introduction to the topic of profiling in SEA programs. The next section reviews the background and policy context for the SEA program in the United States and the role that profiling mechanisms were designed to play in this program. The third section summarizes key findings from an evaluation report on the SEA program mandated by Congress as part of the 1993 legislation. The use of profiling in state SEA programs and its implications is the focus of the fourth section, which includes descriptive information from conversations with states that have implemented SEA programs, a review of operational issues arising from the use of profiling in those programs and how states have responded to these issues, and a discussion of how profiling-type techniques might be applied to other aspects of the program. The final section of the chapter draws some conclusions from the analyses presented in the preceding sections and also discusses their implications for the future directions for the now-permanent SEA program and the role(s) that profiling can continue to play in the program.

BACKGROUND AND POLICY CONTEXT
FOR THE SEA PROGRAM

Self-Employment as a Reemployment Option

One alternative for promoting the reemployment of UI recipients who are dislocated workers is self-employment. The growing recognition of the contribution of very small businesses to the creation of employment opportunities, as well as the relatively modest financial and managerial requirements of self-employment for participation by workers, have generated interest in using self-employment as a tool for assisting unemployed workers in returning to work. Unlike other services to assist the unemployed in obtaining jobs, SEA is designed to promote direct job creation for unemployed workers—to empower the unemployed to create their own jobs by starting small business ventures. These very small start-up firms, which are called "microenterprises," are typically sole proprietorships with one or, at most, a few employees, including the owner/operator of the business.

During the 1990s, increasing numbers of dislocated workers in the United States have been coming from professional, technical, and managerial occupations—occupations which provide skills and experience that may make these workers particularly well-suited for entering self-employment.[2] While the primary goal of SEA/microenterprise programs is direct job creation for unemployed workers (or other specific target groups), the microenterprises started by these individuals may also generate additional jobs that could be filled by other workers. Thus, the SEA program provides an opportunity to integrate labor market policy and economic development policy in a dynamic relationship, helping participants to enter employment while simultaneously providing a modest boost to job creation and economic growth in their communities.

Self-employment assistance programs for unemployed workers were first implemented in several western European nations during the early 1980s. These programs were designed to help unemployed workers to "create their own jobs" by starting small businesses, which usually meant microenterprises. The two best known self-employment programs at the time were those in Great Britain and France. The French self-employment program, *Chômeurs Créateurs*, provided eligible individuals with a single, lump-sum payment for business start-up capital; the British program, the "Enterprise Allowance Scheme," provided eligible individuals with biweekly payments to supplement their earnings during the first year of business operations. In designing the UI Self-Employment Demonstration in 1988, DOL and state representatives visited France, Great Britain, and Sweden to observe firsthand the SEA programs in those countries. The British and French programs provided models of how unemployed workers could become self-employed; these models appeared to be transferable to the United States and were subsequently adapted for testing in two demonstration projects.

The Self-Employment Demonstration Projects

Ultimately, DOL conducted two experimental demonstration projects, in the states of Washington and Massachusetts, that tested the viability and cost-effectiveness of self-employment as an alternative reemployment option for unemployed workers. These projects were designed to assist UI recipients interested in self-employment to "create their own jobs" by starting a business venture. The Washington demonstration project was initiated by DOL in early 1987, and all costs were funded by DOL research resources. The Massachusetts demonstration project was authorized by the Omnibus Budget Reconciliation Act of 1987.

These demonstration projects provided a basic model of a self-employment assistance program for unemployed workers. The program model includes two key components: financial assistance and business development services, modeled loosely on the British and French self-employment programs. The Massachusetts project was based on the United Kingdom's Enterprise Allowance Scheme and paid out biweekly cash self-employment allowances that provided microentrepreneurs with a source of income while they started their business. The Washington State demonstration generally followed the French *Chômeurs Créateurs* model and gave a lump-sum payment to unemployed workers interested in developing a microenterprise. In both programs, the financial assistance provided to participants equaled the total amount of unemployment insurance benefits to which workers would be normally entitled. In addition, both projects delivered business development services including entrepreneurial training, one-on-one business counseling, technical assistance, and peer support groups.

The results from the final evaluation of these demonstration projects clearly indicated that self-employment is a viable reemployment option for some unemployed workers. The evaluation found that while only about 2–3 percent of UI benefit recipients are interested in SEA, over half of this subset actually start a business. A final report on the UI Self-Employment Demonstration projects in Massachusetts and Washington was completed and published by DOL (Benus et al. 1995). The report includes a benefit–cost analysis from three different perspectives: project participants, the government, and society as a whole. The key findings from the evaluation of the UI Self-Employment Demonstration are as follows.

- SEA significantly increased the probability that unemployed workers would start a microenterprise. Compared with the control group, Massachusetts participants were 11 percent more likely to start a business; Washington participants were 22 percent more likely to start a microenterprise than their control counterparts.

- 61 percent of Washington participants and 74 percent of Massachusetts participants that had started a business sometime during the demonstration were still in business nearly three years later. These rates were similar to control group participants that had started businesses.
- Over the three-year follow-up survey period, SEA participants were employed longer than those in the control group by 1.9 months in Massachusetts and by 1.1 months in Washington.
- When both self-employment and wage and salary earnings are considered, the Massachusetts project dramatically increased the total annual earnings of participants: on average, project participants earned $5,940 more than those in the control group.

This evaluation also makes a determination as to the cost-effectiveness of the SEA program models tested from the perspectives of project participants, the government, and society as a whole. The benefit–cost analysis conducted as part of the final report showed that while both program models proved cost-effective interventions for participants and society as a whole, only the Massachusetts model proved to be cost-effective to the government. As a result, the evaluators concluded that for the Massachusetts model,

> These results indicate that SEA is a cost-effective approach to promote the rapid reemployment of unemployed workers and should be permanently incorporated into the U.S. employment security and economic development system (Benus et al. 1995, pp. x–xi).

National SEA Legislation and Key Features of the SEA Program

Based on the preliminary impact results from the UI Self-Employment Demonstration available in mid 1993, a provision allowing states to establish SEA programs as part of their UI programs was enacted into federal law as part of the North American Free Trade Agreement (NAFTA) Implementation Act (Public Law 103-182).[3] This provision allows states the option to offer SEA as an additional tool to help speed the transition of dislocated workers into new employment. States need to enact legislation that conforms to the federal legislation to establish SEA programs (Orr et al. 1994).

State SEA programs provide participants with periodic (weekly or biweekly) self-employment allowances while they are getting their businesses off the ground. These income support payments will be the same weekly amount as the worker's regular UI benefits, but participants can work full time on starting their businesses instead of searching for wage and salary jobs, and they can also retain any earnings from self-employment. In effect, this provision removes a barrier in the law—one that forced unemployed workers interested in self-employment to choose between receiving UI benefits and starting a business.

Under this legislation, in states that operate SEA programs, only those UI recipients identified through profiling as likely to exhaust their UI benefits are eligible for SEA. Self-employment program participants are also required to work full time on starting a business, as well as participate in SEA services—such as entrepreneurial training, business counseling, and other activities—to ensure that they have the skills necessary to operate a business.

DOL issued federal guidelines regarding self-employment programs in an Unemployment Insurance Program Letter in early 1994. States have the flexibility to establish their own programs within these guidelines. To do so, states first need to enact conforming state legislation to establish their self-employment programs, develop a state plan describing how their SEA program will operate, and then submit the state plan to DOL for review and approval.

The 1993 legislation allowed the SEA program to run for five years, and the initial five-year authorization period for the SEA program was due to expire in December 1998. Ultimately, the program was made permanent by Public Law 105-306 (The Noncitizen Benefit Clarification and Other Technical Amendments Act of 1998), which was signed into law on October 28, 1998.

The Role of Profiling in the Demonstration Projects and in the SEA Program

Self-employment and microenterprise development programs have proliferated since the time that DOL began its demonstration projects testing self-employment as a reemployment option for the unemployed. Most of these microenterprise programs, however, focus their efforts on self-employment for welfare recipients and other disadvantaged individuals; that is, on using self-employment as an antipoverty strategy. The SEA program has been and still is one of the few self-employment programs targeted specifically to unemployed workers who have significant labor market experience yet are unlikely to return to jobs similar to those they had prior to layoff. Furthermore, SEA is the only such program that provides such individuals with a period of guaranteed income support while they are starting and operating their own businesses. Profiling, the mechanism used to identify dislocated workers eligible for the SEA program out of the broad UI claimant population, helped the SEA program to be both cost-effective to the government and politically viable for several key constituency groups, particularly employers. Profiling helps ease the concern of employers who want their former employees to be available for recall and are not being subsidized to establish microenterprises that might compete with them (U.S. Department of Labor 1994).

The use of profiling to identify eligible individuals for the SEA program is designed to target the program on the subset of UI claimants who have been permanently laid off from their previous jobs and who are most likely to experience extended spells of unemployment and thus likely to exhaust their UI benefits. Profiling uses a set of criteria, called a "profile," to identify those UI claimants who are likely to be dislocated workers out of the broad population of all UI claimants. Typically, profiling models include both individual characteristics (e.g., an individual's level of educational attainment) and economic variables (e.g., whether or not employment in a particular occupation is growing or declining). The rationale for this targeting is that claimants identified as likely to exhaust UI through profiling are those most in need of reemployment services to be able to return to work; thus, the self-employment assistance provided by the SEA program is merely one alternative in an array of tools designed to assist dislocated workers in their efforts to become reemployed.

As in the WPRS initiative, profiling in the SEA program targets dislocated workers for self-employment assistance because they are considered to be most in need of services. In addition, however, targeting on dislocated workers may be particularly appropriate for the SEA program because an increasing proportion of all dislocated workers are now coming from professional, technical, and managerial occupations—occupations that require knowledge and skills that may be particularly applicable for self-employment. The experiences of the UI Self-Employment Demonstration provide evidence supporting this approach. In Washington State, 37 percent of all participants came from professional, technical, and managerial occupations, and in Massachusetts, more than half of all participants (57 percent) came from these occupations.

SUMMARY ASSESSMENT OF STATE SEA PROGRAMS

Descriptive Information on State SEA Programs

There are currently SEA programs in eight states: listed in chronological order of program implementation, they are New York, Oregon, Maine, Delaware, New Jersey, California, Maryland, and Pennsylvania. These programs are broadly similar but with several identifiable differences. Table 5.1 provides information on detailed aspects of the programs.

Six of the eight states operate statewide programs, meaning UI claimants at any local office may participate if eligible. Entrepreneurial training and other support services are not necessarily available locally, but participants control the decision regarding whether or not to travel to the sites where services are offered. California and Pennsylvania are exceptions regarding geographic coverage.

All programs are required to use profiling to select eligible SEA participants. The individual profiling threshold probabilities (i.e., the minimum likelihood of benefit exhaustion for SEA program eligibility) range from no minimum threshold probability in the eight Pennsylvania service-delivery areas (SDAs) that offer SEA to a high of 70 percent in New York.[4]

States follow differing practices in contacting potential SEA participants. As indicated in Table 5.1, five states send letters informing claimants of the SEA program and inviting them to attend an initial informational meeting. The other three provide information during an

Table 5.1　SEA Intake Procedures, Provisions, and Financing of Support Services and Anticipated Enrollment

Characteristic	California	New York	New Jersey	Oregon	Maine	Delaware	Maryland	Pennsylvania
Geographic extent of SEA program	6 of 52 SDAs	Statewide	Statewide	Statewide	Statewide	Statewide	Statewide	8 of 28 SDAs
Profiling cutoff								
Probability of exhaustion (%)								
1995	NA	75	NA	60	40	68	NA	NA
1997	64	70	42	55	40	68	NA	NA
1999	64	70	42[a]	33	40[a]	68	40	None[b]
Primary method of contacting eligibles	Letter	Letter	Benefit rights interview	Profiling session	Letter	Profiling session	Letter	Letter
Location of initial information meeting	Local SDA office	Local UI-ES office	Regional ES office	Regional ES office	One-stop center	One-stop center	Statewide service vendor	One-stop center or vendor
Types of services								
Entrepreneurial training	Yes	Yes	Yes	Yes	Yes	Yes	Yes	Yes
Counseling	Yes	Yes	Yes	Yes	Yes	Yes	Yes	Yes
Technical assistance	Yes	Yes	Yes	Yes	Yes	Yes	Yes	Yes
Peer support	No	Yes	No	No	No	No	Yes	No
Financial support	No	No	No	No	No	No	No	No
Funding of services								
JTPA-Title III-state grant	Yes	Yes		Yes		Yes		
JTPA-Governor's reserve monies		Yes					Yes	Yes
Small Bus. Dev. Centers (SBDC)		Yes	Yes	Yes		Yes		
State-financed training budget			Yes					

General revenues					Yes			Yes
UI special admin. expense fund	Yes				Yes	Yes		
In-kind services		Yes						
Anticipated enrollment	500–1,000	1,000	750–1,000	200	250–300	75	100	1,000
1996 SEA enrollment	2	2,195	156	111	134	17	NA	NA
1997 SEA enrollment	INA	2,266	776	38	101	INA	INA	560[c]

NOTE: NA = not applicable, no SEA program that year. INA = information not available.

[a] State is considering lowering the cutoff threshold.

[b] All persons who are profiled receive an information letter on SEA.

[c] 1998 enrollment data.

SOURCE: State Annual Self-Employment Assistance Reports, correspondence with DOL, and conversations with state officials as of 1998.

initial face-to-face meeting (benefits rights interview or profiling session). While the latter approach may take more time per client, it seems more efficient in making early identifications of those with definite interests in self-employment. Oregon, in fact, changed its procedures so that screening now occurs at the profiling session and avoids situations where individuals go to small business development centers (SBDCs) with little background and/or little serious interest in self-employment.

In five of eight states, the initial informational meeting where SEA is fully described occurs in offices of the employment service or in one-stop centers. Exceptions are California, where the informational meeting occurs in local SDA offices, and Maryland and Pennsylvania, where the offices of the service provider are used.[5]

All SEA programs provide a similar set of basic services to support those interested in pursuing self-employment. Entrepreneurial training, counseling, and technical support are offered universally. Initial assessment often occurs at an SBDC. Specialized services may be recommended, and counseling may also be available. The SBDCs further provide assistance in developing and reviewing business plans prepared by participants. Three states also indicated that peer support sessions are provided to participants (at least in some local geographic areas). However, given the low levels of SEA enrollment (to be discussed presently), the number of such meetings and total participation is extremely limited.

Financial support other than weekly SEA allowances may be needed to start up new enterprises. Potential sources available to individuals include personal savings, other family sources, or loans from financial institutions. Often SBDCs advise on loan availability and loan application procedures, but loans are currently being made by SBDCs or other SEA service providers. State SEA reports for 1996 typically showed that a very small number of loans had been received.[6]

Table 5.1 also identifies how each state pays for support services provided to clients. Most commonly, client services were financed with Job Training Partnership Act (JTPA) Title III monies, a source used in six states. This financing included JTPA discretionary monies controlled by the governors in three states. New Jersey finances most training activities with monies from its Workforce Development Partnership, a state payroll tax–financed reemployment program. Pennsylvania uses monies from its general revenue-supported Projects for

Community Building, a state economic and community development program with eight separate components.

Support services are also commonly provided by SBDCs. In Maine, SBDC support is provided through a contract with the Maine Department of Labor. The Labor Department monies are derived from the penalty and interest account (or special administrative expense fund) of the unemployment insurance agency. Table 5.1 identifies this source of financing in Maine. SBDC activities in four other states are supported by their SBDC's own resources.

Less common funding sources include in-kind services. Services provided by the Service Corps of Retired Executives (SCORE) in three states have included help in preparing contracts, counseling program participants, and assistance in preparing business plans. In New York, the Internal Revenue Service also conducts seminars informing participants on tax obligations of small businesses.

Thus, for six of eight SEA programs, financial support for SEA services to clients is derived from more than a single source. Monies are most often derived from JTPA (now WIA) and SBDC. The two exceptions are New Jersey and Maine, where financing is predominantly provided by the Workforce Development Partnership program and the UI penalty and interest account, respectively.

The final feature of the SEA programs covered by Table 5.1 is their size in terms of their anticipated and actual numbers of enrollments. The NAFTA Implementation Act specified that enrollment in SEA could not exceed 5 percent of those receiving regular UI benefits. Each program in its planning stages was to indicate the anticipated number of clients. These numbers are shown at the bottom of the table, along with actual 1996 and 1997 enrollments (1998 enrollments in Pennsylvania). With the exceptions of New York and New Jersey, the SEA states have had many fewer enrollees than originally anticipated. Thus, it is clear that SEA is a small program, both relative to the regular UI program and in the absolute numbers of participants.

Personal and Economic Characteristics of SEA Program Participants

Table 5.2 shows the 1996 and 1997 personal and economic characteristics of SEA participants in the first five states to implement SEA

Table 5.2 Personal and Economic Characteristics of SEA Participants, 1996 and 1997

	New York			New Jersey			Oregon			Maine			Delaware	
	SEA participants		Insured unemployed (thousands)	SEA participants		Insured unemployed (thousands)	SEA participants		Insured unemployed (thousands)	SEA participants		Insured unemployed (thousands)	SEA participants	Insured unemployed (thousands)
Characteristic	1997	1996	1996	1997	1996	1996	1997	1996	1996	1997	1996	1996	1996	1996
Year														
Total	2,266	2,195	208.1	832	156	108.2	38	111	44.2	101	134	14.6	17	8.1
Age														
Under 22		10	45.0	1.0	1	4.6	0.0	0	3.3		0	0.5	0	0.2
22–24		35	10.0	2.0	2	6.8	0.0	1	3.3		2	0.9	0	0.4
25–34	605	460	49.5	155.0	30	31.3	6.0	18	12.9		31	4.0	2	2.4
35–44	777	788	45.2	287.0	56	28.9	13.0	42	12.8		52	4.0	9	2.6
45–54	587	654	32.5	241.0	44	20.9	9.0	40	8.0		39	2.8	4	1.5
55–59		137	11.4	86.0	15	7.2	8.0	7	2.2		10	0.9	2	0.5
60–64	297[a]	63	7.9	44.0	5	5.0	1.0	2	1.0		0	0.6	0	0.3
65+		30	6.4	17.0	3	3.6	1.0	1	0.6		0	0.3	0	0.2
Unknown		18	0.4									0.6		
Average age	43.0	42.2	36.6	44.0	43.0	39.9	45.3	43.1	37.5	INA	41.4	39.6	42.7	39.7
Gender														
Women	1,135	957	89.7	319	63	47.4	19	50	17.6	47	72	6.0	5	3.8
Men	1,131	1,231	117.9	513	93	60.7	19	61	26.6	54	62	8.0	12	4.3
Unknown		7	0.5									0.6		

Women (%)	50.1	43.7	43.2	38.3	40.4	43.8	50.0	45.0	39.8	46.5	53.7	42.9	29.4	46.9
Ethnicity														
White	1,269	1,503	112.8	680	134	66.4	34	106	37.3	99	130	13.8	14	5.2
Black	543	292	27.0	105.0	13	20.7	0	3	1.0	0	2	0	3	2.6
Hispanic	159	68	22.3	22	4	18.4	2	0	3.5	0	0	0	0	0.2
Other	68	28	46.1	25	5	2.6	2	2	2.4	2	2	0.8	0	0.1
Unknown	227	304				0.2					0.1			
Black (%)	26.6	15.4	13.0	12.6	8.3	19.1	0.0	2.7	2.2	0.0	1.5	0.3	17.6	32.0
Hispanic (%)	7.8	3.6	10.7	2.6	2.6	17.0	5.3	0.0	8.0	0.0	0.0	0.2	0.0	2.4
Occupation														
Prof/tech/mgr.	1,029	707	36.8	141	21	47.9	22	71	9.5	27	50	1.9	10	1.8
Clerical	707	Note b	43.3	49	17	17.2	8	15	8.4	19	39	2.6	1	2.3
Sales	Note b		Note b	11	9	Note b	4	7	Note b	15	10	Note b	1	Note b
Service	151		23.9	24	12	9.2	0	3	5.3	6	12	1.9	0	0.9
Ag/forest/fish	0		0.4	1	22	2.7	1	1	2.9	2	1	0.4	0	0.1
Industrial	308		102.2	564	75	30.1	3	14	18.0	31	22	6.1	5	2.9
Unknown			1.2	42		1.0				1		1.7		0.1
Prof/tech/mgr (%)	46.9	17.8	17.8	13.5	44.7	57.9	64.0	21.5	27.0	37.3	14.7	58.8	22.5	
Industrial (%)	14.0	14.0	49.5	71.4	48.1	28.1	7.9	12.6	40.8	31.0	16.4	47.3	29.4	36.3
Education														
Less than high school	122	INA	29	8	INA	1	5	INA	7	6	INA	2	INA	
High school	INA	638	INA	229	32	INA	16	38	INA	74	57	INA	6	
More than high school	1314													INA

Table 5.2 (Continued)

Characteristic	New York SEA participants	New York Insured unemployed (thousands)	New Jersey SEA participants	New Jersey Insured unemployed (thousands)	Oregon SEA participants	Oregon Insured unemployed (thousands)	Maine SEA participants	Maine Insured unemployed (thousands)	Delaware SEA participants	Delaware Insured unemployed (thousands)
Education (cont.)										
Some college	INA	INA	256	50	9	29	6	46	5	INA
4-yr. college	INA	INA	279	55	7	29	14	23	4	INA
Adv. degree	INA	INA	39	11	5	19	0	2	0	INA
Unknown	21									
More than high school (%)	63.4	69.0	4.4	55.3	64.2	19.8	53.0		52.9	
UI WBAᶜ ($)	246 249	206	INA 326	258.5ᵈ	274 241	191	165 179	171	271	224
SEA WBA differential (%)	20.8		26.2		26.5		4.9		21.1	

NOTE: INA = information not available.

ᵃ Aged 55 and over.
ᵇ Sales combined with clerical.
ᶜ Weekly benefit amount; statewide WBA from *UI Financial Handbook*.
ᵈ WBA in 1997.

SOURCE: SEA data from state reports, counts of participants. Insured unemployment data from required reports, in thousands.

programs. For comparative purposes, the table also shows information on the characteristics of the insured unemployed (regular UI claimants) in these states in 1996.[7]   SEA participants differ from regular UI claimants in several respects. Table 5.2 provides comparative information on age, gender, ethnicity, occupation, education, and UI weekly benefits for the two groups.

SEA participants in every state are, on average, older than the insured unemployed. The differences in average age range from a low of 1.8 years in Maine in 1996 to a high of 7–8 years in New York and Oregon. These systematic age differences mirror the age differences typically observed between the self-employed and wage and salary workers.[8]   The likelihood of self-employment increases among workers as they attain older ages. SEA participants share this characteristic with the wider self-employed population.

Among the five states there are no dramatic patterns of gender differences between SEA participants and the insured unemployed. The 1996 percentages of women in the two groups were nearly identical in New York. SEA participants had a noticeably higher representation of women in Maine and Oregon but had a lower representation in Delaware.

Ethnic differences between SEA participants and the insured unemployed also are apparent in Table 5.2.   In both New Jersey and Delaware, the percentages of blacks in SEA are lower than among the insured unemployed. New York, the other state with a sizeable black population, had somewhat higher participation in SEA than among regular UI claimants. For Hispanics, on the other hand, SEA participation has been consistently low.

The occupational distributions in Table 5.2 reveal a consistent pattern for four of the five states. In New York, Oregon, Maine, and Delaware, a very high percentage of SEA participants were from the professional, technical, and managerial occupations, while low percentages were drawn from industrial occupations. In New York, for example, 46.9 percent of SEA participants in 1996 were professional, technical, and managerial, compared to just 17.8 percent among the insured unemployed. The industrial occupations in New York supplied just 14.0 percent of SEA participants in 1996 but 49.5 percent of the insured unemployed.

New Jersey appears to be an outlier in its SEA occupational distribution.   Compared with the insured unemployed, SEA participants were less likely to be professional, technical, and managerial, but more likely to be from industrial occupations. Conversations with New Jersey officials did not identify an explanation for this situation. Note that this pattern was observed in both 1996 and 1997.

In all five states, SEA participants showed a relatively high level of educational attainment. For the eight education distributions appearing in Table 5.2, the percentage whose schooling exceeded 12 years (high school) exceeded 50 percent in seven (Maine in 1997 was the exception). In four instances, the percentage exceeded 60 percent. While the regular UI programs' reporting systems do not record educational attainment for the insured unemployed, their average attainment is undoubtedly lower than for SEA participants.

Data from New York's 1996 SEA report are instructive regarding the link between educational attainment and SEA participation and SEA completion (Vroman 1998, Appendix B). The average participation rate among those profiled and identified as likely UI exhaustees was 0.93 percent (2,195 participants out of 235,126). By education level, however, the participation rates were 0.28 percent for those with less than high school education, 0.64 percent for those with high school education, and 1.59 percent for those with more than a high school diploma.

SEA completion rates in New York were also linked to educational attainment. The overall completion rate was 0.80 (i.e., 1,751 of 2,195) as shown in Table 5.2. Completion rates by education levels were 0.66 for those with less than high school, 0.76 for those with a high school education, and 0.82 for those with more than high school. From the New York data, it is clear that the probability of entering and the probability of completing SEA both increase with the level of educational attainment.

For all five states in Table 5.2, it can be inferred that SEA participants had much higher pre-unemployment wages than the wages of the insured unemployed. Weekly benefits in UI programs are based on high quarterly earnings or average weekly wages during the base period.[9] The weekly benefit amount (WBA) of SEA participants in 1996 ranged from 4.9 to 26.5 percent higher than the average WBA for the insured unemployed, and four percentage differentials exceeded 20 percent. The smaller proportional differential in Maine could reflect the high percentage of women (and associated lower earnings) among its SEA participants. While the SEA reports do not indicate the pre-unemployment levels of earnings among participants, their percentage differentials vis-à-vis the insured unemployed undoubtedly exceed the percentage differentials in weekly benefits shown in Table 5.2.[10] Thus, for four of the five states, SEA enrolled relatively high-wage workers, i.e., workers with much higher wages than the wages of the insured unemployed.

To summarize, there were clear differences in 1996 and 1997 between the characteristics of SEA participants and the insured unemployed. On average, SEA participants were older, substantially less likely to be Hispanic, and more likely to be drawn from the professional, technical, and managerial occupations and from the higher ranks of the educational attainment distribution.[11] SEA participants also earned considerably more on average than the insured unemployed prior to the onset of unemployment.

Clearly, SEA participants are not a random group drawn from the pool of eligibles identified as likely exhaustees through state profiling models; rather, SEA participants are a self-selected subgroup of likely UI exhaustees. Participation rates are systematically higher for whites, those with higher educational attainment, and those from the professional, technical, and managerial occupations.

Early SEA Program Outcomes and Costs

SEA programs are required to report on the economic outcomes of program participants for each year that SEA operated for more than six months. This requirement applied to four SEA states in 1996 (New York, Oregon, Maine, and Delaware) and to one state in 1997 (New Jersey). Due to the small scale of Delaware's program, it will not be included in the present discussion.

Data on economic outcomes for program participants were obtained from questionnaires, sent by mail. Interview data are particularly important for the self-employed because such persons are not covered by the UI system and self-employment earnings are not subject to UI reporting. However, self-employment income is frequently episodic, especially at the early stages of new business ventures. Data on self-employment earnings are subject to the twin problems of faulty recall and misreporting (underreporting). Survey-based estimates of self-employment earnings provide systematically downward-biased estimates of actual earnings.

Table 5.3 displays selected data on economic outcomes for participants in four states in 1996 and 1997. The table shows estimates of labor force status, self-employment business activity, and post-SEA wage and salary earnings of participants. Wages and salaries are also shown for the fourth quarter of 1996 and 1997.[12] In New York, the data distinguish SEA program completers from dropouts.

The respondents to follow-up interviews in New York represented just less than half of all SEA program participants. Lacking information from other sources, however, the analysis will use these data. Note also the generally small sample sizes, especially in Oregon.

The data in Table 5.3 are seriously incomplete. Even if these data were complete and based on much larger samples, there is still the issue of the short elapsed interval between program completion and the time when these state surveys were undertaken. From the demonstration project results, it would be expected that important adjustments would still be occurring two or three years following SEA participation.

The data from New York and Maine both recorded the employment situation of SEA participants using three employment categories: self-employed only, wage and salary employment only, and both types of employment at the same time. New York further noted those unemployed and retired. At the time of the interviews, the vast majority of SEA participants were employed, with employment proportions of 89 percent and 86 percent for participants in Maine and 89 percent for SEA completers in New York. Of the New York dropouts, 66 percent were employed. The latter group also had high unemployment, 28 percent of all dropouts. Among New York SEA completers not employed, about half were retired and the proportion unemployed was only 2 percent.

In both Maine and New York, about three-quarters of those employed were working exclusively as self-employed or working both as self-employed and as wage and salary workers. Only the New York dropouts were working mainly as wage and salary workers. At the time of the interviews, about half of the dropouts were working exclusively as wage and salary workers, while less than one-tenth were exclusively self-employed.

Among all states, a consistently high proportion of SEA participants started businesses. The proportions in Table 5.3 range from 65 to 77 percent in New Jersey, Oregon, Maine, and New York (among SEA program completers). For New York dropouts, the business start-up proportion was only 21 percent.

Business start-ups were heavily concentrated in two broad industry groupings, services and trade (wholesale plus retail). For the three states that reported the industry of the start-up businesses, the percentages in these two industries combined were as follows: New York, 83.4 percent; New Jersey, 66.7 percent; and Oregon, 72.0 percent. In New York, where information was also given on previous industry of SEA participants, there were large employment increases in services (increasing from 33.0 percent to 68.3 percent) and decreases in employment in finance, manufacturing, transportation and utilities, and "industry not available." The combined percentage for these latter four industries decreased from 47.1 percent to 12.9 percent. Clearly, many of the business start-ups involved large changes in the types of work activities now being undertaken by SEA participants compared with their previous jobs (Vroman 1998).

The gross income data from three states indicate that annual business sales were low in all three: $26,429 in New Jersey, $37,049 in Oregon, and less than $10,000 in Maine. Note that net business income was less than $7,000 in both New Jersey and Oregon. Thus, for these three states there is a consistent picture of relatively low levels of business sales and net business income. This is similar to findings from the self-employment demonstration projects.

Each state reported on the number of jobs added by the new businesses, besides those for the entrepreneurs. Table 5.3 indicates that there were significant indirect employment effects in all four states. The average number of added (or indirect) jobs ranged from 0.8 per business start-up in Maine and New Jersey to more than 1.4 per business start-up in New York. These added employment effects were larger than those reported in the Washington State demonstration.

In addition to the self-employment outcomes, substantial numbers of participants worked as wage and salary workers following enrollment in SEA. The proportions in the interview data at the top of Table 5.3 were 30 percent in 1996 and 54 percent in 1997 in Maine, 30 percent for New York completers (255 of 853), and 58 percent for New

Table 5.3 Labor Market and Business Outcomes for 1996 and 1997 SEA Participants

Outcome	New York Completers (1996)	New York Dropouts (1996)	New Jersey (1997)	Oregon (1996)	Oregon (1997)	Maine (1996)	Maine (1997)	Delaware (1996)
Completed questionnaires	853	173	136	40	15	53	72	8
Labor force status								
Self-employed only	506	15	INA	INA	INA	31	23	INA
Self-employed and wage and salary emp.	154	22	INA	INA	INA	9	22	INA
Wage and salary emp.	101	78	INA	INA	INA	7	17	INA
Unemployed	15	48	INA	INA	INA	INA	9	INA
Retired	45	3	INA	INA	INA	INA	0	INA
Other	17	5	INA	INA	INA	INA	1	INA
Not known	15	2	INA	INA	INA	INA		INA
Number employed	761	115	INA	INA	INA	47	62	INA
Proportion employed (%)	89	66	INA	INA	INA	89	86	INA
Business activity								
Business start-ups	660	37	98	26	10	40	44	8
Proportion with start-ups (%)	77	21	72	65	67	75	63	100
Business start-up loans	276[a]	Note a	10	3	3	3	INA	1
Business closings	INA	INA	INA	3	3	INA	INA	2
Gross sales ($, 000)	INA	INA	2,590.1	963.3	INA	291.9	INA	75.0
Average gross sales ($)	INA	INA	26,429	37,049	INA	7,298	INA	9,370
Self-employment income ($, 000)	INA	INA	650.5	160.7	INA	INA	INA	INA
Average self-employment income ($)	INA	INA	6,637	6,180	INA	INA	INA	INA
Added jobs	Note a	Note a	82	24	14	32	INA	5

Wages of SEA participants								
Number, fourth quarter		154[b]	10	7	3	48[b]	56	4[c]
Proportion with wages	0.23	0.35	0.07	0.18	0.20	0.48	0.55	050
Total quarterly wages ($, 000)	2,648.1	1,004.9	47.4	24.8	2.3	150.2	200.1	19.8
Average participant wages ($)	6,443	6,525	4,743	3,538	773	3,130	3,573	4,956
Avg. wages of all UI covered workers[c] ($)	9,405	9,405	9,314	6,637	7,005	5,775	6,059	7,726
Ratio of participant wages to covered wages	0.69	0.69	0.51	0.53	0.11	0.54	0.59	0.64

NOTE: INA = information not available.

[a] Combined data for completers and drop-outs. New York's report stated that more than 1,000 additional jobs were created by SEA firms.

[b] Numbers based on all 1996 SEA participants in New York and participants from the first three quarters of 1996 in Maine. New York data from six tax files. Maine data from UI wage records.

[c] Calculated as 13 times the average weekly wage.

SOURCE: Data from 1996 and 1997 SEA state reports.

York dropouts (100 of 173). A second perspective on this phenomenon is provided by the data in the bottom rows of the table. These show counts of those who worked as wage and salary workers during the fourth quarter of 1996 and 1997 based on administrative data. Five of the six proportions range from 18 percent to 55 percent, with only New Jersey's proportion being lower. Thus, both survey data and administrative data show sizeable proportions working in wage and salary employment.

For all four states, the amounts of wages and salaries earned by SEA participants during the fourth quarter were reported. These amounts and the per-person averages appear in the bottom panel of Table 5.3. Five of the six averages range from $3,130 in Maine to $6,525 for New York dropouts.[13] Since wage levels differ widely among states, it seemed more appropriate to compare these averages with average wages in the same states. Estimates of average quarterly wages in UI-covered employment are shown for each state. Finally, the bottom line shows the ratio of the SEA average to the all-worker average. These ratios range from 0.53 in Oregon (1996) to 0.69 in New York.

For SEA participants with wages and salaries in the fourth quarter of 1996 and 1997, the averages represent substantial amounts of earnings. Recall from Table 5.2, however, that SEA participants in all four states earned more than the average for all UI claimants prior to the onset of unemployment (as indicated by above-average weekly UI benefits). Thus, the quarterly averages in Table 5.3 represent much lower average earnings for participants than they earned before unemployment. This finding is consistent with previous work on dislocated workers, such as findings based on the CPS dislocated worker surveys.

The data examined in Table 5.3 suggest the following four conclusions:

1) the vast majority of SEA participants were employed at the time of their interviews;
2) in New York, where SEA completers and dropouts could be compared, the dropouts had lower rates of employment, higher rates of unemployment, higher rates of wage and salary employment, and lower rates of self-employment;
3) in all four states, SEA program participation was followed by a

high rate of business start-ups. The start-up proportions were 65 percent or higher; and

4) in each state, a sizeable proportion of SEA participants (ranging from 18 to 50 percent) had wage and salary earnings during the fourth quarter of 1996.

The average wage and salary earnings for these persons generally ranged from 0.51 to 0.69 of statewide average wages for the quarter.

Some caveats in the SEA outcomes data also should be emphasized. First, most data on labor market outcomes came from surveys with low response rates. The nonrespondents may have had inferior outcomes vis-à-vis the outcomes reported by the respondents. Second, a longer time interval following SEA participation would be more appropriate for measuring labor market outcomes. Measurement over a longer time period would probably reveal larger numbers of business start-ups, business failures, and moves to wage and salary employment. Finally, unlike the self-employment demonstrations, there is no control group against which the labor market outcomes for participants can be compared.[14] Thus, no easy way exists to assess the impacts of SEA. Instead, the outcomes that are summarized in Table 5.4 should be characterized as gross outcomes, not as net impacts.

The 1996 and 1997 SEA program annual reports from the states provided information on the costs of SEA. No quantitative estimates of costs were supplied by California, New York, and Delaware. Limited data were supplied by Oregon and Maine. Only New Jersey provided a reasonably complete accounting of costs. Reporting instructions directed the states to provide information on two main kinds of costs: the added costs of UI program administration and the costs of providing entrepreneurial training and other services to SEA participants. The states were instructed not to report on allowances paid to SEA participants.

A summation that includes the variable costs of SEA training and other support services plus UI administrative costs can be done only in New Jersey. The average cost per enrollee was $1,127 in 1997. Given the limitations of the cost data supplied by the states, we hesitate to make strong conclusions about program costs.

From the data supplied in the 1996 and 1997 annual SEA reports, two tentative conclusions may be drawn. First, New Jersey's average variable costs of $1,127 in 1997 did not differ widely from the costs of self-employment demonstrations, where inflated estimates from Massachusetts and Washington were $1,213 and $474, respectively.[15] Second, there would probably be a wide range of estimates of average costs related to the scale of the SEA program. The estimates of UI agency costs in Oregon in 1996 and 1997 illustrate this point, i.e., $801 in 1997, compared with $384 in 1996.

It should also be noted that, from the 1996 and 1997 data reported by the states, there is no way to undertake a benefit–cost analysis of state SEA programs such as the one completed as part of the evaluation of the UI Self-Employment Demonstration projects.

THE USE OF PROFILING IN SEA PROGRAMS AND ITS IMPLICATIONS

How Profiling Is Being Used in SEA Programs

Since profiling is used to select persons eligible for SEA, some description of the use of profiling in SEA programs is warranted. Table 5.4 provides details of profiling in six states with SEA programs.[16] The table highlights four aspects of SEA profiling: 1) the screening criteria used in the first stage of the profiling process to exclude UI claimants from the second stage of profiling (the statistical model); 2) the variables used in the statistical model; 3) information on updating the statistical model; and 4) the profiling probability of exhaustion threshold used to determine if persons are eligible to participate in SEA programs.

Profiling has two main operational functions in UI programs: to provide rankings of claimants to local UI offices (used to select persons to receive enhanced reemployment services), and to identify persons eligible to participate in SEA. The state criteria used to screen out people in the first stage of the profiling process are identified in the top rows of Table 5.4. Claimants with definite dates of recall and those hired through a union hiring hall are excluded from profiling in all states. These exclusions are based in authorizing statutory language. Persons involved in labor–management disputes and persons with part-time employment are also often screened out during the first stage of the profiling process, as they are job-attached. Most states also exclude persons with interstate claims.[17] Table 5.4 shows these latter three exclusions are not universally applied in the six states. Less common are exclusions based on potential duration of benefits and nonpayment of benefits within 35 days of claim filing. Each of the latter variables is used in just one of the six states.

The profiling statistical model in SEA states typically includes variables reflecting the person's industry and occupation and educational attainment. Of the six states, Oregon does not include industry while Pennsylvania does not include occupation.

States also use a wide variety of variables in their statistical models reflecting aspects of base period earnings and benefit entitlements. Among the six states, only New York does not utilize at least one such variable. Note that two states utilize information on the length of the delay in filing a claim for UI benefits to predict probability of exhaustion.

Job tenure (the length of time the individual spent working in their previous job) and reason for separation are utilized in three and two states, respectively. Besides these personal characteristics, the unemployment situation in the local labor market enters four of the six states' profiling statistical models. In short, the profiling models in these six states rely on a variety of explanatory variables to predict the probability of benefit exhaustion.

The labor market of the late 1990s has much lower unemployment rates than the mid 1990s, when most profiling algorithms were first estimated. Between 1993 and 1998, the nationwide exhaustion rate for regular UI programs declined from 39 percent to 31 percent. Table 5.4 shows two aspects of change in the profiling models being used in 1999. All states have updated time-dependent variables such as the local unemployment indicator, industry employment growth, and variables related to benefit entitlements. It would be interesting to know how closely the time path of the average of the state profiling scores (the predicted probabilities of exhaustion) matched the actual decreases during the period.

However, the specifications of the underlying profiling models have been unchanged in three states and changed only once in two states. In New Jersey the statistical model was reestimated in early

Table 5.4 Details of Profiling in Six SEA Programs

	Maine	Maryland	New Jersey	New York	Oregon	Pennsylvania
Criteria to screen out claimants						
Definite recall date	X	X	X	X	X	X
Exclusive hiring hall	X	X	X	X	X	X
Labor-mgt. dispute				X		X
Part time employment[a]		X	X		X	X
Interstate claim	X	X	X	X		
Potential duration	X					
No first pay within 35 days	X					
Variables in profiling function[b]						
Industry, industry growth	XX	XX	X	X	X	X
Industry exhaustion rate						X
Occupation, occ. growth	XX	X	X	X	XX	
Education	X	X		X	X	XX
Wage replacement rate	X					XX
Weekly benefit amount						
Base period earnings (BPE)					X	
Potential duration			X			
BP wages for 26 weeks					X	
High quarter earnings/BPE	X					
Filing delay	X				X	
Job tenure		X		X		X
Mass layoff status				X		

Indefinite recall			X			
Reason for separation	X				X	X
Local unemployment rate		X	X	X	X	X
Updating of profiling function						
Specification changes						
Number of times	0^d	0	0	1	2^c	1
Date(s)		1997–98	1997–98		1996, 1998	1995
Updating variables	X	X	X	X	X	X
SEA profiling threshold (%)	40	40	42	70	33	None

[a] Equivalent to a partial first payment.
[b] Number of X's indicates the number of variables.
[c] Reestimation planned in 2000.
[d] Reestimation planned in 1999.

SOURCE: Conversations with professional staff in the six states, as of 1998.

1997, but the revised function was first used in January 1998. Two states had plans to reestimate their model in either 1999 or 2000. The changes in specification in Oregon have been more substantial, in part because of changes in the state's base period eligibility criteria. Oregon used to rely on weeks of employment but now uses earnings (with base period hours worked used in a second eligibility calculation) in its monetary determinations. The relative infrequency of these changes is somewhat surprising since the unemployment rates in the states have changed so much since the mid 1990s.

The final aspect of Table 5.4 is the variation in the probability of exhaustion threshold used by the states. New York is at the high end of the distribution, using a probability threshold of 70 percent. In contrast, Pennsylvania uses no probability threshold for persons who pass the initial set of screens in the first stage of the profiling process. Oregon has the next lowest threshold, at 33 percent. It should also be noted that the proportion of UI claimants who are identified through profiling as likely exhaustees varies widely among states. For example, under its 70 percent probability threshold for SEA, New York identified 235,126 likely exhaustees in 1996, while Maine only identified 2,475 using its 40 percent threshold. These numbers represented about 42 percent and 5 percent, respectively, of UI first payments in the two states.

Operational Issues Arising from Profiling in SEA Programs and State Responses: The New York State Experience

SEA programs were implemented in eight states between 1995 and 1998, beginning with a prototype SEA program in the state of New York. At the same time, all states were required to implement worker profiling to identify UI customers who were likely to exhaust benefits as part of the federal requirement to establish Worker Profiling and Reemployment Services (WPRS) systems. The states that simultaneously implemented both WPRS and SEA had an interesting challenge before them. Not only did staff have to acclimate to a profiling model with WPRS services, they also had the added challenge of having their SEA programs tied into profiling. This section provides a look at the operational experiences of the first and largest of the state SEA programs—New York—including some comparisons with other SEA states where comparable information is available.

Under normal circumstances, when the profiling model is applied, UI claimants are not cognizant of the mechanics behind profiling. They are told to report to the UI office for a WPRS orientation (called a "profiling" orientation in New York). Although state staff explain to profiled claimants identified as likely exhaustees that they have been "selected" because they have been determined as likely to exhaust benefits, the assumption they often make is that the computer has randomly selected participants for a WPRS orientation. Very few claimants question why they have been selected for reemployment services, and they generally are quite appreciative of the information gleaned from the profiling orientation.

Customarily, during profiling orientations in SEA states, several options are given to the claimants who have been identified as likely exhaustees via profiling and referred to services. The first choice is reemployment services. These services can range from job search workshops to resumé preparation assistance to career testing and counseling. The vast majority of profiled and referred UI customers choose to take advantage of reemployment services. Statistically, most of these WPRS participants are interested in seeking a wage or salary position, but they have not been in the job market for a number of years and just need assistance with their job search.

The second choice offered to UI claimants in a WPRS orientation is retraining. This option allows profiled and referred UI customers to be excused from the full-time work search requirement in order to take advantage of a full-time training course. The training could be in a Workforce Investment Act (WIA) class (e.g., in a community college), a college course, or training in a private vocational school. This is also a popular option with profiled and referred claimants because in a number of states, getting into a training class extends unemployment benefits for an additional one to six months. It is important to note that even individuals interested in starting a business may choose the training option as more colleges establish degrees and certificates in entrepreneurism.

The third available option (at least in the eight SEA states) is exploring the SEA program. Generally, less than 3 percent of profiled claimants identified as likely exhaustees are interested in going to an SEA orientation session. In many of the SEA states, supplemental letters are sent to all UI customers identified as likely exhaustees to inform them about the SEA program. Even with this, there is still a very small percentage of profiled customers taking advantage of SEA—less than 1 percent of all UI claimants. Thus, SEA is an option for a small number of people with the motivation and skills necessary to start their own business.

The primary problem with profiling and SEA does not occur with an individual who has been profiled and identified as likely to exhaust UI benefits, it occurs when an individual does not meet the probability threshold for SEA eligibility but still wants to participate in SEA. Not all applicants are eligible to participate in the SEA program, and this has proved to be a point of contention in some states, leading to disputes of both nonmonetary determinations and appeals decisions denying SEA eligibility. One source of operational problems has derived from the use of a minimum probability of exhausting UI benefits as a condition of eligibility for the SEA program. Some claimants have not understood (or do not agree) that likelihood of exhaustion is a necessary element in determining eligibility. There have also been more general disputes over applicants' profiling scores and whether these scores reflect their true likelihood of being unemployed for 26 weeks or more. Generally, however, the volume of disputes has declined in more recent periods.

In New York state, the probability threshold (or "cutoff") for SEA program eligibility is 70 percent (which has been lowered from 75 percent when the program first started). UI customers with a profiling probability score below the 70th percentile are told in the local UI office that they have been found ineligible for the SEA program. When they inquire why they are ineligible, the topic of profiling inevitably comes into discussion. From the claimant's perspective, suddenly a statistical, computerized model stands between them and their ability to be able to start their own business and still collect benefit payments. Although the situation has improved since the beginning of the SEA program, most local office staff still have difficulty understanding profiling models, whether it is one using characteristics screens or a statistical model (or, most typically, a two-stage process similar to the DOL profiling model, which uses both screens and a statistical model).

In an attempt to explain why the profiling "score" is not high enough to participate in SEA, the situation becomes even more complicated and potentially confusing to the claimant. This is due to the fact that, to the lay person on the street, when they hear the word "score" they make the assumption that there has been a test given and they did not pass. States vary as to what statistical percentage they use as the threshold (or cutoff) probability for SEA eligibility. Inevitably though, whenever there is an eligibility cutoff, there will be individuals on the other side of the cutoff who do not qualify for the program and who are frustrated and unhappy.

Note that officials in several SEA states have indicated that the profiling cutoffs used in their SEA programs may be too high. As the labor market has strengthened in the late 1990s and state-level unemployment rates declined, the number of initial claims for UI benefits also declined. This decrease in the intake volume for the regular UI program affected the numbers identified as SEA eligibles via profiling. Two states currently operate with lower threshold probabilities than contemplated when their SEA programs were being formulated: New York, at 70 percent rather than 75 percent, and Oregon, at 33 percent rather than 60 percent. Two others, New Jersey and Maine, have considered reducing their thresholds. Finally, as noted earlier in this chapter, Pennsylvania has no probability threshold for SEA eligibility; all of those claimants who pass the screens in the first stage of Pennsylvania's profiling process are informed about the SEA program.[18] Further reductions in the cutoff percentages can be anticipated if labor markets become as robust as they were in the late 1990s.

Administratively, UI claimants with a low statistical probability of exhaustion present a real challenge to the SEA states. The easy way out would be to lower the profiling threshold to a point where nearly anyone could participate in the SEA program. This approach, however, presents the following problems. First, to lower the score to such a point compromises the integrity of the profiling system in terms of its ability to identify claimants who are likely to exhaust UI benefits. Not all UI claimants are likely to exhaust their benefits. As a matter of fact, New York has estimated that, in times of full employment, only 15 to 30 percent of all claimants will be highly likely to exhaust benefits. In the late 1990s in New York State, because the UI recipiency rate was so low (averaging approximately 5 percent), the proportion of claimants who were likely to exhaust benefits dropped even lower to only 11 percent of the total UI claimant population in the state.[19]

A second issue regarding reducing the profiling threshold arises in those states where employers' benefit rating is charged back to a specific firm, thus affecting the employer's experience-rated UI tax liability. In this situation, the use of profiling helps to ensure that only those who will truly have a difficult time becoming reemployed will be eligible for the SEA program and thus receive self-employment allowance payments. This helps in assuring employers that they will not be paying for benefits that claimants would not otherwise have received, and that there will be fewer instances of direct competition against the former employer; in fact, for workers laid off through a mass layoff or plant closing, quite often there is no existing former employer.[20]

CONCLUSIONS AND FUTURE DIRECTIONS

Conclusions Regarding Targeting in the SEA Program

As we have seen, the use of profiling in state SEA programs has had both positive and negative effects on these programs. On the positive side, the use of statistical profiling models in the SEA program has targeted the program on a subgroup of UI claimants who have the characteristics typically associated with dislocated workers. Moreover, in those states where outcomes data are available, those dislocated UI claimants (selected through the profiling process) who participated in the SEA program have generally shown positive outcomes, in terms of both high rates of business start-ups (65 percent or higher) and also entry into wage and salary employment (with employment rates of between 18 and 50 percent). It was difficult, however, to estimate self-employment earnings, and wage and salary earnings of SEA participants were generally lower (0.51 to 0.69 percent) than statewide average wages.

The ability of the profiling models to meet their objective of targeting the SEA program solely on individuals who are permanently separated from their previous job is less ambiguous. As Table 5.4 clearly shows, all states have included a variable in their worker profiling process that screens out those UI recipients who are on recall status, although a WPRS evaluation report to Congress shows that states varied in how they defined "recall status" (Dickinson, Kreutzer, and Decker 1997, p. II-2). Of course, these recall status screens will not be 100 percent accurate. For example, over 45 percent of the states screened out not only those individuals who did not have a definite date of recall to their former employer, but also claimants who indicated that they expected to be recalled but did not have a definite date (Dickinson, Kreutzer, and Decker 1997, p. II-2). Moreover, it is clear from the results of state follow-up surveys of SEA participants described earlier that many of the business start-ups involved large changes in the types of work activities being undertaken by SEA participants compared with their previous wage and salary jobs. Thus, it appears that the presence of these permanent layoff/recall status screens have served to minimize any potential the SEA program might have for disrupting an employer/employee relationship. Also, because SEA program participants are likely to draw no more in SEA allowances than they would have drawn anyway in regular UI benefits, it appears unlikely that SEA will have a significant impact on employers' experience-rated UI tax liability.

The requirement that profiling be used in SEA programs, however, has not been without its downsides. There are at least two major problems that states have experienced in using some type of profiling method in their SEA programs. First, profiling has restricted the access of some UI claimants to the SEA program who might otherwise be good candidates for self-employment. This is not surprising, since individuals identified by profiling as likely to exhaust their UI benefits are likely to be individuals who have *more* barriers to reemployment than UI claimants in general. Thus, although there are obviously exceptions, profiling will identify a group of the unemployed who, on average, are less likely to have the knowledge and skills necessary for self-employment.

For this reason, state economic development agencies and microenterprise practitioners interested primarily in promoting microenterprise and small business development have often viewed profiling as the wrong approach to targeting individuals who would be successful in business. However, their concern about the conflict between targeting SEA on likely UI exhaustees and service providers' desire to focus on those most likely to succeed in business has failed to materialize because of the self-selection factor in SEA. That is, even if a particular claimant is judged to be likely to exhaust UI benefits, they must still be interested in pursuing self-employment, and if so, be motivated enough complete the sequence of self-screening activities (e.g., the orientation and "reality check" about the pros and cons of self-employment).

The characteristics of SEA participants presented above clearly show that SEA participants are not a random group drawn from the pool of eligibles identified as likely exhaustees through state profiling models. Rather, SEA program participants are a self-selected subgroup of dislocated UI claimants. SEA participation rates are higher for whites, individuals with higher educational attainment, and those from the professional, technical, and managerial occupations. This evidence, in combination with the very small proportions of likely UI exhaustees (i.e., as eligible for SEA) who actually apply for SEA, demonstrates that this strong self-selection process is at work in current state SEA programs, just as in both of the UI Self-Employment Demonstration projects. The end result of this process is that, while the use of profiling in SEA targets the program on dislocated UI claimants, the self-selection process used for SEA appears to be further targeting SEA participation on a subset of dislocated claimants who have the knowledge and skills necessary for self-employment.

For program operators, the restriction on access to the SEA program resulting from the use of profiling has also created a second problem—dealing with those individuals who are interested in self-employment but are not eligible for the SEA program due to their (relatively low) profiling scores. By restricting the access of individuals with (relatively) low profiling scores to the SEA program, profiling can generate administrative headaches for SEA program operators as they attempt to explain to these individuals why they are ineligible for the SEA program, what the profiling model is and does, and how profiling relates to self-employment in the first place (which, as noted earlier, is far from an obvious relationship). The experience of the first and largest SEA program, the New York program, provides an illustration of how the use of profiling as a targeting mechanism for SEA can result in unhappy and frustrated claimants, as well as additional work for the few SEA program staff. It is certainly possible that the reductions in the probability of exhaustion thresholds for SEA eligibility that occurred in state SEA programs in the late 1990s was due in part to a desire to minimize the administrative burden on state staff by reducing the proportion of claimants interested in SEA who do not qualify for the program. On the other hand, it is just as likely that this occurrence was simply a temporary response by states to attempt to maintain SEA program enrollments in a time of declining UI caseloads.

Future Directions

Some future directions that the permanently reauthorized SEA program may take are as follows:

- The use of profiling will remain an important feature of SEA programs as a dislocated worker program. The use of profiling is essential for targeting SEA on a subpopulation of UI claimants who are dislocated workers, and it remains a requirement for SEA programs under federal law. The continuing concern about employer attachment issues means that this situation is not likely to change anytime soon. However, the specific variables used in profiling models for SEA are likely to change over time and eventually may be more customized to SEA needs.

- There will be interest in looking at which SEA participants succeed in their business ventures over the long term. Even with the very small numbers of SEA participants, the program has already provided a pool of well over 6,000 individuals who can be studied to see if there are common characteristics of "typical" entrepreneurs that can be developed. New York plans to look at this issue over the next several years to see if any conclusions can be drawn on the elements of the "typical" entrepreneur for future use in developing customized profiling models for the SEA program that take into account these "entrepreneurial" characteristics, in addition to those factors associated with the likelihood of benefit exhaustion.

- Now that SEA has become a permanent program, DOL's direct oversight role in the SEA program will likely diminish. Changes to the SEA program in a UI Program Letter (UIPL 11-99) that eliminated the requirement for states to submit a state SEA plan to DOL for review and approval prior to implementing a SEA program mean that it is easier than ever for states to establish programs. The fact that a state's SEA legislation conforms to the basic tenets of federal SEA legislation, including the requirement that profiling be used in selecting SEA program participants, will now be sufficient for DOL approval of a state's approach to implementing SEA.

- The SEA program will gradually expand to additional states. In fact, three additional states, Arkansas, Washington State, and Massachusetts, have been working on enacting the conforming state legislation necessary to establish their own SEA programs.
- There may be a need for a self-employment program that serves a broader population of the unemployed, so that individuals who are not dislocated workers would be eligible to participate. Such a program could not use WIA dislocated worker funding for business development services (e.g., microenterprise training), but states would have the option to fund such services for a broad range of jobseekers. Such a program, however, would have the potential problem of employer opposition if nondislocated UI claimants are permitted to participate.
- The availability of technical assistance to additional states interested in implementing SEA programs will be critical in creating effective programs. With diminishing direct involvement of DOL staff in the planning process, a "how-to" manual for states to assist them in developing and operating these programs becomes a particularly critical need.
- If SEA programs are to be successful in the long-run, states will have to strengthen the interprogram linkages between UI programs and self-employment service providers. In particular, state SEA programs will need to establish strong working relationships with both microenterprise training providers under the Workforce Investment Act and with the Small Business Administration's network of small business development centers, which can provide SEA program participants with extensive business counseling and technical assistance services.

Notes

This paper represents the views of the authors and does not necessarily reflect the policies or positions of the U.S. Department of Labor, the New York State Department of Labor, or the Urban Institute. Jacob Benus and Wayne Gordon provided substantive comments which helped improve on a prior version of this paper.

1. Based on data from the series of BLS Displaced Worker Supplements to the Current Population Survey (Wandner 1997, p. 96). Also see U.S. Department of Labor (1998).
2. Based on data from the biannual displaced worker surveys conducted by the Bureau of Labor Statistics (BLS), "blue-collar workers," in particular those workers in manufacturing industries, accounted for half of all displaced workers in the early 1980s. However, the most recent BLS displaced worker survey (February 1998) indicates that slightly more displaced workers were from managerial, professional specialty, and technical occupations (30 percent) compared with those "blue-collar" occupations more typically associated with worker displacement (defined here as precision production, craft, and repair workers plus operators, fabricators, and laborers).
3. For an in-depth review of these preliminary results and their impact on federal SEA program legislation, see Messenger and Wandner (1994).
4. Like many states, Pennsylvania uses screens in the first stage of their profiling process to exclude claimants who do not meet certain criteria; e.g., claimants with definite dates of recall. However, all claimants who reach the second stage of the profiling process (the statistical model) are informed about SEA in the eight SDAs with active SEA programs.
5. Maryland has one statewide vendor who hosts the initial meeting. However, correspondence from the UI agency precedes this meeting. Claimant letters are forwarded to the service vendor, who then extends invitations to attend an information meeting. Pennsylvania's SDAs follow different procedures including holding the initial meeting at the vendor's site.
6. For example, the 1996 annual reports indicated that very few loans were received in Oregon, Maine, and Delaware. In that year, loans were relatively common only in New York, but many of them came from personal sources, not from financial institutions.
7. Note that SEA participants are counts of individuals, whereas insured unemployment refers to weekly averages measured in thousands.
8. In 1996, household data from the monthly Current Population Survey (CPS) indicated that the average age of those working as self-employed in nonagricultural industries was 44.4 years, compared with 38.4 years for wage and salary workers.
9. Typically the base period is the first four of the five most recent fully completed calendar quarters preceding the UI claim.
10. The presence of WBA maximums places an upper limit on weekly benefits for many high wage workers. There is no similar upper limit on weekly and quarterly earnings. Thus, the earnings differentials would be larger than the differentials in WBAs that have a constrained maximum.
11. New Jersey and Maine present partial exceptions to this statement.
12. In New York, 1996 fourth-quarter wage and salary data are based on state income tax records.
13. In 1997, only three people participated in Oregon's SEA program. This explains the low figures.

14. There is a question of whether new businesses started by SEA participants displace existing businesses. Although the potential displacement effect is likely to be quite small given the small number of SEA participants, it is impossible to estimate this effect with existing data.
15. The variable cost estimates shown in Benus et al. (1995, Table 10.2) have been inflated by a ratio of 1.1938, which represents the ratio of the 1997 all items consumer price index (CPI) to the 1990 level of the CPI.
16. While California and Delaware have enacted all the necessary legislation to operate SEA, the programs in both states were inactive in 1998. During 1997, these states reported 19 and 40 weeks compensated by their respective SEA programs. Both reported zero weeks compensated in 1998 (ETA report 5159). It should be noted that the Delaware SEA program actively enrolled participants in previous years, but SEA has never been actively pursued in California. States also curtailed their SEA operations due to the scheduled expiration of SEA in December 1998.
17. A profiling process for interstate claimants has not yet been established.
18. It should be noted that among states with an SEA program, only Pennsylvania does not use a probability threshold determining program eligibility. Many states do not establish explicit probability thresholds as part of their profiling procedures for WPRS. Typically, claimants who pass the initial screens in the first stage of the profiling process are ranked in order of their probability of benefit exhaustion, from those with the highest exhaustion probabilities to those with the lowest probabilities. Then, individuals are referred to services beginning with those at the top of the ranking (with highest exhaustion probabilities) and proceeding down the list until the supply of available reemployment services is exhausted.
19. Data provided by the New York State Department of Labor, Unemployment Insurance program office.
20. See the discussion on profiling and employer attachment in the second section of this chapter for an analysis of this issue.

References

Benus, Jacob M., Terry R. Johnson, Michelle Wood, Neelima Grover, and Theodore Shen. 1995. *Self-Employment Programs: A New Reemployment Strategy, Final Report on the UI Self-Employment Demonstration.* Unemployment Insurance Occasional Paper no. 95-4, Washington, D.C.: U.S. Department of Labor.
Dickinson, Katherine P., Suzanne D. Kreutzer, and Paul T. Decker. 1997. *Evaluation of Worker Profiling and Reemployment Service Systems: Report to Congress.* Washington, D.C.: U.S. Department of Labor, Employment and Training Administration.

Messenger, Jon C., and Stephen A. Wandner. 1994. *Self-Employment as a Reemployment Option: Demonstration Results and National Legislation.* Unemployment Insurance Occasional Paper no. 94-3, Washington, D.C.: U.S. Department of Labor.

Orr, Larry, Stephen A. Wandner, David Lah, and Jacob M. Benus. 1994. "The Use of Evaluation Results in Employment and Training Policy: Two Case Studies." Paper presented at the annual research conference of the Association of Public Policy Analysis and Management, Chicago, Illinois, October 26–29.

U.S. Department of Labor. 1994. *The Worker Profiling and Reemployment Services System: Legislation, Implementation Process, and Research Findings.* Unemployment Insurance Occasional Paper no. 94-4, Washington, D.C.: U.S. Department of Labor.

———. 1995. *What's Working (and What's Not): A Summary of Research on the Economic Impacts of Employment and Training Programs.* Washington, D.C.: U.S. Department of Labor, Office of the Chief Economist.

———. 1998. "Worker Displacement: 1995–1997." Washington, D.C.: U.S. Department of Labor, Bureau of Labor Statistics, August 19.

Vroman, Wayne. 1998. "Self Employment Assistance (SEA) Program." Report to Congress. Washington, D.C.: Unemployment Insurance Service, Employment and Training Administration, U.S. Department of Labor.

Wandner, Stephen A. 1997. "Early Reemployment for Dislocated Workers in the United States." *International Social Security Review* 50(4): 95–112.

Comments on Chapter 5

Jacob M. Benus
IMPAQ International

The chapter by Jon Messenger, Carolyn Peterson-Vaccaro, and Wayne Vroman effectively describes the likely benefits and the potential problems generated by the implementation of profiling in self-employment assistance (SEA) programs. The chapter also speculates about the impact of profiling on SEA programs. I believe that the impact of profiling on SEA programs can and should be analyzed more rigorously. In fact, the U.S. Department of Labor (DOL) may already have the data to measure this impact. Before describing how DOL might evaluate the impact of profiling on SEA programs, I will first briefly review the contents of the chapter.

The first section of the chapter describes the UI Self-Employment Demonstrations project.[1] These demonstrations were part of an experimental design project to evaluate the impact of SEA programs on the unemployed. The project was funded by DOL and implemented in the states of Washington and Massachusetts.

To reduce the potential for "excess costs," the Massachusetts demonstration incorporated a UI exhaustion algorithm. Only those above a cutoff probability (i.e., 0.25) were invited to participate in the program (this cutoff eliminated 12 percent of the UI claimants). This exhaustion algorithm was included in the demonstration largely in response to legislative requirements and states' concerns about excess costs. Another feature of the Massachusetts demonstration was the withdrawal of the work search waiver after 24 weeks. That is, after 24 weeks, participants had to drop out of the SEA program and search for regular wage and salary employment in order to remain eligible for the remaining 6 weeks of UI benefits (approximately $1,500).

Between these two features of the demonstration (i.e., profiling and the 24-week benefit cutoff), I believe that the 24-week benefit cutoff was much more important in promoting budget neutrality. If this assertion is correct, the chapter's statements about the effectiveness of profiling on budget neutrality may not be warranted. The problem is that without a rigorous evaluation, we cannot be certain about the impact of profiling.

The chapter next goes into an assessment of the implementation of SEA in eight states. Essentially, the findings in this section confirm the results of the Self-Employment Demonstrations. That is, highly educated individuals from professional, technical, and managerial occupations with high prior earnings make up the bulk of SEA participants. Following this discussion, the chapter describes the use of profiling in the state programs, the implementation of profiling, and the operational issues that profiling raises.

One of the more interesting operational issues described in the chapter is reprofiling. That is, UI claimants who are determined to be ineligible for SEA as a result of a low profiling score may request that their score be recalculated in an effort to become eligible. In New York, the only state to permit reprofiling, one-third of the 1,800 participants in 1997 came into the program after having been reprofiled.

The chapter concludes with the authors pointing out the positives and negatives of profiling for SEA programs. One of the positives claimed for profiling is that profiling results in, or at least enhances, budget neutrality. This conclusion is partly based on evidence from the Massachusetts demonstration. This evidence, however, is weak and, in my opinion, not convincing.

I believe we can get more definitive evidence on this issue from data available in the UI Self-Employment Demonstrations. To analyze the impact of profiling, we can apply a profiling model to the Washington State sample (where profiling was not used). That is, we can profile the treatment and control group members in the Washington sample and eliminate those who fall below the threshold. Using this approach, we can estimate excess costs with and without the eliminated group. This exercise can quantify the impact of profiling. If profiling has no impact on budget neutrality, we should reconsider the assertion that profiling is essential to promote budget neutrality in SEA programs.

The above analysis can be enhanced by altering the threshold level. For example, we can alter the threshold level from 0.25 to 0.50. If profiling reduces excess costs, one might expect excess costs to be lower under the 0.50 threshold than under the 0.25 threshold. This is clearly a testable hypothesis, and the data for testing the hypothesis are available from the UI Self-Employment Demonstrations.

My main conclusion is that the argument in favor of profiling in SEA programs rests heavily on the presumed impact of profiling on budget neutrality. Let's measure whether this presumption is correct. DOL has the data to do it! It would be a shame to leave such an important issue unanswered.

Note

1. For a description of this project, see Benus et al. (1995).

Reference

Benus, Jacob M., Terry R. Johnson, Michelle Wood, Meelima Grover, and Theodore Shen. 1995. *Self-Employment Programs: A New Reemployment Strategy, Final Report on the UI Self-Employment Demonstration*. UI Occasional Paper no. 95-4, Washington, D.C.: U.S. Department of Labor.

Comments on Chapter 5

Wayne Gordon
U.S. Department of Labor

It should first be understood that the self-employment assistance (SEA) program is small, as measured by the number of states having implemented programs in the six years since authorization. Eleven states took the first step of implementation by changing legislation, but only eight can claim any significant effort. Of the eight, three started relatively late in the initial five-year authorization.

Achieving widespread state commitment to the program was made difficult because of uncertainty about the continuation of the program after December of 1998. Now that the authorization is permanent, the U.S. Department of Labor (DOL) expects several more states to implement SEA programs soon, and DOL is encouraging more states to consider doing so. This is vital to long-term survival of the program.

An important question that the chapter fails to address is: With profiling thresholds so low in many of the SEA states, what role does profiling play? It appears that the first step of the profiling process, which applies screens to exclude those with union hiring hall and employer attachment, as well as self-selection, are the more powerful determinants of who enrolls in SEA programs. For example, many people express an interest in SEA-type programs. DOL handles many letters and phone inquiries about how to get into the SEA program. Second, the profiling models exclude some demographic characteristics that are key predictors of successful entrepreneurial success. Third, not all entrepreneurial activity in SEA is in direct competition with past employers. Finally, if it can be shown that the self-employed hire new workers, then widening the SEA offer to more initial claimants would not threaten trust-fund solvency if these employers are paying UI taxes on behalf of new employees.

Under the Workforce Investment Act, new administrative relation-ships are being forged between the public employment service and oth-er agencies like small business development centers and the Service Corps of Retired Executives. It would be interesting to hear more in the chapter about what states are doing to make these specialized ser-vices available to SEA participants, and how continuous improvement principles can be achieved. In relation to such supplementary services, it would be useful to 1) identify which entrepreneurial services would be useful in promoting success of SEA recipients, 2) determine the costs of these services which are often provided "in kind," and 3) es-tablish a feedback loop between these new service providers and the UI system to ensure that SEA claimants are satisfying eligibility require-ments.

State and federal reporting of SEA activity needs to be revisited to determine the best type of information for policymakers and the gener-al public. Currently, since only a small number of states have pro-grams, the annual report method described in the chapter is adequate. However, if many more states were to operate SEA programs, this type of reporting would be excessively burdensome. Furthermore, not all successful outcomes for SEA participants can be captured under cur-rent WIA performance measures. Separate measures will need to be in-corporated under WIA to properly capture performance outcomes that are unique to SEA. A specialized program such as SEA, which targets a small slice of the UI claimant population, requires regular evaluation to ensure effectiveness and use of best practices. Performance moni-toring should be the first system in this continuous improvement loop.

6
Targeting Reemployment Bonuses

Christopher J. O'Leary
W.E. Upjohn Institute for Employment Research

Paul T. Decker
Mathematica Policy Research, Inc.

Stephen A. Wandner
U.S. Department of Labor

Field experiments to evaluate the potential for using cash bonus of-fers to promote early return to work by unemployment insurance (UI) claimants were conducted in four states between 1984 and 1989. The first experiment was initiated by the Illinois Employment Security De-partment and yielded encouraging results. This led the U.S. Depart-ment of Labor to include a bonus treatment in the New Jersey reem-ployment experiment. Even though evidence from New Jersey was not strongly positive, to further clarify the findings from Illinois, the Labor Department sponsored multitreatment experiments in Pennsylvania and in Washington State. Results from the latter two experiments were not supportive of the idea that the reemployment bonus could be a cost-effective way to promote rapid reemployment, and policy momentum for the bonus idea faded.

In 1994, the Clinton administration proposed to Congress a federal reemployment bonus program to be narrowly targeted to dislocated UI claimants by a worker profiling mechanism based on objective charac-teristics such as level of education and length of work experience.[1] The previous year, a profiling mechanism of this type had been incorporat-ed into federal legislation which authorized programs to provide job search assistance and self-employment allowances. Clinton's 1994 reemployment bonus proposal died in Congress, and reemployment bonuses are not presently available in the United States. However, any future legislative initiative on bonuses would likely include a targeting mechanism.

By 1995, mechanisms for early identification of UI beneficiaries who are likely to experience long jobless spells were implemented in all states. These procedures are called profiling models and are part of state Worker Profiling and Reemployment Services (WPRS) systems required by the 1993 federal law. The models are designed to identify UI beneficiaries who are most likely to exhaust their benefit entitlement, so that reemployment services can be delivered quickly and prolonged unemployment can be forestalled.

Since WPRS profiling models currently being used by the states identify potentially dislocated workers, they offer a natural means for targeting reemployment bonus offers. This chapter summarizes recent findings from simulation analysis using data from the Pennsylvania and Washington experiments. These experiments were financed with money that Congress earmarked in 1987 to investigate methods for promoting reemployment of workers dislocated from their jobs because of structural change in the economy. While the first evaluations found little evidence that the reemployment bonus is an effective intervention for dislocated workers, our simulation results suggest that targeting reemployment bonus offers with state profiling models may appreciably improve the cost-effectiveness of the bonus.

The analysis of this chapter yields positive evidence consistent with findings from targeting studies for other employment programs that targeting services can increase reemployment success. For example, Corson and Decker (1996), who applied a similar simulation analysis to the job search assistance intervention for dislocated workers in the New Jersey experiment, estimated a significant improvement in program effectiveness.

THE REEMPLOYMENT BONUS EXPERIMENT

The first reemployment bonus experiment was conducted in Illinois during 1984–1985. It found that a $500 reemployment bonus offer to UI claimants for returning to work within 11 weeks (the *qualification period*) and staying employed at least four months (the *reemployment requirement*) reduced the duration of UI compensated unemployment by 1.15 weeks and saved more than two dollars in UI benefit payments for every dollar paid out in bonuses and administration of the bonus offer (Woodbury and Spiegelman 1987). Treatment designs for the four experiments are given in Table 6.1, and mean net impact estimates are in Table 6.2.[2]

Encouraging results from the Illinois reemployment bonus experiment led to replication trials in other states to test if the large effects found in Illinois could be duplicated. The other experiments varied the bonus amount and the qualification period in an attempt to find the optimal bonus.

The reemployment bonus offer in the 1985–1986 New Jersey experiment also had a four-month reemployment requirement, but it had a

Table 6.1 Treatment Designs for the Reemployment Bonus Experiments

State	Bonus amount ($)	Qualification period (weeks)	
Illinois	500	11	
New Jersey	Declining[a]	12	
Pennsylvania		6	12
	3 × WBA	Low bonus, short qualification	Low bonus, long qualification
	6 × WBA	High bonus, short qualification	High bonus, long qualification
	Declining[a]	—	Declining[a], long qualification
Washington		(0.2 × potential UI duration) + 1 week	(0.4 × potential UI duration) + 1 week
	2 × WBA	Low bonus, short qualification	Low bonus, long qualification
	4 × WBA	Medium bonus, short qualification	Medium bonus, long qualification
	6 × WBA	High bonus, short qualification	High bonus, long qualification

[a] Declining means an initial bonus offer of half the remaining U.I. entitlement payable for reemployment within two weeks and then declining by 10% per week.

Table 6.2 Mean Net Impacts on Weeks and Dollars of UI in the Benefit Year across Four Experiments

Experiment	Net impact on weeks of UI benefits	Net impact on dollars of UI benefits
Illinois	−1.15** (0.29)	−194** (47)
New Jersey	−0.69** (0.23)	−101** (45)
Pennsylvania	−0.54** (0.21)	−95** (37)
Washington	−0.40** (0.21)	−63** (33)

NOTE: The impact estimates reported in this table are based on the full analytic samples examined in each experiment. Eligibility conditions for these samples are summarized in Table 6.3. The remaining estimates in this chapter for Pennsylvania and Washington are based on samples restricted by profiling considerations. Standard errors are in parentheses.

12-week qualification period and a bonus amount that decreased as the duration of insured unemployment lengthened. Net impacts on UI receipt in the New Jersey experiment were much smaller than in Illinois, with the bonus offer yielding only a 0.69 week reduction in UI payments. This raised questions about the appeal to the UI system of such a bonus offer (Corson et al. 1989).

The states of Pennsylvania and Washington each conducted separate reemployment bonus experiments in 1988–1989 involving a total of 11 different treatments, as described in Table 6.1. The Washington experiment had a mean bonus offer of about 3.5 times the weekly benefit amount (WBA) and a qualification period that averaged about 7.5 weeks long. Pennsylvania paid either three or six times the WBA and had qualification periods of either 6 or 12 weeks. There was also a long qualification period treatment with a declining bonus in Pennsylvania. Some of the bonus offers in Pennsylvania and Washington were nearly identical. These were the short qualification/high bonus offer and long qualification/high bonus offer treatments (Decker and O'Leary 1995, p. 536). As a result, it was hoped that the evaluation findings from the two experiments would be complementary and reinforcing.

The Pennsylvania and Washington treatments were intended to supplement information provided by the Illinois experiment by identifying which bonus amount and qualification period was most effective.

Among the five treatments in Pennsylvania and six treatments in Washington, only four were cost-effective from the perspective of the UI system (Decker and O'Leary 1995). As reported in Table 6.2, the mean net impact of the five Pennsylvania treatments of –0.54 weeks of UI and the mean net impact of the six Washington treatments of –0.41 weeks of UI were even more modest than the New Jersey results.

Other analyses have examined the individual experiments and their relationship to one another. The Illinois results were found to be stronger than the other experiments because of the opportunity to reduce much longer potential durations of benefits since extended benefits were available during roughly the first half of the operation of the Illinois experiment (Davidson and Woodbury 1991; O'Leary, Spiegelman, and Kline 1995). New Jersey impacts were found to be weaker than those in Illinois because of the differences in the behavioral responses to fixed versus declining reemployment bonus offers (Decker 1994). Slightly stronger results in Pennsylvania than Washington were attributed to tighter labor markets in Pennsylvania than in Washington during the operation of the two experiments (O'Leary, Spiegelman, and Kline 1995). Differences in impact estimates among the experiments may be further reconciled by examining the alternative targeting of offers resulting from the differing eligibility conditions among the experiments.

It is important to note that each of the four experiments compared reemployment earnings of those offered a reemployment bonus with those in control groups not offered a bonus. Despite spells of compensated unemployment, which were shorter on average, reemployment earnings were no lower for those offered a bonus. Treatment and control reemployment earnings were virtually identical in all of the experiments, suggesting that the offer of a reemployment bonus does not induce job seekers to accept lower quality jobs as measured by the rate of compensation. Long-term follow-up evidence from the New Jersey experiment is particularly compelling on this point. Earnings were tracked in each of six years immediately following the experiment, and neither in any particular year nor cumulatively over the six-year period was there a significant difference in earnings between those offered a bonus and those in the control group (Corson and Haimson 1995, p. 36).[3]

ELIGIBILITY FOR THE EXPERIMENTS

Previous analyses of the reemployment bonus experiments have examined neither the effects of targeting bonus offers nor the effects of differences in eligibility conditions. In most analyses, the implicit targeting resulting from eligibility criteria for the experiments has been accepted as a contextual datum. Each of the four experiments had slightly different eligibility requirements for unemployed workers to participate as members of treatment or control groups. The experiments were mainly focused on permanently separated employees who were going to have difficulty finding new employment. However, the degree of sample screening varied; this was because of a conscious effort to coordinate designs to increase the information provided by the collection of experiments.

Eligibility criteria for the four experiments separated into UI and dislocated worker criteria are summarized in Table 6.3. The requirements were intended to assure that workers opened a UI benefit claim, dealt with UI administrative rules, and experienced some degree of displacement from work.

To elicit the maximum possible bonus impact, offers should be made as soon as possible after a claim for UI benefits is opened. The offer was made after employment service (ES) registration in Illinois, after a first UI payment in New Jersey, and after claiming a UI waiting week in Pennsylvania.[4] In the Washington experiment, the bonus offer was made during the initial UI claim interview, which is well before receipt of the first benefit payment. Furthermore, bonus payments in Washington were sometimes made to persons who never even filed for waiting-week credit.[5] The other experiments required UI payment for bonus payment eligibility.

The presence and extent of dislocated worker criteria varied greatly across the experiments. Screening was extensive in New Jersey, while it was nonexistent in Washington. In terms of this design feature, the Illinois and Pennsylvania experiments fell in between. In Illinois, New Jersey, and Pennsylvania, offers were aimed mainly at permanently separated unemployed workers. Those awaiting recall and union hiring hall members were either explicitly or indirectly excluded. No such

Table 6.3 Eligibility Criteria for the Reemployment Bonus Experiments

State	UI eligibility criteria	Dislocated worker criteria
Illinois	Initial UI claims only	Eligible for a full 26 weeks of potential duration Registered with Job Service (to exclude temporary layoffs and union hiring hall members) At least age 20, not older than 54
New Jersey	First UI payments only	Three years tenure on prior job Age 25 or older Union hiring hall exclusion Exclude temporary layoffs: recall expected on a specific date
Pennsylvania	Initial UI claims only Regular UI claims Initially satisfied monetary eligibility conditions Not separated from job due to a labor dispute Signed for a waiting week or first payment within 6 weeks of benefit application date	Union hiring hall exclusion Exclude employer attached: must not have a specific recall date within 60 days after benefit application
Washington	Initial UI claims only Eligible to receive benefits from the state UI trust fund Monetarily valid claims at the time of filing	

exclusion was imposed in Washington, where the sample design provided that more restrictive screens could be imposed on the experimental data as part of the subgroup analysis. Results from Washington indicate that targeting offers to dislocated workers, defined as those with three or more years of prior job tenure, would modestly increase treatment effects.[6] Additionally, requiring a waiting week in Washington would probably have increased net impacts of the bonus offer.[7]

STATE PROFILING MODELS

In all states, profiling done as part of a WPRS system involves a two-step process. The first step excludes UI claimants expecting recall by their previous employers and those who are members of full-referral union hiring halls. These exclusions are applied to focus services on dislocated workers, and because such UI beneficiaries are not required to actively seek reemployment on their own. The second step identifies those among the remaining group who are most likely to exhaust UI benefits. Almost all states perform the second profiling step using a statistical model that predicts the probability of benefit exhaustion.

The factors used to help predict exhaustion in state WPRS models usually include education, job tenure, change in employment in the prior industry and occupation, and the local unemployment rate. Federal civil rights law prohibits UI benefit eligibility screens based on age, race, or gender, so these factors are excluded. When workers open a new claim for UI benefits, their personal and labor market characteristics are used in a profiling equation to predict their individual probability of UI benefit exhaustion. State WPRS systems then quickly refer UI claimants with a high probability of exhausting benefits to special reemployment assistance (Wandner 1997).

As seen in Table 6.4, the profiling models in Pennsylvania and Washington also include variables summarizing beneficiary UI entitlement. The profiling models in these two states have similar elements, but the Washington model includes more variables in the education and industry categories.[8] Furthermore, because of the great differences in Washington labor markets, three different models are used in that state. Our simulation analysis was based only on the model for the Puget

Table 6.4 Variables in the Pennsylvania and Washington WPRS Profiling Models[a]

Variable	Number of categories in Pennsylvania	Number of categories in Washington
Education	2	5
Job tenure	1	1
Industry	2	17
Local economic conditions	1	1
UI entitlement	2	2

[a] Variables for age, race, and gender are prohibited by federal civil rights law.

Sound area, which is home to more than half of the state's profiled UI claimants.

TARGETING THE BONUS OFFER

Bonus targeting simulations were performed using both the parameters in the actual Pennsylvania and Washington models set in 1994 and new models for each state estimated on the control group data from the experiments.[9] The newly estimated models used similar methods and prediction factors as the original state models.[10] Results from the two sets of models were broadly consistent. In this chapter, we present only results from the new models estimated on data gathered during the experiments in Pennsylvania and Washington.

Predicted exhaustion probabilities were computed for UI claimants in both the treatment and the control groups. Cases were then sorted from the highest to lowest exhaustion probability. The net impacts of the bonus offer were then computed for different groups defined by deciles of the distribution of predicted exhaustion probabilities. Alternative possible target groups were formed by gradually lowering the exhaustion probability threshold. Impact estimates were computed by contrasting benefit receipt by treatment group members with control group members in the same deciles of *ex ante* predicted probability of

UI benefit exhaustion.   Estimates for both the incremental decile groups and the cumulative samples were examined.

The estimates provided in Table 6.5 do not provide clear guidance about which probability threshold generates the largest impacts.   Impacts are relatively large when the offer is made to either the top 20 or 50 percent of the exhaustion probability distribution.   For the Pennsyl-

Table 6.5 Impacts of Combined Treatments on UI Benefit Dollars Paid per Claimant by Predicted Probability of UI Benefit Exhaustion

Exhaustion probability group	Pennsylvania		Washington	
	Cumulative percentage group	Decile group	Cumulative percentage group	Decile group
Top 10% of predicted	−245	−245	−106	−106
exhaustion probabilities	(216)	(216)	(165)	(165)
Top 20%, 9th decile	−244	−235	−176	−264*
	(153)	(219)	(113)	(154)
Top 30%, 8th decile	−175	−34	−95	92
	(124)	(206)	(91)	(148)
Top 40%, 7th decile	−199*	−246	−91	−29
	(108)	(219)	(78)	(141)
Top 50%, 6th decile	−161*	−16	−117*	−213
	(95)	(193)	(69)	(129)
Top 60%, 5th decile	−174**	−260	−112*	−51
	(85)	(192)	(62)	(120)
Top 70%, 4th decile	−119	193	−57	107
	(78)	(185)	(56)	(113)
Top 80%, 3rd decile	−100	12	−35	32
	(72)	(188)	(51)	(108)
Top 90%, 2nd decile	−105	−165	−32	45
	(67)	(183)	(47)	(94)
Total, 1st decile	−115*	−196	−30	48
	(63)	(187)	(44)	(73)
Sample size	5,201	5,201	12,144	12,144

NOTE: Standard errors are in parentheses.   ** = Statistically significant at the 95 percent confidence level in a two-tailed test; * = statistically significant at the 90 percent confidence level in a two-tailed test.

vania experiment, the 10th, 9th, 7th, and 5th deciles have the largest estimated impacts. For the Washington experiment, the 9th and 6th deciles have the greatest estimated impacts. In the Washington experiment the lower five deciles all have smaller impacts, while for Pennsylvania the lowest two deciles have substantial effects. All of this suggests that narrowly targeting a bonus offer to those most likely to exhaust, may not be the best strategy to maximize the overall response. Based on these findings, we choose to examine the effects of bonus offers made to the top quarter and the top half of the exhaustion probability distribution.

NET IMPACTS OF TARGETED BONUS OFFERS

Net impact estimates of all Pennsylvania and Washington treatments on dollars of UI payments in the benefit year are reported in Table 6.6 for the full sample, the top 50 percent most likely to exhaust UI benefits, and the top 25 percent most likely to exhaust. The results suggest that targeting a reemployment bonus to claimants with high exhaustion probabilities can yield larger reductions in UI receipt than a nontargeted bonus. However, the use of a higher probability threshold for targeting does not necessarily translate into larger UI reductions.

Among the 11 individual treatments in the two states, there is not a consistent pattern of higher treatment impacts for samples above the percentile cutoffs. Targeting to either the top 25 percent or top 50 percent of the distribution yields higher impacts in 9 of the 11 treatments compared to a nontargeted bonus offer. The common factor among the treatments with higher impacts above the thresholds is that in most cases they involve a long qualification period.

For the mean bonus offer in both experiments, impacts are larger and statistically significant when the offer is made to the top 50 percent of the exhaustion probability distribution. Targeting to the top half of the distribution raises the impact on UI benefit payments in the Pennsylvania experiment from –$115 to –$161, and in the Washington experiment from –$30 to –$117.

Our findings suggest that targeting a reemployment bonus to claimants with high predicted exhaustion probabilities can yield larger

**Table 6.6 Summary of Net Impacts on Benefit Year UI Payments
($ per claimant)**

Bonus amt.	Qualif. period	Top 25%	Top 50%	Full sample
Pennsylvania bonus offers[a]				
Low	Short	156	72	−33
		(244)	(173)	(112)
Low	Long	−169	−188	−116
		(199)	(135)	(91)
High	Short	−110	22	−72
		(213)	(147)	(99)
High	Long	−236	−264**	−159*
		(180)	(125)	(83)
Declining	Long	−252	−301**	−147
		(209)	(146)	(100)
Mean	Mean	−152	−161*	−115*
		(136)	(95)	(63)
Washington bonus offers[b]				
Low	Short	−77	−47	32
		(145)	(95)	(61)
Low	Long	−139	−187**	−74
		(136)	(93)	(59)
Medium	Short	−143	−121	11
		(138)	(93)	(60)
Medium	Long	12	−33	1
		(136)	(93)	(59)
High	Short	−135	−126	−87
		(157)	(108)	(67)
High	Long	−279*	−228**	−104
		(158)	(108)	(68)
Mean	Mean	−117	−117*	−30
		(100)	(69)	(44)

NOTE: Standard deviations are in parentheses. ** = Statistically significant at the 95 percent level of confidence in a two-tailed test; * = statistically significant at the 90 percent level of confidence in a two-tailed test.

[a] Pennsylvania bonus amount: low = 3 × WBA; high = 6 × WBA; declining = half the remaining UI entitlement with the initial offer good for two weeks and then declining by 10 percent per week. Pennsylvania qualification period: short = 6 weeks, long = 12 weeks.

[b] Washington bonus amount: low = 2 × WBA; medium = 4 × WBA; high = 6 × WBA. Washington qualification period: short = 0.2 × (potential UI duration) + 1 week; long = 0.4 × (potential UI duration) + 1 week.

reductions in UI receipt than a nontargeted bonus. However, targeting does not guarantee larger reductions in benefit payments. Furthermore, the use of a higher probability threshold for targeting does not necessarily translate into larger UI reductions. In our estimates, the lower threshold (top 50 percent) usually yields larger impacts for the targeted group than the higher threshold (top 25 percent). We also found that the improved response associated with targeting follows more consistently for bonus offers with a long rather than short qualification period.

NET BENEFITS

Net benefits are considered here from three distinct perspectives: the UI system, government, and all of society. The most narrow view of net benefits considered is that of the UI system itself. It is reasonable to assume that in an actual bonus program, bonuses would be paid from the UI trust fund. Costs to the UI system are bonus payments and administrative costs, while benefits are the savings in UI payments to claimants plus any increased UI tax revenue resulting from increased earnings.

A somewhat broader perspective for assessing net benefits is the government taken as a whole. Government represents the collection of all public agencies that levy taxes and dispense public services. Benefits to government from a bonus program include the reduction in UI compensation paid, and additional taxes generated as a result of increased earnings. The latter include income taxes, payroll taxes, and taxes on employee earnings paid by employers. Costs to the government include the cost of administering the bonus offer program and bonus payments.

The ultimate acceptability of a program depends on whether it generates positive net benefits to society as a whole. Society gains from a program if the aggregate value of output increases. For a bonus program, gains to society may be approximated by the increase in compensation paid to claimants who respond to the bonus offer by obtaining jobs more quickly. Societal costs are simply the costs of administering the program.[11]

Previous examinations of net benefits for reemployment bonus offers found results to be increasingly favorable as the perspective was gradually broadened from the UI system itself, to the government, and finally to society as a whole. The bonus offers have generally not been found to be cost-effective from the narrow perspective of the UI system. At best, a nontargeted bonus appears to be a break-even proposition for society as a whole (O'Leary, Spiegelman, and Kline 1995, pp. 264–267).

The estimates of administrative costs used in our net benefit computations probably bound the range of costs that would be experienced in an actual program. The cost per offer in Pennsylvania was estimated at $33, while the cost in Washington was put at $3. The Pennsylvania estimate reflects the administrative cost of running the experiment, while the Washington estimate was provided by the state employment security agency as the likely cost per offer under an ongoing program. Certain costs associated with running an experiment would not be incurred in an operational program, and this largely explains the difference in the two estimates. It is likely that the average administrative cost of an ongoing program would lie between these extremes.

Based on the predicted probability of UI benefit exhaustion, Table 6.7 presents estimates from each of the three evaluation perspectives of net benefits for bonus offers made to the top 25 percent, the top 50 percent, and all of those for whom the model was estimated. That is, union hiring hall members and temporary layoffs awaiting job recall were excluded when making computations.[12] Restricted sample sizes mean that few of the parameters in Table 6.7 were estimated with statistical precision; nonetheless, we proceed to discuss the observed patterns of response to targeted bonus offers.

From the narrow perspective of the UI system, net benefit computations for the Pennsylvania experiment suggest that targeting the bonus offers increases net benefits for all three long qualification period treatments, but diminishes net benefits for treatments with a short qualification period. The improved net benefits for the long qualification bonus offers were large enough to result in the overall mean response to targeted bonus offers having positive point estimates for the Pennsylvania experiment. These results are driven mainly by the reduction in UI benefit payments due to targeting, since the added bonus payment costs from targeting were estimated to be modest in the Pennsylvania sample.

For all government and society, targeting offers in the Pennsylvania experiment improved net benefits for all treatments except the high bonus/long qualification period offer. The result for this treatment was due to lower earnings observed for the targeted group. In Pennsylvania the high bonus/long qualification offer is the only treatment which suggested that a bonus offer might induce reemployment in jobs inferior to the prior one.[13] In contrast, the low bonus/long qualification offer did not have unfavorable impacts on earnings and resulted in very favorable net benefit estimates.

Evidence from the Washington experiment also suggests that targeting to those most likely to exhaust UI benefits can improve the cost-effectiveness of bonus offers. However, the results for Washington are not as pronounced as in the Pennsylvania data. The higher bonus payment costs in the Washington experiment are the reason that treatments with the higher bonus amounts fail to have positive net benefits for either target group.

The most favorable treatment design and targeting plan to emerge from our analysis combines a low bonus amount with a long qualification period, targeted to the 50 percent most likely to exhaust UI benefits: for example, a bonus amount set at three times the weekly benefit amount, a qualification period 12 weeks long, and targeted to the half of claimants most likely to exhaust their UI benefit entitlement. Our estimates suggest that such a bonus offer would promote quicker return to work and save the UI trust funds between $50 and $100 per offer. The net benefits to all government and to society should be significantly greater.

CAVEATS

Targeting with profiling models improves the appeal of the reemployment bonus program for employment policy. However, two potential behavioral effects might reduce cost-effectiveness for an operational program.[14] First, an actual bonus program could have a *displacement effect*. Displacement occurs if UI claimants who are offered a bonus increase their rate of reemployment at the expense of other job seekers not offered a bonus. Second, there is also the risk that an

Table 6.7 Net Benefits of the Bonus Offers above Alternative Percentile Cutoffs of Predicted UI Exhaustion Probabilities ($ per claimant)

Offer		UI system[a]			All government[b]			Society[c]		
Bonus amount	Qualification period	Top 25%	Top 50%	Full sample	Top 25%	Top 50%	Full sample	Top 25%	Top 50%	Full sample
Pennsylvania treatments										
Low	Short	−223	−87	−40	325	65	−48	1,638	432	−57
		(245)	(173)	(113)	(1,022)	(765)	(502)	(992)	(745)	(489)
Low	Long	66	93	28	300	363	147	679	790	331
		(200)	(135)	(91)	(830)	(599)	(401)	(806)	(584)	(391)
High	Short	−37	−148	−54	231	56	0	557	588	133
		(215)	(148)	(100)	(897)	(635)	(421)	(871)	(617)	(409)
High	Long	43	69	−23	−78	80	51	−402	1	191
		(182)	(126)	(84)	(755)	(525)	(355)	(733)	(510)	(345)
Declining	Long	134	186	31	421	603	304	841	1,239**	797
		(211)	(147)	(101)	(890)	(636)	(442)	(865)	(619)	(430)
Mean		19	30	−10	192	227	95	494	567	286
		(137)	(95)	(64)	(584)	(428)	(282)	(568)	(417)	(275)
Washington treatments										
Low	Short	19	−11	−81	91	−183	−434	239	−578	−1,181
		(145)	(95)	(61)	(2,110)	(1,143)	(724)	(2,105)	(1,139)	(721)
Low	Long	59	112	20	241	172	56	602	195	116
		(136)	(93)	(59)	(2,616)	(1,434)	(899)	(2,612)	(1,431)	(897)
Medium	Short	−6	−1	−113*	−533	−177	−471	−1,757	−590	−1,195*
		(138)	(94)	(60)	(1,801)	(1,156)	(720)	(1,796)	(1,152)	(717)

Medium	Long	-221	-151	-143**	-680	-403	-524	-1534	-845	-1,273*
		(137)	(93)	(60)	(1,817)	(1,038)	(659)	(1,812)	(1,034)	(656)
High	Short	-111	-105	-87	-512	-317	-350	-1,339	-708	-879
		(160)	(109)	(68)	(2,221)	(1,265)	(845)	(2,215)	(1,260)	(842)
High	Long	-112	-84	-131*	518	150	-13	2,096	778	387
		(161)	(110)	(69)	(3088)	(1686)	(1027)	(3,084)	(1,682)	(1,025)
	Mean	-56	-32	-86*	-169	-132	-303	-379	-336	-725
		(101)	(69)	(44)	(1,519)	(852)	(528)	(1,516)	(849)	(526)

NOTE: Standard errors are in parentheses. ** = Statistically significant at the 95 percent confidence level in a two-tailed test; * = statistically significant at the 90 percent confidence level in a two-tailed test.

[a] For the UI system, net benefits are UI benefit savings plus UI tax revenues on additional earnings minus the costs of bonus payments and program administration. The current average UI tax rates on earnings are 1.00 percent in Pennsylvania and 1.15 percent in Washington.

[b] For government, net benefits are UI benefit savings plus all added tax revenues due to added earnings (UI taxes, Federal Income Contribution Act tax of 15.02 percent, federal income taxes assumed to be 15 percent, and state income taxes which are 2.80 percent in Pennsylvania and zero in Washington) minus the costs of bonus payments and program administration.

[c] For society as a whole, net benefits are simply additional earnings minus administrative costs since taxes and transfer payments cancel from a societal perspective.

operational bonus offer program could induce an *entry effect*; that is, the availability of a reemployment bonus might result in a larger proportion of unemployed job seekers filing for UI, or entering the UI system.

If entry and displacement effects are sizeable, actual program cost-effectiveness will be lowered. However, targeting offers to only those most likely to exhaust UI should reduce both these risks. Targeting would introduce uncertainty that a bonus offer would be forthcoming upon filing a UI claim, which should reduce the chance of a large entry effect. Targeting should also lower any potential for displacement, since a smaller proportion of claimants would receive the bonus offer.[15]

CONCLUSION

Earlier research has indicated that a nontargeted reemployment bonus program is not good public policy since it would not reliably conserve UI trust fund reserves. In this chapter, profiling models similar to those in state WPRS systems are used to reexamine evidence from the Pennsylvania and Washington reemployment bonus experiments.

Targeting offers with WPRS models to UI claimants identified as most likely to exhaust benefits is estimated to increase cost-effectiveness of the reemployment bonus. The best candidate to emerge for a targeted reemployment bonus is a low bonus amount, with a long qualification period, targeted to the half of profiled claimants most likely to exhaust their UI benefit entitlement.

A reemployment bonus targeted with WPRS models is an appealing policy option for a cost-effective early intervention to promote reemployment. It would be administratively simple to implement, it is likely to be cost neutral to the UI program, and it may yield significant positive net benefits to individuals and society. Similar to other reemployment initiatives examined in this volume, targeting services with statistical models based on participant characteristics appears to be a practical and cost-effective strategy.

Notes

For constructive comments that helped to improve this paper, we thank Jennifer War-lick, Jeff Smith, and participants at the Targeting Employment Services Conference, Kalamazoo, Michigan, April 30–May 1, 1999. Kenneth Kline provided excellent re-search assistance. We thank Nancy Mack and Claire Black for clerical assistance. Opinions expressed are our own and do not necessarily represent those of the W.E. Up-john Institute for Employment Research, Mathematica Policy Research, or the U.S. De-partment of Labor. We accept responsibility for any errors.

1. In this chapter, a *dislocated worker* is someone with significant prior job attach-ment who has lost his job and has little prospect of returning to it or to another job in a similar occupation and industry. This is consistent with the program eligibil-ity definition in the Economic Dislocation and Worker Adjustment Assistance Act (EDWAA) of 1988, which amended Title III of the Job Training Partnership Act (JTPA) of 1982, and provides funds to states and local substate grantees so they can help dislocated workers find and qualify for new jobs. The EDWAA defini-tion includes workers who lose their jobs because of plant closures or mass lay-offs; long-term unemployed persons with limited job opportunities in their fields; and farmers, ranchers, and other self-employed persons who become unemployed due to general economic conditions. Leigh (1995) summarized the EDWAA.

2. Local public employment offices served as enrollment sites in each of the experi-ments. They were selected to achieve samples which were representative of UI claimants in the state as a whole. Sampling of claimants within each local office was done by random assignment. Sample sizes were set large enough to achieve the precision needed for estimating individual and subgroup treatment impacts of policy interest.

3. O'Leary, Decker, and Wandner (2001) reported that earnings outcomes were more favorable for the targeted groups, but there was no significant impact. How-ever, groups in the bottom 75 and 50 percent of the exhaustion probability distri-bution in the Washington experiment had statistically significant reductions in earnings. That is, the strongest observed tendency of the bonus to induce reem-ployment in inferior jobs was exhibited by those below the targeting thresholds. Targeting would minimize any tendency in this direction.

4. The *waiting week* is a period of noncompensable unemployment which must pre-cede UI payments in a new benefit year.

5. Spiegelman, O'Leary, and Kline (1992, p. 8) explained the eligibility arrange-ment for people in the Washington experiment who started a new UI benefit year but never claimed a waiting week or benefit.

6. Bonus impacts for UI claimants with three or more years of tenure in the Wash-ington experiment were somewhat larger, but they were not statistically signifi-cantly greater than impacts for the complementary group (Spiegelman, O'Leary, and Kline 1992, pp. 116–119).

7. Interpretation of this result is tentative because of the econometric problem that estimation involves sample selection based on an endogenous variable (Spiegelman, O'Leary, and Kline 1992, p. 110). However, the finding appears to be validated by results under *ex ante* eligibility screens applied in the other experiments.
8. Examples of WPRS profiling models from a number of states are given in Balducchi (1996). Most states with statistical models have chosen to predict UI exhaustion using a logistic regression specification.
9. Both Pennsylvania and Washington use logistic regression models to predict UI benefit exhaustion, since the variable that we are trying to predict is whether individuals exhaust their UI benefits or do not.
10. Details about the original state profiling models, the newly estimated models, and all simulation results are given in O'Leary, Decker, and Wandner (1998).
11. Details of the component estimates for the net benefit computations are provided in O'Leary, Decker, and Wandner (2001).
12. This is the first screen in the WPRS profiling system. Union hiring hall members and those awaiting recall had to be excluded from the Washington sample for computations. As seen in Table 6.2, such beneficiaries were not in the Pennsylvania data at all since they were not given bonus offers.
13. This earnings result for the high bonus offer in Pennsylvania is consistent with the interpretation by Nicholson (2001) of the reemployment bonus as a wage subsidy.
14. As suggested by Meyer (1995).
15. Davidson and Woodbury (1993) found that without targeting displacement could be in the range of 30 to 60 percent, even though bonus offers induce quicker job matches which generates more income growth and new job vacancies. Targeting could significantly reduce this risk.

References

Balducchi, David. 1996. *Worker Profiling and Reemployment Services (WPRS) Systems: National Colloquium, Selected Papers and Materials.* Washington, D.C.: Employment and Training Administration, U.S. Department of Labor.

Corson, Walter, and Paul Decker. 1996. "Using the Unemployment Insurance System to Target Services to Dislocated Workers." In *Background Papers, Volume III.* Washington, D.C.: Advisory Council on Unemployment Compensation, U.S. Department of Labor.

Corson, Walter, and Joshua Haimson. 1995. *The New Jersey Unemployment Insurance Reemployment Demonstration Project: Six-Year Follow-up and Summary Report.* Unemployment Insurance Occasional Paper no. 95-2, Washington, D.C.: Employment and Training Administration, U.S. Department of Labor.

Corson, Walter, Paul T. Decker, Shari Miller Dunstan, and Anne R. Gordon. 1989. *The New Jersey Unemployment Insurance Reemployment Demonstration Project: Final Evaluation Report*. Unemployment Insurance Occasional Paper no. 89-3, Washington, D.C.: Employment and Training Administration, U.S. Department of Labor.

Davidson, Carl, and Stephen A. Woodbury. 1991. "Effects of a Reemployment Bonus under Differing Benefit Entitlements, or Why the Illinois Experiment Worked." Unpublished manuscript, Michigan State University and W.E. Upjohn Institute for Employment Research.

———. 1993. "The Displacement Effect of Reemployment Bonus Programs." *Journal of Labor Economics* 11(4): 575–605.

Decker, Paul T. 1994. "The Impact of Reemployment Bonuses on Insured Unemployment in the New Jersey and Illinois Reemployment Bonus Experiments." *Journal of Human Resources* 29(3): 718–741.

Decker, Paul T., and Christopher J. O'Leary. 1995. "Evaluating Pooled Evidence from the Reemployment Bonus Experiments." *Journal of Human Resources* 30(3): 534–550.

Leigh, Duane. 1995. *Assisting Workers Displaced by Structural Change: An International Perspective*. Kalamazoo, Michigan: W.E. Upjohn Institute for Employment Research.

Meyer, Bruce D. 1995. "Lessons from the U.S. Unemployment Insurance Experiments." *Journal of Economic Literature* 33(1): 91–131.

Nicholson, Walter. 2001. "The Reemployment Bonus Experiments: A Suggested Interpretation." Paper presented at the American Economic Association meetings, January 6, 2001, New Orleans, Louisiana.

O'Leary, Christopher J., Paul T. Decker, and Stephen A. Wandner. 1998. *Reemployment Bonuses and Profiling*. Staff working paper no. 98-51, Kalamazoo, Michigan: W.E. Upjohn Institute for Employment Research.

———. 2001. "Reemployment Bonuses and Profiling." Paper (revised) presented at the American Economic Association meetings, January 6, 2001, New Orleans, Louisiana.

O'Leary, Christopher J., Robert G. Spiegelman, and Kenneth J. Kline. 1995. "Do Bonus Offers Shorten Unemployment Insurance Spells? Results from the Washington Experiment." *Journal of Policy Analysis and Management* 14(2): 245–269.

Spiegelman, Robert G., Christopher J. O'Leary, and Kenneth J. Kline. 1992. *The Washington Reemployment Bonus Experiment: Final Report*. Unemployment Insurance Occasional Paper no. 92-6, Washington, D.C.: Employment and Training Administration, U.S. Department of Labor.

Wandner, Stephen A. 1997. "Early Reemployment for Dislocated Workers in the United States." *International Social Security Review* 50(4): 95–112.

Woodbury, Stephen A., and Robert G. Spiegelman. 1987. "Bonuses to Workers and Employers to Reduce Unemployment: Randomized Trials in Illinois." *American Economic Review* 77(4): 513–530.

Comments on Chapter 6

Jennifer Warlick
University of Notre Dame

This chapter considers the desirability of using profiling to target reemployment bonuses to those displaced workers expected to have the most difficulty finding new employment and hence the longest spells of unemployment. It reports on simulations conducted by the authors that utilize parameters estimated in experiments conducted in Washington and Pennsylvania. Their analysis is very interesting and first rate. Moreover, the chapter is clearly and concisely written. By limiting the description of the technical aspects of the microsimulations, the authors focus the reader's attention on the policy issues at hand: can targeting with profiling enhance the power of reemployment bonuses? If so, how is the target group best defined? Which combination of sample selection and bonus eligibility criteria maximizes the impact of reemployment bonuses?

My primary impression is that this chapter is too short. Indeed, my comments focus more on what the authors do not say than on what they do say. The chapter left me wanting to know more; not more about the experiments or the simulations themselves—I trust that there is little improvement that could be made in the technical area. Rather, I want to know more about the unemployed workers who were treated by the experiments and whether the bonuses were in their best interest. I want to know more about the motivations of the unemployed, how they approach the search for a new job, and what goes through their minds as they decide whether to accept jobs that might be offered to them. Do they weigh short-run gains against long-run payoffs? Does the prospect of a reemployment bonus in a time when every penny counts prompt them to choose a different job than they would have in its absence? When a bonus is available, do they accept the first offer they receive rather than continue the search for a job that might better match their skills and could lead to greater long-run payoffs? And if this is the case, does the policy of reemployment bonuses promote the best interests of the unemployed? Can the outcomes be labeled "reemployment successes," to borrow a term from the chapter, or is it in the best interest of the UI program that the bonuses seek to promote?

The analysis of the net benefits of the reemployment bonuses focuses on entities other than the unemployed individual. For example, in the section entitled "Net Benefits," the authors state:

> Previous examinations of net benefits for reemployment bonus offers found more favorable results as the perspective broadened from the UI system, to all government, to society as a whole. The net benefits to the UI system of a reemployment bonus offer are the reduction in UI benefit payments, minus the cost of bonus payments, minus any additional costs that result from administering a reemployment bonus.

If the best interests of the individual were the primary focus, I suspect that the net benefits would be the difference in the discounted flow of future earnings between the treatment and control groups. This measure would take into account both differences in wage and salary levels and the expected tenure on the jobs. Yes, I worry that the bonuses could affect not only the type of job accepted but also the length of employment on that job.

It may be that it isn't possible to calculate this measure with the data from the Washington and Pennsylvania experiments. From the description in the chapter I could not tell whether and how long the experiments followed the unemployed after they returned to work. If these are not available, it is understandable that the potential effects of bonuses on earnings and job duration are not investigated empirically here.

It has also occurred to me that the effects of the bonuses on worker well-being lie beyond the scope of this chapter but are addressed in other chapters of this volume. My comments may reflect the fact that I read only one-tenth of the total manuscript. If I had read the whole manuscript, would my questions be answered?

Similarly, would I have bothered to raise these questions if I were more familiar with this literature? Experts in this area may be able to tell me that other studies not included in this volume have examined my questions and demonstrated that bonuses do not affect job search, job choice, or job tenure. Does the fact that bonuses are targeted at the unemployed workers most likely to exhaust benefits suggest a different sort of mental calculus? How do these workers see their choices? Is the decision rule I suggested above—that of weighing the short-run gains of accepting a "bird in the hand" plus bonus versus the long-run payoffs of continued search for a better placement—inappropriate for them? Or might you tell me that the rules of UI programs eliminate this issue by requiring that UI beneficiaries accept the first job offer they receive. I hope not, because that too would seem a shortsighted policy.

If the issues I have raised are not answered elsewhere in this volume or are not common knowledge among the audience targeted as readers of this book, then I urge the authors to acknowledge this line of questioning. Perhaps this could be done in the Caveats section, or maybe at an earlier point in the chapter in a discussion of the meaning of "reemployment success." Only then could I agree with their conclusion that "a reemployment bonus targeted with WPRS models is an appealing policy option for a cost-effective early intervention to promote reemployment. It . . . may yield significant positive net benefits to individuals and society."

In the absence of such a discussion, I am left with a lingering impression that the reemployment bonuses share with welfare reform an emphasis on reducing expenditures even if it means sacrificing the well-being of the targeted group. My understanding of the UI system is that it was designed to give unemployed workers an opportunity to search not only for a job, but also for a job that was right for them. In contrast, a system of bonuses that encourages UI beneficiaries to rush through the search process seems to have cost savings as its goal. If this emphasis on cost saving is not the message that the authors want to send, I think it would be prudent for them to give equal time to the best interests of the unemployed.

7

Measures of Program Performance and the Training Choices of Displaced Workers

Louis Jacobson
Westat

Robert LaLonde
The University of Chicago

Daniel Sullivan
The Federal Reserve Bank of Chicago

Passage of the Workforce Investment Act (WIA) has focused policymakers' attention on measuring the performance of employment and training programs. Explicit performance measures can provide timely information to policymakers and program operators for assessing and improving their policies and programs.

Under WIA's predecessor, the Job Training Partnership Act (JTPA), policymakers relied on two approaches for obtaining this information. First, they used formal program evaluations, including the National JTPA Study. These evaluations estimated the "value added" or the return on investment (ROI) of these programs and their net benefit to participants, taxpayers, and governments.

Second, policymakers implemented a system of performance standards. Under this system, they assess the performance of their programs by whether measures of participants' output, such as their entered employment rate, employment retention rates, or postprogram wage levels, exceed pre-designated targets or standards (Barnow 1992). Policymakers intend that these performance standards would substitute for more costly and less timely formal ROI evaluations. Although the relative merits of these approaches for measuring program performance has been hotly contested, one purpose that both share is that they provide policymakers and program operators with an objective basis for assessing and improving their programs.

It is our contention in this chapter that timely and accurate value-added performance measures not only help policymakers improve the effectiveness of their programs, but these measures also can help improve programs by providing likely participants with better information. This information should affect their participation decisions and lead to more efficient use of both their own and government's training resources. To understand this point, consider that participation in many employment and training programs often involves (at least) a two-stage decision process in which individuals decide whether to apply for programs, and program operators decide whether to admit them to the program. Individuals' decisions to apply for or enroll in a program depend on the net benefits that they expect to receive from them. Therefore, program performance measures should improve individual decision-making and improve program performance by ensuring that those who apply to the program in the first place are those most likely to benefit from it.

In this chapter, we show how information about the training decisions made by unemployed adults and the impact of the programs in which they enrolled can improve program performance by potentially improving individual decision making. We base our analysis on the experiences of dislocated workers in Washington State, some of whom enrolled in community college courses around the time of their job losses.

In the remainder of the chapter, we describe the factors that individuals should take into account when deciding whether to participate in training. Here we observe that the cost of retraining displaced workers is likely larger than the cost for other training participants, such as youths and economically disadvantaged persons. Therefore, this population likely requires that training generate larger impacts in order for it to be worthwhile. We next examine how individuals' characteristics relate to their propensity to enroll and complete such courses. We assume that improving labor market prospects is the dominant factor influencing dislocated workers' decisions to enroll in community college courses. Accordingly, information about the characteristics of individuals who enroll in these courses provides information about the types of individuals who are most likely to benefit from retraining. We then present estimates of the impact of alternative community college curricula on earnings based on a formal evaluation of the returns to classroom training. We believe that this information is helpful not only to policymakers who subsidized community college schooling, but also to displaced workers. Finally, we discuss how to use this information to improve program performance by improving individuals' decision-making.

DECIDING WHETHER TO PARTICIPATE IN TRAINING

We base our analysis of the training or schooling decisions of displaced workers on the simplifying assumption that dislocated workers view attending school as a way to improve their labor market prospects. Accordingly, we can judge the success of public investments in these workers' training or schooling on whether this goal is met. This section discusses two frameworks presented in the academic literature for characterizing the decision to invest in training following the loss of a job (Heckman, LaLonde, and Smith 1999).

A broader view of school attendance would include the possibility that dislocated workers attend school for their own immediate enjoyment or to create job opportunities that are more enjoyable, even if not higher paying. Because most displaced workers can attend school and not search for work without jeopardizing their unemployment insurance (UI) benefits, it is possible that substantial numbers decide to take a break from work to pursue personal interests. This motivation for attending school can be productive from a social point of view, because it lowers the cost of job loss, and thereby the cost born by firms and society from making production more efficient. The importance of investment versus consumption motives might be assessed by surveying dislocated workers about their motivation for seeking retraining. We know of no such survey data with which we could examine this contention. Accordingly, in this chapter we focus solely on the implications of economic motives for seeking training.

Training Augments Human Capital

In the more familiar "human capital" framework, individuals view training as an investment. Accordingly, individuals decide to participate in training when the benefits they expect to receive exceed the costs of training. Further, when choosing among alternative courses of study, individuals will choose the one with the greatest net benefit.

In most settings, analysts measure the benefit of training as the difference between participants' postprogram earnings and the earnings they would have received had they not participated in training. This earnings impact could result from either increased wage rates or increased hours worked. Therefore, in order for displaced workers to make productive decisions about whether to participate in training and what to study, they should know what the likely impact of training is and whether this impact varies among programs or alternative courses of study.

The impact of classroom training reported in studies of economically disadvantaged persons or the returns to community college schooling reported for young adults may provide a misleading basis for displaced workers' training decisions. First, displaced workers are older than the other training participants, and the impact of retraining may differ by age. Second, they are also better educated and already possess more vocational skills on which to build. Finally, if the impact of retraining varies among individuals in a population, then the average impact for a group whose cost of participation is low is likely to be lower than for a population whose cost of participation is high. In the latter case, the only persons who participate in training are those who expect the benefits of retraining to outweigh the more substantial costs. If displaced workers based their training decisions on the average annual impact measured for young community college students or economically disadvantaged trainees, they may understate the likely benefits of training. Individuals who have had difficulty finding and keeping any job may participate in a training program that they expect to yield relatively small impacts, whereas a corresponding displaced worker would not. As a consequence, the impact of training as measured by the average of the individual benefits for all young participants is likely to be lower than for a sample of displaced workers. A related point is that evidence showing that displaced workers receive larger benefits from training than younger individuals does not imply that training is more effective for displaced workers.

Another determinant of displaced workers' decisions to participate in retraining is the cost of these programs. There are three components of the cost of training. First, there are the direct costs, which include tuition, fees, supplies, transportation, and care for children and elderly relatives. Next, there are the personal costs, which include the emotional impact of returning to a classroom setting and the toll that time spent in training might take on a person's family. These costs might be negative for some participants if they consider schooling a form of consumption or entertainment. In any case, these emotional costs are difficult to quantify. As a result, although they are acknowledged, analysts usually do not explicitly take them into account. Finally, the largest cost of retraining can be the lost earnings that displaced workers experience if they delay their return to work in order to invest in new skills. If displaced workers decide to return to school to acquire new skills, they are likely to search for new jobs less intensely. As a result, while they are in school they lose earnings that they would have received had they found a new job. These lost, or forgone, earnings constitute a cost of training. Further, displaced workers who return to school also may forgo, at least for the time being, both the formal and informal on-the-job training that they would have received at a new job. Under these circumstances, the labor market experience that they lose while in school also is a cost of training.

Compared with other individuals whom policymakers encourage to receive training, the foregone earnings costs of training are likely to be especially high for displaced workers. Forgone earnings are likely lower for economically disadvantaged workers and for teenagers and young adults, whose likelihood of being employed and earnings power are lower. The upshot is that in order to justify their higher costs of training, displaced workers must experience larger impacts (in terms of dollars gained) from retraining programs than other training participants.

Training Facilitates Job Search

A second way to characterize the training decisions of displaced workers is based on the idea that access to training may facilitate job search. In this setting, unemployed persons seek to enroll in training because they believe that this opportunity increases their chances of receiving an acceptable job offer. What distinguishes this framework is that training may facilitate productive networking by the unemployed. The increased contacts that they experience at a training center or community college may increase the likelihood that they receive an offer of a new job. In this case, training does not increase skills but would increase employment rates and possibly wages if this networking led to better job matches between displaced workers and employers.

According to the job search characterization of training, evidence that displaced workers have high early dropout rates from training programs or community college courses would not necessarily indicate that these programs or courses were ineffective. Instead, this evidence may simply indicate that displaced workers use training opportunities to facilitate their job search and that they leave training once they are reemployed.

DETERMINANTS OF TRAINING PARTICIPATION

In order for displaced workers to make productive decisions about training participation, they need to know more than the likely impacts of training. According to the human capital framework outlined earlier in this chapter, individuals participate in training only if the benefits exceed the costs. Evidence on how different personal characteristics affect the propensity to participate in training provides information about what characteristics make individuals more likely to benefit from training.

The evidence that we present in this chapter on the determinants of displaced workers' decisions to participate in training comes from studying all persons displaced from UI-covered jobs in Washington State during the first half the 1990s. The evidence is largely based on the subsample of persons who filed a valid claim for unemployment insurance benefits following the loss of a job that they had held for at least six quarters, and who were consistently attached to the state's workforce during the period that we studied. Our sample is unusually large for this kind of study, containing over 121,000 persons.

The workforce attachment restriction reduced our sample by nearly one-half. One implication of this fact is that many displaced workers, including those who attend a community college around the time of their job loss, do not remain consistently attached to the state's UI-covered workforce. We find that such persons are more likely to be women and to be older. Neither of these groups are known for high rates of geographic mobility and are likely to still be residing in the state after their displacements. Therefore, if policymakers subsidize training for the purposes of raising worker productivity, a significant amount of community college schooling must generate extremely low returns because many participants do not work very often following training.

Nonetheless, our results on the propensity to participate in training are not sensitive to our restricting the sample to displaced workers who remain consistently attached to the state's workforce. In results reported elsewhere, we find that the influence of factors that are associated with community college participation among displaced workers who remain consistently attached to the state's workforce is the same as it is for displaced workers who are not consistently attached to the state's workforce following their job loss (Jacobson, LaLonde, and Sullivan 1999).

The training that we consider here are courses at 25 of Washington State's community colleges in which dislocated workers enrolled around the time of their displacements. About one-fifth of our sample, or approximately 25,000 persons, enrolled in at least one community college course around the time of their job loss. We define the period around the individual's job loss to encompass the three quarters leading up to the quarter that they separate from their employer and the 11 quarters following the quarter of their job loss. Our sample consists primarily of prime-age workers, so the participation behavior and impacts that we report here are for a population that is not often studied in this literature. The average age of our sample members is approximately 37, and their wage rate prior to the quarter of their job loss was about $18 per hour.

Washington's dislocated workers were not restricted in making choices about their selection of courses or which colleges to attend. In particular, there were no entrance restrictions based on education levels or prior success in school. However, schools did enforce the usual prerequisites for attendance in more advanced courses. There also were no requirements to enter a degree- or certificate-granting program, but only a very small fraction of workers in our sample appeared to pursue a new credential.

Dislocated workers were aided in attending school by low in-state tuition, as well as counseling programs, particularly those supported by unions and firms in the aerospace and timber industries. Some workers obtained financial support through JTPA, but very few qualified for substantial amounts of federal Pell Grants or Stafford Loans. Perhaps most important, starting in late 1992, Washington State routinely permitted UI recipients to attend school without having to satisfy any requirement to search for work. In addition, in 1994, the state began funding a special program that provided financial assistance to community colleges that expanded their enrollments of displaced workers and developed new, more relevant curricula.

We found that nearly one-half of Washington's displaced workers who enrolled in community college courses dropped out or otherwise did not complete a single course with a passing grade. As a result, only 11 percent of the state's displaced workers completed one or more community college courses around the time of their job loss. These students who completed at least one course acquired on average 28 community college credits. The state's community college system operates on a quarter system in which the typical course is worth five credits and an associate's degree requires 90 credits. Hence, even among this subset of trainees, the average number of credits obtained amounts to slightly more than one-half of a year of full-time schooling.

We also considered the types of courses completed by displaced workers. Of the 28 completed credits, approximately 12 were completed in courses teaching more technically oriented vocational skills or in academic math and science classes. These courses included those teaching skills in the health fields, such as a respiratory therapist or a dental hygienist, and in the construction trades.

In our analysis, we found that these types of courses generated larger earnings impacts. As a result, we refer to them as "high-return" classes. We arrived at this grouping of courses after we first considered the returns associated with courses in nine different subject areas. From this analysis it was apparent that the impacts of community college schooling were concentrated entirely in a subset of these subject areas. Within these particular subject areas, completing more courses was associated with increased earnings. We refer to all other courses as "low-return" classes. These courses included academic courses in the humanities and social sciences, as well as relatively nonquantitative vocational courses.

As shown in Table 7.1, the distribution of completed credits among displaced workers is skewed. Approximately one-half of those who complete at least 1 credit complete no more than 10 credits. This amounts to about two classes. The table also indicates that most displaced workers completed 10 or fewer credits in high-return classes. The main point is that very few displaced workers who enroll in com-

Table 7.1 Total Credits Completed by Washington State Displaced Workers

All community college credits

	Mean number (std. dev.)	Number of completed credits (% distribution)					
		1–5	6–10	11–20	21–40	41–75	76+
Males	28 (30)	0.27	0.15	0.16	0.17	0.15	0.10
Females	25 (28)	0.32	0.15	0.15	0.14	0.15	0.08

By type of community college credits

	Mean number (std. dev.)	Number of completed credits (% distribution)			
		0	1–5	6–20	21+
Group 1[a]					
Males	15 (23)	0.30	0.23	0.22	0.24
Females	9 (15)	0.42	0.25	0.20	0.13
Group 2[b]					
Males	13 (19)	0.31	0.22	0.27	0.20
Females	16 (21)	0.18	0.27	0.29	0.27

[a] Group 1 credits are from courses teaching more technical academic and vocational skills.
[b] Group 2 credits are from all other courses, including basic skills classes.
SOURCE: Authors' calculations from a sample of workers dislocated from UI covered jobs between 1990 and 1994. Each worker had filed a valid UI claim, accumulated at least six quarters of tenure with his or her former employer, and had remained consistently attached to the state's workforce during the period that we studied.

munity college courses complete enough classes to obtain even a certificate. If community college schooling is a productive investment, it must be because of the benefit stemming from completing only a few courses.

Determinants of Training Participation

As we discussed in the previous section, evidence that displaced workers who possess particular characteristics are more likely than others to receive training suggests that these types of persons are more likely to view the benefits of training as outweighing its costs. We begin by considering how different personal characteristics are associated with the rates that displaced workers enroll in and complete community college schooling. In our analysis, we hold constant differences among individuals' gender, whether they are non-Hispanic whites, their age at displacement, prior schooling levels, years of service with prior employer, prior industry, whether their prior employer was located in the Seattle metropolitan statistical area (MSA), the state's other MSAs, or the rural regions of the state, the year and calendar quarter of displacement, and earnings prior to displacement.

We summarize our analysis in Table 7.2. As shown in the first row of the table, women's enrollment rates are eight percentage points greater than observationally similar males. In other words, if we were to observe a sample of male and female displaced workers who were all non-Hispanic whites, the same age, the same number of years of prior schooling, the same tenure at displacement, who were displaced from the same industry, located in the same region of the state, and at the same time, we would predict that the enrollment rates of the women would be eight percentage points greater than those of their male counterparts. Given that the average enrollment rate for the entire sample is approximately 20 percent, this impact is substantial. In the second column of the table, we observe that women also are more likely than males to both enroll in and complete some community college schooling. The gap in training rates between the genders is four percentage points. Given that the average training rate for the entire sample is 11 percent, this impact also is substantial. These results indicate that dislocated females are more likely than males to view training as beneficial either as a vehicle to improve their skills or as a vehicle to facilitate their job search.

**Table 7.2 Impact of Demographic Characteristics on Enrollment and
Training Rates of Displaced Workers in Washington State
(percentage point difference)**

Characteristics	Enrollment rate[a]	Training rate[b]
Females vs. males	8	4
Non-Hispanic whites vs. minority	–2	1
Age at displacement (yr.)		
22–24 vs. 55–60	12	9
25–29 vs. 55–60	9	6
30–34 vs. 55–60	7	5
35–39 vs. 55–60	6	5
40–44 vs. 55–60	6	4
45–49 vs. 55–60	5	3
50–54 vs. 55–60	3	2
Prior education		
High school dropout vs. some college	–8	–8
High school graduate vs. some college	–6	–5
College graduate vs. some college	–4	–4
Tenure at displacement		
3–6 yr. vs. 1.5–3 yr.	1	1
6 or more yr. vs. 1.5–3 yr.	3	3

NOTE: Workers displaced during 1990 through 1994 from UI covered employment in Washington. Because of our sample is large, these results are generally statistically significant at conventional levels of statistical significance. For information on the standard errors associated with these estimates see Jacobson, LaLonde, and Sullivan (1999).

[a] The "enrollment rate" measures the percentage of persons who enrolled in a community college course during the period between three quarters prior to the quarter of their jobs loss until the 11th quarter after their job loss.
[b] The "training rate" measures the percentage of displaced workers who enrolled in and completed at least one community college credit around the time of their job losses.

The reason that women complete more training than men is that they are more likely to enroll in community college courses in the first place. However, once they enroll, they are not more likely than are their male counterparts to complete a course. Indeed, we find that among displaced workers who enroll in community college courses, women are, if anything, less likely to complete at least one course.

This finding suggests that the factors which determine and motivate displaced workers' enrollment decisions may differ from their decisions to complete training. In light of our previous discussion about the varied motivations for training participation, this finding is not surprising.

Turning to the second row of the table, we observe that the enrollment and training rates of both minority and non-Hispanic white displaced workers are similar. The results indicate that non-Hispanic whites are slightly more likely to complete some training, while minorities are more likely to enroll in community college courses following their job loss. In work not summarized in the table, we find that the reason for this result is that although minorities are more likely to enroll in community college schooling, once they have enrolled they are approximately 15 percent less likely to complete at least one course. Although this result may suggest that minorities have more difficulty adapting to a classroom training environment, this may not be the correct interpretation of this finding. As our discussion in the previous section suggested, the networking opportunities associated with being at a community college may be greater for minorities, whose transition rates from unemployment to new jobs in the absence of training are usually lower than are those of whites.

Beginning in the third row of Table 7.2, we observe that participation in training declines with age. Enrollment and training rates are the largest for the youngest displaced workers in their early twenties and decline with age. The probability that displaced workers in their early twenties enroll in community college courses is approximately 12 percentage points greater than observationally similar workers who are in their late fifties. Participation rates drop sharply with age until individuals are in their mid thirties. At this point participation rates decline slowly but steadily as individuals approach their sixties. As shown in the table, the enrollment rates of displaced workers in their thirties and forties is approximately 6 percentage points greater than the enrollment rates of displaced workers in their late fifties. This difference implies that the enrollment rates in community college schooling is approximately one-third less for displaced workers in their late fifties compared to those in their thirties and forties.

This relationship between displaced workers' ages and participation rates in training is consistent with the human capital rationale for training. Younger displaced workers are more likely to enroll in training because their forgone earnings are likely lower and they have a longer time frame to realize returns to their investments. At the very least, our findings indicate that displaced workers who are older have less incentive to participate in training or perhaps encounter greater barriers to acquiring skills through community colleges.

One of the most interesting sets of results in the table is the relationship between displaced workers' prior schooling and their participation rates in community college. The displaced workers who are most likely to enroll in these courses are those who previously had acquired some postsecondary schooling. Enrollment and training rates among high school graduates are approximately 6 and 5 percentage points lower, respectively, than those with some postsecondary schooling. The gap between high school dropouts is even larger. Further, those with some prior postsecondary schooling also are more likely to receive training than those with college degrees.

The foregoing relationship between displaced workers' prior schooling and training participation also holds among the subset of displaced workers who enroll in at least one community college course. In results not reported in the table, we find that displaced workers with some prior postsecondary schooling are approximately 33 percent more likely to complete at least one community college course than high school dropouts who enroll in courses. They also are more likely to complete at least one course than enrollees who have only a high school degree or who have a higher degree.

These results suggest that community college retraining is more attractive to displaced workers with prior postsecondary schooling than it is for other dislocated workers. Because we account for many productivity-related characteristics, such as individuals' prior industry, years of service, and earnings, our result implies that among workers with approximately the same productivity, those who had acquired some prior postsecondary schooling benefit more from community college retraining. Further, since we attempt to account for the magnitude of displaced workers' earnings losses in our analysis, it is unlikely that differences between individuals' forgone earnings could explain our result. Instead, our result suggests that displaced workers with prior postsecondary schooling are a good match for community college–based retraining.

There are a couple of reasons why displaced workers with prior postsecondary schooling may find attending community colleges to be an attractive option following their job loss. First, the emotional costs associated with enrolling in community college courses may be less for displaced workers who acquired this type of schooling in the past. An advantage that these displaced workers have is that they know more about community colleges and their programs. Second, these individuals also may benefit more from returning to school than those with postsecondary degrees or those who have no more than a high school education, because they may be able to quickly obtain a degree or some other credential. This possibility would influence displaced workers' training decisions if employers viewed having a credential as an important factor when making hiring decisions. However, when we took into account the number and type of credits displaced workers completed, we did not find evidence that obtaining a degree worked to their advantage.

What Determines the Number of Completed Credits?

Another measure of displaced workers' participation in retraining is how intensely they participated in community college schooling. To address this question, we examined how the personal characteristics of displaced workers predicted the number of credits that they completed in Washington State's community colleges. For this analysis we limited our sample to displaced workers who completed at least one course. As we noted above, this group of trainees completed on average approximately 28 credits.

We found that the personal characteristics that are associated with greater participation rates in retraining also are associated with greater intensity of participation. However, these relationships are often not very strong. Accordingly, these results highlight the importance of the enrollment decision in explaining differences in the amount of training acquired by displaced workers. As shown in Table 7.3, women complete on average two more credits than observationally similar men. Given that this subsample of displaced workers complete an average of 28 credits, this difference is relatively modest. By contrast, we observed above that women were substantially more likely than men to enroll in community college courses.

Table 7.3 Impact of Demographic Characteristics on the Number of Credits Completed by Displaced Workers in Washington State (difference between groups' credits)

		Total credits	
Characteristics	Total credits	Males	Females
Females vs. males	2	—	—
Non-Hispanic whites vs. minority	2	3	1
Age at displacement (yr.)			
22–24 vs. 55–60	6	5	8
25–29 vs. 55–60	7	5	9
30–34 vs. 55–60	7	6	7
35–39 vs. 55–60	8	7	8
40–44 vs. 55–60	7	5	8
45–49 vs. 55–60	4	3	5
50–54 vs. 55–60	3	2	4
Prior education			
High school dropout vs. some college	–4	–6	–2
High school graduate vs. some college	0	0	0
College graduate vs. some college	–6	–6	–6
Tenure at displacement			
3–6 yr. vs. 1.5–3 yr.	3	3	2
6 or more yr. vs. 1.5–3 yr.	4	3	4

NOTE: See Table 7.1 for average number of credits and description of sample. Difference between the number of credits completed by groups indicated in the rows of the table.

The relationship between the age of displaced workers' when they lost their job and the number of credits they complete also is weaker. As shown in the table, the youngest displaced workers complete six more credits than the oldest displaced workers, but they complete about the same number of credits as displaced workers in their early forties. These results indicate that young displaced workers acquire more training than their prime-age counterparts, because they are more likely to enroll and complete at least one course. However, among displaced workers who complete at least one course, age is not a strong predictor of how much training they acquire.

We reach a similar conclusion when examining the relationship between prior schooling and the intensity of retraining. Once again this relation is much weaker than the relation between this characteristic and enrollment or training rates. Displaced workers with some prior postsecondary schooling complete approximately the same number of credits as those with a high school degree and approximately one more course than their counterparts who were high school dropouts or who had a college degree. These results indicate that the reason displaced workers with some prior postsecondary schooling receive more training is that they are more likely to enroll in community college courses and complete at least one course. Once they have completed that course, they take additional training only modestly more intensely than other dislocated workers.

IMPACT OF COMMUNITY COLLEGE SCHOOLING ON SUBSEQUENT EARNINGS

Measures of the value-added of community college courses provide information on the average impact of training. Such measures alone, however, are not sufficient to guide displaced workers' training decisions (Hollenbeck 1992; Kane and Rouse 1993; Leigh and Gill 1997). The impact of training received by displaced workers who are indifferent about participating in community college schooling, and who require encouragement from counselors, may differ from the impact for the average participant. More importantly, information about the impact of training is insufficient because training decisions depend on individuals' perceptions of both the impacts and the costs of training.

Nevertheless, before we can assess the net benefits of retraining, we must document the likely gains from community college schooling. To arrive at our estimate, we developed a statistical model of individual earnings that took account of differences among individuals' observed characteristics and unobserved characteristics that were fixed through time. Accordingly, our framework controls for differences among displaced workers' prior schooling, prior work experience, and family background characteristics that could account for differences in the amount of community college schooling that they acquire around the time of their displacements. Further, we also account for differences in the rate of growth in earnings as a function of gender, ethnicity, and the likely size of the earnings loss that is connected with their displacements.

We identify the impact of community college schooling essentially by comparing the postschooling earnings of displaced workers who are observationally similar but who had acquired more or fewer community college credits. In this framework, information about displaced workers who did not acquire any schooling is not required to estimate the impacts of schooling, although it does help us obtain more precise estimates.

Average Impact of Community College Courses

As shown in Table 7.4, male displaced workers who acquired community college schooling around the time of their displacement saw their annual (long-term) earnings rise by approximately $24 per completed credit. For females we estimate an impact of $20 per completed credit. Therefore, a male displaced worker who completed the average number of credits (among those who completed at least one credit) experienced an earnings increase of approximately $672 ($24 per credit × 28 credits). The average annual earnings of these displaced workers in the postdisplacement period was approximately $20,000. Hence, this impact of retraining constitutes approximately 3–4 percent of total earnings.

Turning to the impacts of community college schooling for selected demographic groups, we observe that minority men benefited less from the training that they received than white men, whereas among women the impacts for minorities and whites were about the same. Community college schooling increased the earnings of very young displaced workers by more than the earnings of their older counterparts. This result is consistent with our earlier finding that younger displaced workers are more likely to participate in training.

The values in Table 7.4 also suggest that the estimated impact of community college schooling is larger for those who are more experienced and better educated to begin with. In general, low-tenure displaced workers are less productive than their counterparts with longer tenure with their former employers. Among those who had acquired

Table 7.4 Impact of Community College Credits on Annual Earnings

Group	Males ($)	Females ($)
Total	24	20
Demographic group		
Minority	8	20
Age 22–24	32	36
Less than six years' tenure	16	12
More than high school degree	28	28
Type of course		
High-return courses[a]	64	68
Low-return courses[b]	−36	−12

NOTE: This table shows the average impact of a completed credit on earnings three years after completing last community college course.

[a] More quantitative vocational courses or academic math and science courses.

[b] All other courses including less quantitative vocational courses or humanities and social sciences courses.

SOURCE: Authors' calculations based on Washington State administrative data (see Table 7.1). For information about the standard errors associated with these estimates, see Jacobson, LaLonde, and Sullivan (1997, 1999).

relatively little tenure, the estimated impact of a community college credit is approximately one-third less than the average impact for all displaced workers. Similarly, we find that the impact of schooling is modestly higher among displaced workers who had more prior schooling. These results help to explain why high-tenure displaced workers with more prior schooling are more likely to participate in training, despite probably having higher costs of participation.

Despite these positive earnings gains, our results indicate that community college schooling usually helped displaced workers offset only a fraction of the losses associated with their displacements. Trainees completed on average about one-half of a year's worth of community college schooling. We observed above that this investment subsequently translated into an approximately 3–4 percent earnings increase. Extrapolating further, we would expect one year of community college schooling to raise the typical displaced worker's earnings by about 6 percent. In our sample, it is unusual for displaced workers to complete this much schooling. As other research has shown, however, long-term earnings losses associated with displacement range from 15 to 25 percent per year and can be larger for workers from some industries (Ruhm 1991; Jacobson, LaLonde, and Sullivan 1993; Schoeni 1996). Therefore, our results suggest that it would take three to four years of full-time community college-style retraining in order for displaced workers to obtain the skills necessary to offset the long-term losses associated with displacement.

Average Impact of Different Types of Courses

Our analysis of community college schooling indicates that it can generate modest earnings impacts for a variety of displaced workers. However, as we analyzed our results more closely, it became clear that the impact of community college schooling resulted almost entirely from large impacts associated with courses in the health-related fields, in more technically oriented vocations including the trades, and in academic math and science classes. As shown by Panel C, the impact of community college schooling appears to depend more on the types of courses that individuals complete than on their characteristics. Displaced workers who complete what we call high-return courses experience very large earnings increases per completed credit. Extrapolating from the values in the table, we estimate that a displaced worker who completed 15 high-return credits (just three to four courses) experienced nearly a $1,000 rise in their annual earnings.

All other categories of courses, including those that taught less technically oriented vocational skills or academic subject matter, usually generated small or even negative earnings impacts. These results imply that such courses probably make displaced workers financially worse off. Indeed, male displaced workers appear to be made substantially worse off on average by enrolling in school and completing low-return courses. This result could be spurious if displaced workers who experienced larger earnings losses in connection with their job losses also tended to complete more low-return courses. However, our statistical framework takes this possibility into account. One way to interpret our finding for low-return courses is that when displaced workers invest in such training, they not only may fail to acquire any productive skills, but they also may lose valuable labor market experience.

To explore further our finding about the adverse impacts of low-return courses, we limited our analysis to the subsample of displaced workers who had completed 15 or more high-return credits. This group of displaced workers was on average more skilled than other training participants. We then asked whether this more skilled group experienced any earnings gains from completing low-return courses? Once again, we found that even among this group of displaced workers, the numbers of low-return courses completed were not associated with increased earnings. We interpret this result as strong evidence that our findings on the disparate impacts of high- and low-return courses are not due to differences in the types of individuals who enroll in these kinds of classes.

The impacts of high-return courses that we report here help explain why more productive and younger displaced workers experience larger average impacts of schooling. We find that both more-skilled displaced workers and younger displaced workers are more likely than other displaced workers to enroll in such courses. Consequently, they gain more from training partly because they complete training in areas that are better rewarded in the labor market. These results also are consistent with a general finding in the training literature indicating a complementarity between skills and the receipt of training. In the private sector, employers are much more likely to train their most skilled workers, probably because the gains from training are largest for this group.

PROGRAM PERFORMANCE AND INDIVIDUAL DECISION MAKING

Whether displaced workers' retraining is likely to pay off depends on the types of courses that they complete and the costs that they incur in order to be retrained. As we observed in the previous section, a displaced worker choosing to complete low-return courses is likely to be worse off as a result of participating in training. Individuals unaware of this tendency would make better decisions, if they received this information around the time of their displacements. By contrast, those who complete some of the high-return courses may benefit from training, depending on its costs.

To assess whether the benefits of high-return courses likely exceed their costs, we consider a hypothetical example. Suppose that a displaced worker enrolled in community college courses for one full academic quarter. During that quarter, she completed 15 credits in high-return classes. We estimate above that this training might increase her annual earnings by an average of $1,000 per year. If this displaced worker could expect to earn $20,000 a year in the absence of training and she loses one-quarter of that pay because she enrolls in school full time, then the forgone earnings cost of her retraining is about $5,000. Alternatively, if she works part time while going to school, the forgone earnings cost of her retraining might be closer to $2,500. We also assume that the cost of tuition, fees, transportation, and child care amounts to $2,000. Ignoring the emotional costs of training, total training costs for the trainee who works part time amounts to $4,500. The question now becomes, is a $1,000 annual impact sufficient to justify a $4,500 investment in training? The answer is that it depends. If the displaced worker is relatively old, her working career may not be long enough for the impacts to offset the costs. Further, if a displaced worker's newly acquired skills depreciate, over time her annual earnings impacts from this retraining will diminish so that the cumulative impacts may be insufficient to cover the cost of retraining.

The answer also depends on how we discount the future earnings gains from retraining. We must discount future gains because a $1,000 gain in earnings ten years from now is not worth the same to an individual as a $1,000 gain in earnings one year from now. If we use an interest rate of 5 percent, an individual should be indifferent between receiving $1,000 ten years from now or $614 today.

In this example, we discount future gains according to a rate of 5 percent. We also assume that during the first year after leaving training, displaced workers did not experience any earnings gains. We impose this assumption because we found in our study, that earnings impacts during the first year after training were often either negative or zero.

We now consider the calculation of net benefits of high-return community college courses for four hypothetical displaced workers whose ages were 25, 35, 45, and 55 when they lost their jobs. We also show how the calculation is sensitive to assumptions about the depreciation rate of displaced workers' newly acquired skills by assuming 1) no skill depreciation, and 2) a 5 percent rate of skill depreciation. In Table 7.5, we present the net benefit calculation based on these assumptions. In the third row, we report the adjustment that we make to annual earnings gains to account for 1) these gains continuing through the remainder of a person's career, 2) the possibility that the skills acquired in community college courses depreciate, and 3) the discount rate. The present value of the gains from schooling at the time a displaced worker makes the decision to enroll in courses is given by the product of the average annual impact times the adjustment factor. The net benefit of schooling is the difference between the total impact and the costs.

As we can see from Table 7.5, if newly acquired skills do not depreciate, the net benefits of retraining for all but the oldest displaced workers are very substantial. The net present value for a 35-year-old, the approximate mean age of our sample of displaced workers, completing an academic quarter of high-return courses is $14,400. Given the assumed costs of this retraining, this gain implies an (internal) rate of return on investment of approximately 20 percent. Even by the standards of the late 1990s stock market, this gain is substantial. By con-

Table 7.5 Computing the Net Benefits of High-Return Community College Courses

Variable	Age at displacement						
	—25—		—35—		—45—		55
Annual impact ($)	1,000	1,000	1,000	1,000	1,000	1,000	1,000
Depreciation rate (%)	0	5	0	5	0	5	0
Adjustment factor[a]	16.2	8.4	14.4	8.1	11.5	7.3	6.8
Total impact[b] ($)	16,200	8,400	14,400	8,100	11,500	7,300	6,800
Costs ($)	4,500	4,500	4,500	4,500	4,500	4,500	4,500
Net benefit ($)	11,700	3,900	9,900	3,600	7,000	2,800	2,300

NOTE: The calculations are based on a discount rate of 5% and an assumption that individuals' working lives end when they are 65.
[a] These numbers are the product of the annual impact and the adjustment for the time value of money, skill depreciation, and years left in career.
[b] The adjustment factor accounts for the time value of money, skill depreciation, and years left in career.

trast, the same $1,000 gain in annual earnings translates into a smaller $6,800 present value for displaced workers in their mid fifties. If the forgone earnings associated with training participation were double their assumed levels, the net benefit of completing an academic quarter of high-return courses would be negative. Under these circumstances, older displaced workers would be better off not enrolling in training.

The foregoing calculations in Table 7.5 depend on several assumptions. We assumed that skills did not depreciate. Some analysts of private sector training have reported evidence of skill depreciation (Lillard and Tan 1992). If the value of newly acquired skills depreciate at a rate of only 5 percent per year, the net benefit of retraining declines substantially. As shown in Table 7.5, the present value of the gain for a 35-year-old displaced worker falls from $9,900 to only $3,600.

Another important assumption underlying our calculations concerns how much displaced workers would have earned had they not been in school. In a depressed labor market, the likelihood of receiving a job offer may be so low that the forgone earnings associated with retraining are insubstantial. By contrast, the cost of retraining displaced workers is greater when labor markets are tight and unemployment rates are low, as they have been during recent years. If there are no forgone earnings costs associated with training, the net benefits of retraining would rise by an additional $2,500 for each age group in the table. The internal rate of return from training also would then rise substantially for each group. Nevertheless, an important point to recognize is that even if the retraining costs depicted in the table are too large, the net benefits are always larger for younger displaced workers.

We believe in general there are some forgone earnings costs associated with retraining. In our data, we find that displaced workers earn less when they are in enrolled in school than when they are out of school. Those who enroll in community college courses earn less than observationally similar persons who did not enroll in such classes. Further, those who enroll in more courses during any given time period earn less than their counterparts who enroll in fewer courses (Jacobson, LaLonde, and Sullivan 1997). On one hand, this evidence may indicate that those who train more intensely are those who had not yet received an acceptable job offer. On the other hand, it also may indicate the potential for substantial forgone earnings costs associated with retraining.

CONCLUDING REMARKS

The preceding discussion outlines a framework that program operators, counselors, and displaced workers can use to assess whether retraining in a college environment is likely to raise earnings. We have contended in this chapter that policymakers can enhance program performance not only when program operators understand the benefits of training, but also when individuals themselves have better information to make more informed decisions. Displaced workers who are contemplating retraining should be aware of all the costs of their decisions as well as the benefits that they are likely to receive from different curricula.

By having this information, dislocated workers are likely to direct their energies toward more productive activities, which may include forgoing training and focusing on a job search. For many displaced workers, policies designed to facilitate reemployment are likely more beneficial than those designed to encourage retraining. Among those displaced workers who opt for retraining, policies that encourage more-skilled persons to acquire more quantitatively oriented skills are likely more beneficial than those that encourage them to acquire less quantitative or more general skills.

Although our results indicate that the subset of high-return courses generate substantial gains for displaced workers, this finding does not imply that those displaced workers who are inclined to enroll only in less quantitative courses would experience the same large returns if instead they enrolled in the high-return courses. Our results measure the impact of high-return courses among those displaced workers who actually enrolled in them. Indeed, our findings suggest that because these persons were more skilled to begin with—more tenure with their former employer and higher predisplacement earnings—they would experience higher returns from these types of classes. We would expect that those inclined to enroll only in the low-return courses would not experience gains as large if policymakers encouraged them instead to enroll in more high-return courses.

At the same time, we should note that we found that those who benefit from the high-return classes do not appear to benefit from completing additional low-return courses. Therefore, the substantial gains that we report in this chapter for high-return courses are not simply a result of the skills of the individual, but an interaction between the individual and the type of courses (or programs) that they complete.

Our empirical results apply to displaced workers from Washington State who enrolled in community college courses around the time of their job losses in the early 1990s. Obviously, the impacts could be different for other displaced workers in other time periods, in other parts of the country, or for those who matriculated into private training institutions. We have performed a similar analysis for workers who were displaced from firms in Allegheny County, Pennsylvania, in the early 1980s and obtained similar results (Jacobson, LaLonde, and Sullivan 1997). With the growth in popularity of vocational programs in community colleges during the last two decades, it would be surprising if the benefits associated with retraining in private institutions were substantially larger. In any event, even for individuals considering enrolling in private training institutions, our framework and results are still valuable. If applied, it would ensure that applicants for such programs are those who expected to obtain the largest net benefits from retraining.

Finally, we contend that the impact of this study on dislocated workers' decisions to enroll in community colleges and select specific courses of study would depend on the extent to which

- their personal goal is to increase their earnings power,
- the accuracy of their assessments of the returns to various courses, and
- the accuracy of their assessment of the costs of attending school.

The social value of providing this information would be highest if dislocated workers 1) do not have an accurate view of the benefits and costs of attending school, and 2) are attending school primarily to increase their future earnings.

Importantly, the value of the information to dislocated workers would be even greater if they are interested and able to excel in high-return courses. However, from society's viewpoint, the cost-effectiveness of training also would increase if policymakers and program operators simply discouraged from taking training those displaced workers who are likely to make themselves financially no better off or even worse off by attending school. One way to discourage such persons from taking training is to provide them with accurate information about the likely costs and benefits of specific types of training. If the cost of providing this information is sufficiently low, it could constitute an exceptionally effective way to raise both the private and social returns to government-subsidized training. Such information would help individuals self-select into training in a way that would make it more likely that public training resources are directed toward those who are likely to derive the greatest benefit from retraining. Clearly, the value of providing such information should be assessed in future research.

Note

We thank Kevin Hollenbeck for comments on an earlier version of this paper. The views expressed in this paper are solely those of the authors and do not reflect those of the U.S. Department of Labor. This research has been supported by the Employment and Training Administration under contract number K-630707-00-80-30.

References

Barnow, Burt. 1992. "The Effects of Performance Standards on State and Local Programs." In *Evaluating Welfare and Training Programs*, Charles F. Manski and Irwin Garfinkel, eds. Cambridge, Massachusetts: Harvard University Press, pp. 277–309.

Heckman, James, Robert LaLonde, and Jeffrey Smith. 1999. "The Economics and Econometrics of Active Labor Market Policies." In *Handbook of Labor Economics, Volume 3A*, Orley Ashenfelter and David Card, eds. Amsterdam: Elesvier Science B.V., pp. 1865–2097.

Hollenbeck, Kevin. 1992. "Postsecondary Education as Triage: Returns to Academic and Technical Programs." Working paper no. 92-10, W.E. Upjohn Institute for Employment Research, Kalamazoo, Michigan.

Jacobson, Louis S., Robert J. LaLonde, and Daniel G. Sullivan. 1993. "Earnings Losses of Displaced Workers." *American Economic Review* 83(4): 685–709.

———. 1997. "The Returns from Classroom Training for Displaced Workers." Working paper series (WP-99-28), Federal Reserve Bank of Chicago, December.

———. 1999. "Participation and the Effects of Community College Schooling for Displaced Workers: A Study of Displaced Workers from Washington State." Draft prepared for the U.S. Department of Labor, K-6307-700-80-30.

Kane, Thomas, and Cecila Rouse. 1993. "Labor Market Returns to Two- and Four-Year College." Photocopy, Princeton University.

Leigh, Duane E., and Andrew Gill. 1997. "Labor Market Returns to Community Colleges: Evidence for Returning Adults." *Journal of Human Resources* 32(2): 334–353.

Lillard, Lee A., and Hong W. Tan. 1992. "Private Sector Training: Who Gets It and What Are Its Effects?" In *Research in Labor Economics, Vol. 13*, Ronald Ehrenberg, ed. Greenwich, Connecticut: JAI Press, pp. 1–62.

Ruhm, Christopher. 1991. "Are Workers Permanently Scarred by Job Displacements." *American Economic Review* 81(1): 319–323.

Schoeni, Robert. 1996. "Wage Losses of Displaced Workers." Photocopy. Santa Monica, California: The RAND Corporation.

Comments on Chapter 7

Kevin Hollenbeck
W.E. Upjohn Institute for Employment Research

The general policy issue being discussed at this conference is targeting of services. This chapter delves into the question of the appro-
priateness of investment in formal education at community colleges for
unemployed individuals. It tangentially addresses targeting to the extent that it identifies characteristics of individuals who tend to have investment successes and the educational experiences that tend to have a
payoff. In the Workforce Investment Act (WIA), as I understand it, local boards will provide individual training accounts (ITAs) to or will
enter into on-the-job-training contracts for adults or dislocated workers
who do not or cannot find employment after receiving core and intensive services. But also, boards are obliged to provide information on
eligible training providers to *anyone* under core services. As boards
implement these policies, the central questions they must address are
how much and what type of information about which providers should
be supplied to which individuals. Furthermore, boards need to determine the size of the ITAs—should the targeting be narrow with a relatively large voucher or wider with a relatively smaller voucher? This
chapter provides some information that will be useful to boards as they
wrestle with these issues; however, the information is highly limited in
scope and usefulness.

Jacobson, LaLonde, and Sullivan have accessed a very rich data
source on community college attendance of displaced workers in the
state of Washington from 1990 to 1994. They have quarterly earnings
records, unemployment insurance claimant data, administrative data
from the Job Training Partnership Act (JTPA) for all persons who received community college subsidies, and data from a special survey of

community college students. The inclusions that they place on the data are as follows:

- had six or more quarters of tenure prior to separating from their employer between 90:3 and 94:1,
- had an active unemployment insurance (UI) claim one quarter after their job loss (coverage issue),
- were between the ages of 22 and 60 (inclusive) during the quarter that they separated, and
- had positive earnings during each calendar year between 1987 and 1995, except during the eight quarters following their job loss (displacement).

The last criterion is important because it cut the useable sample in half from about 250,000 to 121,000, and because it meant that individuals who never became employed (or became self-employed or moved out of state) after training are not observed or analyzed.

I liked the fact that Jacobson, LaLonde, and Sullivan use three measures of community college "behavior." First, *enrollment* is defined as completing an application form. About one-quarter of the analysis sample enrolled in community colleges. *Training* is defined as having completed at least one course. Incredibly, less than half of the individuals in the sample who enrolled received training under this definition. In other words, more than half of the individuals who enrolled did not complete even a single course. *Intensity of training* is the number of credits completed. The conditional mean (on having completed at least one course) is 28 credits (slightly more than one-quarter of what it takes to complete an associate's degree in a quarter system).

The authors first present and discuss estimates of equations that explain participation behavior—i.e., enrollment, conditional training, and intensity. They then determine the wage returns to each of these types of behavior, and, finally, they suggest a process and even some wording of information that is provided to individuals who encounter an employment center. Some interesting findings about the enrollment rate and training rate are as follows:

- Women are more likely than men to enroll in a community college; however, they are no more likely to complete at least one course given enrollment.
- Minorities and non-Hispanic whites are equally likely to enroll

in a community college, but minorities are less likely to complete at least one course given enrollment.

- Age has a monotonically inverse relationship to enrollment and training, although the relationship is not smooth. Individuals in their twenties are most likely to enroll and be trained; the rates are smaller but level off for individuals in their thirties and forties, and then drop off considerably for individuals in their late fifties.

- Individuals who had some prior postsecondary schooling but not a bachelor's degree (which the authors refer to as "some college") were more likely to enroll and be trained than individuals with just a high school diploma or less and individuals who were college graduates.

They suggest that their findings regarding intensity of training, i.e., number of credits completed, are similar to the enrollment and training findings, but the strength of the relationships is not as great.

What I really like about the chapter is its attention to the "full return" to formal education, not just its impacts on earnings. Usual practice in estimating the returns to education is to estimate an earnings equation that has educational variables as covariates and to call the coefficient on education the returns to education. However, as Jacobson, LaLonde, and Sullivan point out, this is the benefit side of the investment, and an accounting of costs needs to be performed in order to determine the full return on investment. They point out that attending community colleges has direct, emotional, and opportunity costs in the form of forgone wages.

In their estimates of the impact of attending community college on annual earnings, i.e., the benefit side of the equation, the authors find that the average annual impact of completing one credit is about $20 for women and $24 for men. At the conditional mean intensity of 28 credits, they point out that this works out to about 3 to 4 percent. Minority males earned a lower return; young individuals having more than six years of (prior) job tenure and more educated individuals earned a higher return.

In attempting to analyze the impact of particular educational experiences at community colleges on earnings, the authors make what I believe is an unfortunate choice in how they characterize curriculum options. They show that the returns to "quantitative vocational courses or academic math and science courses" are higher than the returns to "less quantitative vocational courses or humanities and social sciences courses." It is an unfortunate choice for a variable because community college students don't have much of an opportunity to choose courses once they have selected whether they are going to pursue an occupational or a transfer program and once they have selected which program they're going to pursue. It would be far more useful to potential community college students to know the (average) returns to a transfer program of studies (and an Associate of Arts or an Associate of Science degree) versus an occupational program (and an Applied Associate of Science degree). Next in importance would be particular program or concentration areas (i.e., political science, administrative assistant, dental assistant, library science, etc.). My experience is that once students have chosen their program and degree option, their course selections are rather limited. They do have a choice about how quickly they pursue their program area, so sequencing patterns, or even quarters enrolled, would have been more relevant.

Furthermore, the authors say that they control for observed and time-invariant unobserved characteristics, but there must be unobserved characteristics (which must be time-varying) that are not controlled in their specification. How much one learns or benefits from a quantitative or nonquantitative course must depend on tastes, preferences, talent, quality and quantity of educational background, aptitudes, learning style, occupational awareness, and a host of other variables. I am very uncomfortable using these results to recommend that any and all individuals should pursue quantitative course work without regard to their own interests, aptitudes, and educational background.

There is a discernible change in tone and rigor in the chapter when the authors consider the cost side of the investment decision. Basically, they no longer rely on any data; rather, they present (simulated) scenarios. Their base case is a woman who pursues a community college program on a full-time basis for one quarter. They simulate a benefit of $1,000 in annual earnings. On the cost side, they suggest that direct costs (including tuition, fees, transportation, and child care) would be $2,000 and that forgone earnings would be $5,000 (three months at annual earnings of $20,000). They ignore emotional costs. Table 7.4 in the chapter shows the lifetime net benefit of this investment assuming a

5 percent discount rate, varying the annual depreciation rate of the skills learned between 0 and 5 percent, and varying the age at displacement from 25 to 35 to 45 to 55. My basic quibble here is whether the cost assumptions are realistic. Jacobson, LaLonde, and Sullivan report having extensive community college surveys, and I'm wondering what those data report in the way of direct, out-of-pocket costs to students. Furthermore, they have quarterly earnings data, so they should be able to provide mean differences in earnings between observationally equivalent students and nonstudents. I suspect that forgone earnings are very small, because most community college students are employed while attending school. Additionally, the benefit is assumed to be a one-time shift of $1,000 in annual earnings, but the earnings advantage will most likely grow over time as trained individuals receive more on-the-job training and have higher promotion likelihoods. On the other hand, I suspect that 5 percent is a low discount rate for community college students.

The final major point I want to make is the question of the generalizability (or external validity) of these findings. Recall that they are specific to displaced workers in the state of Washington who chose or were directed into community college programs in the early 1990s. Community colleges are only one type of eligible training institution out of many types of training institutions, and displaced workers are only one type of client who will be seeking information on the benefits (and costs) to training at a one-stop employment center.

8

Using Statistical Assessment Tools to Target Services to Work First Participants

Randall W. Eberts

W.E. Upjohn Institute for Employment Research

This chapter describes the design and evaluation of a recently completed Work First pilot, funded by the Employment and Training Administration of the U.S. Department of Labor, which uses statistical methods to assess each customer's employability and then uses the assessment to refer them to services. The pilot addresses the need for early identification of employment barriers faced by welfare recipients and for the targeting of services. Welfare-to-work programs typically treat all recipients the same, providing the same basic services regardless of a participant's skills, aptitudes, and motivation. Yet, barriers vary widely. Some customers require little assistance in finding a job, while others have multiple barriers and stand to benefit from more intensive, targeted services.[1] However, most Work First programs do not have sufficient funds to provide case managers for all customers who need more specialized attention and advocacy.

This pilot develops administrative tools to target services to customers without changing the nature of the program or significantly raising costs. Statistical techniques were developed to estimate the likelihood of employment based on participants' demographic and work history information found in administrative records. An employability score was computed for each customer and was then used to assign each participant to one of three providers. Each provider offered the same basic set of services but differed in the mix of services and in their approach to delivering services. The pilot used these differences to determine the best provider for each customer. The pilot was designed by the W.E. Upjohn Institute for Employment Research and conducted in Michigan at the Kalamazoo/St. Joseph Workforce Development Board (WDB), which is administered by the Institute.

The evaluation, based on random assignment, provides evidence that the pilot was successful in using statistical tools to improve program outcomes by placing more welfare recipients into jobs. It showed that the statistical assessment tool successfully distinguished among participants with respect to barriers to employment. It also found that referring participants to service providers according to their individualized statistical needs assessment (employability score) increased the overall effectiveness of the program as measured by the program goal of customers finding and retaining a job for 90 consecutive days.

MICHIGAN'S WORK FIRST PROGRAM

Program Overview

The purpose of Michigan's Work First Program is to move welfare recipients into jobs as quickly as possible. It was developed from waivers to Aid to Families with Dependent Children (AFDC), approved by the Clinton Administration in 1994 and 1996, and has continued under Temporary Assistance for Needy Families (TANF). The program provides welfare recipients reemployment skills, support, and opportunities to obtain employment, and it offers instruction in the proper techniques for writing resumes, completing applications, and interviewing for jobs. All enrollees receive similar services regardless of their needs. More intensive skill training is available only to those who hold a job or those who have repeatedly failed to find employment. After clients complete the core services, they are expected to search intensively for work and accept offers that provide at least 20 hours of work per week at or above minimum wage.[2] Customers employed for 90 consecutive days in a qualified job are considered a successful outcome, and they are terminated from the program. As an incentive for finding work, participants are allowed to keep the first $200 earned each month and 20 percent over that without reducing benefits. Participants also receive transportation, child care, and Medicaid for a limited time.

This statistical assessment model was based on the outcomes of participants entering the program during 1996. Table 8.1 displays the characteristics of Work First participants who enrolled in the program in 1996. Participants were predominantly single parents who had not completed high school and who had been on welfare for less than 36 months during the last five years. Some of the participants had completed a general equivalency diploma (GED), but few received vocational training.

Work First participants engaged in a variety of activities as part of their requirement for successfully participating in the program. Most participants began with assessment and employability planning (code 12). As shown in Table 8.2, 83 percent of all participants received these services in 1996. The percentage was higher for those who were not employed prior to entering Work First, about 90 percent. Around half of the participants engaged in group or individual job-search assistance, which includes counseling, job-seeking skills training, and may include support on a one-to-one basis (code 13). Fifty-three percent were employed in a job (code 1) that paid minimum wage or more and the employment was for 20 hours or more per week (or 35 hours if a working spouse). Another 6 percent were employed in unsubsidized employment that did not meet the requirements of code 1. Nineteen percent of the participants were in unsubsidized employment when referred, obtained subsidized employment meeting the requirements of code 1 prior to reporting, or obtained the appropriate employment prior to reporting to the first activity. Only a handful of participants (2 percent) were referred to community service programs or vocational educational training.

Differences in Activities among Providers

The Kalamazoo/St. Joseph WDB contracted with three organizations to provide employment services to participants of the Work First program. The providers delivered services that met state and federal requirements regarding content and duration. However, there was some flexibility within the requirements. WDB staff observed that providers differed in their styles and philosophies in delivering services

Table 8.1 Variables Used in the Work First Statistical Assessment Model

Name	Description	Mean (%)
sglprnt	=1 if single parent	82.7
age	Age at time of enrollment (yr.)	29.7
age2	Age squared	
noschl	No formal schooling	3.8
grlt9	Completed less than 9th grade	5.6
gr9	Completed 9th grade	5.6
gr10	Completed 10th grade	8.9
gr11	Completed 11th grade	19.1
gr12	Completed 12th grade (omitted from analysis, thus reference)	38.7
post1	Completed one year of postsecondary	1.2
post2	Completed two years of postsecondary	1.6
post3	Completed three years of postsecondary	0.4
post4	Completed four years of postsecondary	0.1
ged	Earned GED certification	16.1
YOU	Youth Opportunities Unlimited	18.9
Goodwill	Goodwill Industries	17.9
foundat	Behavioral Foundation	30.3
comstock	Comstock	4.5
sturgis	Sturgis	4.0
rivers3	Three Rivers	24.0
voced	Attended postsecondary vocational education program	1.4
notarget	Not a target group, which includes AFDC received in any 36 of preceding 60 months, youngest child 16–18, or custodial parent under 24 and who has not completed high school or with little or no work experience	52.8
AFDC36	Received AFDC any 36 of preceding 60 months	34.3
code20_1	Qualified unsubsidized employment prior to assignment	19.0
code20_2	Qualified unsubsidized employment prior to assignment in previous enrollment	0.3

Table 8.1 (Continued)

Name	Description	Mean (%)
nocmpl	Terminated as noncompliant in previous enrollment (code 59, 60, or 61)	5.7
employed	Terminated as employed in qualified unsubsidized job	42.7
Observations		1,546

SOURCE: Author's calculations of Kalamazoo/St. Joseph Work First administrative data, 1996–1997.

Table 8.2 Selected Activities of Work First Programs

Activity	Code	Mean (%)	Standard deviation	Minimum	Maximum
Unsubsidized employment	01	53	0.50	0	1
Job readiness	10	9	0.28	0	1
Assessment and employ-ability planning	12	83	0.37	0	1
Job search	13	55	0.50	0	1
Part-time employment	19	6	0.24	0	1
Employment prior to assignment	20	19	0.39	0	1
Community service	33	1	0.11	0	1
Voc. ed. training	34	1	0.09	0	1

SOURCE: Author's calculations of Kalamazoo/St. Joseph Work First administrative data, 1996–1997.

and in the number of hours in which participants were engaged in specific activities. These observed differences were critical to the pilot by providing the opportunity to refer participants to the provider, and thus the mix and style of services, that best met their needs.

The length of time that Work First enrollees engaged in activities varied by type of activity and by subcontractor. For example, as shown in Table 8.3, 38.1 percent of the participants spent two hours in the assessment and employability planning activity, while 39.6 percent spent 20 hours in the same activity. Of the three subcontractors within the Kalamazoo area, Youth Opportunities Unlimited (YOU) averaged 7.3 hours, the Behavioral Foundation 11.2 hours, and Goodwill 16.0 hours in this activity. The higher average for Goodwill results from a much larger percentage of participants spending time in the services than those assigned to other providers. More than three-quarters of those going to Goodwill spent 20 hours in this service. Only 27 percent of the participants receiving services from either YOU or the Foundation

Table 8.3 Distribution of Hours Engaged in Assessment and Employability Planning

Hours	Percentage			
	All	Foundation	Goodwill	YOU
1	5.9	1.9	1.9	14.6
2	38.1	38.3	19.0	52.8
3	0.2	0.5	0.0	0.0
4	0.4	0.5	0.5	0.0
5	0.1	0.0	0.5	0.0
6	0.1	0.0	0.0	0.4
7	0.0	0.0	0.0	0.0
8	0.1	0.0	0.0	0.4
9	0.0	0.0	0.0	0.0
10	0.1	0.0	0.0	0.4
11	0.7	0.0	0.5	1.9
12	0.2	0.5	0.0	0.0
13	0.0	0.0	0.0	0.0
14	0.2	0.5	0.0	0.0
15	4.8	11.1	0.0	0.0
16	9.3	19.6	0.9	1.9
17	0.0	0.0	0.0	0.0
18	0.0	0.0	0.0	0.0
19	0.0	0.0	0.0	0.0
20	39.6	26.9	76.8	27.7

SOURCE: Author's calculations of Kalamazoo/St. Joseph Work First administrative data, 1996–1997.

received 20 hours of this service. For those going to YOU, two-thirds of the participants received two hours or less of assessment and planning. Time spent in this activity for those receiving services from the Foundation were split between 2, 15 or 16, and 20 hours. The wide distribution may indicate that these individuals have more discretion in how much time they spend in various activities.

Hours spent in group or individual job-search activities were much more uniform. Ninety-seven percent of the participants spent 20 hours, and there was no significant difference in the amount of hours the three subcontractors devoted to this activity.

Providers also differed in their approaches to delivering services. For instance, one provider stressed a goal-oriented approach to job search, requiring that participants call a given number of employers each day until they found a job. Another provider offered more assistance to customers in conducting phone inquiries and interviewing for jobs. Staff would work directly with customers to show them how to find employment postings and telephone numbers, how to inquire about the job posting, and how to present themselves during interviews. This same organization would also provide more intensive training at times to those who were not able to find a job during their initial several weeks in the program.

STATISTICAL ASSESSMENT MODEL

The purpose of the statistical assessment (or statistical profiling) model is to use information commonly collected during the intake process to identify Work First participants who are likely to obtain employment with minimal intervention (or conversely, to identify individuals who need the most assistance in finding and maintaining employment). The following information is available at intake and is used as explanatory variables in the statistical assessment model: age, parental status, educational attainment, AFDC history, service provider, target group, employment prior to enrolling in Work First, and compliance history of participant if they were previously enrolled in the program. During the operation of the pilot, a successful outcome was defined as working in a qualified job for 90 consecutive days (with a grace period of no longer than a week if they changed jobs). A qualified job must offer a single parent at least minimum wage and 20 hours a week.

Data were obtained from the intake forms and the tracking system developed and maintained by the Kalamazoo/St. Joseph WDB. For most participants, multiple activities were recorded. The type of activity, the number of hours engaged in each activity, and the starting and ending dates of each activity were included in the files. Consequently, it was possible to piece together a sequence of activities between the time participants entered and left the program.

A logistic statistical procedure was used to estimate the relationship between a Work First participant's personal characteristics and the likelihood of finding qualified employment. The dependent variable in this statistical model is discrete, taking on the value of 1 (if employed) or 0 (if not employed). The probability of employment lies between 0 and 1 (that is, 0 percent and 100 percent). A logistic estimation procedure transforms the discrete event into a smooth functional form bounded by 0 and 1 and estimates the effect of specified variables on the probability of employment.

Estimates were based on a sample of Work First participants from the Kalamazoo/St. Joseph WDB who enrolled in the program during 1996. The 1996 period was used because all who enrolled in Work First during that time had completed the program before the start of the pilot and thus their outcomes were known.[3] The variable definitions and sample means are displayed in Table 8.1.

Results of the logit estimation are shown in Table 8.4. Focusing on the signs of the statistically significant coefficients, Work First participants are more likely to complete 90 consecutive days of employment if they had completed 12th grade (the omitted variable in the equation), were older, were employed prior to first assignment, enrolled in the program earlier in the year rather than later, and were not out of compliance if they had previously enrolled in Work First.[4]

The only variable that may need an explanation for its inclusion in the model is the date of admission into Work First. The coefficient on this variable is negative and statistically significant. Therefore, those who enrolled in Work First in more recent periods experienced a lower probability of finding and maintaining employment for 90 consecutive days. The percentage of Work First participants reaching this status

Table 8.4 Logit Estimates of the Basic Statistical Assessment Model

Variable	Coefficient	Standard error	z	P>|z|	95% Confidence interval Lower limit	Upper limit
sglprnt	0.223	0.156	1.429	0.153	−0.083	0.528
age	0.115	0.041	2.790	0.005	0.034	0.196
age2	−0.002	0.001	−2.602	0.009	−0.003	−0.000
noschl	−1.801	0.555	−3.244	0.001	−2.889	−0.713
grlt9	−0.454	0.304	−1.495	0.135	−1.049	0.141
gr9	−0.167	0.252	−0.662	0.508	−0.661	0.327
gr10	−0.775	0.218	−3.553	0.000	−1.203	−0.348
gr11	−0.431	0.157	−2.744	0.006	−0.739	−0.123
ged	0.174	0.162	1.074	0.283	−0.143	0.492
voced	−0.591	0.487	−1.212	0.225	−1.546	0.364
post1	0.079	0.501	0.159	0.874	−0.903	1.062
post2	0.162	0.438	0.371	0.711	−0.695	1.020
post3	0.011	0.884	0.013	0.990	−1.721	1.744
goodwill	−0.463	0.187	−2.485	0.013	−0.829	−0.098
foundat	−0.560	0.164	−3.406	0.001	−0.883	−0.238
sturgis	0.005	0.300	0.017	0.986	−0.582	0.593
comstock	0.127	0.302	0.421	0.673	−0.465	0.719
rivers3	−0.454	0.172	−2.641	0.008	−0.791	−0.117
notarget	0.064	0.116	0.555	0.579	−0.163	0.292
addate	−0.003	0.001	−5.424	0.000	−0.004	−0.002
code20_1	1.107	0.144	7.683	0.000	0.825	1.390
code20_2	−0.393	1.055	−0.373	0.709	−2.46	1.674
nocmpl	−0.750	0.281	−2.672	0.008	−1.301	−0.200
Constant	36.921	7.260	5.086	0.000	22.693	51.150

No. observ.   1,546
Pseudo R^2 0.1010

NOTE: Dependent variable: employed for 90 days = 1; log Likelihood = −948.47621; $\chi^2(23) = 213.10$; Prob > χ^2 = 0.0000.
SOURCE: Author's calculations of Kalamazoo/St. Joseph Work First administrative data, 1996–1997.

steadily declined from the first quarter of 1996, when the sample began. During the first and second quarters of 1996, 53 percent of participants in the sample were employed for 90 days, after which the percentage dropped to 50 percent during the third quarter, 31 percent during the fourth quarter, and 24 percent during the first quarter of 1997. The admission date variable can be interpreted as a proxy for attributes of Work First participants that are not captured in the characteristics included in the model. Work First staff observed that as the pool of welfare recipients going through the program diminished, enrollees were increasingly less qualified to find and hold jobs. The variable may also capture changes in the program and changes in local labor market conditions over time.

Applying the estimated coefficients to the characteristics associated with each Work First participant yields predictions of the probability of employment for each individual. Consequently, each Work First enrollee can be ranked according to their estimated probability.[5] For heuristic purposes, one can view the distribution of employability scores as representing participants lined up to enter the Work First program according to their probabilities of finding employment. If the door is envisioned to be on the left side of the graph in Figure 8.1, those with the least propensity to find a job are at the front of the line, and the participants with the highest propensity are at the end of the queue. According to our model, the estimated probabilities of employment range from a low of 0.02 to a high of 0.85. Therefore, the person at the head of the line has almost no chance of finding a job and would need considerably more assistance than the person at the end of the line, who is almost certain to find employment without much help. Although 43 percent of the Work First participants in the sample found employment, the model did not assign anyone a probability of 100 percent. However, the spread is quite large, spanning most of the range from 0 to 1.

The assignment of participants to a provider was based on the participant's employability score. The distribution of scores was divided into three groups, as shown in Figure 8.1. For evaluation purposes, participants were randomly assigned to a treatment group or a control group. Based upon prior analysis and the opinions of WDB staff, those in the treatment group with low employability scores were assigned to Goodwill, those in the middle group were referred to Youth Opportunities Unlimited (YOU), and those in the high employability group were

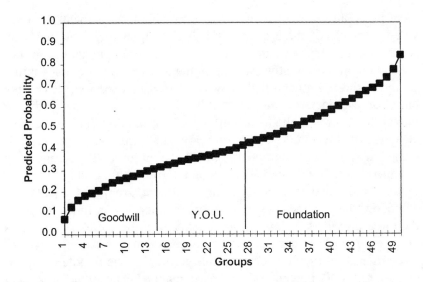

Figure 8.1   Referral of Participants to Providers Based on Employability Scores

assigned to the Behavioral Foundation. The assignment of participants in the control group will be discussed in the next section.

EVALUATION OF THE KALAMAZOO/ST. JOSEPH WORK FIRST PROFILING PILOT

Design of the Evaluation

The Kalamazoo/St. Joseph Work First profiling pilot was evaluated using a random assignment approach. The evaluation included participants who entered the program from March 1998 to March 2000. During the two-year period, nearly 3,600 welfare recipients who were single parents were assigned to the three providers serving the Kalamazoo area.[6]

The computerized intake process was designed so that welfare recipients referred to Work First from the Family Independence Agency (FIA) were randomly assigned to various groups. The random assignment procedure took place in three steps. First, participants were divided into one of three groups, depending upon their employability score. Assignment of participants to the three employability groups was based on their relative ranking in the distribution of employability scores of those who enrolled in Work First at that session. It was not based on a predetermined cutoff value. Those participants with employability scores in the lowest 40 percent of the distribution were assigned to the low employability group (L), the next 20 percent were assigned to the middle group (M), and the highest 40 percent were assigned to the high group (H). Second, those within each group were randomly divided into control and treatment groups of equal size. Third, enrollees in the control group were randomly assigned to one of the three providers. Those in the treatment group were assigned to a predetermined provider that was considered to be most effective for those in each of the three employability groups. The middle group included only 20 percent of the participants because the treatment provider for that group, YOU, could accommodate only that percentage due to capacity constraints.[7] The number of participants in each group is displayed in Table 8.5.

The primary outcome measure for the evaluation is the retention rate; that is, whether or not the participant was employed 90 consecutive days. Table 8.6 shows the retention rates of those in the control and treatment groups by employability group and provider. In this case, there is considerable variation both between groups and within groups. Note that the actual retention rate averaged for each group increases from the lowest employability group to the highest. For the control group, it increases from 11.6 percent for the lowest group to 21.7 percent for the highest employability group. The treatment group also follows the pattern of increasing retention rates from low to high employability groups. The same monotonic increase is exhibited for each provider except YOU. However, as shown in Table 8.7, the upper and lower bounds of the 95 percent confidence intervals overlap across the various groups.[8]

Retention Rates by Various Combinations of Providers

In order to determine whether different combinations of assignments of employability groups to service providers yield different out-

Table 8.5 Number of Participants Assigned to Each Provider

| | Employability group | | | | | | Total | |
| | Low | | Middle | | High | | | |
Provider	Contr.	Treat.	Contr.	Treat.	Contr.	Treat.	Contr.	Treat.
Goodwill	144	402	73		164		381	402
Foundation	177		83		211	402	471	402
YOU	59		26	194	54		140	194
Total	380	402	183	194	429	402	992	998

SOURCE: Author's calculations of Kalamazoo/St. Joseph Work First administrative data, 1998–2000.

Table 8.6 Retention Rates, by Provider and Employability Group (%)

| | Low | | Middle | | High | |
Provider	Contr.	Treat.	Contr.	Treat.	Contr.	Treat.
Goodwill	15.3	15.4	21.9		22.6	
Foundation	7.9		14.5		22.3	23.4
YOU	13.6		37.0	17.0	16.7	
Average	11.6		20.8		21.7	

SOURCE: Author's calculations of Kalamazoo/St. Joseph Work First administrative data, 1996–1997.

comes, we examined six combinations.[9] The effects of the various combinations are measured by computing the number of participants within each employability group who retained their jobs if everyone in that group received services from the same provider. To illustrate this approach, consider the first combination listed in Table 8.8. The designation "gyk" refers to the combination in which all participants in the low employability group (the left-most group in Table 8.6 is hypothetically assigned to Goodwill [g]; all participants in the middle employability group are assigned to YOU [y]; and all participants in the high employability group are assigned to Behavioral Foundation [k]). Since participants in the control group were randomly assigned

Table 8.7 Upper and Lower Bounds of the 95 Percent Confidence Intervals for the Retention Rates of Each Provider (%)

| | Employability group | | | | | | | | |
| | Low | | | Middle | | | High | | |
Provider	Lower	Mean	Upper	Lower	Mean	Upper	Lower	Mean	Upper
Control group									
Goodwill	9.4	15.3	21.2	12.4	21.9	31.4	16.2	22.6	29
Foundation	3.9	7.9	11.9	6.9	14.5	22.1	16.7	22.3	27.9
YOU	4.9	13.6	22.3	18.8	37.0	55.2	6.8	16.7	26.6
Treatment group	11.9	15.4	18.9	11.7	17.0	22.3	19.3	23.4	27.5

SOURCE: Author's calculations of Kalamazoo/St. Joseph Work First administrative data, 1996–1997.

Table 8.8 Number of Participants Employed 90 Consecutive Days by Combination of Providers

Combination of providers		Employability group			Total	Ranking
		Low	Middle	High		
1	gyk	58	68	96	222	1
2	gky	58	26	72	156	5
3	ygk	52	40	96	188	3
4	ykg	52	26	97	175	4
5	kyg	30	68	97	195	2
6	kgy	30	40	72	142	6

NOTE: Providers are designated as letters: "g" = Goodwill; "k" = Foundation; and "y" = YOU. The combination "gyk" refers to the low employability group assigned to Goodwill, the middle employability group to YOU, and the high employability group to the Foundation.
SOURCE: Author's calculations of Kalamazoo/St. Joseph Work First administrative data, 1996–1997.

to each of the providers within each of the three employability groups, using the subgroup assigned to a particular subcontractor to represent the effects for everyone in that employability group is a sound approach.

Using this approach, the appropriate retention rate for each employability group is multiplied by the total number of participants in the control group to compute the number of participants within that group who retained their job for 90 consecutive days. For instance, for the first combination, the retention rate of 0.153 for Goodwill is multiplied by 380, the size of the control for the low employment group (see Table 8.5). This yields 58, which indicates that 58 participants in the control group of the low employability group would have retained their jobs if all were assigned to Goodwill. The same calculation is performed for the middle group, multiplying 0.370 by 183, which yields 68, and for the high group, multiplying 0.223 by 429, which yields 96. Summing these three numbers yields the total number of participants in the three control groups who retained their jobs, 222. Dividing by the total number of participants in the control groups results in the hypothetical retention rate if the combination "gyk" were used to assign participants.

Performing these calculations for all six combinations provides a convenient measure of the effectiveness of the various combinations. As shown in Table 8.8, the number of retentions ranges from a high of 222 for the combination "gyk" to a low of 142 for "kgy." The difference between the highest and lowest is 80 retentions, or 56 percent. The difference between the highest number and the average is 47, or 27 percent. The results indicate that using the statistical tool to assess and refer Work First participants can increase the effectiveness of the program without increasing cost. The optimal combination of providers "gyk" yields a 27 percent higher retention rate than if the participants were randomly assigned to the providers.

Differences between any of the various pairs of combinations are statistically significant at the 95 percent significance level. Table 8.9 displays the difference in the retention rates and the t-statistics for each pair of combinations. For instance, the difference between the retention rate for combination "gyk" and for combination "gky" is 0.066 (e.g., $65 \div 992$). The t-statistic for this pair is 5.26, which is much greater than the critical value of 1.96 for a 95 percent significance level. Note that 10 out of the possible 15 pairs are statistically significant. Only those with differences in the retention rates of less than 2 percentage points (approximately 20 participants out of 992) are not statistically significant.

Based upon the analysis of the effectiveness of the combinations of providers, it appears that Goodwill had a comparative advantage in serving low employability participants, YOU in serving middle employability participants, and Behavioral Foundation in serving high employability customers. This combination of assignments was the same as the treatment group, which was determined by staff knowledge of the approaches taken by each provider and an analysis of welfare recipients who had participated in the program before the pilot began. However, it is beyond the scope of the pilot to determine the specific aspects of each provider's approach that led to this outcome.[10]

Benefit/Cost Analysis of the Statistical Assessment and Referral System[11]

The benefits of using the statistical assessment and referral system can be quantified by taking into account the earnings received by those

**Table 8.9 Differences in Retention Rates between Pairs of
Combinations of Providers**

Providers	1	2	3	4	5	6
Differences in retention rates						
1 gyk	—	0.066	0.034	0.046	0.026	0.080
2 gky		—	−0.031	−0.019	−0.039	0.014
3 ygk			—	0.012	−0.008	0.045
4 ykg					−0.020	0.033
5 kyg					—	0.053
6 kgy						—
t-Statistics of difference in retention rates						
1 gyk	—	5.260	2.671	3.654	2.028	6.487
2 gky		—	−2.603	−1.618	−3.245	1.244
3 ygk			—	0.986	−0.644	3.842
4 ykg				—	−1.630	2.860
5 kyg					—	4.481
6 kgy						—

NOTE: Standard deviation derived according to the following formula:

$$\sqrt{\hat{p}\hat{q}\left(\frac{1}{n_1} + \frac{1}{n_2}\right)}$$

where $\hat{p} = \dfrac{x_1 + x_2}{n_1 + n_2}$; $\hat{q} = 1 - \hat{p}$; and x_1 and x_2 are the number of successes in the

samples of size n_1 and n_2.
SOURCE: Author's calculations of Kalamazoo/St. Joseph Work First administrative data, 1996–1997.

additional participants who retained their jobs. As shown in the previous section, the optimal assignment rule yielded a net increase of 47 participants who retained their jobs 90 consecutive days over the number retaining their jobs in the group created by random assignment. Consequently, the net effect of the statistical assessment and referral system is computed by considering the difference in retention rates and earnings of the two groups. A benefit-to-cost ratio is then calculated by dividing the net effect by the cost of the pilot.[12]

The earnings are comprised of two components: the number of participants who retained their jobs (R) and the average weekly earnings of each participant in that group during the 90 days (calculated here as 13 weeks) of employment (E). As shown in Table 8.10, the average weekly earnings of those in the optimal assignment group (referred to as the treatment group and denoted by subscript T in this section) is $192 and of those in the randomly assigned group (the control group denoted by subscript C) is $195. The difference in earnings of the two groups ($B_T - B_C$) can be decomposed in the following way, using the control group as the base of comparison:

$$B_T - B_C = [(R_T - R_C)E_C] + [(E_T - E_C)R_C] + [(R_T - R_C)(E_T - E_C)]$$

This decomposition yields the net effect in terms of additional earnings to program participants as a result of the statistical assessment and referral system. It is assumed here that the earnings difference continues for eight quarters, with two possible scenarios considered. The first scenario assumes that the difference in the number of participants retaining their jobs for 90 days persists throughout the 8 quarters. The

Table 8.10 Average Weekly Earnings by Different Combinations of Providers

Combination of providers	Average weekly earnings ($)
gyk (treatment group)	192
gky	211
ygk	181
ykg	175
kyg	165
kgy	189
Randomly assigned (control group)	195

NOTE: Providers are designated by letters: "g" Goodwill; "k" Foundation; and "y" YOU. The combination "gyk" refers to the low employability group assigned to Goodwill, the middle employability group to YOU, and the high employability group to Foundation.

second scenario assumes that the difference in job retention narrows throughout the eight-quarter period until the two series are equal. In both scenarios, wages are assumed to grow by 3 percent per year, and a 10 percent annual discount rate is used when computing the net present value of the earnings streams. As shown in Table 8.11, under the first scenario, the net present value of the difference in the earnings streams of the treatment and control groups is $840,827; under the second scenario, it is $471,054.

The additional costs incurred to develop and operate the statistical assessment and referral system for the two-year life of the pilot totaled

Table 8.11 Difference in Earnings between Treatment and Control Groups and Benefit-to-Cost Ratio of the System

| Quarters after leaving program | Treatment group earnings minus control group earnings ($) | |
	No narrowing of earnings gap	Narrowing of earnings gap
1	112,179	112,179
2	113,666	98,706
3	115,165	85,073
4	116,675	71,279
5	118,197	57,321
6	119,730	43,197
7	121,274	28,906
8	122,830	14,445
Net present value ($)	840,827	471,054
Program cost ($)	145,000	145,000
Benefit-to-cost ratio	5.8	3.3

NOTE: The first column of earnings assumes that the retention rates remain the same throughout the eight-quarter period while the average weekly earnings converge. The second column of earnings assumes that they converge until they are equal in the ninth quarter. Wages are assumed to increase 3 percent per year, and a 10 percent discount rate is assumed for the net present value calculation.

$145,000. This expense included designing and integrating the system into the existing Work First program, which cost roughly $105,000, and hiring a part-time person to administer the system during the intake and orientation process, which amounted to another $40,000 during the two-year period. Dividing the net present value for each scenario by the program costs of $145,000 yields a benefit-to-cost ratio for the first scenario of 5.8 and a ratio for the second scenario of 3.3.

CONCLUSION

The purpose of the Work First pilot was to determine the benefits of using a statistical assessment tool to target employment services to meet the needs of Work First participants more effectively. The statistical assessment tool estimated the probability that a participant would be employed for 90 consecutive days by relating this outcome to the personal characteristics and work history of former Work First participants. Estimates were based on administrative records of welfare recipients who had participated in the Work First program prior to the time of the pilot.

The evaluation yielded the following results. First, the statistical model exhibited sufficient precision to distinguish among participants according to their likelihood of working 90 consecutive days. Second, there was considerable variation in the retention rates among the various combinations of providers offering services to participants in the three employability groups, as identified by the assessment tool. The retention rate of the combination of providers that yielded the highest rate was 56 percent higher than the combination yielding the lowest rate, and 27 percent higher than if the participants were randomly assigned to providers. Third, the benefit-to-cost ratio of the pilot project ranged from 3.3 to 5.8, depending on the assumptions regarding the persistence over time of the earnings differences between the treatment and control groups.

The results of the Kalamazoo/St. Joseph Work First pilot provide evidence that the statistical assessment and referral system can be successful in identifying needs and in targeting services to help meet the needs of customers in finding jobs. By using the system developed for the pilot, more Work First participants can have successful outcomes without increasing the cost of the program. The pilot opens the possibility for statistical tools to be used to help improve the effectiveness and efficiency of other employment programs and service delivery systems.

Notes

The author acknowledges the valuable assistance of Stephen Wandner, Ronald Putz, and Jon Messenger of the U.S. Department of Labor and of Timothy Bartik, Christopher O'Leary, Lillian Vesic-Petrovic, Radika Rajachar, Kris Kracker, Robert Straits, Craig Schreuder, Phyllis Molhoek, Claire Black, and Nancy Mack of the W.E. Upjohn Institute.

1. For example, Gueron and Pauly (1991), from their evaluations of welfare-to-work demonstrations, suggest that increased service intensity improves employment rates of clients and that spreading resources too thinly reduces program effectiveness. In addition, the evaluation of programs such as California GAINS (Freedman et al. 1996) suggests the importance of assessment in getting welfare recipients into jobs.

2. Allowable work activities include 1) unsubsidized employment; 2) subsidized private sector employment; 3) subsidized public sector employment; 4) on-the-job training; 5) job search and job readiness training and activities up to six weeks; 6) community service programs; and 7) no more than 12 months of vocational educational training.

3. Individuals can and do enroll in Work First several times. However, only about 8 percent of those who enrolled during 1996 enrolled more than once. We included each enrollee only once in the sample and included their latest appearance so that we could use any previous history in the analysis.

4. These results are consistent with previous studies that examine employment prospects of welfare recipients. Estimates based on the national SIPP survey found that education and prior employment history were important determinants of the likelihood of leaving welfare for employment (see Eberts 1997, Appendix). A study for the state of Texas also found these factors to be important (Schexnayder, King, and Olson 1991). The Texas study also found that the number of children, the age of the welfare recipient, the duration on welfare, and the use of the employment service and participation in job-training programs also affected the likelihood of employment in the expected direction. The employment- and training-related results from Texas are consistent with our results from Work First that prior employment and compliance with previous Work First enrollment positively affect the likelihood of qualified employment.

5. Several criteria can be used to judge the ability of the model to distinguish among

Work First participants as to their likelihood of finding employment. Two measures are considered here: 1) the relative steepness of the distribution of each individual's employment probabilities, and 2) the width of the confidence intervals. The model satisfies both criteria, as described in Eberts (2002).

6. About half of the participants went through the program at least twice. For purposes of the evaluation, we included only the last time the person appeared in the program, if they appeared more than once. We adopted this approach to avoid biasing the evaluation toward multiple enrollees. One could argue that including the same person more than once in the evaluation overweights that person's experience relative to those who entered the program only once. More will be said about this approach in a subsequent section.

7. The actual assignment of employability scores was slightly different from the way in which the statistical assessment model was originally estimated. The model was estimated based on the entire set of individuals who participated in and completed the program during a year's time. The computation of the employability score, based on the coefficients from the model, was done at each intake and orientation session. These sessions took place twice a week. Obviously, only a small number of people who participated in the program each year attended each session.

Because of the small number of participants at each session, it may be the case that individuals in attendance on any given day were not fully representative of the Work First population. In examining the distribution of employability scores for each session, we found that on some days the employability scores would cluster on the high side, while on other days they would center on the low side of the distribution. Since the cutoffs were determined by dividing the distribution of scores of individuals who showed up on a given day, it could be the case that individuals with lower-than-average employability scores were assigned to the "high" employability group, while on another day individuals with higher-than-average employability scores were assigned to the "low" employability group. It depends upon who was referred to a particular session.

Another difference between the employability scores as originally estimated and those assigned to participants during the pilot was the magnitude of the score. We recognized that the employability scores declined over the year in which the statistical assessment model was estimated. This relationship was consistent with the general observation by the WDB staff that as an increasing number of Work First participants found jobs, those remaining would have lower skills and be harder to place into jobs. To account for this trend, we included in the model the date that the participant enrolled in the program. The coefficient on this variable (addate), as shown in Table 8.4, was relatively large and highly statistically significant. The value of the coefficient (–0.003) was large relative to the mean of the variable (approximately 14,460, which is the date expressed in machine language).

However, it turns out that as time increased from the date in which the model was estimated to when it was used to assign the employability scores, the coefficient played a much larger role in determining the size of the predicted value.

The mean value of the employability score fell from about 0.30 in the original model to 0.05 in the evaluation. Most of the difference is due to the more advanced date. When the date is rolled back to its average value during the period in which the model was estimated, the mean employability score for the sample used in the evaluation increases to 0.46.

    Further investigation shows that the rank ordering of employability scores computed with and without the adjustment for the time is highly correlated. The correlation coefficient of the actual employability score assigned to participants during the evaluation and the hypothetical one when the date of enrollment is rolled back by two years is 0.82.

8. The overlap is not as great between the low and middle employability groups as it is between the middle and high groups. The difference in the average retention rates for the low and middle employability groups is statistically significant at the 95 percent significance level. On the other hand, the difference in the average retention rates for the middle and high employability groups is not.

9. More than six combinations are possible with three providers and three groups by assigning more than one employability group to a provider. However, we adhered to the WDB's contractual arrangement during the pilot that all three providers delivered services. Therefore, we eliminated from consideration combinations that assigned two or three groups to one service provider.

10. As previously noted, the retention rate for those in the middle employability control group assigned to YOU is higher than the rate for the treatment group assigned to YOU. If, as intended, individuals were randomly assigned to the treatment and control groups, and those within the control group were randomly assigned to the providers, one would expect the two retention rates to be similar. We tried two alternative approaches of deriving retention estimates for the different combinations that may mitigate the problem. The first approach controlled for factors that could be responsible for the significant difference between the treatment and control groups assigned to a specific provider. One possible factor is the date on which participants enter the program. It could be the case that because of the small number enrolled during each session and the nonrandom nature of referrals from FIA, the time of enrollment may lead to these differences. The second method combined the outcomes of both the control and the treatment groups. In this way, we reduced the effect of the timing of enrollment by considering outcomes from both groups. Both approaches yield results that are similar to the original approach.

11. I thank Kevin Hollenbeck and Jeff Smith for suggestions and guidance on conducting the benefit/cost analysis.

12. The social value of the new system may be less than the value computed here because of displacement effects among the welfare population. It is conceivable that the additional retention by participants of the program with the new system may displace other welfare recipients from their existing jobs or preclude new Work First participants from finding jobs since the additional retentions reduce the job vacancies.

References

Eberts, Randall W. 1997. "The Use of Profiling to Target Services in State Welfare-to-Work Programs: An Example of Process and Implementation." Staff working paper no. 98-52, W.E. Upjohn Institute for Employment Research, Kalamazoo, Michigan.

———. 2002. *Design, Implementation, and Evaluation of the Work First Profiling Pilot Project.* Final report prepared by the W.E. Upjohn Institute for Employment Research for the Employment and Training Administration, U.S. Department of Labor, March.

Freedman, S., D. Friedlander, W. Lin, and A. Schweder. 1996. *The GAIN Evaluation: Five-Year Impacts of Employment, Earnings, and AFDC Receipt.* New York: Manpower Demonstration Research Corporation.

Gueron, Judith, and Edward Pauly. 1991. *From Welfare to Work.* New York: Russell Sage Foundation.

Schexnayder, Deanna, Christopher King, and Jerome Olson. 1991. "A Baseline Analysis of the Factors Influencing AFDC Duration and Labor Market Outcomes." Report to the Center for the Study of Human Resources and the Bureau of Business Research, the University of Texas at Austin.

9

Targeting Job Retention Services for Welfare Recipients

Anu Rangarajan, Peter Schochet, and Dexter Chu
Mathematica Policy Research

The Personal Responsibility and Work Opportunity Reconciliation Act of 1996 (PRWORA) terminated the welfare program known as Aid to Families with Dependent Children (AFDC). The federal government now provides states with block grants to provide cash assistance under the Temporary Assistance for Needy Families (TANF) program. States have wide discretion to structure TANF eligibility, but federal law imposes a lifetime limit of 60 months on benefit receipt and imposes work requirements on adult recipients after a maximum of two years of benefit receipt.

These changes mean that welfare recipients must now find jobs and stay employed. To help welfare recipients reach these goals, many state welfare agencies are setting up (or are considering setting up) job retention programs. However, because large numbers of welfare recipients are moving into the workforce, states may not have sufficient resources to provide job retention and advancement services to all welfare recipients who become employed. Therefore, states may want to target job retention services to those groups of newly employed welfare recipients who are at high risk of losing their jobs and who can most benefit from these services.

This chapter examines the feasibility of targeting clients for job retention services. In particular, we give states and programs some guidance on how they can identify welfare recipients for job retention services. We do not address what specific services should be offered or targeted, rather, we provide a general statistical framework that can be used to rank clients by their likelihood of having poor labor market outcomes. States can then use these rankings to target clients who are in need of services and who can benefit from them.

This chapter is in two sections. First, we provide a framework for agencies that may want to develop targeting mechanisms and discuss the key steps they must take to target clients. Then, using data from the National Longitudinal Survey of Youth (NLSY), we present a targeting strategy that can serve as a useful guide for programs that want to use it to target clients or to conduct their own targeting analysis.[1]

Using the NLSY data, we find that it is feasible to successfully identify clients who are at high risk of having labor market problems so they may be targeted for more intensive job retention services. This is because we observe diversity in the characteristics of welfare recipients and the types of jobs they find, diversity in their employment patterns over a longer period, and some association between these individual and job characteristics and long-term employment outcomes. These modest associations allow us to predict which cases are likely to have poor employment outcomes and are in particular need of job retention services. It is worth emphasizing that initial job characteristics are good predictors of job retention, and using these characteristics largely accounts for the success of our targeting analysis.

The remainder of the chapter is organized as follows. The first section describes the data and sample used in our empirical application. Next, we discuss our methodological approach to targeting and provide a framework for agencies that want to develop their own targeting mechanisms. We lay out, in six steps, how agencies or programs can conduct their own targeting. In the third section, we use the NLSY data to illustrate our approach to targeting. The data or resources to develop targeting mechanisms may not be currently available in some states or local areas, so the targeting strategy based on the NLSY data can serve as a useful guide for programs that may want to attempt to target clients before conducting their own analysis. The last section provides some concluding comments.

DATA AND SAMPLES

Our targeting analysis attempts to identify cases at high risk of adverse labor market outcomes and provide decision rules for programs to select these individuals for services. This analysis uses data from the 1979–1994 NLSY.[2] The NLSY selected a nationally representative sample of youths who were between the ages of 14 and 22 in 1979 and followed the sample members for the next 15 years, until they reached ages 29 to 37.[3] The data include detailed information on sample members' program participation, labor force participation, and other socio-demographic and economic variables.

Our sample includes 601 young women who, at some point during the panel period, started a job either while receiving AFDC or within three months after ending an AFDC spell. To observe employment experiences over the long run, the sample also includes only those welfare recipients for whom we have five years of follow-up data after initial job start.

The welfare recipients in our sample are fairly disadvantaged, although there is some diversity in their demographic characteristics. Our sample members were on average about 23 years old at the time their jobs started (Table 9.1); however, over 17 percent were teenage mothers. About 64 percent had an infant or toddler less than two years of age. About one-third of sample members did not have a high school credential. In addition, more than 50 percent scored in the bottom 25 percent of those taking the Armed Forces Qualifying Test (AFQT), although more than 15 percent scored in the upper half of test takers nationally.[4]

In general, our sample members found fairly unstable, entry-level jobs that provided low pay, offered few fringe benefits, and had high turnover. Sample members earned an average of $6.60 per hour (in 1997 dollars), and about 33 percent held jobs that paid less than $5.50 per hour; only about 20 percent found jobs that paid $8.00 or more per hour (Table 9.2). Just under half of the sample held full-time jobs (defined as jobs with 35 or more hours of work per week). In addition, just under half reported working in jobs that offered paid vacation, and about 42 percent had jobs that offered some health insurance. Finally, about 48 percent worked in evening or variable-shift jobs.

Job retention was a problem for most welfare recipients in our sample. Nearly 45 percent ended their initial employment spells within four months, and more than 75 percent ended them within one year (not shown). However, many of those who lost their jobs found new ones. For example, about 60 percent found another job within one year.

We find that because of the cycling in and out of employment, there is some diversity in the employment experiences of our sample mem-

Table 9.1 Characteristics of the Sample

Characteristic	All welfare recipients who find jobs (%)	Averages
Age at start of job (yr.)		
Less than 20	17.4	
20–24	57.1	
30 or more	2.6	
Average age		22.5
Age of youngest child (yr.)		
0–2	63.8	
3–5	28.6	
6 or older	7.6	
Average age		2.2
Child care arrangement		
Relative care	47.1	
Nonrelative care	22.5	
Center-based care	15.3	
Other arrangements	14.1	
Lives with mother/partner	55.9	
Degree attained		
High school diploma	53.6	
GED	13.0	
AFQT scores (percentile)		
Less than 10	23.9	
11–25	28.7	
26–50	31.6	
More than 50	15.8	
Average score		28.7
Has a valid driver's license	71.0	
Health limitations	6.1	
Sample size	601	

NOTE: All estimates are weighted using the 1979 sample weights. Data pertain to the start of the first observed employment spell while case was on welfare or within three months after case left welfare. Sample includes those for whom we have a five-year follow-up period.
SOURCE: Data from the 1979–1994 NLSY Surveys.

Table 9.2 Characteristics of Initial Jobs Obtained by Sample Members

Characteristic	All welfare recipients who find jobs (%)	Averages
Hourly wages (1997 $)		
Less than $4.50	21.1	
$4.50–$5.49	11.9	
$5.50–$6.49	24.2	
$6.50–$7.99	22.0	
$8 or more	20.8	
Average wages		6.59
Hours worked per week		
1–19	20.3	
20–29	16.0	
30–34	11.5	
35–39	10.1	
40–more	42.1	
Average hours worked		31.2
Weekly earnings (1997 $)		
Less than $100	21.2	
$100–$174	21.5	
$175–$249	25.1	
$250–$324	17.6	
$325 or more	14.5	
Average earnings		214.09
Fringe benefits available		
Health insurance	41.9	
Life insurance	29.1	
Paid vacation	47.1	
Shift workload		
Regular day shift	52.3	
Evening shift	31.5	
Variable shift	16.2	
Occupation		
Manager/professional/technical	7.1	
Sales	4.2	
Clerical	24.6	
Operators	12.6	
Service	36.8	

Table 9.2 (Continued)

Characteristic	All welfare recipients who find jobs (%)	Averages
Occupation (continued)		
Private household	10.1	
Other	4.5	
Sample size 601		

NOTE: All estimates are weighted using the 1979 sample weights. Data pertain to the start of the first observed employment spell while case was on welfare or within three months after case left welfare. Sample includes those for whom we have a five-year follow-up period.
SOURCE: Data from the 1979–1994 NLSY Surveys.

bers during the five-year period after they found their initial jobs. For example, as seen in Table 9.3, about 25 percent of the sample were employed in less than 25 percent of the weeks over the five-year period after initial job start, whereas about 30 percent worked more than three-quarters of the weeks during the five-year period.

Because our analysis uses data obtained before the passage of PRWORA, some of these findings should be viewed with caution. For example, the work requirements and time limits imposed by the new law may affect the number of people who enter the labor force, as well as their employment patterns. However, while the law may affect individuals' employment experiences, we do not believe that it will affect the more fundamental relationships between individual or job characteristics and employment experiences, which lie at the core of the targeting analysis.

METHODOLOGICAL APPROACH: KEY STEPS FOR MAKING TARGETING DECISIONS

Step 1: Identify Individual Characteristics

Targeting involves identifying key individual characteristics that programs can use to determine who will receive certain services. In se-

Table 9.3 Employment Experiences during the Five-Year Period after the Start of the First Employment Spell

Variable	Sample members (%)	Averages
% of total weeks employed		
Less than 25	25.8	
25–50	22.1	
50–75	22.8	
More than 75	29.3	
Average pecentage of weeks employed		52.5
Number of employment spells		
1	16.1	
2	29.9	
3	20.9	
4 or more	33.2	
Average number of spells		3.0
Sample size 601		

NOTE: Figures pertain to the percentage of sample members in the specified categories. For example, 25.8 percent of sample members worked fewer than 25 percent of weeks during the five-year period after job start.
SOURCE: Data from the 1979–1994 NLSY Surveys.

lecting characteristics, agencies must choose those perceived to be good predictors of labor market outcomes. The choices can be made on the basis of past research or on the experience of the program staff in working with clients, as well as their perceptions of who succeeds and who does not. It is important to select characteristics that can be easily identified at low cost, are readily available to program staff, and are perceived as fair. Programs might consider such characteristics as educational attainment, presence of young children, presence of supportive adults, available transportation and time to commute to a job, as well as job characteristics. In contrast, programs might want to avoid using such characteristics as test scores even if they predict outcomes well, because obtaining them on a systematic basis for all might be difficult. It is also important to minimize the number of data items that program staff will have to consider.

Step 2: Define Outcomes and Goals That Describe Risk Status

Agencies must make decisions on what they consider adverse outcomes, to define the group they intend to target for specialized services. For instance, our study shows considerable diversity among welfare recipients who find jobs. Some recipients are able to maintain their jobs more or less continuously or with only short breaks in employment. Others cycle in and out of low-paying jobs, whereas others lose their jobs and have difficulty obtaining other ones. The risk criteria that state and local agency staff use may be related to the proportion of time welfare recipients are employed during a given period, the number of jobs they hold during a given period, the proportion of time they receive welfare after job start, or other outcomes considered important for targeting of services.

Step 3: Select among Potential Characteristics

Agencies will have to choose from the list of potential characteristics for targeting, as not all identified characteristics will be good predictors of outcomes. Characteristics should only be used if they can effectively distinguish between persons with a high risk of job loss (those more likely to benefit from specialized services) and those with a low risk of job loss.

Efficiency is a key criterion for assessing whether a characteristic is a good predictor of outcomes. An efficient targeting characteristic is one that describes many high-risk cases and only a few low-risk ones. Therefore, programs that target using this variable will ensure that few resources are spent on those who are unlikely to need services. As an example, consider people who have health problems. If most people who have health problems are likely to have poor labor market outcomes, this would be an efficient characteristic on which to target. However, if many with health problems do well in the labor market, targeting on this variable may not be an efficient use of resources.

An efficient characteristic is also one that enables a program to serve a higher proportion of needy clients than would be the case if services were allocated randomly. For example, suppose that two-thirds of all welfare recipients who obtain employment were high-risk cases who likely would lose their jobs quickly. If programs randomly selected 100 clients for services, 67 (two-thirds of the 100) would be high-risk cases who may benefit from additional services. Thus, in this case, a characteristic should be selected only if more than two-thirds of those targeted for services on the basis of the characteristic were high-risk cases. Otherwise, programs could do just as well by randomly serving clients.

It is important to keep in mind that the targeting strategies we discuss here do not address the issue of effectiveness of services in promoting job retention. In selecting characteristics, programs may want to consider whether targeting on the specific characteristic has promise and whether the kinds of intervention that can be implemented for the targeted group have the potential to improve outcomes.

Step 4: Decide Whether to Use Single or Multiple Characteristics

Programs can target people for services on the basis of a single characteristic or a combination of characteristics. Under the single-characteristic approach, an agency would examine each characteristic in isolation and then would use the methods described in Step 3 to select efficient characteristics. The multiple-characteristic approach considers combinations of characteristics that individuals possess and determines how these combinations relate to the risk of adverse outcomes.[5] Programs using the single-characteristic approach would target anyone who has the characteristic for program services. With the multiple-characteristic approach, programs would consider a variety of characteristics and would select those individuals who have one or more of the characteristics, recognizing that those who face multiple barriers are likely to be at higher risk for facing adverse outcomes.

Single-characteristic approach

The main advantage of this approach is that the rules are simple to define and easy to implement. After an agency has identified a characteristic to target, any individual with that characteristic will be selected to receive special services. A second advantage is that, depending on the characteristic selected, the approach may simplify the decision of what services to provide. For example, if people with health limitations are targeted, programs may want to ensure that this group has health insurance or access to medical services.

One of the drawbacks of the single-characteristic approach is that it is less effective than the multiple-characteristic approach in identifying all high-risk cases or in ranking cases according to their need for services. Second, it is somewhat less flexible with respect to enabling programs to select different numbers of clients for possible service receipt. For instance, certain characteristics, such as health limitations, may describe only a small proportion of the overall group of individuals at high risk. Finally, program staff may consider this method unfair because it selects only individuals with certain characteristics for program services.

Multiple-characteristic approach

The main advantage of the multiple-characteristic approach is that it is better able to identify and distinguish those at high-risk for adverse outcomes. If programs make decisions on whom to target for services on a periodic basis after collecting information on a group of clients, this approach also can rank people in order of their risk of having poor outcomes and, consequently, in order of their need for services (see Step 6). This ranking feature allows programs to better select the number and types of individuals who are to receive program services. Finally, program staff may perceive it as a more equitable approach to sharing resources.

The main drawback of this approach is that it is slightly more complex than the single-characteristic approach to implement. For each individual, program staff will have to determine the combination of characteristics he or she possesses, and whether that individual needs special services.

Step 5: Select the Numbers and Types of Clients to Serve

Programs may want to have the flexibility to choose the numbers and types of clients to serve, as program resources or client needs may dictate these choices. For example, agencies confronting tight resource constraints might have to decide in advance what fraction of clients they will serve. With respect to whom to serve, some agencies may choose to serve the neediest set of individuals. In contrast, other agencies may decide that this approach is not the best use of their resources; they may prefer to spread those resources among a middle group of welfare recipients who may face fewer barriers, but who may be more likely to benefit from services. As discussed previously, because the multiple-characteristic approach allows programs to rank individuals according to their risk of having adverse outcomes, it more readily allows programs to choose the number and types of clients they want to serve.

Step 6: Time the Identification of Clients for Targeting

Program staff also have to determine the timing of targeting decisions. For instance, decisions could be made either on a periodic basis, after information on a group of clients has been collected, or on a case-by-case basis, as soon as each client is ready to receive services. This choice will depend on a number of factors, including caseload size, staff size, how quickly services can be provided, assessments of how quickly clients need services, and how quickly the decision rules can be applied.

The timing choice does not affect the way the single-characteristic approach is applied, but it does affect the way the multiple-characteristic approach is applied. If programs make decisions periodically, clients can be ranked on the basis of their likelihood of being high-risk cases, and programs could use these rankings to select cases for services. The rankings would be constructed by using aggregate "scores" for each person that are based on several characteristics (see the appendix). States use this procedure to profile unemployment insurance (UI) claimants who are likely to exhaust benefits (Wandner and Messenger 1999). Programs that make decisions on a case-by-case basis would not be able to rank cases. Instead, they would provide services to an individual if the person's aggregate score were higher than some predetermined cutoff value (see the appendix).

TARGETING STRATEGY USING NATIONAL DATA

To apply the targeting approach most effectively, each state or local agency should attempt to identify targeting characteristics appropriate to their local areas, and program staff must use local data to determine the most appropriate set of decision rules for their own location. Local area circumstances differ to varying degrees, as do the characteristics of individuals who live in each area. Consequently, agencies can create the best decision rules by using data specific to their own areas and identify the most efficient characteristics for targeting purposes.

In this section, we use data from the NLSY sample to identify targeting characteristics for programs that are considering providing job retention services to welfare recipients who find jobs.[6] This analysis has two purposes. First, for agencies that want to conduct their own targeting analysis, this discussion illustrates how to use the proposed targeting framework discussed in the previous section. Second, for agencies that currently lack the data or tools required to conduct targeting analyses but that may be interested in targeting, the NLSY provides preliminary decision rules.

It is important to recognize that our decision rules are based on national data and on our definition of high-risk cases. Caseload characteristics in any given locality might differ from the characteristics of the individuals in our sample. Moreover, the relationship between individual characteristics and employment outcomes may differ across localities. Program staff who choose to use the rules proposed in this report should consider these findings as broad guidelines, and should adapt them to their local circumstances to the extent possible.

Using the NLSY data, we examined eight potential characteristics that programs could use to select individuals for targeting job retention services:

- was a teenage mother at the time of initial employment;
- was employed less than half the time in the year preceding initial employment;
- has no high school diploma or GED;
- has a preschool child;
- received less than $8 per hour (in 1997 dollars) as starting pay in job;
- receives no fringe benefits on the job;
- does not have a valid driver's license;
- has health limitations.

In defining outcomes, we focus on sustained employment during the five-year period after job start. We defined a high-risk case as one who worked less than 70 percent of the weeks during that period.[7] We now summarize the findings from our analysis.

- It is possible to identify single characteristics by using the univariate procedure to identify and target services to high-risk cases.

Table 9.4 shows the efficiency measures of the eight potential targeting variables. The first column presents the sample means (that is, the percentage of individuals who have each characteristic), and the second shows the proportion in that group who need services (that is, who had poor employment outcomes). We find that three-quarters or more of those in three of the eight groups (age less than 20 years, high school dropout, and health limitations) are high-risk cases. For instance, programs that targeted people younger than 20 years of age at the time of initial employment would serve about 17 percent of all welfare recipients who found employment. However, more than 80 percent of those served would be high-risk cases. Similarly, by targeting those with health limitations, programs would serve only 6 percent of all cases, but about 88 percent who receive services would be high-risk cases. If programs wanted to serve high school dropouts, they would serve about 34 percent of all cases. About three-quarters would need services.[8]

Targeting on most of the other variables individually produced either no better or only slightly better results than would have been obtained if the programs were to serve a random set of individuals who find jobs. This finding is driven in part by the fact that a high fraction of the sample members have these characteristics. For instance, more than 90 percent have a preschool child. However, according to our definition of high risk, only two-thirds of the full sample are likely to need services. Therefore, by targeting this group, programs will serve many more cases than need services, which will lead to inefficient use of resources.

- Programs can do better by using a combination of characteristics and applying the multiple-characteristic procedure for targeting.

By using the same set of eight characteristics, the multiple-characteristic or multivariate procedure produced decision rules that were

Table 9.4 Selecting Individual Characteristics for Targeting Purposes Using the Univariate Procedure

Characteristic	% of sample with characteristic	% with characteristic that needs services[a]	% of all high-risk cases receiving services
Age younger than 20 yr.	17.4	80.6	21.7
Employed less than half the time in year prior to job start	79.2	66.6	83.0
No high school diploma/GED	34.2	74.8	39.3
Presence of preschool child	92.4	64.4	93.6
Wage less than $8 in 1997 dollars	79.2	65.6	83.2
No fringe benefits	81.1	70.0	87.8
No valid driver's license	29.0	71.8	32.6
Has health limitations	6.1	88.1	8.3

NOTE: Characteristics are defined at the start of the initial employment spells.
[a] Refers to those in the group who are at high risk for adverse employment outcomes.
SOURCE: Data from the 1979–1994 NLSY Surveys.

able to distinguish between high- and low-risk cases reasonably accurately. Table 9.5 displays findings on how well the multivariate method performed for different fractions of overall caseloads that programs might want to serve.[9] From Columns 1 and 2, we see that if programs serve 10 percent of their caseloads, more than 90 percent of those served will need services (assuming that programs serve the cases at highest risk for negative employment outcomes). Similarly, if they choose to serve 50 percent of their caseloads, more than 80 percent of those served will be high-risk cases who may benefit from services. The values in Column 2 suggest that as programs become more selective with respect to the numbers to serve, they are better able to identify the highest-risk cases.[10]

Compared with the single-characteristic decision rule, the multiple-characteristic decision rule will serve a greater proportion of high-risk

Table 9.5 Efficiency of the Multiple-Characteristic Approach for Targeting Purposes Using the Multivariate Procedure

Fraction of cases served, ranked according to highest level of risk (%)	% that need services[a]	% of all high-risk cases
10	91.1	12.6
20	90.2	27.3
30	87.8	39.2
40	84.6	50.0
50	82.1	60.8
60	79.9	72.7
70	77.9	80.8
80	74.4	88.2
90	71.5	95.1

[a] Refers to those in the group served who are at high risk for adverse employment outcomes.
SOURCE: Data from the 1979–1994 NLSY Surveys.

cases for the same total number of people served. For example, programs that want to serve about 20 percent of their cases could choose to serve teenage mothers (see Table 9.4), or they could use the multivariate method to choose the 20 percent with the highest probability of poor outcomes. By targeting the single characteristic, 80 percent of those served will be high-risk cases; according to the multivariate methods, more than 90 percent will be high-risk cases (Tables 9.4 and 9.5).

- Implementing decision rules is straightforward. However, programs must take into account their own goals and area characteristics when applying these rules.

If programs choose to use the single-characteristic decision rules, implementation is straightforward. Program staff would identify cases with a particular characteristic and would provide services only to those cases.

Program staff could implement the multivariate decision rule in two stages. In the first stage, program staff would calculate an aggregate score for each individual based on the characteristics the individual possesses. The weights attached to each characteristic, displayed in Table 9.6, would be used to construct these aggregate scores.[11] For example, a high school dropout who has a wage of $6 per hour and no fringe benefits, but none of the other characteristics listed in Table 9.6, would receive an aggregate score of 10 (3 + 2 + 5). Individuals with higher aggregate scores are more likely to be high-risk cases than are those with lower scores.

In the second stage, programs would use the aggregate scores to identify cases requiring special services. If program staff decide to make targeting decisions periodically, after collecting information on a group of clients, they would rank all these clients on the basis of their aggregate scores and would select those with the highest scores. However, if program staff decide to make targeting decisions sequentially, on a case-by-case basis, they would have to measure an individual's aggregate score against a cutoff value and provide services if the aggregate score were higher than that cutoff value. The cutoff values are dis-

Table 9.6 Checklist for Multivariate Targeting

Barriers	Weight	Check characteristic	Associated points
Age younger than 20	✓✓	☐	—
Employed less than half the time in year prior to job start	✓✓	☐	—
No high school diploma/GED	✓✓✓	☐	—
Presence of preschool child	✓✓	☐	—
Wage less than $8 in 1997 dollars	✓✓	☐	—
No fringe benefits	✓✓✓✓	☐	—
No valid driver's license	✓✓	☐	—
Has health limitations	✓✓✓✓	☐	—
		Total score	_____

NOTE: Discussion of the calculation of the weights is contained in the appendix.
SOURCE: Data from the 1979–1994 NLSY Surveys.

Table 9.7 Cutoff Scores for Multivariate Targeting

Fraction served (%)	Cutoff levels
70	10
50	12
30	14
20	15
10	17

NOTE: Discussion of the calculation of the cutoffs is contained in the appendix.
SOURCE: Data from the 1979–1994 NLSY Surveys.

played in Table 9.7 and depend on the fraction of the caseload that the programs want to serve. In particular, the fewer cases a program wants to serve, the higher the cutoff value it will have to use. Thus, if the program had the goal of serving at least 70 percent of cases, a client with an aggregate score of 10 would receive services (because the cutoff value would be 10). If the goal was to serve only 50 percent of cases, this person would not receive services (because the cutoff value would be 12).

As we have mentioned, the decision rules described here were created using information on a nationally representative sample of youths who received welfare and found a job at some point between 1979 and 1990. The caseload characteristics in any locality might differ from the characteristics of the individuals in our sample. Moreover, the relationship between the characteristics and being a high-risk case may differ among localities. Program staff are encouraged to work with researchers to generate their own set of weights and cutoff values using local data. However, program staff who decide to use our results as guidelines should adjust them based on good-sense judgments of local area characteristics (in the absence of data for analysis). For instance, in urban areas with mass transit, programs may want to ignore whether or not a welfare recipient has a driver's license in calculating weights, as this characteristic is unlikely to form a barrier to work. Furthermore, program staff may want to adjust their cutoff values downward because they are dropping this characteristic from consideration.

CONCLUSIONS

Our analysis has shown that programs can successfully identify high-risk cases using data on individual and job characteristics that are likely to be available to program staff. Programs can use single characteristics (such as age, education levels, or health problems) to identify high-risk cases. Alternatively, they can more accurately identify high-risk cases by targeting on a combination of client characteristics. The decision rules we construct can provide guidance to programs that want to target clients, and the programs can use the framework to develop their own decision rules.[12]

The challenge for program operators as they decide to go ahead with targeting is how to select cases so that resources can be put to the best use. Differences in program goals and resources, local circumstances, and area and client characteristics all determine whom programs might want to target. Because of these differences, each state or local area ideally should conduct its own assessments of the feasibility of targeting and should identify the key characteristics most appropriate for targeting in its local area. Conducting these assessments and formulating targeting decisions at the state or local level will require data, both on the characteristics of welfare recipients and on the outcomes, so that a determination can be made of how characteristics relate to outcomes.

Before attempting to target individuals for job retention services, programs have to consider several factors. First, programs should consider whether there is sufficient diversity among welfare recipients' characteristics, the types of jobs they find, and their employment experiences. For example, if all welfare recipients who find jobs have a hard time holding on to their jobs, targeting would not be very meaningful. However, if some groups of individuals can hold sustained employment on their own, while others cannot, programs may want to know who the latter are so they can focus resources more intensively on those who most need them. A second factor that may determine whether or not a program targets clients for services depends on whether it has resource constraints. If a program has no resource constraints, it can serve all clients. By doing so, it will ensure that everyone who potentially needs services is covered. However, if programs want to use their resources efficiently, they may want to allocate their resources to those who most need services. Finally, the types of services being provided may guide whether targeting makes sense. If a program is considering delivering intensive services that are costly and require extensive outreach, it may be worth considering targeting. However, if a program is considering a more passive approach to service delivery (for example, making available job search assistance or child care subsidies, where service use may be driven by client demand), targeting may be less relevant.

Notes

This research was supported by Department of Health and Human Services Contract Number 282-92-0044 (21). We are grateful to Lawrence Wolf, Nancye Campbell, Howard Rolston, and Kelleen Kaye at DHHS, Stuart Kerachsky, Alan Hershey, and Phil Gleason at Mathematica, and Chris O'Leary and Timothy Bartik from the Upjohn Institute for useful comments. We also thank Tim Novak for skillful programming support, Laura Berenson, and Patricia Ciaccio for skillful editing, and Jennifer Baskwell for exemplary production support.

1. Some government agencies are already profiling clients so they can be targeted for services. For example, since 1994, all states have identified those cases who file for benefits under the Unemployment Insurance (UI) program who are likely to exhaust their UI benefits (Eberts and O'Leary 1996). In this volume, Eberts (see p. 221) discusses the use of profiling to target services in state welfare-to-work programs.
2. To increase sample sizes, the random and supplemental samples were used for the analysis.
3. Our sample excludes the small fraction of older women who receive welfare. For instance, in 1995, about 14 percent of households receiving welfare were headed by individuals over 40 years of age.
4. More detailed information on characteristics of sample members, the jobs they found, and their employment experiences can be found in Rangarajan, Schochet, and Chu (1998).
5. The appendix briefly discusses the methods by which agencies can implement the single- or multiple-characteristic approach.
6. In this section, we focus on targeting welfare recipients who have found jobs for job retention services. The general targeting approach, however, can be used by agencies that may want to consider targeting clients for other types of services.

7. Nearly two-thirds of the NLSY sample members were classified as being at high risk for adverse labor market outcomes. The 70 percent cutoff is based on the results of "cluster analysis" that split the sample into those who had low earnings and intermittent jobs (the high-risk cases that were employed less than 70 percent of the time) and those with higher earnings and more stable employment (the low-risk cases).

8. The third column of Table 9.4 shows the percentage of all high-risk cases who would be served by targeting on each characteristic. For example, by targeting on those people younger than 20 years of age at time of initial employment, programs would serve about 22 percent of all high-risk cases.

9. The purpose of Table 9.5 is to indicate how well the multiple-characteristic approach performs (compared with the single-characteristic approach described in Table 9.4).

10. The multivariate decision rule also gives programs the flexibility to decide whom to serve or the types of services to provide. For example, programs may choose to provide the most intensive services to the top 5 percent of the highest-risk cases and to provide less intensive services to the next 20 or 30 percent of the cases that may benefit from certain types of job retention services.

11. The weights are calculated from a simple regression model and reflect the relative magnitudes of the coefficient estimates from the model. The estimation of the model is described in the appendix.

12. To some extent, programs may already be targeting clients for job retention services, although they may not explicitly call it targeting. For instance, programs may allow clients to "self-select" into programs, or case managers may conduct assessments and then decide who receives what type of assistance. The targeting tool presented in this chapter can help case managers as they decide how to direct clients to appropriate services.

Appendix:

Statistical Methods for the Multivariate Targeting Analysis

The multivariate targeting procedure provides decision rules to target cases for postemployment services on the basis of a combination of their individual and job characteristics. This appendix provides details on the statistical aspects of how this procedure can be implemented by program staff who choose to create multivariate decision rules using their own caseload data. This same procedure was used to create the decision rules using the NLSY data that we describe in this report.

To construct decision rules using the multivariate procedure, programs must first identify individual and job characteristics that potentially can be used for targeting. In addition, programs must decide who the group is that they consider at risk of adverse employment outcomes. Finally, they must collect data on a representative sample of their caseload—the test sample—so that decision rules constructed using this sample will apply to cases they will serve in the future. The data must include information on the targeting variables *and* on employment outcomes so that programs can define which cases in the sample are high-risk cases (using their own definitions of a high-risk case).

The tools necessary to construct decision rules are 1) weights needed to assign to each targeting variable, and 2) cutoff values to determine which cases should be targeted for services. These tools are obtained from a regression model, where the targeting variables are used to predict whether a case in the test sample was a high-risk case. Program staff can then use these tools to determine whether the cases that programs serve in the future should be targeted for specialized postemployment services.

The tools necessary to construct decision rules using the multivariate approach can be obtained in the following three steps.

1) *Estimate a logit regression model.* Using data on the test sample, programs should regress the probability that a case was a high-risk case on the selected targeting variables (such as individual and job characteristics).[1] The parameter estimates from this model represent the effects of each targeting variable on the likelihood that a case should be targeted for services. Many statistical software packages can be used to estimate the model. Targeting variables that have little ability to predict who is a high-risk case (that is, that are statistically

insignificant) should be removed from the model, and the model should be reestimated. The overall predictive power of the final model should be assessed using the criteria presented in this report.[2]

2) *Construct weights to assign to each targeting variable.* The weights are the parameter estimates from the logit model. Program staff may want to scale each of the weights by a fixed factor (for example, 10 or 100) and then round them to make the weights user-friendly.[3]

3) *Construct cutoff values for different assumptions about the proportion of the caseload that programs may want to serve.* To construct the cutoff values, programs first need to construct an "aggregate score" for each case in the test sample. The aggregate score for a particular case is a weighted average of measures of the case's characteristics, where the weights are those constructed in step 2.

The cutoff values can then be constructed using these aggregate scores. Suppose that a program aims to serve 10 percent of the caseload. The cutoff value for that program is selected so that 10 percent of those in the test sample have an aggregate score greater than the cutoff value, and 90 percent have an aggregate score less than the cutoff value. Similarly, the cutoff value for a program that aims to serve 40 percent of the caseload is that value such that 40 percent of those in the test sample have an aggregate score greater than that value.

Once these weights and cutoff values have been obtained using the test sample, programs can use these tools to target cases in the future for specialized postemployment services. The process of assigning cases, however, will differ depending on how sites choose to time the selection process. Programs may choose to target after collecting information on a large number of cases. In these instances, aggregate scores should be constructed for each case by taking a weighted average of the case's characteristics near the job start date and using the weights constructed in step 2 above. Cases should then be ranked on the basis of their aggregate scores, and programs should select cases with large scores. Alternatively, programs may choose to assign a case in isolation as soon as they have information on the case. In these instances, a case should be targeted for services if the case's aggregate score is above the selected cutoff value (created in step 3 above). The relevant cutoff value to use will depend on the proportion of the caseload the program desires to target.

Appendix Notes

1. For example, the following logit model could be estimated using maximum likelihood methods:

$$\text{Pr(case was high risk)} = \frac{e^{x'\beta}}{1 + e^{x'\beta}}$$

   where x is a vector of characteristics for an individual, and β is a vector of parameters to be estimated. Alternatively, a probit regression model could be estimated.

2. Specifically, this assessment can be performed in four main steps: 1) predicted probabilities should be constructed for each individual using the equation in the previous footnote based on the estimated parameters; 2) individuals should be sorted on the basis of their predicted probabilities; 3) a prespecified percentage of individuals with the largest predicted probabilities should be "selected" for services; and 4) the proportion of those selected for services who are actually high-risk cases should be calculated. The model has sufficient predictive power if the proportion calculated in step 4 is larger than the proportion that would occur if all cases were randomly assigned to services. The assessment should be performed for various prespecified percentages used in step 3.

3. This procedure was used to create the checklist of weights in Table 12 of Rangarajan, Schochet, and Chu (1998), where the logit model was estimated using data on the NLSY sample.

References

Eberts, Randall W., and Christopher J. O'Leary. 1996. "Design of the Worker Profiling and Reemployment Services System and Evaluation in Michigan." Staff working paper no. 96-41, W.E. Upjohn Institute for Employment Research, Kalamazoo, Michigan.

Rangarajan, Anu, Peter Schochet, and Dexter Chu. 1998. *Employment Experiences of Welfare Recipients Who Find Jobs: Is Targeting Possible?* Volume I. Princeton, New Jersey: Mathematica Policy Research, Inc.

Wandner, Stephen A., and Jon C. Messenger. 1999. *Evaluation of Worker Profiling and Reemployment Services Policy Workgroup: Final Report and Recommendations.* Washington, D.C.: U. S. Department of Labor, Employment and Training Administration.

Comments on Chapter 9

Timothy J. Bartik

W.E. Upjohn Institute for Employment Research

The chapter by Rangarajan, Schochet, and Chu develops a simple model that uses data from the National Longitudinal Survey of Youth (NLSY) to predict whether a welfare recipient who gets a job will be employed less than 70 percent of the weeks during the five years after starting the job. These individuals are considered at risk or in need of services.

The chapter outlines how data on individuals can be used to estimate a single- or multiple-characteristic model that can target who is most likely to be at risk. The multiple-characteristic model does better in predicting who is at risk. The authors estimate a logit model predicting which ex-welfare recipients will have employment retention problems and then restate these logit coefficients as simple weights, which can be used to assign points to each client. This approach could easily be implemented by agencies. An agency would measure each client's characteristics, multiply by the weight on each characteristic to get a certain number of points, and add up all these points to determine which clients are the neediest. In the model estimated here, risk is best predicted by whether the person has health limitations, whether the job lacks fringe benefits, and whether the person lacks a high school diploma or GED. Less importance is estimated for other characteristics, such as the job's wage, the client's age, prior employment, or possession of a driver's license. All these characteristics could easily be measured by a social agency, so it would be straightforward for the agency to predict which clients out of a group of potential clients would be most likely to have employment retention problems.

From my perspective as a social scientist, I would like to see an appendix that gives the actual estimates of the logit model. Of course, agencies don't need the actual point estimates and standard errors to implement the model, as long as they have the weights. But the main issues I want to raise go beyond the authors' model to consider the possible purposes of targeting models. In addition, I want to consider how such purposes might vary between targeting unemployment insurance (UI) services and targeting welfare services.

One purpose of targeting models is to best allocate a limited social program budget among potential clients. Given the shortage of funds, we can't serve everyone who might need services. We would prefer to have some rational basis for targeting services. Targeting based on need is appealing, both politically and morally, and the authors have developed an algorithm for this, for which they are to be commended. Targeting based on need is better than simply flipping a coin.

In addition to moral or political purposes, targeting might have the purpose of maximizing the total "value-added" of social services. Targeting might help social programs maximize their value-added in two ways. First, for a given service, a targeting algorithm might identify those who would gain the greatest value-added from the service. Second, if the program offers several services, targeting algorithms might identify those clients who would most gain from a particular service or mix of services.

Compared with targeting based on client need, targeting to maximize program value-added is much more difficult. Ideally, such targeting would be based on estimates of the effects of program participation on outcomes in a model that allows such effects to vary with the characteristics of the person or job. If we want to target different services to different persons, such a model would need to be estimated separately for program participation in different services. This type of targeting is more difficult than what the authors have tried to do, or what most of the targeting literature has tried to do, because the models needed for such targeting are more difficult to estimate. As is well known, there are generally big issues of selection bias in estimating the effects of program participation, as persons who participate in a program may self-select or be selected by the programs. Without some corrections for this selection bias, the estimated effects of program participation may instead represent the effects of this selection.

If we could predict client need extremely accurately, and some people had zero need for services, obviously there would be some correlation between predicted need and value-added: for those with zero need for services, there can be no value-added of services. But in the authors' research, and in the research of others, our predictions of need are usually quite imperfect. Given this imperfection, it is unclear whether predicted need has any correlation with program value-added.

There are some differences between recipients of UI and welfare that make targeting more difficult for welfare recipients. First, I suspect that there is less of a correlation between need and value-added for welfare recipients than for UI recipients. Some people do fine in the labor market on their own and don't need services. Others, who may be a bit needier could benefit greatly from services. Other people do horribly in the labor market, and the kinds of services we can afford to offer don't help. In other words, I have a triage view of the effectiveness of services in improving clients' labor market outcomes. Among UI recipients, I suspect we mostly have persons from the first and second group: people who don't need services, and somewhat needier people who could benefit from services. Hence, it is intuitively plausible that targeting on need could proxy for targeting on value-added, although one would like studies to confirm this. Among welfare recipients, I suspect we have many recipients who fall into the third group and are very needy, but are perhaps too needy for the services we can offer to really help them. So I suspect targeting based on need is less of a proxy for targeting based on value-added. The authors recognize this possible problem, but they need to discuss it further.

A second difference between UI recipients and welfare recipients is the difference in possible services to offer. For UI, the targeting issue is whom to target for mandatory job search assistance. The evidence suggests that such a service probably helps a wide variety of persons gain employment more quickly. For welfare, there is more uncertainty about what services should be offered and more actual variation in services offered. In my view, the services offered to welfare recipients should differ quite a bit, because welfare recipients are a very needy population. Tolstoy's opening sentence in *Anna Karenina* claimed that "Happy families are all alike; every unhappy family is unhappy in its own way." Perhaps we can adapt this observation to social programs to say that the deeper the problems of a potential client of a social program, the more complex and diverse are their needs for services.

Because different welfare recipients will benefit from different services, the type of targeting we do for welfare recipients should depend on what services we are able to offer. Targeting services based on whether the welfare recipient is disabled makes more sense if we have services that provide support for people with disabilities. If we lack such services, I doubt whether targeting based on disability will improve program value-added. Targeting clients based on whether their job placement has fringe benefits makes sense if we have a postemployment service that can help clients find better jobs, or help clients get the Medicaid benefits to which they are entitled. This suggests another possible use of the authors' estimates, which is to decide what services should be offered, not which clients to target. We should seek to adjust our services to what the clients need, not simply adjust the clients served to what we happen to offer.

For highly needy populations such as welfare recipients, doing targeting right requires much more than a statistical targeting algorithm for choosing clients. Welfare reform is already providing the simple services of mandatory job search and work activities. We have already thrown off welfare most of the welfare recipients who can readily find a job if forced to do so. Those who remain on welfare probably need a very diverse set of intensive services. This requires at least two stages to targeting: first, through some simple targeting algorithms, determining who needs more intensive tests to determine specific service needs, and second, based on these more intensive tests, determining what mix of specific services to provide to each client.

For example, work by Sandra and Sheldon Danziger and their colleagues indicates that many welfare recipients are clinically depressed (Danziger et al. 2000). Some welfare recipients may need antidepressants as much or perhaps more than they need job training, but we can't prescribe antidepressants based on a statistical targeting algorithm or a short intake interview. We can use the targeting algorithms to allocate the scarce resource of expensive diagnostic tests. These more expensive diagnostic tests, such as medical exams, would then be used to target specific services.

In sum, the chapter by Rangarajan, Schochet, and Chu is a well-done first step toward the important goal of being able to target job retention services based on need. But we have much more work to do to accomplish the more important but complex goal of targeting the right services to the right clients in order to maximize program value-added.

References

Danziger, Sandra K., Mary Corcoran, Sheldon Danziger, Colleen Heflin, Ariel Kalil, Judith Levine, Daniel Rosen, Kristin Seefeldt, Kristine Siefert, and Richard Tolman. 2000. "Barriers to the Employment of Welfare Recipients." In *Prosperity for All? The Economic Boom and African Americans*, R. Cherry and W. Rodgers, eds. New York: Russell Sage Foundation, pp. 239–277.

Tolstoy, Leo. 1878. *Anna Karenina*. Available on-line at http://www.literature.org/authors/tolstoy-leo/anna-karenina/part-01/chapter-01.html; last accessed December 2001.

Comments on Chapters 8 and 9

Don Oellerich
U.S. Department of Health and Human Services

These chapters are quite timely and important. They address an issue for welfare that has received limited attention—the profiling and targeting of employment-related services to recipients of cash assistance. While not new to the welfare world, the emphasis on work began in the late 1960s with the Work Incentive program and was further emphasized in the 1984 amendments, which created the Job Opportunities in the Business Sector program. Welfare reform of 1996 and the creation of the Temporary Assistance for Needy Families (TANF) marked a giant step in welfare by placing an increased emphasis on work. Both chapters focus on targeting a defined at-risk group for services, moving systematically from the greater welfare population to a smaller group of needy recipients.

Peter Schochet commented that the U.S. Department of Health and Human Services (HHS) is relatively new to reemployment services. While this is true, we have been involved in a large number of random-assignment welfare-to-work experiments since the 1980s. While neither targeting nor profiling was a focus of these experiments, identifying who would benefit from a given set of services has been part of the agenda. Program administrators need to be able to target different types of programs and services to those clients most in need and most likely to benefit. This is particularly true for high-cost services and differentially targeting very disadvantaged and long-term recipients. An example of an early targeting approach was a model employed in Riverside, California. The initial placement into either job search or basic needs training was made based on objective assessment of the applicant's education level—if she had a high school diploma, she was referred to job search. For those with high school degrees, their success or failure in the labor market was the screener for the need for training. This model has become known as the Work First model and has gained wide acceptance with states in operating their TANF programs. Work First has proven to be effective in moving welfare recipients to work very quickly.

Both of the previous chapters take positive steps in moving forward the idea that we can make valid predictions for welfare recipients and identify those who are likely or not likely to succeed in the labor force. Chapter 8, by Eberts, focused on Work First, which in my mind is the dominant model used by states for the treatment of welfare recipients, particularly as they enter the program. Chapter 9, by Rangarajan, Schochet, and Chu, deals with the other end. That is, how to maintain employment for those welfare recipients who manage to get a job, and how to help them leave welfare. Both chapters make the case that targeting could provide a useful tool for defining who might be in need of services, or who is at risk of failing. I don't think the authors go far enough. We need to extend this work to not only identify those at risk but also to identify points of intervention; that is, identify the service needs of clients and identify the strengths that clients bring with them. This is a lot to ask from such models.

HHS is very interested in targeting services, and it is developing several new projects in that direction. These projects are looking at both welfare-to-work strategies for entering and current recipients (the focus of Chapter 8) and job retention and advancement (the focus of the Chapter 9). Hopefully we will learn more over the coming years. An example of a project focused on the former is one jointly sponsored by the Office of the Assistant Secretary for Planning and Evaluation and the Administration for Children and Families (ACF). This project has two components. The first is to get a broad sweep of what is currently going on in the welfare world in terms of identifying disadvantaged clients and targeting them for services. The second piece of this project is more in depth; we will go to 8 to 10 states and observe what the localities are doing. A second project is in the area of retention and advancement; here again, targeting and profiling will come in handy. In the past, the approach has been for those who leave welfare for work to be terminated from the program with little or no employment related services. Today, retention and advancement is an important part of our agenda for ensuring the success of welfare reform. If you start off in a job that is not great or even one that is just okay, we want to provide a set of services that will help you advance in that job, earn a higher wage, and move to a new and better job if that is what is needed. The track record thus far for advancement and retention services is not very positive. ACF, as a first phase in furthering our understanding, is currently awarding planning grants to 13 states to work on retention strategies. From these 13 states it is hoped that we can secure at least several random assignment sites for evaluation purposes of the various strategies that are developed.

A last project I want to mention is one being carried out in Maryland, sponsored by ACF. In this project, they are examining the implementation of assessment practices by line workers at client intake. The aim is to document the information that line workers have for supporting decision making and to find out what changes in this information base would make line workers more effective.

A key point, which has already been mentioned, is that welfare reform has made fundamental changes in the way welfare operates. Eligibility determination and check-writing used to be the main job of line workers. Tools were developed so they could do that job right, and they did it very well. Now they have a new role. Not only do they have to work on eligibility, they have to work on being a job coach, an employment counselor, a needs assessor, and a referral person to direct clients into the right services. Front-line staff need a whole new set of tools that are not yet in welfare offices.

Part of the reason for the increased focus on work is the Personal Responsibility and Work Opportunity Reconciliation Act (PRWORA) of 1996. People who are on welfare have to go to work to maintain their benefits, and there is pressure on the states to get people to work. The initial target is to have 25 percent of the caseload in work-related activities, with this target rising to 50 percent of the caseload in 2002 and thereafter; that is, half the people on the welfare roles have to be in work activities. Also, the hours that these people must be participating has gone up, along with the participation rate. The requirement started at 20 hours and is now at 25, and it will soon go up to 30 hours a week. Part-time work will no longer help meet performance targets. The pressure is on the line worker to make decisions about who needs what, and when to move them to the right place.

There are some additional incentives for states to do the right things. Our financial incentives for high performance total $200 million per year. These payments reward work outcomes, job placement, and success in the labor force. Success in the labor force has two components: job retention and wage growth. Again, there is an incentive to provide what we call postemployment services. You want to get people into work and move them along. A targeting strategy that would help us to identify those people in need and what they need would come in very handy. Models such as the one demonstrated by Eberts or one that could be developed based on the results of Rangarajan, Schochet, and Chu may help to fill this need.

Peter Schochet raised some good questions. Do the associations between the variables estimated in the models still hold, or have they changed? I believe that the associations have changed, and one of the things that I heard through the day is the need to develop the models and periodically update them so they are in tune with what is happening.

Welfare recipients always went to work. There was always a portion of the caseload that left very quickly, went to work, but unfortunately came back. So the data from the analysis show about half of the people leaving welfare, with about half of those leaving for work and half of them coming back onto public assistance within a year. Preliminary data on trends since PRWORA was enacted in 1996 suggest that things are changing. People are still leaving for work, but in higher proportions: instead of half, about 60 to 65 percent are getting jobs at exit. That is as high as anything that we have seen in any of the welfare-to-work experiments. It is just phenomenal as far we are concerned.

Equally important is the fact that people who leave are much less likely to come back onto the welfare rolls. Previously, half of the people would return within a year. In some states, the fraction has now dropped to 20 percent. People are going out, finding, and keeping a job. How well are they doing? We are studying that in 13 or 14 different locations. A number of states are also doing their own evaluations. We have what we call the "welfare leavers" studies, because the first question that was asked after welfare reform is, what is happening to all of these people leaving? The caseload in late 1998 was 44 percent lower than it was in 1993. There were about 2.2 million fewer families on in December 1998 compared with January 1993.

Not only is work effort up for people who are leaving welfare rolls, but it is up for the people still receiving assistance. It used to be that in any month, about 8 percent of the caseload was engaged in work. The recent data indicate that this fraction is up to 18 percent. Beyond PRWORA, we believe that these results are due to a combination of a strong economy and changes in the way that states figure earnings disregards. The old rules likely discouraged work. Newer policies such as Michigan's, where they are allowed to keep the first $200 plus 20 percent of anything beyond, encourage work. So we are seeing more work happening all of the time.

We would like to target people for additional services while they are on the caseload so they can increase their labor supply and move on. Many welfare recipients have characteristics that would classify them as at-risk. Schochet said that in his data, two-thirds of his sample could be considered at-risk. The question that needs to be addressed is, what are the service needs of this large group of at-risk clients?

Tim Bartik mentioned, and I know Sheldon Danziger talks about this fact, that people with mental disabilities, mental health problems, and learning disabilities are a very large share of the welfare caseload. People with cognitive impairments, developmental disabilities, substance abuse problems, and victims of domestic violence are all clients. About half of the caseload can be considered long-term, meaning that they have received assistance for 30 months or more. People who have been on welfare for 30 months or more don't do a lot of working. They don't have a strong labor force attachment. About 45 percent of this group have neither a GED nor a high school diploma. Reading and math skills are an employment barrier for between 40 and 50 percent, physical disability hinders 20 to 35 percent, about 15 percent have debilitating substance abuse problems, and domestic violence affects 20 to 30 percent of the caseload in any given year.

As Schochet pointed out, if there is no variability in the caseload, you cannot target services. As caseloads decline, I expect that the variability in client types will diminish on the welfare rolls and that remaining clients will be increasingly harder to serve. In terms of observable characteristics, the trends observed for entry cohorts from 1988 to 1997 are the age of the mother at entrance, the age of the mother at first birth, and education of the mother and youngest child. There had been no change in program entrance, but the caseload itself is changing slightly, meaning that there is a distinct population of those leaving.

State-by-state variation in client populations is quite large: some states have had caseload reductions of 90 percent. That is, they have 10 percent of their former caseload from just 1993 to 1998. Other states may have seen caseload reductions of 11 percent. The big states of California and New York have reduced caseloads by about 25 percent.

We will certainly have variation among the states, rather than one size fits all. I like the idea of the Upjohn Institute model, where it could be adapted to other states and reestimated because it uses information that is readily available. When I look at Eberts's model, I noticed that it only explained about 10 percent of the variation. What that tells me is that 90 percent of the variation is still left unexplained by the set of variables. So there is a lot of randomness in this selection process, even when your probability is spread. Additional variables might help reduce this unexplained variation. I liked the implementation plan. It was simple and straightforward.

I think that the model Eberts presented with the personal computer-based operating system is really nice and slick. For a line worker to have something like that at their disposal to help direct clients would be a great help. It's a great advance over what is currently done. On the welfare side, we clearly have a tendency to ask, what do clients need? That requires a systematic plan for assessment and referral.

I conclude with two final thoughts. One concern I have is the time required for assessment; the distribution appears to be bimodal. Clients appear to require either 2 hours or 20 hours for assessment. Is it the case that those requiring 20 hours have more risk factors? I was unclear about what's going on in the assessment box. It would be helpful if you tell us about that. Also, it would be helpful to know how the reemployment probability correlates to the time required for assessment.

Part III

Canadian Approaches for Targeting Employment Services

10
Targeting Reemployment Services in Canada
The Service and Outcome Measurement System (SOMS) Experience

Terry Colpitts
Human Resources Development Canada

The Service and Outcome Measurement System (SOMS) was developed by Human Resources Development Canada (HRDC) to be a tool for promoting employment. SOMS was intended to help frontline staff in local public employment service offices counsel job-seekers about the best strategies for gaining employment and to assist analysts and managers in determining the best employment and/or training strategies for specific client groups. A microcomputer-based prototype of SOMS was built in 1994. It had three main elements: 1) a relational database of client specific information for employment insurance beneficiaries and/or participants of HRDC employment or training programs, 2) a means for examining the results of past services provided by the public employment service, and 3) a computerized model to predict what services would most benefit a particular job-seeker. In 1997, an algorithm was added to SOMS for predicting what service would best promote employment among groups defined by geographic and demographic characteristics.

While SOMS has not been adopted in Canada, many useful lessons were learned in the course of its development and pilot testing. This chapter attempts to communicate the most important of those lessons while telling the story of SOMS. We begin by describing the policy context of SOMS. We then briefly explain the technical structure of SOMS, how SOMS could be used by frontline staff to assist jobseekers, and how the model could be used to manage job-seeking by groups. The chapter concludes by reviewing some recent events in SOMS development, and reflecting on SOMS prospects for the future.

BACKGROUND

SOMS originated as a contribution by the Strategic Policy branch to the effort within HRDC known as the Knowledge Product Strategy.[1] SOMS built upon the multitude of evaluation studies performed by Strategic Policy's Evaluation and Data Development (EDD) branch during the prior 15 years. EDD viewed SOMS as a user-friendly vehicle for letting scientific research inform the management and practice of employment service delivery. Relying on an extensive client database summarizing past patterns of client services and outcomes, SOMS was intended to inform the choice of employment services for over four million annual customers of HRDC's nationwide network of local Canada Employment Centers (CEC).

Leading-edge evaluation techniques used within EDD formed the foundation for SOMS. However, to ensure that SOMS resulted in a user-friendly tool for management and practice, three development principles were established: 1) to link internal and external files to provide a detailed, sole source, multiple-year record of interventions provided to clients, their labor force participation and earnings history, as well as standard sociodemographic characteristics; 2) to develop and test statistical models to determine "point-in-time" intervention impacts at the client-specific level of detail; and 3) to incorporate the data and models in an interactive, micro-based system.

The SOMS prototype delivered to senior HRDC executives in the fall of 1994 was faithful to these principles as well as to the overriding objective of using research to inform practice. A series of SOMS demonstrations made to various groups in HRDC's national headquarters and many regional offices resulted in strong positive support for the SOMS initiative. There was so much support for the project and hopes were so high that SOMS developers tried to cool expectations.

SOMS was not intended to serve as an "expert system" to replace employment security officers, a potential trumpeted by some executives but feared by local office staff.

Concerns were also expressed about the privacy of client information held in the SOMS database, which was sometimes referred to as the "Big Brother" database. Some critics took the alternative position that the SOMS database was faulty, despite extensive data-checking and scrubbing routines employed by EDD. These criticisms and how they were addressed are explained in the following discussion of the four main system components and their historical development.[2]

SOMS RELATIONAL DATABASE

The core of SOMS is a large relational database system. In the absence of highly reliable and credible data that can be accessed quickly, SOMS's other components would not be acceptable to practitioners. The SOMS topology of data sources and preparation are summarized diagramatically in Figure 10.1.

The initial step in the data-building process was extraction of information from 19 different administrative silos. Sources for these data included HRDC, provincial, and external mainframe systems. This compilation required 18 months and was completed by EDD staff in December 1995. The data is longitudinal in nature, meaning it contains information on individual clients over time. Nine years of data covering the period 1987–1995 were originally archived in SOMS. Programming specifications were defined for more than 2,000 variables grouped into four modules—individual, interventions, providers, and outcomes.

Extensive data-scrubbing routines were used in creating the longitudinal client database. In 1996, Oracle database software was selected as the HRDC standard for the regional database system, and by early 1997, an Oracle-based SOMS regional database system was operational. This database accommodated about 250 of the most important variables from the large longitudinal file on over 10 million clients.[3]

Figure 10.1 SOMS Topology

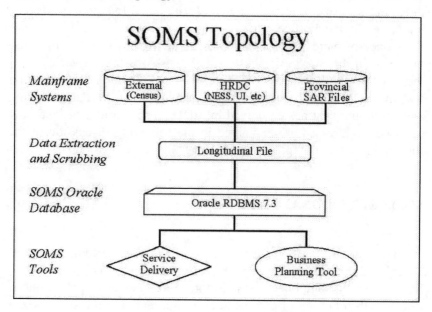

SOMS SERVICE DELIVERY TOOL

While the SOMS database was being constructed between 1994 and 1997, a prototype called Client Monitoring System (CMS)[4] was being used for focus-group testing in 30 Human Resources Centre of Canada (HRCC) offices located in six main metropolitan areas. Figure 10.2 shows a graphical user interface screen from SOMS, similar to that used in the CMS prototype, which is used for reviewing client data.

CMS contained 6,000 records of HRDC clients who had been surveyed in 1994 as the first step in an evaluation of an initiative called the Employability Improvement Program. The focus group testing occurred during a sensitive period. HRDC had been formed only three months earlier by combining all or part of four previous federal departments. At the same time that its reorganization was under way, the federal government announced a workforce reduction of 25,000 full-time

Figure 10.2 SOMS Graphical User Interface to Review Client Data

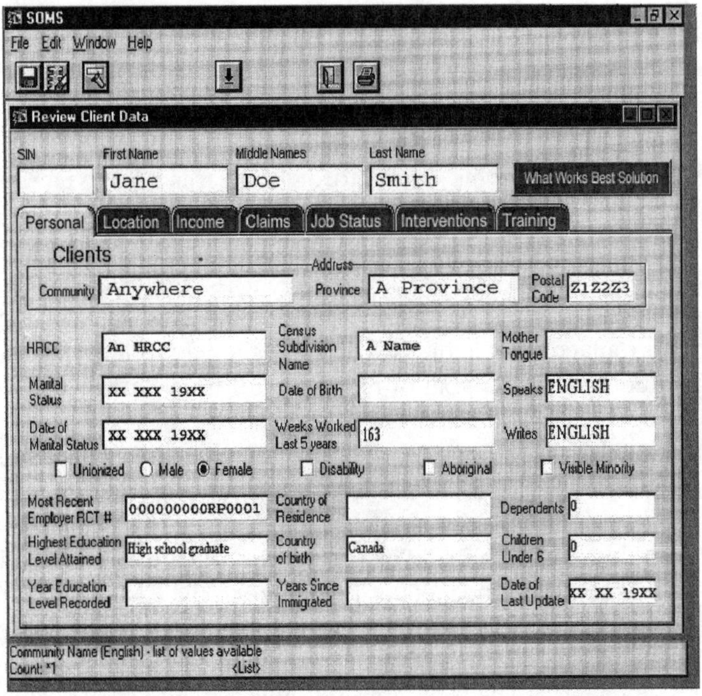

NOTE: By entering a Social Insurance Number into this screen, the service delivery person obtains access to a rich data source on a client's sociodemographic characteristics (Personal); data from the 1991 Census on the area in which they presently live (Location); income, earnings, unemployment insurance (UI), and social assistance benefits received over a multiple-year period (Income); detailed information on UI claims over a multiple-year period (Claims); a multiple-year record of employment, unemployment, and not in the labor force spells (Job Status); a multiple-year record of HRDC interventions provided (Interventions); and a multiple-year record of training provided (Training). Each of these information sections is shown as a file tab near the top of the record. The Personal tab (highlighted) is the one active in the screen above. At the far right and near the top, there is a button labeled "What Works Best Solution." By pressing this button, it is possible to view which of about 25 possible HRCC interventions will lead to the best result for the client in terms of improving income, earnings, saving employment insurance, improving time employed, or reducing dependency on employment insurance. The solution is unique to the individual. The "What Works Best Solution" can be of assistance in making a service delivery decision but it is not a replacement for the good judgment of the counselor.

staff equivalents with HRDC's share of the reduction set at 5,000 persons.[5]

The initial reaction of many service delivery staff to CMS was one of skepticism and suspicion, as it came on the heels of a major workforce reduction. Simultaneously, a policy of devolving employment policy responsibilities from the federal to the provincial governments was being pursued. This added to the concerns of service delivery staff for their own job security. CMS, although being touted as an aid to service delivery by improving the effectiveness of program targeting, was viewed as a possible replacement for the case management approach. In the minds of some, it was viewed as an expert system that could replace counselors in HRCCs as a way to help the national headquarters achieve its goal of reducing full-time staff equivalents by 20 percent.

Despite the unfortunate context, focus group tests proceeded as planned. Interviews with HRCC staff after exposure to CMS features in focus groups indicated that most participants could imagine themselves working with a refined version of the software. Despite this majority view, there were pockets of resistance to the CMS approach that included two distinct camps: the "philosophically opposed" (or "Luddites," about 5 percent of participants) and the "threatened pessimists" (about 33 percent).[6] The former group saw CMS as a challenge to their counseling methods, while the latter group feared CMS as a replacement for their services. Nonetheless, some constructive suggestions did surface from the focus group participants. These included the following:

1) Change the name Client Monitoring System, especially the word *monitoring*, which was viewed as threatening to both staff and clients because it implied "Big Brother."

2) Link CMS data with other key HRDC systems in various stages of development.

3) Ensure that management and service delivery staff have a shared understanding of how CMS would be used in improving the day-to-day operations at the HRCCs.

As a consequence of the focus group testing, an "alpha" version of the system was developed. The system name was changed from CMS to SOMS. Attempts were also made to link SOMS with other data and accountability systems. However, these efforts failed because of incompatibility with the older data structures.

In 1996, after the successful business case presentation of SOMS to the Project Review Committee, Strategic Policy, and Systems branch formed a joint partnership to further SOMS development. Later that year, "beta" focus group tests of the SOMS system were planned for 10 of the 30 alpha HRCC sites. Around this time, devolution of employment programs from the federal government to the provinces was being done through bilateral agreements. As provincial management took over, several of the selected beta test sites dropped out of the plans for focus groups. In the end, only two of the selected local HRCC offices were left to participate in the beta tests, which went ahead in late 1996 and early 1997.

As a result of the sharp decline in the number of beta test sites, the methodological design for live system testing was modified. The test period was shortened to include only a comparison of the pretraining questionnaire data against that collected one month after system training.[7] Focus group participants were positive about the quality of the information, the organization and presentation of client data in easily navigable screens, and the high level of security for confidential information. On the negative side, they downplayed the value of SOMS in helping to improve the quality of their work with clients. They also expressed concerns about the reliability and completeness of the data.

Despite the sometimes negative perceptions of SOMS's service delivery tool, in a March 1997 presentation of the system to an Assistant Deputy Minister with primary responsibility for all HRDC training and employment programs, the Assistant Deputy Minister suggested that SOMS replace the existing antiquated data-entry processing system used by local HRCCs. However, SOMS was not designed as a data-entry system. The time and resources needed to make the necessary changes were judged too large. In addition, resistance to a new system during a period of high uncertainty with respect to HRDC's role in the local labor market was likely to be strong. Rather than risk the entire project, which had in early 1997 received Treasury Board support and multiyear funding as an accountability system for HRDC, efforts were turned toward marketing and implementing SOMS's business application tool.

SOMS'S BUSINESS PLANNING TOOL

The other component of SOMS, its management reporting/accountability tool, was still relevant in a devolved department and development of this component, including the maintenance and updating of the relational database that supports the tool, continued. This component loaded directly on the end user's desktop computer and permitted managers and analysts to review summarized group data for the 10.8 million clients at various levels of detail and for different outcome measures. All of the national data were available at a glance in either spreadsheet or graphical format. Users could rapidly and easily explore the data of any multi-dimensional cube at any level of detail by filtering on the client (age, sex, education, unemployment compensation claim, etc.) and geographic dimensions. Users could also choose the outcome measure(s) to use in analyzing the effectiveness of service provided and its impact on clients served. The accountability portion of SOMS provided the manager or analyst with a powerful tool to review performance in order to make strategic decisions on where and to whom resources should be targeted.

Three data "cubes" (data sets) were developed and tested in the beta evaluation of SOMS: annual income information, employment insurance claims information, and intervention and results information. To build the cubes for analyzing grouped client data, data was first extracted and packaged in a format suitable for building the cubes by using software called Transformer. In Transformer, the analyst defines the data elements that need to be extracted from the source database and the important relationships between the elements. This forms the data model, which, after extensive testing for data consistency and correct relationships between the variables, is executed against the SOMS database to produce a number of PowerCubes. Each PowerCube contains a selection of extracted data, structured to show defined relationships, and stored in a proprietary format.

A six-week pilot test of the business application tool was conducted in Ontario during the summer of 1997. The test revealed that while the software was not as user-friendly as other "spreadsheet/analysis" software used, its graphical interface was far superior. Moreover, in comparison to other data sources available, SOMS was found superior, as was the data quality and its organization. Shortcomings were noted in SOMS's geographic structure, the presence of "stale" data, and its querying ability.

Since the testing of SOMS's business application ended, agreements were reached with an HRDC partner—The Canadian Labour Force Development Board—and two provincial governments to test SOMS's business application tool on a trial basis. Other provincial governments also expressed an interest in testing SOMS.

SOMS'S PREDICTIVE MODELING COMPONENT[8]

The predictive modeling component, which slowed SOMS's acceptance by frontline delivery staff, was the system's Achilles' heel. The predictive models were designed to calculate which of the many programs and services delivered by HRDC had the best probability of improving the employment and earnings prospects for a client based on their sociodemographic characteristics and their past history of employment, earnings, and service receipt. The models were intended to allay criticisms often directed by local managers with respect to evaluation studies; namely, that although relevant to making policy decisions at a national level, such studies were viewed as irrelevant to frontline staff making day-to-day service delivery decisions.

To develop predictive "what works best" models at the level of the client, it was necessary to reorient the standard program evaluation strategy. In a traditional quasi-experimental evaluation, the net program effect is computed in a statistical model as the difference between the labor market outcome of program participants and nonparticipants, while adjusting for differences between the two groups. In the SOMS approach, all of the previous interventions received by a client are also included in the statistical model as independent variables, along with variables that measure standard sociodemographic variables, and various periods of elapsed time since the interventions were provided. Lagged dependent variables were also used as predictors of outcomes. Finally, to make the model relevant at the level of the individual, a number of interactive terms were also added using a "stepwise" regression procedure.

From each of the four regression outcome models specified—earnings, weeks of employment, savings in unemployment compensation, and probability of employment—predictive models were then developed for each of 25 interventions identified. To determine what works best, the predictive models use the regression outcome for a particular individual and increment the intervention by 1 (employment interventions) or by a specified typical number of weeks (training interventions) and estimate the outcome. The difference between the predicted and regression outcome measures equals the value of an additional unit of the intervention. By comparing the effect of each of the 25 interventions for any one individual, it is then possible to say which intervention will have the best effect.

While this approach was judged theoretically sound by leading econometricians, considerable difficulties were encountered in attempting to arrive at findings that could be generalized to the population and adequately differentiated between competing interventions. In early model rounds, although it appeared that the models could isolate the best intervention for a client, the predictive models often resulted in a majority of the clients (as much as 70 percent) being targeted to the same intervention. Furthermore, each of the outcome models tended to favor a different intervention.

Several refinements were adopted to improve the ability of the models to discriminate among alternative interventions. The revised models were able to identify more than one favorable intervention for each outcome, but confidence intervals for the program effect estimates were too large to precisely state which intervention was best. Moreover, the effect estimated for a number of the service outcomes was not statistically significant. While our efforts did not yield a tool to assist in service delivery, a number of findings which arose from the modeling efforts are important to consider.

First, in attempting to develop participation models to account for self-selection bias, it was found that there were such extreme differences between those who were past clients of HRDC and those who had never received service, that the participation models could not be built. The inability to construct a comparison group that both had not received an intervention at some time since 1987 and resembled those who did receive services strongly suggests the existence and operation of dual labor markets in Canada. That is, distinct markets for workers who are usually job-attached and radically different markets for those who rely on the public employment service to assist them during jobless spells.

Secondly, missing data on key variables for large proportions of the sample populations resulted in large and significant bias in the estimation of program effects. This finding illustrates the importance of valid and complete client data entry in administrative systems, especially for those variables which are strong predictors of success. It also suggests that it would be useful to modify administrative data systems to capture certain information that, although not essential for program administration per se, is highly relevant in measuring success and maintaining accountability.

A number of reasons were postulated for our inability to predict reliably what would work best for a particular client in a given labor market area. In addition to the phenomena reported above, other potential reasons, which are backed up by the analysis conducted and/or the empirical research, suggest that the problem may result from the presence of unknown or unmeasurable attributes of clients, i.e., unexplained heterogeneity. In effect, people differ with respect to certain behaviors in ways that we cannot comprehend or model using available data. Also, individual programs have become more heterogeneous over time due to 1) dilution of selection criteria, 2) increasing devolution of service delivery from the federal to provincial governments, and 3) tailoring of interventions to match the characteristics of local labor markets. Increasing variation in the content and intensity of programs delivered can, by itself, result in imprecise estimates of intervention effects since the interventions themselves are imprecise.

Finally, the unavailability of precise cost data means that a cost-effectiveness ranking of net impacts for alternative interventions cannot be produced. If reliable cost data were available, the uncertainty about program referral resulting from overlapping confidence intervals might be greatly reduced.

RECENT SOMS DEVELOPMENTS

SOMS has moved far beyond the prototype stage. It is a fully tested, leading-edge, multifaceted accountability and targeting system ready for wide-scale deployment throughout HRDC. Increased use of SOMS by national and regional headquarters for quickly constructing participant and/or comparison group samples affirmed it to be a reliable database for quick sample design and construction. Heightened interest in the SOMS business application tool by provinces and regions lent strength to the planned conversion of SOMS's programming code and an update of the SOMS database.

SOMS modeling revisions, which were completed in early 2000, succeeded in dramatically narrowing the confidence intervals, thus permitting much more precise statements about what works best. As a result, the SOMS modeling component was much more useful than at any prior stage of development. However, recent developments regarding the use of personal information for research and evaluation purposes that entailed the linking of databases from various sources have slowed the development pace, as multiple approvals are required by senior officials in more than one federal department or agency. Since patterns of program participants change over time, model estimates of what works best for whom have a finite useful lifetime. Unless the required approvals are sought and granted to build a new SOMS relational database system with refreshed current data, SOMS's potential as a service delivery and resource allocation tool will be lost.[9]

CONCLUSION

In the development of any accountability and targeting system, the highest importance must be placed on developing a reliable and credible database. If the results are to be meaningful and accepted, the data foundation must be trusted. Nonetheless, even after the best efforts to achieve this ideal, data anomalies will crop up in a system where the data is subdivided in so many ways to produce program effect estimates.

Building a system to meet many competing needs across a large organization is a challenging task. Constant testing and validation must be done to ensure that needs are met in terms of functionality, simplicity, and system compatibility.

Sometimes, as was found with SOMS, a system can be so technologically advanced that it is hard to link it with older systems. A new system can also pose a threat to the status quo and, as a result, be cast in a bad light or discredited entirely. Sufficient attention must be given to such factors for proper planning of a system with the size and complexity of SOMS. However, even the best planning cannot foresee all contingencies, and timing may play an overly significant role in deciding the fate and acceptance of a system.

Finally, "what gets measured, gets done (and gets attention)." In HRDC's case, the important measures following the announcement of the new accountability system for the Employment Benefits and Support Measures (EBSM) were the short-term (3-month postprogram) unemployment insurance savings and return to work. SOMS reported on both in annual time increments. Instead of focusing on SOMS as a short-term EBSM outcome monitoring system, an effort was made to simply add that functionality to SOMS's other features. In retrospect, concentration on a simple outcome monitoring system would probably have had the greatest effect on improving the acceptance of SOMS at the field level. However, besides being wasteful of resources, a second monitoring system would have increased confusion in HRCC's trying to determine which system was best.

To avoid systems proliferation, efforts focused on linking and partnering the SOMS effort with other parts of the HRDC organization. This was seen as a means of reducing the total number of systems in use, while simultaneously improving their impact on the clients served and the results achieved.

Notes

This paper does not necessarily represent the views and opinions of the Government of Canada, nor those of the Department of Human Resources Development Canada.

1. In 1995, with the introduction of a revised program structure, Employment Benefits and Support Measures (EBSM), a formal accountability structure was introduced, requiring HRDC to report annually to Parliament on EBSM performance in meeting its short-term objectives of generating employment and saving employment insurance funds. Medium-term measures of employment stability, in-

come enhancement, etc. were also specified, but reporting on these measures needed the EBSM to have been in operation for a number of years before measures could be taken.

2. These points were brought out in various presentations made by the SOMS development team and were reinforced by the findings from focus group testing of various SOMS components over the 1995–1998 period.

3. A client is defined by SOMS to be anyone who had an employment insurance claim and/or a training or employment intervention at some point since 1987.

4. At the time of the focus group testing, and until early 1996, SOMS was called the Client Monitoring System (CMS). Focus group testing revealed the need for a change in the system's name.

5. In 1994, the Department of Employment and Immigration Canada (EIC) was reorganized as part of a major restructuring of the federal government. EIC lost its immigration component. All or part of four other federal departments were added to the remaining EIC. The newly formed HRDC accounts for almost all of the federal labor market and social programming. With spending of almost $70 billion annually, HRDC accounts for one-half of total federal government spending.

6. Human Resources Development Canada (1995).

7. In each of the two offices, one manager was separately trained in using SOMS's PowerPlay business application.

8. Full model details are provided in the appendix.

9. In May 2000, the SOMS database was wiped out in response to concerns raised by the Office of the Privacy Commissioner regarding the extensive data holdings of HRDC.

Appendix

Details of the Modeling Approach for SOMS

In the past, program evaluations undertaken by HRDC have focused on determining the net effect of a program on a particular outcome indicator, by the use of a pre/post comparison group methodology and the estimation of a regression model, which took the form of

(A.1) $Y_i = \beta_0 + X_i\beta_1 + P_i\beta_2 + \mu_i$

In this equation, the dependent variable Y is the outcome indicator; β_0 is the intercept term; the vector X_i contains the environmental and demographic variables of the program participants and comparison group members, and β_1 denotes their coefficients; P_i is a 1,0 variable indicating whether the individual participated in the program or not; β_2 is the marginal effect of a program; and μ_i is a random error term.

While the β_2 coefficient provides information on the incremental impact of the program being evaluated, it does not provide frontline HRCC staff with an answer to the question of whether the program would work for their clients, or, in the limit, for a particular client. Also, and as is normally the case, the delineation of individuals as participants or comparison group members is based on receipt or nonreceipt of a program. There may well be differences between the two groups in terms of the quantities of other programs received in the past. The implicit assumption of the standard equation for estimating program impact in a quasi-experimental research design is that the two groups are similar in terms of past programs and there is no bias in the estimate of the impact of the program under consideration.

In order to answer the question of which of the many available HRDC interventions would maximize the benefits received by a client, it was necessary to significantly alter the standard regression equation noted above. The heart of the SOMS predictive capability is a regression equation of the form:

(A.2) $UI_{i,95} = \beta_0 + UI_{i,(95-T)}\beta_1 + T_{ij}\beta_2 + X_i\beta_3 + I_i\beta_4 + Z_i\beta_5 + \psi_i\beta_6 + \mu_i$

for $i = 1, \ldots, 93{,}026$

where,

- $UI_{i,95}$ is unemployment insurance benefits paid in 1995 for the ith individual.

- β_0 is the intercept term.
- $UI_{i,(95-T)}$ is a vector of three values, representing lagged UI benefits paid in years $T - 1$, $T - 2$, and $T - 3$, where T is the year of the first recorded intervention on file for the ith client. The coefficient vector for $UI_{i,(95-T)}$ is denoted by β_1.[1]
- The vector T_{ij} measures weeks since the last occurrence of intervention j for the ith client. T_{ij} consists of up to three elements, representing the distribution of times in separate linear pieces. This approach provides a flexible method of dealing with nonlinear relationships in the elapsed time since an intervention occurred in the past and the residual effect of the past intervention on the outcome indicator. The number of components and their precise definitions varies across interventions. The corresponding coefficient vector is β_2.[2]
- The vector X_i contains environmental and demographic variables, and β_3 denotes their coefficients.
- I_i is the vector of intervention variables whose coefficients are β_4. The vector, comprising 25 intervention variables (10 employment and 15 training), captures data on receipt of interventions over the period 1987–1994. Employment interventions are measured in terms of the frequency of occurrence over the time period, while training interventions are measured as the duration of training, in weeks. Both types are represented in the model by up to three component variables, where each component represents a piece of the distribution of the observed frequencies or durations as either a dummy variable or a linear approximation. The purpose of including components of this kind is to identify nonlinear relationships between the quantity of the intervention and the observed effect on the outcome indicator.[3]
- The variable denoted by Z_i captures the time elapsed between the receipt of the earliest intervention on record for the ith client and January 1, 1994. The coefficient β_5 gives the relationship between this time variable and the outcome indicator.
- Terms representing the Kronecker product of the demographic, environmental, time, and lagged dependent variables (X_i, Z_i, and $UI_{i,(95-T)}$) with the intervention variables (T_{ij}) are denoted by ψ_i. The coefficients of these interaction terms are denoted by β_6.
- Finally, μ_i is a random error term.

The model is estimated by ordinary least squares (OLS). All variables except the interaction terms are forced into the model. For the interaction terms, a forward stepwise procedure is applied and only those interaction terms (components of ψ_i) which meet or exceed a 0.20 significance level are included in the model. Before the stepwise procedure is applied, a total of 1,809 interactive terms are available to the model. Variables entered on a step may be dropped at a later point in the procedure if their calculated significance level falls below 0.22. The significance levels set for model inclusion and exclusion were chosen to achieve a balance between competing concerns. That is, to include a sufficient number of interaction terms to allow for differing estimates of what works best for clients, while at the same time trying to avoid the problem of multicollinearity. The resulting OLS estimates of the coefficients β_1, $\beta_2, \ldots, \beta_6$ are denoted by $b_1, b_2, \ldots, b_6$.

The model described above can be used to estimate the reduction in UI benefits paid that results from the receipt of any given type of intervention. These savings can be assessed on an individual basis or on any level of aggregation (e.g., HRCC, region, province, etc.). The calculation requires several steps, as follows:

1) Estimate unemployment compensation receipt by the ith person, $UI_{i,95}$ by substituting the OLS estimates $b_1, b_2, \ldots, b_6$ for $\beta_1, \beta_2, \ldots, \beta_6$ into Equation A.2 and evaluating the equation for the ith person's characteristics $(T_{ij}, X_i, I_i, Z_i, \psi_i)$.

2) Increment the value of the particular intervention j received by person i (T_{ij}). The intervention is increased by one unit if the intervention is measured as a frequency, or by the historically observed average number of weeks per occurrence if it is measured as a duration (e.g., the average duration of a training course).

3) Recalculate values of all explanatory variables $(T_{ij}, X_i, I_i, Z_i, \psi_i)$ which depend on the value of the intervention.

4) Reestimate $UI_{i,95}$ using the recalculated explanatory variables and the original OLS parameter estimates $(b_1, b_2, \ldots, b_6)$.

5) The estimated effect of the intervention is then produced by subtracting the result of step 1 from that of step 4.

In addition to the savings in UI benefits paid, models were specified and tested for three other dependent variables: earnings in 1995, weeks of employment in 1995, and probability of employment in 1995. For the first two of these outcome indicators, a process similar to the one described above was followed to arrive at the final predictive equations. In the third case, a logistic regression model was used instead of OLS. The stepwise selection of interaction terms was different for each of the four outcome indicators.

Effects were estimated for 22 of the 25 interventions.[4] The estimation, therefore, required 88 predictive equations—i.e., 4 outcomes by 22 interventions. Since the predictive models use interactive terms consisting of environmental and demographic variables specific to the client, SOMS can estimate the impact of any one of the 22 interventions in terms of its predicted impact on a client's earnings, income, etc. In so doing, SOMS brings evaluative information down to the service delivery level and answers the question of "what works best" for a specific HRCC client.

The SOMS models are continually being refined and reestimated as a consequence of the dynamic nature of the data and the interventions upon which the SOMS models are based. New data, in addition to permitting reestimation of models, can also suggest changes in the formulation of the SOMS outcome models. Consequently, SOMS should be viewed as a dynamic model exercise which is sufficiently flexible to adapt to changes in the underlying data, as well as changes in HRDC's requirements for accountability and for information on what works best.

Appendix Notes

1. Previous SOMS models had only one lagged dependent variable term, defined for the period $T - 1$.
2. In previous SOMS models, T_{ij} was linear in construction, implying an assumption that the effect of past interventions was constant and not influenced by the time elapsed since receipt. The assumption of linearity runs counter to empirical literature, which suggests that the attenuation of effects is best depicted by a nonlinear curve.
3. Previous SOMS models accounted for possible nonlinear relationships between the intervention and its effect on the outcome indicator by using squared values of the main intervention variables, measured as either frequencies or durations.
4. Three of the interventions were residual categories for interventions that either were not captured specifically in the data (e.g., "other" purchased training) or occurred too infrequently to be modeled as separate interventions. These interventions were included in the models to compensate for their effects on the outcome indicators, but the process to estimate effects was not applied to them because such information would offer no guidance with respect to identifying an optimal intervention for a client or group of clients.

Reference

Human Resources Development Canada. 1995. "Focus Group Testing of the Client Monitoring System [SOMS] with CEC [HRCC] Staff." Ottawa: Human Resources Development Canada.

Comments on Chapter 10

Jeffrey Smith
University of Maryland

The Service and Outcome Measurement System (SOMS) represents an important advance in attempts to use statistical models to guide the assignment of participants in social programs to particular interventions. Such efforts are important given that what little evidence we have suggests that caseworkers may not do particularly well at this task (see Bell and Orr forthcoming; Plesca and Smith 2001; and Lechner and Smith 2001). The lessons that Human Resources Development Canada (HRDC) learned from developing the SOMS should provide useful guidance to similar efforts in the United States to develop the Frontline Decision Support System (FDSS) to guide the assignment of individuals to services provided under WIA (the Workforce Investment Act).

Using statistical models to target (or profile) participants into alternative services is the administrative innovation *de jour* in the public sector agencies that provide these services. Like earlier administrative innovations *de jour*, such as performance standards, statistical targeting is proceeding much faster in practice than the research base that should support and guide its development. One of the things that has remained foggy in much of the small literature on statistical treatment rules (STRs), of which SOMS and FDSS are examples, is the importance both conceptually and practically of the choice of variable on the basis of which to allocate individuals to services. This issue is discussed at length in Berger, Black, and Smith (2000).

In the U.S. unemployment insurance (UI) system, the variable used to target services is the predicted probability of UI benefit exhaustion. In the welfare-to-work programs described in Chapter 8, it is predicted levels of employment. The thing that makes SOMS relatively unique is that it is explicitly designed to allocate participants to services based on the predicted impacts of those services rather than on expected outcome levels in the absence of service. By targeting based on the expected gains from alternative services rather than on predicted outcome levels, the SOMS maximizes the efficiency gains from the program, thereby providing (it is hoped) the largest bang per long-suffering (and in Canada they are indeed long-suffering) taxpayer dollar. These gains may come, of course, at some equity cost, as persons who would do poorly in the absence of expensive services will not receive those expensive services if their predicted benefit from them is small.

In addition to highlighting the conceptual value of basing an STR on predicted impacts, the SOMS also serves to illustrate the fact that constructing automated systems to assign participants to services represents a very difficult task indeed. SOMS and other similar systems represent an attempt to create an automated, ongoing, non-experimental program evaluation of a large number of alternative services. Automated in this context means that, once established, the system can reliably generate impact estimates without the frequent intervention of an econometrician. The parameters of interest in the evaluation implicit in the SOMS include predicted subgroup impacts for a nearly infinite number of subgroups defined by observable demographic characteristics, past service receipt, and past transfer payment receipt. The difficulty of the task is recognized when it is considered that we really do not yet have a robust methodology for conducting one-shot non-experimental evaluations (see, for example, the discussion in Heckman, LaLonde, and Smith 1999). Thus, it is not at all surprising that the SOMS developers had some troubles along the way.

In the remainder of my remarks, I would like to briefly discuss some specific issues that were raised in the course of developing SOMS. Some of these are mentioned in Chapter 10 and some are not. The first issue concerns the econometric method used to generate SOMS's impact estimates. This method consists more or less of "one grand regression." The implied comparison group is persons with low intensity services rather than persons who never receive any services but would be eligible for them. As Colpitts notes in the chapter, this was due in part to the fact that persons who were eligible but did not participate during the long period covered by the SOMS database were an unusual group. This reflects the fact that the eligible population is more saturated with employment and training programs in Canada than it is in the United States.

This econometric strategy relies on the assumption of what Heckman and Robb (1985) call "selection on observables." The idea here is that conditioning on observable characteristics—in this case quite a lot of them but with some notable omissions, such as years of schooling—will control for all selective differences between participants in any of the different services. This is a tall order for a non-experimental estimator in an evaluation examining only one service; it is perhaps an even taller one in the case of a system that seeks to generate credible impact estimates for more than a dozen services.

The virtues of this econometric strategy are threefold. First, it is readily understood by agency staff and can be explained in a simple manner (at least relative to other available evaluation strategies). Second, unlike the currently popular matching strategies examined in, e.g., Heckman et al. (1998) and Heckman, Ichimura, and Todd (1997), the SOMS econometric strategy uses off-the-shelf software. This is important for a system that, once launched, should require little in the way of expensive econometric maintenance. Third, it uses the data at hand, which do not include any obvious sources of exogenous variation that could be used as instruments in models that attempt to take account of selection on unobservables (e.g., motivation and ability) as well as selection on observables. It remains an important open question whether it would be possible in future versions of SOMS or in other systems of this type to adopt more ambitious econometric strategies.

The second issue worth raising is how to code the extremely heterogeneous interventions commonly offered to the disadvantaged and the unemployed. These include somewhat standardized services such as job clubs or job search assistance, as well as quite heterogeneous services such as classroom training in occupational skills. For the latter, should the system treat all classroom training of this type as one service, thereby leaving the case worker with substantial discretion about what specific occupation to have the participant train for? Or should it define training more narrowly, and attempt to produce separate impacts for specific occupational groups? This is complicated by the fact that not all types of training will be available in all localities. This issue was not addressed in great detail in SOMS, where existing administrative categories were taken essentially as given. The optimal way to approach this question remains an issue for future research.

Related to this issue is the question of how to deal with multitreatment paths. In many programs of the type offered in Canada during the time that SOMS was created, participants may receive a sequence of services rather than just one. In some cases, these sequences may be preplanned, as when it is expected that job search assistance will follow classroom training for those who have not already located a job. In other cases, they may reflect a search for a good match between the participant and the service being provided. In these cases, the initial services received resemble the "tasters" built into the New Deal for Young People in the United Kingdom. These tasters explicitly allow New Deal participants to try out the different types of services offered by the program in the hope that additional information will lead to a better match between participant and service and thereby to a larger impact.

If the sequences are preplanned, a particular sequence of services (if sufficiently common) can simply be treated as a separate service, for which a separate impact estimate is generated. In the case where the sequences represent "search" among possible service matches, things become trickier, both in the predictive sense and in the sense of what services received by past participants to include in the impact estimation model. This aspect of the design of service allocation systems would also benefit from further analysis, both conceptual and empirical.

The final issue pertains to which set of services to attempt to estimate impacts for at all. Another way to think of this issue is how to incorporate prior information that certain services, such as orientation interviews or individual counseling sessions, are unlikely to have detectable impacts. Attempting to estimate impacts for services that are known in advance to have impacts too small to measure will reduce the credibility of the system and may lead to some embarrassing numbers (as indeed it did in some early versions of SOMS). It is important in designing these systems to focus on key services and not to attempt too much, especially in the first round of development.

In looking to the future it is useful to consider two lines of development for statistical treatment allocation systems such as SOMS in Canada and FDSS in the United States. The first is their transformation into true expert systems. We already have a lot of knowledge from both social experiments and from high-quality non-experimental evaluations about what works and for whom. As noted by Manski (2001), the data sets from some of these evaluations could usefully be mined to extract even more information along these lines. This information is ignored in SOMS, which relies solely on its own internal impact estimates—estimates based on a methodology that emphasizes ease of automation over econometric appeal. Combining the evidence from other evaluations with the internal estimates from SOMS (or other similar systems) would substantially increase the likelihood that the system would actually fulfill its appointed task of helping to associate participants with the services that would benefit them the most.

Second, the service allocation component of SOMS or of other similar systems could be used to generate useful exogenous variation in service receipt that would then in turn reduce the bias associated with future internal impact estimates from the system. The basic idea is to introduce some randomization into the set of services recommended as a permanent feature of the system. The randomization would not require that anyone be denied service, only that some systematic variation in service receipt be introduced by varying the set of services recommended or their ordering in a way unrelated to the observable characteristics of the participant. In technical terms, the system would be creating an instrument that could be used to help in evaluating the program. Building this aspect into the system would relatively painlessly increase the credibility of, and reduce the bias associated with, the impact estimates used to guide service allocation.

In conclusion, it should be clear that statistical treatment allocation systems such as SOMS display great promise at improving the efficiency of service allocation in social programs. At the same time, the research base underlying these systems is woeful, a situation that the chapters in this volume only begin to address. Much remains to be done.

Disclaimer

The author worked as an occasional paid consultant to Abt Associates of Canada (now Applied Research Consultants) in the course of their work on the Service Outcomes and Monitoring System (SOMS) under contract to Human Resources Development Canada (HRDC). The views expressed in this comment do not necessarily represent those of any person or organization other than the author.

References

Bell, Stephen, and Larry Orr. Forthcoming. "Screening (and Creaming?) Applicants to Job Training Programs: The AFDC Homemaker-Home Health Aide Demonstrations." *Labour Economics*.

Berger, Mark, Dan Black, and Jeffrey Smith. 2000. "Evaluating Profiling as a Means of Allocating Government Services." In *Econometric Evaluation of Labour Market Policies*, Michael Lechner and Friedhelm Pfeiffer, eds. Heidelberg: Physica, pp. 59–84.

Heckman, James and Richard Robb. 1985. "Alternative Methods for Evaluating the Impact of Interventions." In *Longitudinal Analysis of Labor Market Data*, James Heckman and Burton Singer, eds. Cambridge, England: Cambridge University Press for Econometric Society Monograph Series, pp. 156–246.

Heckman, James, Hidehiko Ichimura, and Petra Todd. 1997. "Matching as an Econometric Estimator: Evidence from Evaluating a Job Training Programme." *Review of Economic Studies* 64(4): 605–654.

Heckman, James, Hidehiko Ichimura, Jeffrey Smith, and Petra Todd. 1998. "Characterizing Selection Bias Using Experimental Data." *Econometrica* 66(5): 1017–1098.

Heckman, James, Robert LaLonde, and Jeffrey Smith. 1999. "The Economics and Econometrics of Active Labor Market Programs." In *Handbook of Labor Economics, Volume 3A*, Orley Ashenfelter and David Card, eds. Amsterdam: North-Holland, pp. 1865–2097.

Lechner, Michael, and Jeffrey Smith. 2001. "What Is the Value Added by Caseworkers?" Unpublished manuscript, University of Maryland.

Manski, Charles. 2001. "Designing Programs for Heterogeneous Populations: The Value of Covariate Information." *American Economic Review* 91(2): 103–106.

Plesca, Miana, and Jeffrey Smith. 2001. "How Can We Improve Public Employment and Training Programs?" Unpublished manuscript, University of Maryland.

11

Predicting Long-Term Unemployment in Canada

Prospects and Policy Implications

Ging Wong, Harold Henson, and Arun Roy
Human Resources Development Canada

The problem of long-term unemployment—jobless but seeking work for 12 months or more—was persistent throughout the 1980s and 1990s in all 30 member countries of the Organisation for Economic Co-operation and Development (OECD). However, the extent of the problem differed greatly among countries. In Canada, Norway, Sweden, and the United States, the proportion of unemployed who were long-term unemployed (LTU) was relatively low, ranging from 9.5 percent in the United States to 17.1 percent in Sweden in 1996. This compares with 30.7 percent on average in the G7 countries, 34 percent on average for the 30 OECD countries, and 49.3 percent for the 15 members of the European Union (Organisation for Economic Co-operation and Development 1998b, 1998c). Nevertheless, these lower rates in North America and northern Europe represent significant increases over rates observed a decade earlier.

Targeting of reemployment services to the LTU became part of national employment policy in both the United States and Australia during the 1990s (Organisation for Economic Co-operation and Development 1998a). In the United States, the Worker Profiling and Reemployment Services (WPRS) system, established by 1993 legislation, required early identification and referral to services of unemployment compensation beneficiaries who are predicted as likely to be LTU. In Australia, a formal early identification and intervention strategy was devised and implemented by the Commonwealth Employment Service

(CES) in 1994 as part of their reform policy called "Working Nation." In Australia, the LTU and those determined to be "at risk" are given preferential access to case management and labor market programs delivered by either a public or private provider.

To date, Canada has not developed a policy for targeting services to the LTU. It has not been a pressing concern, because until recently the number of LTU has been low. Instead, Canada has focused its labor market reform efforts to deal with unemployment recidivism. Rather than large numbers of LTU, Canada has a high incidence of part-year employment in fishing, agriculture, and tourism with consequent seasonal unemployment. Public concern about long-term unemployment surfaced in the 1990s as the ratio of unemployment compensation beneficiaries to all unemployed (the B/U ratio) fell. The B/U ratio declined dramatically from 0.83 in 1989 to 0.42 in 1997. Research revealed that about half of this drop was due to tightening of the unemployment compensation system, but that the other half was due to changes in the nature of the labor market. In particular, B/U has dropped because the share of unemployed Canadians who have not worked for the last 12 months has nearly doubled, from 20.8 percent in 1989 to 38.4 percent in 1997.[1]

The next section of this chapter documents the rise in Canadian long-term unemployment, and the related trends in exhaustion of unemployment compensation entitlement. The chapter then reports on an empirical exercise using Canadian data that attempt early identification of individuals who are at risk of remaining jobless for 52 weeks or more. Such a model, however, is useful only if linked to efficacious employment measures. The next section therefore reports which services are most likely to promote reemployment for those at risk of long-term joblessness. For Canadian unemployment compensation recipients, estimates are provided of how net benefits of interventions vary depending upon the timing of the intervention. A summary and concluding remarks appear in the final section.

THE LABOR MARKET CONTEXT

Labour Force Survey (LFS) data are used to provide descriptive statistics about the magnitude and trends in the growth of long-term unemployment.[2] The LTU increased from 3 percent of all unemployed in 1976 to 5 percent in 1981, to 7 percent in 1991, and reached a peak of 15 percent in 1994. In recent years the LTU has declined, reaching 10 percent in 1998 (Figure 11.1). In spite of declines in recent years, the incidence of LTU doubled between 1981 and 1998 and increased three-fold between 1976 and 1998. In absolute numbers, the size of the LTU has been in the range of 125,000 to 175,000 in recent years. In 1998, the number of workers reported to have been in the LTU category was 126,000.

There is a strong positive correlation between the aggregate unemployment rate and the incidence of long-term unemployment. This means that as the unemployment rate increases in a recession, the incidence of long-term unemployment also increases. It is also evident that the incidence of long-term unemployment declines much more slowly than the unemployment rate during subsequent recoveries.

Among age groups, long-term unemployment is substantially higher among older workers (55 and over) than among prime-age or young workers. The incidence is particularly low for youth because of their high turnover in the labor market.[3] By gender, the incidence of long-

**Figure 11.1 Proportion of Total Unemployment That Is Long-Term and
the Unemployment Rate, 1976–1998**

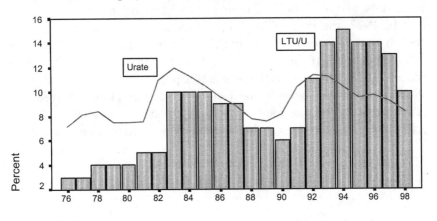

SOURCE: Statistics Canada, LFS

term unemployment is also slightly higher among males than females. The incidence among those with only primary education is substantially higher than the average. But contrary to expectations, long-term unemployment is not lower among those with postsecondary education than among individuals with high school education.

There are some notable variations in the incidence of long-term unemployment among provinces. It is relatively high in Quebec and lower than the average in Ontario, the prairie provinces, and British Columbia. In the Atlantic provinces it has always remained at or below the national average. This is because a significant part of unemployment in the Atlantic provinces is of the seasonal variety (Green and Sargent 1995; Wesa 1995).

In summary, the aggregate data suggest that the LTU carry a large burden of the costs of recession and that this group shares relatively little in the benefits of recovery. The incidence of long-term unemployment appears to be higher for older workers, males, those with primary education, and in the province of Quebec.

Higher levels of unemployment have budgetary implications that operate through lower tax receipts and higher outlays of income support for the unemployed than would have been the case. The unemployment compensation payment cost of long-term unemployment can be estimated as $(B_e - B_I) \times N_e$, where B_e is the average dollar amount paid to UI exhaustees, B_I is the average dollar amount paid to all UI claimants, and N_e is the total number of UI exhaustees.

In 1997, the cost of long-term unemployment was $1.6 billion, which works out to 16 percent of the total benefit payments in that year. This means that if the risk of long-term unemployment could be reduced by 75 percent through more active policies, a savings of $1.2 billion could be generated in the insurance account alone. Figure 11.2 shows that the cost of long-term unemployment varies cyclically, increasing in times of a recession and declining in times of a recovery.

PREDICTING LONG-TERM UNEMPLOYMENT

Our modeling approach for early identification of long-term unemployment draws on the practical experience of the United States and

Figure 11.2 Estimated Cost of Long-Term Unemployment

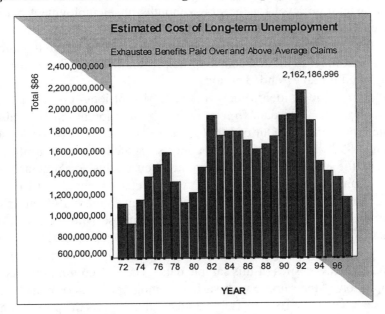

SOURCE: Our own estimates of $(B_e - B_l) \times N_e$ based on data from the HRDC Status Vector.

Australia (Wandner 1997; Chapman 1993). Worker profiling systems in those countries rely on readily observable personal and labor market characteristics as predictors of continuing unemployment. In the United States, the factors include recall status, union hiring hall agreement, education, job tenure, change in employment in previous industry, change in employment in previous occupation, and local unemployment rate. In Australia, seven key predictors are used: age, educational attainment, aboriginal status, foreign country birthplace, disability, English speaking ability, and geographic location.

Neither the U.S. nor the Australian system exploits the fact that the probability of exiting unemployment changes with the duration of unemployment.[4] Our models for Canada do capture this "duration dependence." In most cases the chance of exit falls as the unemployment spell lengthens. Consequently, the LTU find it increasingly difficult to find work. In part, this may be due to a reduction in job search intensity over time. There is evidence in Canada that job search effort remains at a fairly high level for the first 9 months of unemployment but declines steadily thereafter, stabilizing at a much lower level after 18 months.[5] Another reason for the declining likelihood of leaving unemployment may be the reluctance of employers to engage someone unemployed for an extended period.

To try models identifying workers at risk of long-term unemployment, we use 1996 data from a relatively new longitudinal database called the Canadian Out of Employment Panel (COEP) (Crossley and Wong 1997). The COEP survey collects detailed microlevel information on the sampled individuals and their households on a regular basis.

A sample from the 1996 COEP was selected to include UI/EI[6] covered workers who had job separations between October 1995 and September 1996. The sample was restricted to those who were laid off, ended a contract, or were dismissed. A final sample of 8,020 observations was used for regression analysis. Table 11.1 summarizes the statistical characteristics of this sample data. The first column reports the proportion of the sample with various demographic, labor market, and job search characteristics. The second column reports the proportion in each subgroup who experienced long-term unemployment.

Overall, 23.3 percent of the individuals in the analytical COEP sample became LTU. The figures in Table 11.1 suggest several factors which may be relevant in predicting long-term unemployment. For example, 28.4 percent of females were found to become LTU, as were 43.3 percent of older workers, 36.6 percent of disabled, 33.6 percent of those without a recall date, and 39.9 percent of those dismissed from their last job.

We examine two different approaches for predicting long-term unemployment. These alternate models are referred to as the Weibull and the probit (see the appendix for technical details). A practical distinction between the two regards the form of the dependent variable. For the Weibull model, the number of weeks unemployed is the dependent variable, while for the probit model the dependent variable is binary having a value of 1 if long-term unemployment was experienced, and 0 otherwise.

When comparing probit and Weibull results, it should be remembered that probit coefficient signs are opposite those obtained from Weibull formulations. Probit coefficients represent the effect of factors

Table 11.1 Sample Characteristics

Variable	% of Sample	LTU (%)
Demographics		
Males	56.9	19.5
Females	43.1	28.4
Youth (15–24)	15.4	15.8
Prime (25–54)	75.8	22.5
Older 55+	8.8	43.3
More than high school	45.0	21.6
Disabled	7.3	36.6
Not disabled	92.7	22.3
Disabled and old	1.1	46.6
Not disabled and old	98.9	23.0
Has child 3–5 yr. old	6.4	17.5
Canadian-born	86.8	22.6
Not Canadian-born	13.2	27.8
Labor market		
Atlantic	12.0	24.3
Quebec	31.7	26.3
Ontario	30.6	22.2
Prairies	13.9	18.7
British Columbia	11.8	20.2
Primary industry	6.9	19.6
Manufacturing industry	18.7	23.3
Construction industry	12.7	14.0
Services industry	53.3	24.9
Public administration	7.0	32.5
Knowledge occupation	7.0	18.1
Management occupation	4.6	31.5
Data occupation	7.8	28.3
Services occupation	13.2	30.2
Goods occupation	45.3	17.2
Data and service occupation	1.4	35.0
Seasonal job	29.0	15.3
Nonseasonal job	71.0	26.6
Had part-time job	13.2	20.7
Had full-time job	86.8	23.7

Table 11.1 (Continued)

Variable	% of Sample	LTU (%)
Job search		
Had a recall date	55.3	15.0
No recall date	44.7	33.6
Dismissed	4.6	39.9
Not dismissed from last job	95.4	22.5
Had UI/EI in previous year	47.5	18.2
No UI/EI in previous year	52.5	27.9

SOURCE: Statistics Canada (2001).

on the probability of becoming LTU, while the Weibull coefficients represent the effect of factors on the probability of leaving unemployment. Table 11.2 presents the results of model estimation with the influence of each factor listed as a determinant of long-term unemployment. For the probit model, both the variable coefficient estimate and the marginal impact of the variable on the probability of long-term unemployment are given.

Beyond the simple correlations suggested in Table 11.1, the model estimates provide information about the influence of a factor controlling for all other measured factors. The negative sign for males in the probit regression indicates that, *ceteris paribus*, male job losers are less likely to become LTU. For the Weibull regression, the positive sign for males indicates a more favorable prospect for reemployment. The probit models also suggest that older job losers are more at risk of LTU, as are individuals who reported a disability and those who did not have a recall date. Not surprisingly, educational attainment appears to have a significant negative relationship with long-term unemployment. Coefficients on regional location are not significant, except in Atlantic Canada. This may be due to the fact that regional dummies are masking within-region unemployment differentials. Taken at face value, the regression results appear to suggest that once a person becomes unemployed, there is little difference among regions in the probability of becoming LTU.

The U.S. systems for WPRS are based on models predicting UI claimants' exhaustion of benefit entitlement. Table 11.3 presents results of predicting UI/EI benefit exhaustion in the Canadian context. The same set of variables is used to predict benefit exhaustion as were used for the probit and Weibull models given in Table 11.2. Therefore, this Canadian benefit exhaustion model was expected to have many properties similar to those reported in Table 11.2. One interesting difference is that part-time workers in general were less likely to be LTU, but part-time status had no impact on the probability of exhausting UI/EI.

At this exploratory stage of system development, an important question concerns the predictive accuracy of the estimated equations. Predictions were computed from the above equations using estimated parameter values. For the probit model, predicted probabilities greater than or equal to 0.5 were classified as likely to experience long-term unemployment.[7] For the Weibull model, the time until exit from unemployment was predicted for each observation with predicted values greater than 52 weeks classified at risk of long-term unemployment.

In our calculations, the probit prediction success rate of 55.0 percent was better than the 45.5 percent observed for the Weibull. Both models are good improvements on the 21.3 percent point estimate of LTU given by the sample proportions.[8] For the Canadian exhaustion model, the probit prediction success rate of 56.4 percent was much better than the 32.6 percent success rate given by the sample proportions. These prediction reliability rates compared favorably with those obtained for U.S. models. Olson, Kelso, Decker, and Klepinger (see p. 29) reported success rates of 58.8 percent for their effort with U.S. models. Notably, exhaustion in U.S. models occurs at 26 weeks, while the Canadian models must predict 52 weeks into the future.

IMPACTS OF REEMPLOYMENT SERVICES

If a good model for predicting the probability of long-term unemployment can be developed, it could be used as part of a system for early referral to reemployment services in Canada. To make such referrals to services valuable, estimates of the net impacts of reemployment

Table 11.2 Determinants of Long-Term Unemployment

Variable	Probit			Weibull	
	Coefficient	P > |t|	Marginal impact (%)	Coefficient	P > |t|
Demographics					
Male	-0.36	0.00	-10.2	0.24	0.00
Youth	-0.99	0.00	-19.9	0.57	0.00
Prime	-0.71	0.00	-22.5	0.41	0.00
More than high school	-0.21	0.01	-5.7	0.15	0.00
Disabled	0.42	0.00	13.3	-0.29	0.00
Disabled and old	-0.15	0.58	-4.0	0.06	0.70
Has child 3–5 yr. old	-0.05	0.72	-1.3	0.05	0.64
Canadian-born	-0.22	0.03	-6.5	0.15	0.04
Labor market					
Atlantic	0.20	0.03	5.9	-0.25	0.00
Quebec	0.15	0.15	4.4	-0.16	0.03
Ontario	-0.07	0.52	-1.8	0.03	0.69
Prairies	-0.16	0.07	-4.2	0.07	0.29
Primary industry	0.13	0.51	3.7	-0.14	0.24
Manufacturing industry	0.04	0.80	1.2	0.08	0.45
Construction industry	-0.09	0.61	-2.3	0.03	0.74
Service industry	-0.14	0.33	-3.9	0.11	0.21
Knowledge occupation	-0.37	0.22	-8.8	0.27	0.24
Management occupation	-0.14	0.63	-3.7	0.22	0.32

	Coef.	P	%	Coef.	P
Data occupation	−0.14	0.59	−3.9	0.23	0.28
Service occupation	−0.04	0.87	−1.2	0.17	0.41
Goods occupation	−0.39	0.15	−10.8	0.42	0.05
Weeks of work in last 52	−0.13	0.33	−12.8	0.28	0.00
Seasonal employment	−0.09	0.20	−2.6	−0.01	0.77
Had part-time job	−0.26	0.02	−6.7	0.32	0.00
Job search					
Had recall date	−0.63	0.00	−18.1	0.49	0.00
Dismissed	0.15	0.43	4.5	−0.04	0.74
Weeks of UI/EI entitlement	0.00	0.28	0.0	0.00	0.94
UI/EI in previous year	−0.20	0.01	−5.6	0.21	0.00
Constant	1.10	0.00		−4.92	0.00
P				0.94	0.00
N	8,020			8,020	
Pseudo R^2	0.1226				
log Likelihood	−3,771			−3E+06	

NOTE: Estimated with COEP data, $P = 1$ indicates no duration dependence. Coefficients on Weibull indicate the percent change in the probability in leaving unemployment in a week.

Table 11.3 Predicting UI/EI Benefit Exhaustion

	Probit		
Variable	Coefficient	P > |t|	Marginal impact (%)
Demographics			
Male	−0.38	0.00	−13.1
Youth	−0.61	0.00	−17.9
Prime	−0.51	0.00	−18.7
More than high school	−0.32	0.00	−10.8
Disabled	0.20	0.20	7.1
Disabled and old	0.17	0.60	6.2
Has child 3—5 yr. old	0.01	0.96	0.2
Canadian-born	−0.27	0.03	−9.9
Labor market			
Atlantic	0.36	0.00	13.2
Quebec	0.07	0.61	2.3
Ontario	0.11	0.41	3.7
Prairies	0.03	0.82	0.9
Primary industry	0.30	0.15	11.0
Manufacturing industry	0.00	0.99	0.1
Construction industry	0.22	0.27	8.0
Service industry	−0.14	0.45	−4.7
Knowledge occupation	−0.63	0.05	−17.7
Management occupation	−0.55	0.08	−16.3
Data occupation	−0.62	0.03	−19.5
Service occupation	−0.19	0.52	−6.4
Goods occupation	−0.85	0.00	−27.6
Weeks of work in last 52	−0.79	0.00	−27.2
Seasonal employment	0.02	0.81	0.8
Had part-time job	0.08	0.54	3.0
Job search			
Had recall date	−0.39	0.00	−13.6
Dismissed	0.06	0.80	2.2
Weeks of UI/EI entitlement	−0.01	0.08	0.0
UI/EI in previous year	−0.15	0.10	−5.2
Constant	2.26	0.00	
N	4,432		
Pseudo R^2	0.1059		

NOTE: Estimated with COEP.

services for participants from the predicted LTU group and non-LTU group are required. A recently completed project on benchmarking reemployment services for the purposes of setting new baselines for the UI/EI reforms provides some evidence of impact on UI/EI claim durations.

Using administrative data prior to the 1996 UI/EI reform, the net UI savings impact resulting from reemployment services was calculated by comparing the actual UI benefits draw of a claimant with his or her expected draw in the absence of a reemployment service. The expected values for claim duration were derived from UI actuarial tables as the comparison group matched on several characteristics to the reemployment service program participants.

For this chapter, UI savings in terms of UI/EI benefit weeks payout have been recalculated to illustrate the potential of selected reemployment services within time frames that could reduce unemployment time and cost. Savings are measured from the end of participation in the reemployment service and are equal to the difference between actual weeks collected on the claim following participation and the expected remaining weeks estimated from the actuarial tables.[9]

Descriptions of the reemployment services are provided in Table 11.4. Table 11.5 reports estimates of net UI/EI weeks of benefit payments saved for selected reemployment services. Positive values indicate savings relative to the expected claim duration derived from actuarial tables; negative values mean that program interventions exceed the expected duration of benefits for people without interventions. This shows that each intervention has a different schedule in which it could work to generate UI savings.

The following highlights can be drawn from Table 11.5:

- For each service or program appearing in the table, the earlier the program delivery, the greater the net savings. An intervention commencing in the first five weeks of a claim generated at least two weeks of savings in all cases except Self-Employment Assistance.
- Job Creation Projects and Job Opportunities both provide wage subsidies and are both effective in producing savings. In the case of Job Creation Projects, the wage subsidy is in the form of regular UI benefits or enhanced UI benefits. Job Opportunities

Table 11. 4 Canadian Reemployment Services

Employment Assistance Services typically follow from a preliminary client assessment or Service Needs Determination. These include job search strategies (two-day course); job-finding clubs (up to three weeks); group employment counseling (9–15 hours); community-based employment assistance for targeted disadvantaged clients; and diagnostic assessment from a counselor referral.

Feepayers are enrolled in an approved training course but pay their own tuition or course costs. They receive their regular UI benefits for as long as they attend the course. At the end of the course, benefits may be paid for an additional three weeks while the feepayer looks for work.

Direct Purchase Option is an option available to local employment offices in a variety of programs for the purchase of training from public or private institutions.

Job Entry was designed to help youth, particularly those who did not complete secondary school or make the school-to-work transition. It offered a mix of classroom training and work experience.

Coordinating Groups are a component of Purchase of Training, which provides clients with the opportunity to learn new job skills in a classroom setting. Training may be purchased from private or public sector trainers either directly through government-to-government and Canada Employment Center purchases, or indirectly through local coordinating groups. Eligible training must meet the needs of the local labor market and the client's interests and aptitudes.

Job Opportunities are directed to persons who have problems joining the labor force, the objective being to provide job opportunities leading to long-term employment. The program provides employers with a wage subsidy to hire selected clients.

Job Creation Projects provide opportunities for unemployed workers to maintain their work skills during unemployment. Participants receive regular or enhanced UI benefits in place of wages.

Self-Employment Assistance promotes self-sufficiency in the labor market through self-employment. Income support may be paid for a maximum of 52 weeks while a person is starting and running a microbusiness. Counseling, training, and technical support could be provided by a designated community organization.

Table 11.5 Net Weeks of UI/EI Benefits Saved Following Participation in Selected Reemployment Services, 1995

Intervention start week	Employment assistance services	Training				Wage subsidy		Self-employment assistance
		Fee-payers	Direct purchase option	Job entry	Coordinating groups	Job creation	Job opportunities	
0–5	2.53	2.05	3.65	3.44	3.64	2.96	11.88	1.35
6–10	1.47	1.08	2.16	2.28	2.39	1.99	11.35	0.56
11–15	1.35	0.61	1.00	1.85	1.78	1.33	9.02	0.46
16–20	1.01	−0.03	0.45	1.11	1.37	1.07	9.01	0.53
21–25	0.47	−0.34	−0.27	0.34	0.62	0.69	6.22	0.33
26–30	0.71	negative	−0.87	−0.36	−0.10	0.16	6.32	0.26
31–35	0.46	—	negative	−1.12	−0.37	0.08	5.53	0.12
36–40	−0.20	—	—	negative	negative	−0.46	5.74	0.00
41–45	−0.60	—	—	—	—	−0.73	3.19	0.00
Av. duration (weeks)	7	33	26	22	17	14	2 UI weeks[a]	45

[a] Job Opportunities participants spent about 24 weeks in their program. They collected UI for about 2.5 weeks and received a wage subsidy for about 21.5 weeks.

clients stop collecting UI and their wage subsidy derives from other sources. The UI savings are thus much larger for Job Opportunities clients.

- Self-employment assistance (SEA) allows a participant up to 52 weeks of income support. The average in 1995 was 45 weeks. Given the long duration, savings from SEA are small. The savings occurring for programs beginning in the first five weeks of a claim reach 1.35 weeks and apply to clients with SEA programs of relatively short duration (about 25 weeks).

- The three training programs (Direct Purchase Option, Job Entry, and Coordinating Groups) yield about the same net savings when delivered in the first 10 weeks of UI. Feepayers, paid by the participant and typically of longer duration, delivers lower but still positive savings.

SUMMARY AND CONCLUSIONS

To sum up, there is evidence that long-term unemployment is a growing and serious labor market problem in Canada. Having just completed a major structural reform in UI/EI and reemployment services (employment benefits and support measures) to address problems associated with recurrent unemployment spells, the Canadian government is committed to a new prevention strategy for the at-risk populations. In this policy context, there is an interest in discovering what has worked (and what has not) regarding worker profiling and early reemployment services for the LTU.

Our preliminary analysis indicates some modest prospects for success in identifying the probability of long-term unemployment for the newly unemployed. Assuming that the existing array of reeemployment services are appropriate for the LTU, targeting of this at-risk group could produce both labor market efficiency and equity benefits.

Notes

We are indebted to Jeff Smith (University of Western Ontario) and Alice Nakamura (University of Alberta) for invaluable advice on modeling issues, and to Lesle Wesa for producing net impact estimates for employment interventions used in this study. All errors are, of course, ours.

1. See Applied Research Branch (1998, pp. 41 and 43). Note that the number used in the analysis is not the LTU but those not employed for a year, which includes both unemployed and out of the labor force.
2. The Canadian LFS is a monthly survey of the labor market activities of the sampled population and is comparable with the U.S. Current Population Survey. The LFS data covers the entire labor market and thus provides a measure of long-term unemployment at the aggregate labor market level.
3. See Lavoie 1996, Table I.
4. The following discussion draws heavily from Chapman and Smith (1993, pp. 7–9).
5. This appears to be true regardless of UI eligibility (Créémieux et al. 1995a, 1995b).
6. Unemployment insurance was renamed employment insurance in 1996.
7. See Greene (1993, pp. 651-653) for further discussion of this procedure. Note that the results can be improved by using other cutoff values. The use of the mean of the dependent variable improves the results somewhat. A grid search of possible values can raise the 55.0 percent to over 80 percent. However, as the issue of the appropriate cutoff is controversial, it was decided to stay with the value of 0.5.
8. Note that the 21.3 percent LTU is different than the 23.3 percent given in Table 11.1. The results reported here are based on the observations used in the regression, whereas Table 11.1 is based on all observations. The sample used in the regression is different because any observation with even one undefined variable is omitted from the analysis.
9. See Wong and Wesa (1999) for a more complete description of the methodology, in particular the difference strategy that was used to control for self-selection.

Appendix

Estimating the Probability of Long-Term Unemployment

Duration models are typically used to empirically investigate the probability or hazard of exiting unemployment at time t given that the unemployment spell has lasted to time t (Kiefer 1988). Following the formulation of Chapman and Smith (1993), the general specification of the Cox proportional hazard framework is used:

(A.1) $h(t, \mathbf{X}'b, a) = H(\mathbf{X}'b) \times H_0(t, a),$

where $h(.)$ is the hazard function given the unemployment duration t; $H(.)$ is the relative hazard; $H_0(.)$ is the baseline hazard; $\mathbf{X}$ is a matrix of explanatory variables; b is a vector of parameters associated with $\mathbf{X}$, and a is a parameter associated with baseline.

The function is made up of the proportional factor H, which represents the observed heterogeneity effect, and H_0, which captures baseline hazard. Since the chance of leaving unemployment often declines with duration, the efficient estimator is based on the Weibull distribution. The component parts of the Weibull form for Equation A.1 can be written as follows:

$$H(\mathbf{X}'\mathbf{b}) = \exp(b_0 + \mathbf{X}'b)$$

and

$$H_0(t, a) = t^{(a-1)},$$

so that Equation A.1 can be written as

(A.2) $h(t, \mathbf{X}'b, a) = \exp(b_0 + \mathbf{X}'b) \times t^{(a-1)}.$

This general formulation permits both duration dependence and observed heterogeneity. If the value of parameter a is constrained to equal 1, no duration dependence is allowed. On the other hand, values of less than 1 mean there is negative duration dependence.

Probit regression models for predicting the probability of long-term unemployment are also estimated in this chapter. For the probit, the risk of unemployment is assumed to be distributed normally, and the dependent variable is dichotomous. The variable takes a value of 1 representing the event of long-term unemployment for those with 52 or more consecutive weeks of unemployment, and 0 otherwise. The probit model permits measurement of the strength of the relationship between the outcome and independent variables in an equation predicting the probability of long-term unemployment.

References

Applied Research Branch. 1998. *An Analysis of EI Employment Insurance Benefit Coverage*. Ottawa: Human Resources Development Canada.

Chapman, Bruce. 1993. *Long-Term Unemployment in Australia: Causes, Consequences and Policy Responses*. A report prepared for the Department of Employment, Education and Training, Canberra, Australia.

Chapman, Bruce, and Peter Smith. 1993. "Predicting the LTU: A Primer for the Commonwealth Employment Service." Discussion paper 285, Australian National University, Canberra, Research School of Social Sciences, Centre for Economic Policy Research.

Créémieux, Pierre-Yves, Pierre Fortin, Paul Storer, and Marc Van Audenrode. 1995a. *Unemployment Insurance and Job-Search Productivity*. Ottawa: Human Resources Development Canada, Macro-Evaluation Directorate.

———. 1995b. *The Impact of Unemployment Insurance on Wages, Search Intensity and the Probability of Re-employment*. Ottawa: Human Resources Development Canada, Macro-Evaluation Directorate.

Crossley, Thomas, and Ging Wong. 1997. "The Canadian Out of Employment Panels: An Introduction." Photocopy. Human Resources Development Canada, Ottawa.

Green, David, and Timothy Sargent. 1995. *Unemployment Insurance and Employment Durations: Seasonal and Non-Seasonal Jobs*. Ottawa: Human Resources Development Canada, Macro-Evaluation Directorate.

Greene, William. 1993. *Econometric Analysis*. Second ed. Englewood Cliffs, New Jersey: Prentice-Hall.

Kiefer, Nicholas. 1988. "Economic Duration Data and Hazard Functions." *Journal of Economic Literature* 26(2): 646–679.

Lavoie, Claude. 1996. "Special Report: Youth Unemployment." *Quarterly Macroeconomic and Labour Market Review* (Spring): 20–26.

Organisation for Economic Co-operation and Development. 1998a. *Early Identification of Job Seekers at Risk of Long-Term Unemployment*. Paris: OECD.

———. 1998b. *OECD Employment Outlook*. Paris: OECD, September.

———. 1998c. *OECD in Figures 1998*. Paris: OECD.

Statistics Canada. 2001. "Canadian Out of Employment Panel Survey." Available at http://stcwww.statcan.ca/english/sdds/4418.htm; last accessed December 2001.

Wandner, Stephen A. 1997. "Early Reemployment for Dislocated Workers: A New United States Initiative." *International Social Security Review* 50(4): 95–112.

Wesa, Lesle. 1995. *Seasonal Employment and the Repeat Use of Unemployment Insurance*. Ottawa: Human Resources Development Canada, Macro-Evaluation Directorate.

Wong, Ging, and Lesle Wesa. 1999. *Management by Results: Employment Benchmarks and Savings Impacts for Employment Insurance*. Ottawa: Human Resources Development Canada, Strategic Evaluation and Monitoring.

Comments on Chapter 11

Jeffrey Smith
University of Maryland

This chapter presents two separate analyses. The first considers the predictability of long-term unemployment, or its close cousin, exhaustion of unemployment insurance (UI/EI) benefits.[1] The second presents some basic estimates of the impact of particular employment and training services on the duration of unemployment, with the impacts varying both by type of service and by when the services begin in the course of the UI/EI spell. I consider each analysis in turn.

In thinking about predicting long-term unemployment, it is useful to step back and ask an important but sometimes neglected question: why bother? There are two possible reasons. The first is that we might want to allocate some treatment based on predicted probabilities of being long-term unemployed for equity reasons. That is, we may have a limited budget for providing employment and training services to the unemployed, and so we may want to concentrate them on the worse off among the unemployed, where we equate worse off with having a long expected duration of unemployment. Although Berger, Black, and Smith (2000) show that this equation is not as obvious as it might seem, it is surely not unreasonable. Once we decide to focus services on those likely to become long-term unemployed, we would like to find a model that does a good job of sorting persons by expected duration; that is, a model that effectively predicts (out of sample!) long-term unemployment.

The model presented by Wong, Hensen, and Roy appears to do reasonably well at predicting long-term unemployment (within sample, in this case). In future work, it would be nice to go further—in particular, to compare the specification employed here with the specifications used in the various profiling models in the Worker Profiling and Reemployment System (WPRS) for UI recipients in the United States. These range from the very spare specification with only a small handful of variables utilized in the Maryland model to the vast armada of covariates employed in the Kentucky model (see Berger et al. 1997). There are also intermediate models such as those of Pennsylvania and Washington.

Three related questions are important here. First, how well do these models perform in the Canadian context? Second, can evidence on their relative performance based on U.S. data be generalized to the Canadian context? Third, what variables represent the most important predictors of unemployment duration in the Canadian context? The second question indicates the extent to which Canada can rely on U.S. research on predictive models. The third question holds great practical importance, as including additional covariates can substantially increase the cost (if additional data sets must be employed) and complexity of a predictive model.

The second reason for basing service allocation on the predicted probability of long-term unemployment or some close analogue such as UI/EI benefit exhaustion is efficiency. We might imagine that the impact of employment and training services, whether required as in the U.S. WPRS, or optional as in the current Canadian policy environment, varies with the probability of long-term unemployment. Assuming that the cost of providing the services is roughly constant across persons, efficiency dictates assigning the services to those with the largest impacts. In general, the presumption is that the impact of employment and training services will be larger for persons with a high probability of long-term unemployment, although the evidence for this presumption is mixed at best. On this point see, e.g., Black et al. (2001) and O'Leary, Decker, and Wandner in this volume (p. 161).

When efficiency is the aim, the model predicting long-term unemployment has both a different justification and a different goal. It should now seek to do the best job possible of distinguishing persons who will and will not have a large impact from whatever services are to be provided conditional on the predicted probability. This is not quite the same thing as simply doing as well as possible at predicting long-term unemployment. For example, if subgroups among the long-term unemployed have low mean impacts of service, then the model should exclude them from services. The present chapter does not address the conceptual and practical distinctions between the two motivations for predicting long-term unemployment; it would be useful to do so in future work.

Turn now to the authors' analysis of the impacts of reemployment services on the duration of UI/EI claims, conditional on type of employment and training service received and on when in the spell the service is received. This analysis addresses the right questions—what are the impacts of different services that might be provided to the unemployed, and when is the optimal point in a spell to provide a given service. The first of these two questions relates to the discussion of the Service Outcomes and Measurement System and other profiling methods described in Chapter 10. For efficiency reasons, we want to assign unemployed persons to those services that will benefit them the most. The second question is also an important one, and one that has received relatively little study. It is a question that has implicitly been answered in different ways by different programs. On the one hand, the WPRS system in the United States implicitly assumes that early service provision is best. On the other hand, the service allocation scheme embodied in the new Workforce Investment Act program in the United States assumes that expensive services should be deferred until inexpensive ones have been tried. Despite this variation in practice, I am not aware of much evidence on this question in the literature. More evidence, such as that provided here, is of great use.

At the same time, while the chapter asks the right questions, it is difficult to evaluate the quality of the answers. The text omits important aspects of the econometric strategy used to identify the impacts of training, both in terms of broad concepts and specific details. A long literature, including papers such as LaLonde (1986), Heckman and Hotz (1989), Heckman, LaLonde, and Smith (1999), and Smith and Todd (forthcoming), documents the importance of the choice of non-experimental evaluation strategy. While the audience for this book is a nontechnical one, it remains very important to convey the gist of the econometric strategy so that readers familiar with the econometric evaluation literature can judge the likely extent and source of bias in the impact estimates.

The reader should also keep in mind that impacts on UI/EI benefit receipt represent only one component of a complete social cost/benefit analysis. Providing employment and training programs to the unemployed has a number of effects. Some effects are distributional. For example, employed persons paying payroll taxes benefit if the training reduces the amount of benefits paid by an amount that exceeds the direct cost of training. This reduction in benefits comes at the expense of the unemployed persons who would otherwise have received them. Other effects of the program may relate to efficiency, as when the program allows efficient training to occur that would otherwise not have occurred due to credit constraints. These aspects of the social cost/benefit calculation need to be carefully distinguished. In particular, all costs, including the direct costs of training and the net effects of the training programs on the efficiency costs associated with the distortionary taxes used to fund the UI program, should be taken into account in the analysis.

It is also important to keep in mind that there may be general equilibrium effects associated with these programs. For example, such effects could result from skill price changes resulting from increases in the supply of skilled labor due to the training being provided. Partial equilibrium analyses such as that presented in this chapter will not capture these effects. Indeed, the impact estimates provided by a partial equilibrium analysis may be biased in the presence of general equilibrium effects, which may cause the experiences of comparison group members to differ from what they would have been in the absence of the program.

Note

1. A few years ago, Canada took the bold step of changing the name of unemployment insurance (UI) to employment insurance (EI). To avoid confusion, in these comments I will refer to the program as either unemployment insurance or UI/EI.

References

Berger, Mark, Dan Black, Amitabh Chandra, and Steven Allen. 1997. "Profiling Workers for Unemployment Insurance in Kentucky." *Kentucky Journal of Economics and Business* 16: 1–18.

Berger, Mark, Dan Black, and Jeffrey Smith. 2000. "Evaluating Profiling as a Means of Allocating Government Services." In *Econometric Evaluation of*

Labor Market Policies, Michael Lechner and Friedhelm Pfeiffer, eds. Heidelberg: Physica-Verlag, pp. 59–84.

Black, Dan, Jeffrey Smith, Mark Berger, and Brett Noel. 2001. "Is the Threat of Training More Effective than Training Itself? Experimental Evidence from UI Profiling in Kentucky." Unpublished manuscript, University of Maryland.

Heckman, James, and V. Joseph Hotz. 1989. "Choosing among Alternative Methods of Estimating the Impact of Social Programs: The Case of Manpower Training." *Journal of the American Statistical Association* 84 (408): 862–874.

Heckman, James, Robert LaLonde, and Jeffrey Smith. 1999. "The Economics and Econometrics of Active Labor Market Policies." In *Handbook of Labor Economics, Volume 3A*, Orley Ashenfelter and David Card, eds. Amsterdam: North-Holland, pp. 1865–2097.

LaLonde, Robert. 1986. "Evaluating the Econometric Evaluations of Training Programs with Experimental Data." *American Economic Review* 76(4): 604–620.

Smith, Jeffrey, and Petra Todd. Forthcoming. "Does Matching Overcome LaLonde's Critique of Nonexperimental Methods?" *Journal of Econometrics*.

Part IV

New Directions for Targeting Employment Services

12

A Frontline Decision Support System for One-Stop Centers

Randall W. Eberts, Christopher J. O'Leary, and Kelly J. DeRango
W.E. Upjohn Institute for Employment Research

The Workforce Investment Act (WIA) of 1998 emphasizes the integration and coordination of employment services. Central to achieving this aim is the federal requirement that local areas receiving WIA funding must establish one-stop centers, where providers of various employment services within a local labor market are assembled in one location. This arrangement is expected to coordinate and streamline the delivery of employment-related programs and to meet the needs of both job seekers and employers more effectively than did the previous arrangement.

Successful implementation of the one-stop system requires new management tools and techniques to help staff meet the challenges presented by the one-stop environment. A major challenge is the large volume of customers expected to use the system. Increased use of services is expected because of a reduced emphasis on program eligibility as a condition for participation in the workforce investment system. Nonetheless, resources for comprehensive assessment and counseling are limited, and frontline staff have few tools with which to help them make decisions.

A prime challenge for frontline staff is to determine which set of services best meets the needs of customers who enter a one-stop center, and to do this in a consistent, rational, and efficient manner. However, not all one-stop center staff may have sufficient experience to make informed decisions for clients participating in the wide variety of programs offered. The coordination of services under the new one-stop arrangement now requires staff to serve customers with various backgrounds, whereas prior to the creation of one-stop centers, staff typically concentrated in a single program area and saw clients with similar barriers. An additional complication is the emphasis that WIA places on performance outcomes and accountability. WIA requires that program success be measured by employment, earnings, job retention, and knowledge or skill attainment.

The Frontline Decision Support System (FDSS) is a set of administrative tools that is being developed to help frontline staff successfully perform their duties within one-stop centers. The goal of these tools is to assist staff in quickly assessing the needs of customers and in referring customers to services that best meet their needs. FDSS includes new tools to help customers conduct a systematic search for jobs that offer the best match, to set a realistic wage goal, and to assist staff in determining which one-stop center services are likely to be effective in meeting the needs of specific customers in becoming employed.

The W.E. Upjohn Institute for Employment Research is working to design, develop, test, and implement an FDSS in pilot sites within the states of Georgia and Washington. These states were chosen because they offer an opportunity to demonstrate the adaptability and capability of the FDSS within different one-stop center operating environments. Recognizing that the computer operating systems for the one-stop centers vary among states, FDSS is being designed so that states can easily integrate the decision tools into their specific computer systems. The FDSS tools are designed to be used within the data-retrieval and display systems being implemented by states for their one-stop centers.

The design and implementation of FDSS is a cooperative effort of the U.S. Department of Labor (DOL), the state employment agencies of Georgia and Washington, and the W.E. Upjohn Institute. After testing the system at sites in these states, DOL intends to offer FDSS tools to other interested states. With research and operations carried out within the same organization, the Institute is uniquely positioned to coordinate the analytical and administrative tasks required to develop, test, and implement FDSS within the one-stop centers. The Institute not only conducts employment-related research but also administers the state and federal employment programs that are the responsibility of the local Workforce Investment Board. The Institute has served as the administrator of federal and state employment-related programs for the Kalamazoo, Michigan, area since the early 1970s. During that period, the Institute has operated programs under the Comprehensive Employment and Training Act, the Job Training Partnership Act, and currently WIA.

The purpose of this chapter is to present an overview of FDSS and to give examples of the analysis underlying some of the decision algorithms that are the backbone of the FDSS tools. In the next section, we summarize the overall concept of FDSS and provide an outline of the typical client flow through the one-stop centers. We then proceed to describe examples of the statistical models that are used in the systematic job search module of FDSS. These models include estimates of the likelihood of finding a job in the industry in which the worker was employed prior to displacement and estimates of the earnings that a displaced worker might expect when looking for reemployment. We next outline the algorithm that identifies occupations that are related to a worker's occupation held prior to displacement. The purpose of this algorithm is to provide workers who have been frustrated by their initial job search efforts with a list of occupations that have skills and attributes similar to the ones embodied in jobs held prior to displacement. This list of related occupations allows a worker to conduct a more systematic job search effort. Finally, we describe the features of the second FDSS module, the service referral module, which is currently under development. This module assesses the most effective set of services based on the individual's characteristics and employment history.

FRONTLINE DECISION SUPPORT WITHIN ONE-STOP CENTERS

FDSS provides one-stop center staff with client information and assessment tools that can be used in helping clients conduct a systemic job search and in determining the set of employment services that should work best for specific clients. To understand the role of FDSS, it is first necessary to provide a brief overview of one-stop centers, the services they provide, and the way in which staff interact with customers. The operation of one-stop centers varies among states, and even among local areas within states. Consequently, we can provide only a stylized description of one-stop centers, which suffices for our purpose of describing how FDSS can be integrated into the general approach of these centers.

As mandated by WIA, one-stop centers provide a central physical location for the provision of services offered by federal and state employment programs. WIA requires that the following programs be included: unemployment insurance, employment service, dislocated worker and youth training, welfare-to-work, veterans' employment and training programs, adult education, postsecondary vocational education, vocational rehabilitation, Title V of the Older Americans Act, and trade adjustment assistance. Other programs may also be included under the one-stop center's umbrella of services. One-stop centers are designed to serve customers within local Workforce Investment Areas, which usually encompass the population of one or more counties within a state. Workforce Investment Areas with large populations or which span a large geographical area may choose to establish several one-stop centers. WIA required that each state develop a system of one-stop centers that would be fully operational by July 2000. Most states met this target date.

Services provided by the one-stop centers are divided into three levels: core, intensive, and training. Services within each level are characterized by the amount of staff involvement and the extent to which customers can access the service independently. Core services typically have the broadest access and the least staff involvement of the three categories. Many core services are accessible on a self-serve basis. All adults and dislocated workers can access core services, which include assessment interviews, resume workshops, labor market information, and interviews for referral to other services.

Intensive services, the next level of services within a one-stop center, require a greater level of staff involvement, and access is more restricted than for core services. Services within the intensive category include individual and group counseling, case management, aptitude and skill proficiency testing, job finding clubs, creation of a job search plan, and career planning. Training services, the third and final level of services offered by one-stop centers, use staff most intensively and are open to customers only through referrals. One-stop centers typically contract with organizations outside the centers to provide these services. Included in this set of services is adult basic skills education, on-the-job training, work experience, and occupational skills training.

Several challenges must be surmounted for successful implementation of one-stop centers. The first is the large volume of customers expected to use the centers. Nationally, nearly 50 million people are expected to use the one-stop centers each year. Center staff will be faced with serving more people than under previous organizational arrangements. The move toward integrating services raises another challenge: staff will be asked to serve clients who may have unfamiliar backgrounds and needs. For instance, a staff person who worked extensively with dislocated workers under JTPA may now be asked to work with welfare recipients as well. Job search techniques and services that are appropriate for dislocated workers may not be as effective for welfare recipients. The lack of prior experience counseling welfare recipients may hinder staff effectiveness. WIA does not provide additional resources for staffing or significant cross training.

Another challenge for operators of one-stop centers is to refer customers to services in the most effective matter. The efficiency and effectiveness of a center's operations are driven by the difference in cost of providing the three levels of services. As shown in Figure 12.1, the cost of services increases dramatically and the anticipated number of participants falls as one moves from core services to training services. Therefore, the ability to identify the needs of individuals and to refer them to the appropriate service as early as possible in the process will determine the cost-effectiveness of the one-stop centers. FDSS is designed to address the need for more informed decision-making and the strategic referral of services.

FDSS includes two basic modules or sets of tools. Figure 12.2 shows how the two modules fit into the operation of the one-stop center. The first is the systematic job search module. This set of tools provides clients with customized information about several aspects of the job search process, with the purpose of assisting them in conducting a more systematic search. Initial job search activities are concentrated in the core services, and consequently this is where the systematic search module will be incorporated. A large proportion of individuals who come to the one-stop centers are looking for job search assistance in the form of labor market information, assistance with preparing resumes, an initial understanding of the likelihood of finding a job, and what wage or salary level to expect. The first prototype FDSS includes algorithms for five programs: employment service, unemployment insurance, skill training, welfare-to-work, and veterans employment and

Figure 12.1 Use and Cost of One-Stop Career Center Services under the Workforce Investment Act

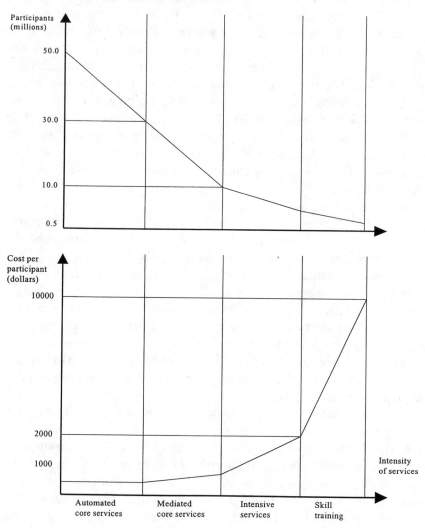

Figure 12.2 One-Stop Center Client Flow

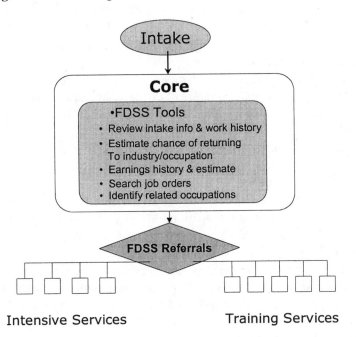

Intensive Services   Training Services

training programs. To illustrate how these algorithms are constructed, this chapter focuses on the tools developed for displaced workers.

The systematic job search module includes three basic components to help job seekers become better informed about their job prospects and expected earnings. The first component, referred to as the industry transition component, estimates the likelihood that a customer can find a job in the industry in which they were previously employed. Obviously, this component is designed primarily to inform displaced workers about their job prospects. Research has shown that displaced workers tend to wait for jobs to open up in the industries in which they worked before displacement. Workers prefer to return to jobs with which they are familiar, and typically salaries are higher for those who stay in the same industry. However, in many cases, a worker was displaced because of general downsizing in that industry, which reduces the chances that a job in the same industry will become available. Waiting for such an event to occur increases the amount of unemployment insurance (UI) benefits the person will draw and reduces the likelihood of finding employment, even in another industry. The purpose of the systematic search module of FDSS is to help inform job seekers as to their prospects for finding jobs and to provide realistic assessments of likely compensation levels.

The need for a realistic assessment of expected reemployment earnings leads to the second component of the systematic search module—the earnings algorithm. The earnings algorithm is a statistical model that uses personal characteristics, work history, prior earnings, and educational attainment to predict earnings upon reemployment.

The third component is the related-occupations algorithm. The algorithm offers job seekers who have exhausted their likely job prospects within their prior occupation with a list of other occupations that are similar to their prior occupation. We offer different algorithms based on available data and show how they differ. More detailed descriptions of these algorithms are provided below.

The second module of FDSS is the service referral module. As mentioned in the overview of one-stop centers, a critical element for successful implementation of one-stop centers is staff ability to identify the needs of customers and to refer them expeditiously to services that best address their barriers to employment. Compounding this challenge is the possible lack of staff experience in serving a wide range of customers. The purpose of the FDSS service referral module is to compile and process information about the effectiveness of various alternative services in a way that better informs staff for referring customers to services. The service referral module uses information about the characteristics and outcomes of individuals who have recently participated in and completed services offered by one-stop centers. This information is used to estimate statistical relationships between personal attributes and outcomes. It should be emphasized that this module does not supplant staff referral decisions. Rather, it provides a means for staff to make better informed decisions.

The service referral module has two basic algorithms. The first is to estimate a person's employability, or likelihood of finding a job; the flip side of this is identifying an individual's barriers to employment. The second algorithm delineates the paths, or sequential combinations of services, that lead to successful outcomes. By conditioning these paths on the employability of a specific customer, the service referral module can rank the likely effectiveness of various programs for individuals having specific observable characteristics.

TOOLS FOR THE SYSTEMATIC SEARCH ALGORITHM

The systematic job search module consists of three tools: 1) the probability of return to the prior industry, 2) likely reemployment earnings, and 3) three alternative approaches to identifying occupations related to a prior one. For the first two tools, examples are provided for both Georgia and Washington using data on UI beneficiaries. The Georgia examples are for metropolitan Atlanta, and the Washington examples are for the south Puget Sound area. The third tool, identification of related occupations, is based on three sources: analyst ratings, national survey data, and Georgia Employment Service job placement data.

Return to Industry

Many one-stop customers, particularly displaced workers, will switch employers. Prior research suggests that earnings losses will be minimized if the new job is in the same industry and occupation. As suggested by Becker's (1964) theory of human capital formation, the quickest way to return to the prior lifetime earnings path is to resume employment and begin building firm-specific human capital in a new job. To help clients more realistically assess job prospects, FDSS provides an estimate of the probability of returning to employment in their prior industry.

Reliable data are available from UI wage records in both Georgia and Washington to identify the industry in which the person was employed before and after displacement. Unfortunately, similar information is not available for an individual's occupation. Table 12.1 shows an industry transition matrix for UI clients in metropolitan Atlanta. Industries are separated into nine categories with the prior industry category in the left column and the reemployment industry along the top row. In each row, the largest element is on the diagonal of the matrix, indicating that the largest share of industry UI recipients return to work

Table 12.1 Industry of Employment Transition Matrix: Percentage of Unemployment Insurance Clients, Metropolitan Atlanta, Georgia

Reemploy. ind. / Prior ind.	Agric., forestry, fishing	Mining, construction	Manufacturing	Transp., comm., utilities	Wholesale trade	Retail trade	Finance, insurance, real estate	Services	Public admin.
Agric., forestry, fishery	26.3	10.1	10.9	4.9	10.5	11.7	3.2	20.6	1.6
Mining, const.	0.5	60.1	5.8	3.9	5.3	5.1	2.5	15.0	1.6
Manufacturing	0.3	3.8	40.1	5.7	11.7	8.9	3.0	24.8	1.6
Transp., comm., util.	0.4	2.9	6.4	41.8	8.0	7.2	4.7	26.6	2.0
Wholesale trade	0.4	4.5	14.2	7.4	28.6	11.7	3.9	27.8	1.5
Retail trade	0.3	2.4	6.2	5.5	7.3	45.5	4.7	26.6	1.5
FIRE	0.3	2.5	4.2	4.7	5.1	6.8	38.3	35.7	2.4
Services	0.3	2.6	6.2	6.2	6.2	8.4	5.9	61.6	25.3
Public admin.	0.5	3.6	5.4	7.9	4.0	7.8	6.1	39.4	25.3

SOURCE: Based on data provided by the Georgia Department of Labor.

in the same industry. These aggregate average return probabilities range from 20.8 percent in agriculture, forestry, and fishery, to 73.3 percent in mining and construction.

Table 12.2 summarizes the percentage change in quarterly earnings for these industry employment changes in the Atlanta metropolitan area. The diagonal of Table 12.2 is positive for all industries except public administration, indicating that those who manage to be reemployed in their prior industry have earnings gains despite changing jobs. Similar patterns can be seen for south Puget Sound, Washington, in Tables 12.3 and 12.4. However, a larger share of UI claimants managed to be reemployed in their prior industry, and earnings growth was somewhat stronger in that region of Washington than in metropolitan Atlanta.

To provide individual estimates of the probability of being reemployed in the prior industry, we estimated logit models for each industry transition.[1] The logit model relates whether or not an individual stays in the same industry to a set of explanatory variables including prior earnings, age, educational attainment, the quarter of the year in which UI was applied for, and indicators for prior occupation.[2] The logit model also included variables that indicated whether an individual was a member of the following population groups: youth, veterans, currently employed, receiving public welfare assistance, and dislocated workers.[3] For Washington we were also able to include an indicator of union membership. Because of eligibility conditions, UI beneficiaries include very few people currently enrolled in school, so that category is not included.

Tables 12.5 and 12.6 provide examples of earnings models estimated on UI recipients in Atlanta and south Puget Sound whose prior job was in the manufacturing industry. Comparing parameter estimates across the two regions in the different states shows a large degree of consistency. In all cases where parameters on similar variables were estimated with adequate statistical precision, the estimates are of the same sign and similar magnitude. As an additional way of comparing the models, Tables 12.5 and 12.6 each consider the same three examples for evaluating the probability of returning to work in the manufacturing industry. Example 1 is a person aged 35, with a high school education, who earned $30,000 per year in a clerical/sales occupation, and applied for UI in the second calendar quarter.[4] The probability of

Table 12.2 Mean Percentage Change in Earnings for the Industry of Employment Transition Matrix, Metropolitan Atlanta, Georgia

Reemploy. ind. / Prior ind.	Agric., forestry, fishing	Mining, const.	Manufacturing	Transp., comm., utilities	Wholesale trade	Retail trade	Finance, insurance, real estate	Services	Public admin.
Agric., forestry, fishery	1.6	1.6	-3.0	-0.9	32.4	-12.1	12.8	-3.5	-16.6
Mining, const.	-30.6	6.4	-7.8	-0.9	-2.1	-25.4	3.3	-9.9	-25.5
Manufacturing	-34.3	-14.3	6.6	-0.5	-2.1	-29.4	-9.0	-15.7	-21.4
Trans., comm., util.	-25.8	0.1	-2.1	6.2	-4.3	-25.2	-9.3	-15.8	-19.0
Wholesale trade	-28.3	-2.0	-2.0	1.3	7.1	-21.4	-0.7	-7.4	-26.8
Retail trade	-12.1	0.8	9.0	6.0	10.1	1.9	10.2	-3.1	-9.7
FIRE	-28.3	-9.9	-6.6	-10.1	1.4	-26.4	8.6	-11.2	-23.4
Services	-20.3	6.3	8.7	9.3	14.4	-20.0	6.7	3.9	-8.4
Public admin.	-22.7	-7.7	1.7	2.2	12.2	-21.5	-8.6	-2.4	-4.2

SOURCE: Based on data provided by the Georgia Department of Labor.

Table 12.3 Industry of Employment Transition Matrix: Percentage of Unemployment Insurance Clients, South Puget Sound, Washington

Reemploy. ind. / Prior ind.	Agric., forestry, fishing	Mining, const.	Manufacturing	Transp., comm., utilities	Wholesale trade	Retail trade	Finance, insurance, real estate	Services	Public admin.
Agric., forestry, fishery	20.8	11.3	13.5	8.8	5.3	12.8	3.5	21.4	2.6
Mining, const.	0.9	73.3	4.5	3.6	3.8	3.7	1.6	7.6	1.1
Manufacturing	1.0	5.7	54.8	4.7	7.1	6.9	1.7	16.9	1.2
Trans., comm., util.	0.7	4.2	4.9	61.0	5.9	5.7	2.3	14.0	1.4
Wholesale trade	0.4	7.7	15.9	7.2	29.2	12.1	3.3	22.8	1.4
Retail trade	0.7	3.7	6.7	4.7	7.2	50.9	3.9	21.0	1.3
FIRE	0.6	3.8	4.3	4.6	2.8	7.2	48.9	26.2	1.6
Services	0.7	3.3	5.9	4.6	4.1	8.9	4.6	65.1	2.9
Public admin.	0.3	5.2	8.2	8.0	6.6	9.2	3.6	28.9	30.0

SOURCE: Based on data provided by the Washington State Employment Security Department.

Table 12.4 Mean Percentage Change in Earnings for the Industry of Employment Transition Matrix, South Puget Sound, Washington

Prior ind. \ Reemploy. ind.	Agric., forestry, fishing	Mining, const.	Manufacturing	Transp., comm., utilities	Wholesale trade	Retail trade	Finance, insurance, real estate	Services	Public admin.
Agric., forestry, fishery	7.4	8.1	11.1	24.4	7.6	-2.5	13.3	-5.1	-4.6
Mining, const.	9.1	9.0	14.1	16.5	13.4	-0.9	16.9	3.7	10.1
Manufacturing	5.5	-0.3	1.2	-8.0	-5.9	-9.5	-0.7	-9.0	1.9
Trans., comm., util.	0.1	8.4	16.9	8.4	1.8	-0.1	7.2	0.6	-2.6
Wholesale trade	4.1	16.9	2.4	3.2	1.6	-3.8	2.5	-2.0	5.0
Retail trade	-1.6	24.7	29.2	20.7	12.5	3.4	10.7	8.3	27.3
FIRE	-15.9	8.8	14.5	10.5	3.5	-1.1	4.3	-4.0	-0.8
Services	-0.5	18.6	22.3	17.8	15.6	2.6	16.2	3.7	11.2
Public admin.	-24.2	-11.5	6.1	3.8	-3.0	-21.1	3.5	-11.9	8.8

SOURCE: Based on data provided by the Washington State Employment Security Department.

returning to the same industry was estimated to be 0.294 in Georgia and 0.346 in Washington. The second example shows the Washington model to be much more sensitive to the prior earnings variable. Doubling prior earnings from $30,000 to $60,000 raised the chance of returning to manufacturing to 0.532 in south Puget Sound and only to 0.327 in the Atlanta area. The third example illustrates the same tendency for a lower prior annual earnings of $10,000, with the probability in Washington falling to 0.114 and that in Georgia falling to 0.172.

Reemployment Earnings

The WIA legislation permits intensive services to include "evaluation to identify employment barriers and appropriate employment goals" and also "the development of an individual employment plan, to identify appropriate employment goals, appropriate achievement, and appropriate combinations of services for the participant to achieve their employment goals."[5] An underlying principle of WIA is that the best training is a job. Moderating wage expectations in order to gain a new job may be the quickest way to return to the prior earnings path. This establishes a need for a system like FDSS and requires that outcomes be judged relative to individual targets. FDSS provides an algorithm to estimate the expected reemployment earnings for each job seeker. By providing the job seeker with a realistic assessment of earnings prospects, he or she can conduct a more informed job search that can hasten employment.

Displaced workers and those who have had little attachment to the workplace, such as welfare recipients, may have little understanding of the earnings level that they might expect to find in the local labor market given their skills and opportunities. Displaced workers, for example, may expect to receive wages in their new jobs comparable to those in jobs they held prior to being displaced. However, recent research has shown that the earnings can drop by as much as 25 percent for workers who have found jobs after being displaced. Most of the loss in earnings is due to loss in value of firm-specific skills (Jacobson, Lalonde, and Sullivan 1993). It is important to point out that the FDSS earnings assessment is only suggestive. Job seekers who find the recommended target to be out of line with their expectations may discuss their differences with a staff person in the one-stop center. The staff

Table 12.5 Logistic Regression Summary for the Probability of Returning to the Same Industry for UI Clients in Atlanta Whose Prior Industry Is Manufacturing

Variable description	Parameter estimate	Std. error	Marg. effect	Hypothetical workers[a]		
				1	2	3
log(max. prior earnings)	0.663**	0.061	0.159	8.923	9.616	7.824
Age as of ref. date	0.017**	0.003	0.004	35	35	35
Education						
Less than high school	0.032	0.058	0.008	0	0	1
More than high school	−0.304**	0.060	−0.070	0	1	0
Youth, ages 14–21	−0.173	0.202	−0.041	0	0	0
Veteran	−0.161**	0.073	−0.038	0	0	0
Welfare recipient	0.052	0.239	0.013	0	0	0
Dislocated worker	−0.123**	0.054	0.029	0	0	0
Employed	−0.036	0.144	−0.009	0	0	0
Reference date						
In 2nd qtr.	−0.043	0.063	−0.010	1	1	1
In 3rd qtr.	−0.086	0.068	−0.020	0	0	0
In 4th qtr.	−0.098	0.073	−0.023	0	0	0
Prior occupation						
Clerical and sales	−0.062	0.092	−0.015	1	1	1
Services	0.408**	0.150	0.101	0	0	0
Agric., forestry, fishing	1.144**	0.436	0.277	0	0	0
Processing	0.937**	0.132	0.230	0	0	0
Machine trades	1.021**	0.096	0.249	0	0	0

Bench work	0.988**	0.106	0.242	0	0
Structural work	1.089***	0.110	0.264	0	0
Miscellaneous	0.795**	0.088	0.196	0	0
Intercept	-7.291**	0.549	-0.400	1	1
Probability of return to same industry			0.294	0.327	0.172

NOTE: ** = Parameter statistically significant at the 95% confidence level in a two-tailed test.

[a] Hypothetical worker 1: age 35, high school education, earning $30,000 per year in a clerical/sales occupation, entering in the 2nd quarter of the year; hypothetical worker 2: age 35, post-high school education, earning $60,000 per year in a clerical/sales occupation, entering in the 2nd quarter of the year; hypothetical worker 3: age 35, less than high school education, earning $10,000 per year in a clerical/sales occupation, entering in the 2nd quarter of the year.

SOURCE: Based on data provided by the Georgia Department of Labor.

Table 12.6 Logistic Regression Summary for the Probability of Returning to the Same Industry for UI Clients in South Puget Sound, Washington, Whose Prior Industry Is Manufacturing

Variable description	Parameter estimate	Std. error	Marg. effect	Hypothetical workers[a]		
				1	2	3
log(max. prior earnings)	0.733**	0.092	0.182	8.923	9.616	7.824
Age as of ref. date	0.026**	0.004	0.006	35	35	35
Education						
Less than high school	0.077	0.095	0.019	0	0	1
More than high school	−0.275**	0.086	−0.068	0	1	0
Youth, ages 14–21	0.208	0.188	0.051	0	0	0
Veteran	−0.167	0.109	−0.042	0	0	0
Welfare recipient	−0.402**	0.148	−0.100	0	0	0
Dislocated worker	−0.102	0.174	−0.025	0	0	0
Employed	0.530**	0.090	0.125	0	1	0
Union	−0.298*	0.168	−0.074	0	0	0
Reference date						
In 2nd qtr.	−0.035	0.097	−0.009	1	1	1
In 3rd qtr.	−0.186**	0.091	−0.046	0	0	0
In 4th qtr.	0.207	0.149	0.051	0	0	0
Prior occupation						
Clerical, sales	−0.306**	0.152	−0.076	1	1	1
Services	0.173	0.221	0.042	0	0	0
Agric., forestry, fishing	1.048**	0.278	0.228	0	0	0

Processing	0.842**	0.160	0.190	0	0	0	0
Machine trades	0.891***	0.142	0.199	0	0	0	0
Bench work	1.064***	0.145	0.230	0	0	0	0
Structural work	0.841***	0.146	0.190	0	0	0	0
Miscellaneous	0.817***	0.134	0.185	0	0	0	0
Had job last quarter	0.618***	0.116	0.157	1	1	1	0
Intercept	-8.419***	0.838	-2.085	1	1	1	1
Probability of return to same industry				0.346	0.532	0.114	

NOTE: ** = Parameter statistically significant at the 95% confidence level in a two-tailed test; * = parameter statistically significant at the 90% confidence level in a two-tailed test.

[a] Hypothetical worker 1: age 35, high school education, earning $30,000 per year in a clerical/sales occupation, entering in the 2nd quarter of the year; hypothetical worker 2: age 35, post-high school education, earning $60,000 per year in a clerical/sales occupation, entering in the 2nd quarter of the year; hypothetical worker 3: age 35, less than high school education, earning $10,000 per year in a clerical/sales occupation, entering in the 2nd quarter of the year.

SOURCE: Based on data provided by the Washington State Employment Security Department.

person may use several means in addition to FDSS to establish a realistic earnings target, including past studies and current labor market conditions.

Quartile regression models are used to estimate earnings. The upper and lower bounds on the earnings range are set at the 25th and 75th percentiles, so one can think of this range as including earnings of half the people with similar measured characteristics. The model relates quarterly earnings to personal characteristics and labor market conditions. Many of these factors may be similar to those used by employment counselors to match job seekers to openings. The model assesses those factors in a systematic and consistent way so that customers with similar needs and characteristics are treated similarly.

The earnings models were developed using quarterly earnings data from UI wage records, which are the most reliable source of earnings data. However, workers do not usually measure their compensation in terms of quarterly earnings. Rather, earnings are typically expressed as hourly, weekly, monthly, and yearly rates of compensation. Converting the quarterly earnings to any of these other units is problematic, since wage records do not indicate the number of hours worked or even the number of weeks worked during a quarter. By using the maximum earnings in the year before and the year after receiving reemployment services, we anticipate that quarterly earnings will reflect full-time hours. Conversion from quarterly earnings to hourly earnings can then be achieved by applying the usual hours of work observed in each occupation and industry group using national survey data.[6]

For consistency of exposition, we report the results from the quartile regression models for the manufacturing sector in metropolitan Atlanta and south Puget Sound, the same regions and industry as used in the "return-to-prior-industry" models discussed above. As shown in Tables 12.7 and 12.8, the model includes variables typically used in earnings models, such as educational attainment, prior job tenure, occupation, and industry. Of course, the industry of reemployment is known only after a person finds a job. Since it is an endogenous variable, it would be appropriate to find an instrument for this variable, such as the industry transition regression described in the previous section. However, since our primary purpose is to construct a relatively simple model that offers the best prediction of future wages, we have not instrumented the variable. Instead, when predicting the earnings for individuals we substitute the prediction of the likelihood the person will find a job in the same industry as a predictor in the earnings equation. Earnings models for Georgia and Washington also include age and age squared to capture the earnings cycle over one's working life.

Georgia data permit the inclusion of additional explanatory variables measuring tenure on the previous job, possession of a driver's license, availability for rotating shifts, employer attachment, current school enrollment status, and an individual's self-reported reservation wage. Washington data contain an indicator of union membership. Both models include indicator variables for population groups that are typically identified with the various programs offered by one-stop centers. These groups include youth, veterans, currently employed, receiving public welfare assistance, dislocated workers, and economically disadvantaged workers.

Results of the median regressions for the two models, as shown in Tables 12.7 and 12.8, are broadly consistent with previous earnings research. In both models, prior earnings, education, and age are positively correlated with future earnings, and occupation variables in prior employment are significant predictors of future earnings. In addition, returning to the industry of prior employment raises earnings by roughly 17 percent in both models, and the coefficient estimates are highly statistically significant. Indicators for the various population groups are not statistically significant except for welfare recipients in Washington and the economically disadvantaged and veterans in Georgia.

Coefficient estimates related to variables unique to each state add further insight into the determinants of a worker's compensation. For Georgia, results show that possession of a driver's license increases earnings. In addition, tenure on the previous job reduces earnings, which supports the results of WPRS models that detachment and subsequent loss of work experience reduces future earnings. On the other hand, those individuals with higher reservation wages receive higher future earnings, possibly because they know of skills and other personal traits not measured in the data that make them attractive to employers. In the Washington model, union membership raises earnings by 9 percent.

The purpose of the earnings algorithm is to estimate an earnings range for each one-stop customer. To do this, the regression coefficients are multiplied by the individual's characteristics. Consider again

Table 12.7 Quartile Regression Coefficient Estimates and Examples of Predicted Earnings from an Earnings Model for Recent Manufacturing Employees among UI Recipients, Metropolitan Atlanta

Variable description	25th Percentile		Median		75th Percentile		Hypothetical worker[a]		
	Param. est.	Std. error	Param. est.	Std. error	Param. est.	Std. error	1	2	3
log(max. prior earnings)	0.412**	0.019	0.466**	0.014	0.503**	0.012	8.923	9.616	7.824
Age as of ref. date	0.009***	0.005	0.003	0.004	−0.001	0.003	35	35	35
(Age)^2	−1.3E−04	5.4E−05	−5.2E−05	4.3E−05	−5.6E−06	3.8E−05	1,225	1,225	1,225
Education									
Less than high school	0.014	0.014	−0.008	0.011	0.012	0.010	0	0	1
More than high school	0.058**	0.014	0.062**	0.012	0.063**	0.010	0	1	0
Youth, age 14–21	−0.039	0.047	−0.057	0.038	−0.122**	0.034	0	0	0
Veteran	0.011	0.017	0.036**	0.014	0.028**	0.012	0	0	0
Welfare recipient	−0.071	0.056	−0.048	0.045	−0.065	0.040	0	0	0
Dislocated worker	0.011	0.013	0.009	0.010	0.006	0.009	0	0	0
Employed	0.003	0.034	−0.012	0.028	−0.014	0.025	0	0	0
Education status	−0.015	0.043	0.002	0.035	−0.011	0.031	0	0	0
Economically disadvantaged	−0.046**	0.015	−0.031**	0.012	−0.031**	0.010	0	0	0
Exhausted prior UI claim	0.014	0.051	−0.006	0.040	0.062*	0.035	0	0	0
Weeks UI collected prior claim	0.002	0.002	0.003**	0.002	0.001	0.001	0	0	0
Workforce/employer attachment	0.053	0.037	−0.002	0.030	0.014	0.027	0	0	0
Does not have driver's license	−0.077**	0.024	−0.079**	0.020	−0.072**	0.017	0	0	0
Available for rotating shifts	0.027	0.017	0.024*	0.014	0.041**	0.012	0	0	0
Months of tenure, most recent job	−0.002**	2.2E−04	−0.001**	1.8E−04	−0.001**	1.6E−04	24	48	8
(Months of tenure)^2	3.2E−06	6.9E−07	3.6E−06	5.9E−07	2.6E−06	5.2E−07	576	2304	64

							12	23	5
Required hourly salary	0.022**	0.002	0.024**	0.001	0.023***	0.001			
Reference date									
In 2nd qtr.	0.014	0.015	-0.002	0.012	-0.001	0.011	1	1	1
In 3rd qtr.	0.005	0.017	0.003	0.014	0.002	0.012	0	0	0
In 4th qtr.	-0.001	0.018	-0.012	0.015	-0.013	0.013	0	0	0
3 qtrs. after max. wage	0.008	0.015	0.004	0.012	0.017	0.011	1	1	1
4 qtrs. after max. wage	0.005	0.016	-0.003	0.013	-0.002	0.012	0	0	0
5 qtrs. after max. wage	0.010	0.015	0.034**	0.012	0.029***	0.011	0	0	0
Days left in current quarter	3.5E-04	2.2E-04	0.001**	1.8E-04	0.001***	1.6E-04	40	40	40
UI ref. date	-0.004	0.003	-0.004*	0.002	-0.006**	0.002	13,581	13,581	13,581
(UI ref. date)^2	1.4E-07	1.0E-07	1.6E-07	8.6E-07	2.2E-08	7.7E-08	184,523,177	184,523,177	184,523,177
Unemployment rate, $t-3$	0.022	0.667	0.135	0.547	1.141***	0.480	0	0	0
Post industry same as prior industry	0.206***	0.013	0.181***	0.010	0.140***	0.009	0.292	0.325	0.171
Occupation									
Clerical and sales	-0.070**	0.021	-0.045***	0.017	-0.031**	0.015	1	1	1
Services	-0.090***	0.036	-0.034	0.029	-0.050***	0.025	0	0	0
Agric., forestry, fishing	-0.320***	0.105	-0.193***	0.087	-0.272***	0.075	0	0	0
Processing	-0.104***	0.033	-0.076***	0.027	-0.017	0.023	0	0	0
Machine trades	-0.059***	0.024	-0.041**	0.019	-0.015	0.017	0	0	0
Bench work	-0.102***	0.026	-0.086***	0.021	-0.056***	0.018	0	0	0
Structural work	-0.015	0.027	0.009	0.022	0.048***	0.019	0	0	0
Miscellaneous	-0.105**	0.022	-0.078***	0.018	-0.038**	0.015	0	0	0
Intercept	30.072	19.087	32.627***	15.802	45.345**	14.170	1	1	1

Table 12.7 (Continued)

	25th Percentile		Median		75th Percentile		Hypothetical worker[a]		
Variable description	Param. est.	Std. error	Param. est.	Std. error	Param. est.	Std. error	1	2	3
Predicted 25th							5,472	9,636	3,020
Predicted 50th							6,728	12,618	3,387
Predicted 75th							8,179	15,557	4,078

NOTE: ** = Parameter statistically significant at the 95% confidence level in a two-tailed test; * = parameter statistically significant at the 90% confidence level in a two-tailed test.

[a] Hypothetical worker 1: age 35, high school education, earning $30,000 per year in a clerical/sales occupation, entering in the 2nd quarter of the year; hypothetical worker 2: age 35, post-high school education, earning $60,000 per year in a clerical/sales occupation, entering in the 2nd quarter of the year; hypothetical worker 3: age 35, less than high school education, earning $10,000 per year in a clerical/sales occupation, entering in the 2nd quarter of the year.

SOURCE: Based on data provided by the Georgia Department of Labor.

the same three examples used above for evaluating the probability of returning to work in the manufacturing industry. Person 1 is 35 years old, has a high school education, earns $30,000 per year (or $7,500 per quarter) in a clerical/sales occupation, and applied for UI in the second calendar quarter. Median reemployment earnings for this individual in metropolitan Atlanta are predicted to be $6,728 per quarter with lower and upper bounds of $5,472 and $8,179. A person with the same characteristics but living in the south Puget Sound area is expected to earn roughly the same amount: $7,164 per quarter, with lower and upper bounds of $5,615 and $8,422. Consider Person 2, who is identical to Person 1 except that her prior earnings are doubled. This change has the effect of raising predicted median reemployment quarterly earnings in metro Atlanta to $12,618 and in south Puget Sound to $12,394. Person 3 has characteristics similar to the first two, except that prior annual earnings are $10,000. For this example, predicted median reemployment quarterly earnings fall in metro Atlanta to $3,387 and in south Puget Sound to $3,450.

Related Occupations

The FDSS algorithm identifying related occupations provides customers and frontline staff with a list of occupations that are related to the occupation that a worker most recently held. The purpose of the algorithm is to provide a customer who does not immediately find a suitable job match with job options in other occupations that require similar skills and aptitudes. Displaced workers are paid less upon reemployment than those who change occupations voluntarily, in part because of the poor match between their current occupational skills and current job. Providing customers with reliable information on alternatives to their previous occupation may improve their reemployment earnings and reduce the amount of time spent unemployed.

A study by Markey and Parks (1989, p. 3) found that "more than half of the workers in the United States who changed occupations did so because of better pay, working conditions, or advancement opportunities; however, about one in eight workers changed occupations because they lost their previous jobs." Fallick (1993) found evidence that displaced workers increase the intensity of their job search in other industries when the employment growth rate in their previous industry is

Table 12.8 Quartile Regression Coefficient Estimates and Examples of Predicted Earnings from an Earnings Model for Recent Manufacturing Employees among UI Recipients, South Puget Sound, Washington

Variables	25th percentile		Median		75th percentile		Hypothetical worker[a]		
	Param. est.	Std. error	Param. est.	Std. error	Param. est.	Std. error	1	2	3
log(max. prior earnings)	0.465**	0.024	0.630**	0.020	0.632**	0.024	8.923	9.616	7.824
Age as of ref. date	0.006	0.007	0.006	0.006	0.002	0.007	35	35	35
$(Age)^2$	-9.1E-05	8.0E-05	-8.2E-05	6.9E-05	-5.0E-05	8.1E-05	1,225	1,225	1,225
Education									
Less than high school	-0.019	0.024	-0.019	0.020	-0.027	0.024	0	0	0
More than high school	0.059**	0.022	0.056**	0.019	0.040*	0.022	0	1	0
Youth, ages 14–21	-0.061	0.053	-0.009	0.045	-0.037	0.054	0	0	0
Veteran	0.040	0.027	0.019	0.023	0.018	0.028	0	0	0
Welfare recipient	-0.170**	0.044	-0.135**	0.039	-0.143**	0.047	0	0	0
Dislocated worker	0.042	0.045	0.036	0.038	0.108**	0.046	0	0	0
Employed	0.084**	0.023	0.025	0.019	0.013	0.023	0	1	0
Union	0.115**	0.042	0.087**	0.036	0.097**	0.044	0	0	0
Economically disadvantaged	-0.009	0.042	0.014	0.037	0.046	0.045	0	0	0
Reference date									
In 2nd qtr.	-0.006	0.024	-0.003	0.021	-0.017	0.025	1	1	1
In 3rd qtr.	0.020	0.023	0.018	0.020	0.051**	0.024	0	0	0
In 4th qtr.	0.062	0.038	0.025	0.033	-0.004	0.039	0	0	0
3 qtrs. after max. wage	0.023	0.023	-0.001	0.020	0.005	0.024	0	0	0
4 qtrs. after max. wage	-0.050*	0.027	-0.053**	0.023	-0.061**	0.028	0	0	0
5 qtrs. after max. wage	-0.010	0.026	-0.023	0.022	-0.003	0.027	0	0	0
Days left in current quarter	4.9E-04	3.5E-04	4.7E-04	3.0E-04	-4.0E-04	3.6E-04	37	37	37
Weeks benefits drawn	-0.011**	0.001	-0.009**	0.001	-0.006**	0.001	1	1	1

Occupation									
Clerical, sales	-0.068*	0.038	-0.064**	0.032	-0.096**	0.039	1	1	1
Services	-0.103*	0.056	-0.101**	0.047	-0.160**	0.057	0	0	0
Agric., forestry, fishing	-0.057	0.068	-0.030	0.058	-0.106	0.070	0	0	0
Processing	-0.120**	0.041	-0.129**	0.035	-0.073*	0.042	0	0	0
Machine trades	-0.094**	0.037	-0.065**	0.031	-0.103**	0.037	0	0	0
Bench work	-0.178**	0.038	-0.138**	0.031	-0.165**	0.037	0	0	0
Structural work	-0.084**	0.037	-0.022	0.032	-0.000	0.038	0	0	0
Miscellaneous	-0.121**	0.035	-0.080**	0.029	-0.093**	0.035	0	0	0
Post industry same as prior industry	0.185**	0.019	0.168**	0.016	0.123**	0.020	0.346	0.532	0.114
Intercept	4.393**	0.238	3.163**	0.198	3.464**	0.238	1	1	1
Predicted 25th							5,615	9,249	3,228
Predicted 50th							7,164	12,394	3,450
Predicted 75th							8,422	14,081	4,087

NOTE: ** = Parameter statistically significant at the 95% confidence level in a two-tailed test; * = parameter statistically significant at the 90% confidence level in a two-tailed test.

[a] Hypothetical worker 1: age 35, high school education, earning $30,000 per year in a clerical/sales occupation, entering in the 2nd quarter of the year; hypothetical worker 2: age 35, post-high school education, earning $60,000 per year in a clerical/sales occupation, entering in the 2nd quarter of the year; hypothetical worker 3: age 35, less than high school education, earning $10,000 per year in a clerical/sales occupation, entering in the 2nd quarter of the year.

SOURCE: Based on data provided by the Washington State Employment Security Department.

low. Shaw (1987) estimated that a 25 percent increase in the transferability of occupational skills leads to an 11 to 23 percent increase in the rate of occupational change, depending on the age of the worker. Taken together, these results suggest that workers concentrate their search efforts in industries and occupations similar to their own. A reasonable reemployment strategy might include identifying related occupations and providing clients with timely information on the prospects for work in those areas.

Two methods are used to identify related occupations. The first methodology, based on the O*Net system, chooses occupations that are considered to be closely related to the previously held occupation with respect to a person's qualifications, interests, work values, and previous work activities, to name several of the attributes. O*Net, developed by the U.S. Department of Labor, incorporates the expert opinions of human resource professionals and analysts as to the characteristics of each of more than 1,000 occupations and then relates the various occupations by prioritizing the importance of these attributes for each occupation. This methodology addresses the decision to change occupations by asking the question, "What occupations are most related to my previous occupation with respect to my qualifications, interests, and aspirations?" This approach assumes that the person was qualified for the job that he or she previously held. O*Net matches the characteristics of the previous job with the characteristics of other related occupations. However, these transfers are hypothetical and are not based on actual occupational transfers. It does not take into account the actual demand for a worker's skills.

The second methodology is based on actual occupational changes and addresses the transfer decision with the following question: "For workers who switch out of my occupation, into which occupations do they most frequently move?" This methodology provides a worker with insights into the set of jobs that people like him most often obtain. It incorporates both the qualifications of workers and the demand for their skills. Two data sets are used to record job changes and to compile the list of occupational transfers. The first data set is the Current Population Survey (CPS), which is a national survey of households taken each month. The second data set is the administrative files from the Georgia employment service, which includes self-reported work histories of each participant. Unfortunately, Washington employment service records could not be used because they do not include occupation codes.

Each methodology has its advantages and disadvantages. The first methodology is based on extensive information about the characteristics required by an occupation. Furthermore, because of its comprehensive assessment of skill requirements for specific occupations, this methodology allows one to link this information to possible course offerings at local training and educational institutions in order to fill specific skill gaps. The information can also be used to assist in determining the services that best meet the individual's needs and then to make the appropriate referral. The tools can help determine not only which programs are appropriate for the customer, but also which services within a particular program may be most effective.

However, one of the major drawbacks of this first methodology is that it does not consider the demand by employers for those skills embodied in the occupation. For instance, the occupation that O*Net determines to be highly related to a worker's previous occupation may be a good match with respect to skills, but there may be little demand for that occupation in the local labor market.

The primary advantage of the second methodology is that it incorporates both supply and demand considerations inherent in job changes. By using local data, it can provide a convenient perspective on the occupations within which a person is most likely to find a job. Its drawback is the lack of detailed information about the occupation. There is little information about the qualifications of those who hold a job in that occupation, except for information about educational attainment. Some of the deficiencies of this methodology with respect to detailed occupation information may be addressed by combining the two approaches.

To illustrate the two approaches, we found occupations related to the occupation of bookkeeping, accounting, and auditing clerks (O*Net Occupation Code 43-3031.00).[7] As shown in Table 12.9, O*Net identified occupations that appear to be closely related in terms of the type of tasks required and the level of autonomy in executing the tasks—elements which O*Net focuses on in categorizing occupations. Table 12.10 shows the matches of people who switched from computing and account recording to other occupations, as recorded in the Georgia employment service records. While the majority of job switchers stayed

Table 12.9 Related Occupations for Bookkeeping, Accounting, and Auditing Clerks

O*Net occupation title	O*Net occupation code
Billing, cost, and rate clerks	43-3021.02
Billing, posting, and calculating machine operators	43-3021.03
Brokerage clerks	43-4011.00
Loan interviewers and clerks	43-4131.00
Secretaries (except legal, medical, and executive)	43-6014.00
Office clerks, general	43-9061.00

NOTE: The O*Net occupation code for bookkeeping, accounting, and auditing clerks is 43-3031.00.
SOURCE: O*Net Online (http://online.onetcenter.org).

within the same occupation, the next most prevalent job change was to the occupation of packaging, and materials handling. This choice of a related occupation seems strange, but it most likely reflects the prevalence of job openings in the area for people with the skills embodied in the occupation of computing and accounting. Changes to occupations more related to record keeping also took place. Job changes recorded using CPS data as reported in Table 12.11 reveal occupations more closely aligned to record keeping than found for the Georgia data. Most of these occupations are considered clerical, except for teachers. The difference between the two data sets results perhaps from the industrial mix of jobs in local labor markets, which is not captured in national data such as the CPS.

SERVICE REFERRAL ALGORITHM

The second module of FDSS is the service referral algorithm. As mentioned in the overview of one-stop centers, a critical element for successful implementation of one-stop centers is the staff's ability to identify the needs of customers and to refer them expeditiously to services that best address their barriers to employment. Compounding this challenge is the possible lack of experience among the center's

Table 12.10 Placements According to JS200 Record and Concordance with JS300 Job Orders File

Placement occupation (JS200)	No. of placements by ES (JS200)	% of total placements (JS200)	Total of past and present openings (JS300)	Total placements (JS300)	Placements as % of openings	Dictionary of occupational titles code
Packaging, materials handling	1,435	13.7	88,542	82,710	93.4	92
Processing food, tobacco	1,125	10.7	50,953	48,472	95.1	52
Miscellaneous sales	948	9.0	23,656	21,397	90.5	29
Stenography, typing, filing	932	8.9	22,135	16,288	73.6	20
Food, beverage preparation, services	904	8.6	25,578	24,053	94.0	31
Information and message distribution	508	4.8	9,890	8,515	86.1	23
Fabrication, assembly, repair of metal products	431	4.1	19,155	17,444	91.1	70
Miscellaneous personal services	260	2.5	7,800	6,381	81.8	35
Miscellaneous clerical	259	2.5	6,802	5,291	77.8	24
Fabrication, repair, textile, leather	243	2.3	7,787	7,499	96.3	78
Computing and account recording	3,443	32.8	22,969	20,690	90.1	21

NOTE: From occupation 21: computing and account recording.
SOURCE: Based on data provided by the Georgia Department of Labor.

Table 12.11 Ten Most Frequent Occupation Changes from Bookkeepers, Accounting, and Auditing Clerks

Title	No. of observations	Census code
Accountants and auditors	22	23
Supervisors and proprietors, sales occupations	13	243
Managers and administrators, N.E.C.	11	22
Secretaries	12	313
General office clerks	7	379
Teachers, elementary school	7	156
Payroll and timekeeping clerks	5	338
Cashiers	8	276
Receptionists	5	319
Administrative support occupations, N.E.C.	6	389
Bookkeepers, accounting and auditing clerks	124	337

NOTE: The Census code number for bookkeepers, accounting, and auditing clerks is 337.
SOURCE: Based on analysis of Current Population Survey (CPS) data.

staff in serving a wide range of customers. The purpose of the FDSS service referral module is to compile and process information about the effectiveness of various programs in a way that better informs staff when referring customers to services.

The service referral module is based on information about the characteristics and outcomes of individuals who have recently participated in services offered by one-stop centers. These data are used to estimate statistical relationships between personal attributes and outcomes. The service referral module uses these models to identify the sequence of services that most often leads to successful employment outcomes for individuals with specific characteristics. It should be emphasized that this algorithm does not replace the staff's referral decisions. Rather, it provides additional information to better inform the decision.

The effectiveness of alternative paths for each customer depends upon their employability. Therefore, the service referral algorithm has two basic components. The first is a model to estimate a person's employability, or likelihood of finding a job. Conceptually, this is the flip side of WPRS models, which identify the chance of UI benefit exhaustion. The second component is a delineation of the paths, or sequential combinations of services, that lead to successful outcomes. By conditioning alternative services on the employability of a specific customer, a ranking can be produced of the effectiveness of various programs for individuals with specific measurable characteristics. This ranking would be a suggested ordering of service participation.

Since it is based on prior values of exogenous variables, the employability index can be viewed as a summary of client characteristics. Interacting the employability index with service indicators is a type of subgroup analysis (Heckman, Smith, and Clements 1997). The planned approach is analogous to that used by Eberts in Chapter 8 of this volume (p. 221) for assigning welfare-to-work clients to alternative bundles of reemployment services. This method is also similar to the procedure applied in this volume by O'Leary, Decker, and Wandner (p. 161), who essentially interacted an unemployment insurance benefit exhaustion probability index with reemployment bonus intervention indicators to identify the best exhaustion probability group for targeting a bonus.

The exercise of O'Leary, Decker, and Wandner reexamined treatment and control group data generated by random trials in a field experiment. However, service referral algorithms for FDSS are based on administrative data in which program participation is subject to selection bias. So that the effectiveness of alternative services may be ranked for customers with different employability scores, impact estimates will be computed while correcting for selection bias. We plan a simple single-equation least squares methodology, which will be validated by a matching approach that accounts for all possible nonlinear influences of observable factors on selection for program participation (Rosenbaum and Rubin 1983; Heckman, Ichimura, and Todd 1997; Heckman, LaLonde, and Smith 1999; and Smith 2000).

Employability Estimates

This algorithm estimates the likelihood of an individual finding employment based upon prior work history, personal characteristics, and educational attainment. The estimate is based on the experience of individuals who have recently enrolled with the employment service or with other programs provided through one-stop centers. However, since we are assessing their initial employability before receiving services, we estimate the model using only those persons who have not yet received services within their current enrollment period.

The data come from the same administrative records that are used to estimate the components of the systematic job search module described in the previous section of this chapter. The employability model is similar to the earnings algorithm, except that employment is used as the dependent variable instead of earnings. Thus, the sample includes individuals who have worked just prior to enrolling in one-stop programs, as well as those who have not held a job prior to enrolling. In this way, we are able to compare the measurable attributes of those with and without recent employment as they enter a one-stop center. The presumption is that those with more recent work experience are more employable, even before they receive services.

For illustrative purposes, an employability model for welfare recipients in the State of Washington is discussed. The explanatory variables include prior work history, educational attainment, participation in public assistance programs, and their primary language. As shown in Table 12.12, the coefficients display the expected signs and many are statistically significant. For instance, people who have experienced longer periods of unemployment are less likely to hold a job at the time of intake. People with more education are more likely to hold a job. Those who are willing to relocate are also more likely to find employment. Based on these variables and others, the probability of employment is predicted for each individual who enrolls in Work First. The next step is to determine whether or not some services are more or less effective for individuals within certain ranges of the distribution of employment probabilities.

Path Analysis

The second component of the service-referral module is an analysis of the various services that individuals receive to assist their efforts in searching for and obtaining a job. As discussed in the section on the flow of clients through one-stop centers, it is apparent that individuals typically receive more than one service during their participation period and that they receive those services in various sequences. For instance, a welfare recipient may start his or her participation in the Work

Table 12.12 Logit Estimates of Employability Model for Welfare Recipients in the State of Washington

Variable description	Coefficient	Std. error	Marginal/ discrete effect
Unemployed in			
One of the four prior qtrs.	–0.849**	0.038	–0.136
Two of the four prior qtrs.	–1.153**	0.041	–0.169
Three of the four prior qtrs.	–1.205**	0.045	–0.174
All four prior qtrs.	–2.407**	0.045	–0.243
Max. quarterly wage in the four prior qtrs.	4.7E–005**	1.0E–005	9.5E–006
(Max. quarterly wage)^2	–2.1E–009**	5.8E–010	–4.1E–010
Education			
Less than high school	–0.206**	0.026	–0.039
GED	–0.018	0.042	–0.004
Some college	0.063	0.047	0.013
Associate's degree	0.080	0.056	0.016
Bachelor's degree	0.147	0.096	0.030
Advanced degree	0.495**	0.176	0.109
Willing to relocate	0.082*	0.044	0.017
Minimum required wage	0.018**	0.006	0.004
On food stamps	–0.038	0.106	–0.008
Not welfare recipient	0.334**	0.043	0.072
Economically disadvantaged	0.072	0.047	0.015
Language spoken at home			
English	0.743**	0.053	0.169
Spanish	1.059**	0.079	0.248
Received deferrals	–0.739**	0.029	–0.122
Intercept	–0.002	0.080	–0.000

NOTE: Sample includes 46,732 individuals aged 14 and above, who had received some services from the Washington State Work First program. ** = Statistically significant at the 95% level in a two-tailed test; * = statistically significant at the 90% level in a two-tailed test.

SOURCE: Computations based on data provided by the Washington State Employment Security Department and the Washington Work First activity file.

First program by being referred to the program by the welfare (or social service) agency, then being referred to a job search workshop, then to a basic education program, and then back to a job search initiative. The final steps would be a job interview and employment. Even after obtaining a job, the individual may participate in postemployment activities. Another welfare recipient entering the same program may take a different route to employment.

Therefore, for programs that offer a sequence of services, the analysis must identify the predominant paths that participants typically follow. Considering a collection of individual activities, such as attending a job search workshop or enrolling in an education program (without taking into account how they relate to other activities) does little to capture the cumulative nature of the delivery of services. Once the pathways, or sequence of service activities, have been identified, the effectiveness of these strings of services will be analyzed with respect to each individual's estimated likelihood of employment. One would expect to find that specific paths are more effective in leading to employment for some individuals than others, depending upon the individual's propensity for employment as measured by the estimated employability.

For Work First, the pathways are relatively short. In some cases, participants receive only one service before finding employment or otherwise exiting the program. Table 12.13 shows a sample of paths from two starting points. The top portion of Table 12.13 includes those who were referred to the Employment Security Department (ESD) during their participation in Work First. The bottom portion includes those who returned to Work First after working for a while but then losing their job. The specific activities are not important for the purpose of illustrating the paths.[8] Rather, the important point is that definite sequences of activities occur and that many of these paths consist of only one recorded activity.

Estimates of the Effect of Services on Employment Outcomes

To illustrate the effect of specific services on employment outcomes, we estimate a model that relates employment in the quarter after exiting from the program to participation in services and other characteristics, including the predicted probability of employment derived from the employability model. We focus on the two most prevalent services received by those returning to Work First—employment retention services and labor market exchange (WPLEX). We interact the predicted employability estimate for each individual with a variable indicating whether or not they received either one of the two postemployment services.

Results in Table 12.14 show that returnees who have participated in WPLEX and postemployment retention services are more likely to find a job and stay off of welfare than those who do not participate. Furthermore, WPLEX is more effective for those who have a higher probability of employment than those with a lower probability, according to the employability estimate. Therefore, while the magnitudes of the effects are small, the estimates do offer information about the appropriate services for individuals with certain characteristics. The service referral algorithm will follow a similar approach in estimating the effect of services offered by other programs.

SUMMARY

The Workforce Investment Act of 1998 calls for the creation of a national network of one-stop centers where intake and referral of job seekers to various programs will be done in a coordinated fashion. Resource constraints dictate that each workforce development program can serve only a portion of the population which might benefit. Funding levels, from state and federal sources, determine how many workers can be served. Choosing which individuals are served depends on decision rules applied by frontline staff in one-stop centers. By targeting services to job seekers who will benefit the most, statistical tools can help make these decisions more cost-effective for society, thereby maximizing the net social benefit of program expenditures.

The Frontline Decision Support System offers a variety of tools that can help inform staff and customers in their job search efforts and in their selection of reemployment services. The tools are based on statistical techniques that use administrative data to estimate likely earn-

Table 12.13 Selected Paths of Component Codes

	Path	Activity 1	Activity 2	Activity 3	Number	%
Following referral to ESD (RI)						
	1	No Show (RN)			422	5.5
	2	Referred back early (RB)			343	4.5
	3	Working full time–30+ hours/wk. (FT)			182	2.4
	4	Working part time–29 or less hours/wk. (PT)			120	1.6
	5	Initial job search (JI)			107	1.4
	6	Sanction (SA)			102	1.3
	7	Referred back early (RB)	Sanction (SA)		94	1.2
	8	No show (RN)	Sanction (SA)		90	1.2
	9	No show (RN)	Processing returned referral (PR)	Sanction (SA)	81	1.1
	10	Job search workshop (JW)	Job search (JS)	Working full time, 30+ hours/wk (FT)	79	1.0
	Total				7,642	
Following nonsubsidized employment (PT or FT)						
	1	WPLEX Contact (PS)			701	16.3
		Employment Retention			321	7.4

2	(RS)		
3	Working full time–30+ hours/wk (FT)	216	5.0
4	ESD (RI)	160	3.7
5	Working part time–29 or less hours/wk (PT)	120	2.8
6	Referred back early (RB)	57	1.3
7	Job search (JS)	54	1.3
8	Counseling/anger management; drug, alcohol or mental health treatment; temporary incapacity, medical treatment (XM)	51	1.2
	No show (RN)		
9	ESD (RI)	50	1.2
10	Other (RO)	50	1.2
	Total	4,291	

SOURCE: Based on the Washington Work First activity file.

Table 12.14 Logit Estimates of Service Impact Model for Work First Participants in the State of Washington

Variable	Coefficients	Std. error	Marginal/discrete effects
Unemployed in all four prior qtrs.	0.249**	0.083	0.053
Age as of ref. date	0.008**	0.003	0.002
Dislocated worker	−0.888**	0.386	−0.141
Referred to ESD	−0.409**	0.086	−0.074
Job Search activity	−0.655**	0.105	−0.111
Job Search workshop	−0.040	0.174	−0.008
Attend HS or GED	−0.306*	0.183	−0.057
Training	−0.610**	0.257	−0.105
On the job training	−0.803**	0.206	−0.130
Pre-employment training	−1.087**	0.327	−0.162
Deferrals	−1.409**	0.110	−0.191
Other referrals (refer to)	−0.069	0.144	−0.014
Sanction	0.261*	0.158	0.055
Referrals (refer back)	0.138	0.087	0.028
Employment retention	0.302*	0.168	0.064
WPLEX	0.361**	0.150	0.078
Predicted employability (PE)	0.426**	0.180	0.085
Employment retention × PE	−0.088	0.382	−0.018
WPLEX × PE	0.551*	0.329	0.110
Intercept	0.161	0.129	

NOTE: Sample includes 9,009 individuals who have found either part-time or full-time employment after entering the Work First program. The dependent variable is 1 if the individual was off TANF after obtaining employment, and 0 if no record shows that he/she left TANF. ** = Statistically significant at the 95% level; * = statistically significant at the 90% level.
SOURCE: Based on data provided by the Washington State Employment Security Department and the Washington Work First activity file.

ings prospects, industry transitions, related occupations, and outcomes associated with participating in specific reemployment services. FDSS is an extension of previous methods like the Worker Profiling and Reemployment Services system, which all states have implemented, and the Work First pilot, which was implemented at the Kalamazoo-St. Joseph, Michigan, Workforce Development Area. At the time of this writing, the W.E. Upjohn Institute is working closely with the states of Georgia and Washington to design and implement FDSS in selected one-stop centers.

Notes

We thank Helen Parker and Richard Hardin and participants at the Targeting Employment Services conference, Kalamazoo, Michigan, April 30–May 1, 1999, for constructive comments that helped to improve this chapter. For research assistance we thank Wei-Jang Huang, Ken Kline, and Kris Kracker. Clerical assistance was provided by Claire Black, Nancy Mack, and Phyllis Molhoek. Opinions expressed are our own and do not necessarily represent those of the W.E. Upjohn Institute for Employment Research. We accept responsibility for any errors.

1. Logit models were widely used by states as a basis for Worker Profiling and Reemployment Services (WPRS) assignment rules. Eberts and O'Leary (1996) provided an example from Michigan.
2. Age, gender, and race were prohibited variables in WPRS models. However, unlike WPRS, the FDSS system does not set criteria for program eligibility. The graphical user interface for FDSS computer screens in one-stop centers will not display age, gender, and race as variables on which "what if" scenarios can be examined. These variables were included because statistical tests indicated that excluding these variables would introduce an omitted variables bias in estimation of other model parameters, following the work of Kletzer (1998) and others.
3. These categories are defined by employment service practice. The dislocated worker definition is consistent with that in the Economic Dislocation and Worker Adjustment Assistance Act (EDWAA) of 1988. The EDWAA definition includes those with significant prior job attachment who have lost their job and have little prospect of returning to it or to another job in a similar occupation and industry.
4. Note that the earnings variables in the models are quarterly figures, not annual figures.
5. Section 133(d)(3)(i) and (ii), Workforce Investment Act, Public Law 105-220–August 7, 1998. U.S. Congress (1998, Section 134[d][3][c]).
6. Using data from the Current Population Survey for a comparable time period, we computed a (9×9) industry-occupation matrix of average hours worked using one-digit industry and occupation groups.
7. In making the comparisons, considerable effort was required in converting the occupation codes from O*Net to the occupation codes used in the CPS and by the Georgia Employment Service. Complete matching was not possible, but we came as close as possible. See DeRango et al. (2000) for more details.
8. A detailed discussion of these paths is given by Eberts, O'Leary, and Huang (2000).

References

Becker, Gary S. 1964. *Human Capital.* New York: National Bureau of Economic Research.

DeRango, Kelly, Randall Eberts, Wei-Jang Huang, Kenneth Kline, Kris Kracker, and Christopher J. O'Leary. 2000. "Development of the Transferable Occupations Algorithm." Unpublished paper, W.E. Upjohn Institute for Employment Research, Kalamazoo, Michigan.

Eberts, Randall W., and Christopher J. O'Leary. 1996. "Design of the Worker Profiling and Reemployment Services System and Evaluation in Michigan." Working paper no. 96-41, W.E. Upjohn Institute for Employment Research, Kalamazoo, Michigan.

Eberts, Randall W., Christopher J. O'Leary, and Wei-Jang Huang. 2000. *Elements of a Service Referral Algorithm for a Frontline Decision Support System for Washington Work First.* Report to Washington State Employment Security Department and the U.S. Department of Labor. W.E. Upjohn Institute for Employment Research, Kalamazoo, Michigan.

Fallick, Bruce C. 1993. "The Industrial Mobility of Displaced Workers." *Journal of Labor Economics* 11(2): 302–323.

Heckman, James J., Hidehiko Ichimura, and Petra E. Todd. 1997. "Matching as an Econometric Evaluation Estimator: Evidence from Evaluating a Job Training Programme." *Review of Economic Studies* 64(4): 605–654.

Heckman, James J., Robert J. Lalonde, and Jeffrey A. Smith. 1999. "The Economics and Econometrics of Active Labor Market Programs." In *Handbook of Labor Economics, Volume 3A*, Orley Ashenfelter and David Card, eds. Amsterdam: Elsevier Science, pp. 1865–2097.

Heckman, James J., Jeffrey A. Smith, and Nancy Clements. 1997. "Making the Most Out of Programme Evaluations and Social Experiments: Accounting for Heterogeniety in Programme Impacts." *Review of Economic Studies* 64(4): 487–535.

Jacobson, Louis S., Robert J. LaLonde, and Daniel G. Sullivan. 1993. "Earnings Losses of Displaced Workers." *American Economic Review* 83(4): 685–709.

Kletzer, Lori G. 1998. "Job Displacement." *Journal of Economic Perspectives* 12(1): 115–136.

Markey, James P., and William Parks. 1989. "Occupational Change: Pursuing a Different Kind of Work." *Monthly Labor Review* 112(9): 3–12.

Rosenbaum, P., and D. Rubin. 1983. "The Central Role of the Propensity Score in Observational Studies for Causal Effects." *Biometrika* 70(1): 41–55.

Shaw, Kathryn L. 1987. "Occupational Change, Employer Change, and the Transferability of Skills." *Southern Economic Journal* 53(3): 702–719.

Smith, Jeffrey. 2000. "A Critical Survey of Empirical Methods for Evaluating Employment and Training Programs." *Schweizerische Zeitschrift fuer Volkswirtschaft und Statistik (Swiss Journal of Economics and Statistics)* 136(3): 247–268.

Comments on Chapter 12

Helen Parker
Georgia Department of Labor

The concept of using statistical profiling (targeting) on the front line of the one-stop system emerging under the Workforce Investment Act of 1998 (WIA) is a significant and timely development. The Frontline Decision Support System described by Eberts, O'Leary, and DeRango will help ensure both effective customer service and efficient use of resources in the new integrated environment. Its dual usefulness as a management tool and a staff/customer resource makes FDSS a versatile and valuable addition to the one-stop service delivery "toolkit."

As Eberts and O'Leary point out, FDSS will be an excellent management tool for resource allocation and continuous improvement. At the same time, it provides a much needed service for staff to help ensure that customers receive the services they really need—no less and no more. At a time when the workforce development system is moving away from "one size fits all" services and toward the customer-focused, customer-led service strategies envisioned by the WIA, this targeting approach should facilitate, perhaps even force, individualized customer-by-customer decision making. With both the customer and the staff armed with better information, service tailored to the unique needs of the individual is not only achievable, but it becomes the norm.

FDSS may also help us prevent what may be an unanticipated consequence of the WIA's perceived "work first" philosophy and delineation of what some call "sequenced" services. The WIA describes three levels of services—core, intensive, and training—and would seem to suggest, as Eberts and O'Leary note, that lack of success in obtaining employment is the criterion for moving from one level to the next. This creates an impossible—and decidedly *not* customer-friendly—scenario that requires a customer literally to fail his way into need-

381

ed services. Because it helps the customer and staff identify both barriers and needed services very early in the service continuum, FDSS
should enable staff to identify situations in which core services clearly
will not suffice, and to help those customers move more quickly into interventions that will lead to employment.

FDSS should also be particularly helpful when there is an economic downturn, when demand will outstrip available resources even more.
Higher unemployment not only increases customer demand for services, it increases the demand for more staff-intensive services. A targeting tool like FDSS can help staff more quickly and more thoroughly
assess and guide their customers.

While FDSS will be an extremely valuable tool for both staff and
management, it does not come "worry-free." The description of this
tool and its potential uses raises several concerns. First, the system
must be designed with maximum flexibility, so that it can be used in a
wide variety of settings and with an equally wide variety of automated
systems. The Upjohn Institute seems to have anticipated this by planning another version of the product for states and local areas that do not
use the federally supported one-stop operating system.

Using wage records both to target jobs and to help determine cost-
effectiveness may prove rather limiting. The wage records by themselves may be inadequate to give a true sense of an earnings range, and
the lack of real-time data will limit the usefulness of that aspect of the
tool. From a customer service standpoint, the wage range itself may
create customer dissatisfaction in screening for jobs: neither the customer who will settle for lower pay nor the one who demands access to
higher wages jobs—and there are many of both—will be satisfied with
the results. Development of a meaningful cost/benefit analysis may
also prove a challenge. While the costs of training have traditionally
been fairly easy to identify, the costs of other "softer" services like
counseling, workshops, and case management may prove difficult. In
the integrated one-stop system envisioned by the WIA, distinguishing
between shared system costs toward which all partners contribute and
program-specific costs for services, which may also be split across
more than one fund source, may well hinder accurate determination of
costs. The benefit side is equally complex; earnings, or "narrowing the
earnings gap," is only one aspect of the benefit measurement and is

likely to be inadequate unless both labor market and wage information are more up to date and more market-specific.

In developing and implementing FDSS, the U.S. Department of Labor and the Upjohn Institute will need to confront the tensions inherent in the service delivery approach mandated by WIA. Perhaps most troublesome is the tension between "most in need" and "most likely to benefit." The pull between these two has always been a frustrating reality in performance-driven systems like those under the Job Training Partnership Act. WIA does not relieve that potential for conflict, and in fact it may exacerbate it as local areas struggle to meet the spirit of the law with limited resources. The ability of a staff member or a local board to target customers and services hinges on determining whether need or benefit receives priority. If developed with an awareness of that dilemma, FDSS may well offer at least a partial solution.

A second tension, and one that FDSS designers may not yet have considered seriously enough, stems from the very clear mandate in WIA for customer choice in decisions about services and training. The concept of targeting and the decision-making tool itself may assume a level of staff intervention or control that could be difficult to achieve. For mandatory customers, such as profiled UI claimants and welfare recipients, staff interventions might be tolerated more readily. But customers who simply want to access some mix of services and/or training, particularly those who already have expectations about the services they want, may require more staff time to guide them than the system has the capacity for or than is cost-effective.

We also need to guard against the use of a tool like FDSS inadvertently reinforcing the tendency of workforce development and human resource development systems to assume that we know better than the customer what is best for him or her. If one goal of WIA is to empower the customer to make informed choices, this new tool needs to be as customer-friendly as possible, and our staff need to be thoroughly trained in what the FDSS is and what it isn't. Indeed, the "selling" of this new tool and staff training on its uses are of paramount importance. As with the development of Service and Outcome Measurement System in Canada, buy-in by management, and particularly by frontline staff, is absolutely critical if the product is to reach its true potential. We must also be sensitive to the very human reactions that staff and customers may have to such a system, and this too must be a part of the selling of and training for the product.

Some staff and customers will feel threatened by such a tool. Other staff are likely to use it as a shield behind which they can hide from interaction with customers; it was, after all, the computer that made the decision, as they see it. Still others will see the system's targeting recommendations as directives, not guidance, and will forego the role that a professional staffer should play in helping a customer make good decisions.

A colleague of mine likes to describe the delivery of employment services as a "high tech, high touch" business. FDSS has the potential to address both. If it is developed as planned, it can add a level of sophistication and flexibility that the emerging workforce development system will need for effective service. It can enable staff to assist and guide their customers, and empower customers to make more informed choices about their service needs. We just need to take care that, with FDSS or any other such tool, "high tech" doesn't substitute for the "high touch" that many of our customers need and want.

13

A Panel Discussion on the Experience and Future Plans of States

Panel Chair: Rich Hobbie
National Association of State Workforce Agencies

Panelists: Jim Finch
Utah Department of Workforce Services

Chuck Middlebrooks
South Carolina Employment Security Commission

Jack Weidenbach
Minnesota Department of Economic Security

Rich Hobbie

Because we are short on time, I will introduce our three distinguished panelists together and ask them to speak in the order in which I introduce them. Jim Finch is Director of Payment Services for the Utah Department of Workforce Services. Chuck Middlebrooks is Unemployment Insurance Director for the South Carolina Employment Security Commission. Jack Weidenbach is Assistant Commissioner for the Minnesota Department of Economic Security. Each of the panelists will share his experience with targeting employment services and his plans for the future. Jim Finch will speak first.

Jim Finch

This conference has been a very interesting experience for me and, I am sure, for everyone that operates at the level I do in the employment security system. Targeting is just one piece of the total package that we have to deal with. While listening the last couple of days, I was reminded of my first experience with profiling, when I was a local office manager in Salt Lake City. Our benefit payment control chief developed a profiling system for people who were apt to commit unemployment fraud. We tried it out for a little while, and it was very accurate.

After I had three or four radio interviews, a couple trips to local television stations, and newspaper reporters questioning me about this profiling system, I realized that profiling can be a two-edged sword. The model was very good at identifying clients and customers who needed specific kinds of services, but it included some elements to identify certain groups having rather vocal public representation. As soon as the word got out that they were being identified on demographic characteristics, and not for any other reason, it created a significant public relations problem. Keep that experience in mind as you are developing your profiling systems.

When Rich Hobbie introduced me, he mentioned that I am director of payment services for Utah's Department of Workforce Services. I just want to touch on that. At one time I was the unemployment insurance director for the department. However, in 1996, Utah's approach to welfare reform was to combine the Office of Family Support—which we used to call the welfare department—with Job Service and the JTPA agency to form a single department. At the same time we established a centralized telephone UI claims center. It didn't take long to realize that the ongoing eligibility function of our welfare activities could also be handled in the telephone center. I was given responsibility for the ongoing eligibility function for welfare services, so my position changed from unemployment services to payment services.

As I listened to Randy Eberts's presentation, and certainly Jim Vollman's luncheon talk yesterday, they very largely described where Utah is now—not where we intend to go, but where we actually are. In Utah, we had 24 job service offices before we combined with the other agencies. The combination created 109 offices statewide, and we have reduced that number to 51. At the same time our customer base has expanded. We have many more people seeking services though this expanded department than we did before. As a consequence we have had to implement Jim Vollman's cone of service, or what we called the Vollman wedge, which was mentioned earlier.

We have set up job connection rooms in our local offices where job seekers use PCs to review job orders. In essence, a routine job search is self-directed with little or no help from an employment counselor. Customers who are determined to need more intensive services would then be referred to the next level of service in the department. For UI, profiling is the entrance to more intensive services, which are offered in employment centers. For that reason, profiling has been an important part of our system. Without going into detail, I will say that some method of profiling has become absolutely necessary within our system because of our very high volume of customers.

Chuck Middlebrooks

When I was UI director in Maryland, we eagerly sought the opportunity from the U.S. Department of Labor to be the profiling test state. We saw profiling as a way to bring together activities of EDWAA (Economic Dislocation and Worker Adjustment Assistance), unemployment insurance, and the job service. Basically what we did was use profiling as an opportunity for selecting people who would be targeted for a 10-hour workshop, provided through the use of EDWAA resources. This provided a new entry into EDWAA for UI claimants. Previously they reached EDWAA services in a haphazard way. We saw the profiling demonstration as a real opportunity, and I believe targeting will continue to be used in the one-stop environment under WIA.

How services might be coordinated for a more generalized intake remains to be seen, but certainly where I am now, in South Carolina, we plan to continue efforts in that direction. I hadn't yet arrived when profiling started in South Carolina. The first attempt was based on a successful prior model which had nine factors. I believe that South Carolina was the state which identified delayed filing for UI as an important predictor; it actually is the second best predictor in our model. I think the relative value is in the 30 percent range. Why that is, I don't claim to know.

About one-third of the people profiled by our model are being served, so we are at the national average in that regard. The service provided to those referred was uneven across the state, and very dependent on the county of residence. The most widespread approach was to bring people in for a one-hour orientation, followed by various one-on-

one services. These included things that you would normally expect or encourage in job search-referrals, use of the phone for job prospects, and things like that. Some people did get into basic readjustment adjustment services in EDWAA, but only a small number of people went into training as a result. Last summer we started looking more closely at profiled client flows. This was my first opportunity to look at the data and make some changes, and I want to give some numbers so you can understand the context.

We had slightly more than 90,000 new initial UI claims. About two-thirds of these were on standby awaiting recall to their prior job, leaving about 30,000 to be profiled by the WPRS system. That 30,000 includes everybody from the lowest to the highest probability of UI benefit exhaustion. The state was calling in 9,000 to 10,000 people, so they were serving about one-third of the people, and most who were called in did come. Most of the referrals did receive the service.

Last summer we looked at the distribution of UI exhaustion probabilities. When I was in Maryland we used 40 percent as the cutoff point for EDWAA eligibility and service. I asked our staff in South Carolina to find out what cutoff probability was being used for referrals. It turned out that at the 40 percent and above level, there were about 10,000 UI beneficiaries, which was about what we were serving. The way the system worked was that profiled beneficiaries were listed in rank order, and the office was required to refer people in that order. They were not allowed to skip people, and I think we had pretty consistent implementation. In most offices we probably served those with predicted exhaustion probabilities of 40 percent or higher. Keep in mind that with 90,000 first initial claims, and 60,000 on standby, 10,000 of the remaining 30,000 had an exhaustion probability of 40 percent or higher.

Last summer we changed the profiling list provided to local offices so that it now only includes the people at or above the 40 percent probability. This required offices to bring in 10,000 clients, minus those excused for good reasons, and refer them to the dislocated worker program where they would start receiving additional services. The practice has not been as uniform as we would have liked, but we are moving toward consistent practice. In South Carolina, we also added a three-hour workshop. This is shorter than the 10-hour workshop tested in Maryland, but it was an expansion of services.

As part of the new three-hour workshops, there was also a simple change in the reemployment work search rule. In workshops, the clients were required to complete a brief work search questionnaire to be used in UI eligibility review (ER). Normally an ER is done in about the sixth week; however, under WPRS they report at about the fourth week so the initial ER is done sooner for WPRS clients. Before, there was no connection between WPRS and the UI eligibility review. I went out into the local offices, and in some cases the person was called in one week for profiling and the next week for eligibility review. Clients complained, so we tied those two together. We plan to improve coordination between these two programs.

We have funded additional positions for local offices to do job search workshops. During the first quarter not much happened, but during the winter quarter that just passed, 40 percent of all clients attended workshops. There were 3,400 participants instead of around 2,500. We increased both participation and the quality of our services. Clients felt like they were getting something more when they came into the office, something beyond a basic registration, and that was good. We had some excellent examples of follow-up service and use of new resource centers; however, we do not yet have the uniformity that we would like.

Future plans are to provide services earlier to profiled clients. I don't think we will go to the first day, as Georgia did, but we will probably do the batch the first night. We won't go to the first day because of the way we take and process UI claims. We plan to produce the profiling scores on the first night and to get people scheduled in either the first or the second week of their claim series instead of the fourth or fifth week. So we do plan to speed up the process.

We also need to smooth the procedures for quickly excusing some clients from the workshop. We plan a standard script for the workshop staff. Things go more smoothly when they understand exactly the order to proceed over material. We didn't want to be overly proscriptive to start with, but we are rethinking our strategy. We will permit reasonable exceptions to our script, but we expect general compliance. In particular, I would like a more objective process from the sixth week on.

Currently, we get a good start with the three-hour workshop, but as clients move along in the claim series, treatment is not consistent. We want to have a plan for staff actions to take place starting after the sixth week, the twelfth week, and so on. We need tracking. Someone made the point that if the frontline people knew exactly what the results are, and what outcomes were being measured on a weekly or monthly basis, they will perform better. We don't have such a system in place, but we want one. We also want more training for the local office staff so they understand objectives of the reemployment effort. Sometimes procedures don't make sense to staff, because they don't know the underlying policies. Staff often regard required procedures as management's effort to complicate their duties. Performance monitoring with well-specified outcomes can improve appreciation for the value of well-designed staff procedures. Certainly we need to do more evaluation.

As an administrator who is always forced to think about program financing, I would like to say a few things about cost models. In South Carolina we serve 10,000 people on an annual basis. An important question is, "How do we pay for these services?" Does that mean $100 a head, or a million dollars that should be budgeted for special services above the normal? Or is the cost $150 or $200 per customer? We need some reliable cost models.

We expect lots of competition for intensive services. UI claimants will be competing in the same way as welfare recipients or anyone else. We estimated services costs in the neighborhood of $100 to $200 for the Maryland evaluation. We had enrollment of about 250 people and the cost turned out to be a little less than $200 per person. We could provide more up-front services, we could do the workshops sooner, and get people through services more quickly. However, if we are also going to review eligibility at 13, 16, and 18 weeks, the caseload will build up. These tensions should be balanced in the case management model.

Jack Weidenbach

In Minnesota, our approach has been somewhat like Utah's. We too have become true believers in the Vollman wedge client flow model, and we have worked very hard to coordinate our services with that model. In Minnesota, much of what we do is determined by the fact that we have a serious labor shortage. Minnesota is a geographically large state with a population of only about 4.4 million. Of those people, 2.7 million are in the workforce, and we have the highest women's labor force participation rate in the nation and the second highest rate for males. This maximization of the workforce means there is pressure on us to get people back to work quickly.

Several years ago we changed the program name from "unemployment insurance" to "reemployment insurance." We are the odd state out, in terms of the name for the program, but the new name suggests our emphasis. We have seen real pressures on the WPRS system that lead us, at the local level, to lean more toward bringing everybody in for workshops instead of restricting services just to the high-quotient profiled. The reason is that the demand for the unemployed workers, who will be eligible for dislocated worker services in many cases, is high in most areas of the state. In many local areas, the WPRS system is almost certain to call in every person who is not job-attached for special job search services. That doesn't mean that we don't operate a WPRS system, but our model doesn't distinguish between claimants in a significant way, meaning that many people get similar services.

Our profiling system is built into the reemployment insurance system. It is a mainframe-based system that runs on the DB 2 database, and we have eight screens that staff can use to record the profiling activity. One computer screen allows on-the-spot profiling. That functionality is rarely used because we don't accept in-person UI claims anymore. It's something that staff would have to see the value in before they would want to go through that extra step. Getting staff to believe in the merits of the WPRS system has been kind of a struggle for us.

We decided around the middle of last year that we had to beef up our efforts in worker profiling for a number of reasons. The strongest was that we were centralizing our reemployment functions and we were worried about losing the connection between claimants and the one-stop services, so we really got serious about the processes. We revisited workflows, began training staff again, and reintroduced the screens as ways to let people see the value of the process. The result was that we provided services to about twice as many people in 1998 as we had in 1996–1997.

At first we had problems with the staff understanding the value of WPRS and why they should go through the extra steps of collecting and entering data. We have improved on that with employment service staff over the last three years. We have, over the same period, become more closely integrated with our Title III partners. We are pushing a lot of "profiled" claimants into the Title III programs, but in that area, we still are unsuccessful in having them report activity in the computerized information system.

I would attribute a lack of success in this area to a couple of factors. One is somewhat cultural. UI tends to be viewed as a hard process. When you say we have this great program to profile claimants, the reaction in the service delivery area (SDA) world is that it's simply another way to avoid paying UI to people. I think this was the basis for an original reluctance to collaborate. The second factor is that SDAs are not familiar with UI automated systems and that staff must exit their normal systems to access the UI system.

We found that in order to change our approach to profiling, we had to change the budget structure. Last summer we took our ES and reemployment budgets for workforce centers (our one-stops), and tied funding to the number of unattached claimants in the area and to the level of services delivered in the area. We are trying to refine the process and expand the number of services for which we track outputs. It appears to have given our middle managers a reason to pay attention. When you tie service funding to positive results, it makes a big difference.

I conclude by saying that Randy Eberts's presentation on FDSS this morning provided a direction where we ought to be going. We really need a common computer operating system for one-stops, and actually, a system that can be expanded outside of the one-stops to our affiliated service providers. That's ambitious, but it's extremely important if we are going to tie this whole effort together, and if we want to do it well.

We have been involved with New Jersey and Utah in developing the first phase of the Workforce Investment System (WINS). We see it as the first part of our one-stop operating system. It is a replacement for the old employment service computer system that will be fully integrated with America's Job Bank. It runs on the same Oracle database and has the same look and feel for customers. We would now like to move the profiling screens into the WINS system. This would provide a first step toward our one-stop operating system. It would be available for everybody in the workforce center to do their business and to get used to starting people through the system at the big end of the Vollman wedge.

I really want to emphasize that the comments made earlier about FDSS are extremely important, and I appeal for a strong self-service component to that since we are moving so many services to self-service. The management role of FDSS should also be appreciated, it will permit us to properly serve the person who is walking in the door, and to treat customers in a consistent way.

Postscript

WIA operations officially began in all states during July 2000. As we go to press with this conference volume in early 2002, we are pleased that the chapters remain timely and relevant. The conference held in spring of 1999 anticipated many of the challenges of WIA implementation. Many states are still grappling with practical implementation issues. Few have completely achieved unified computer operating systems for one-stop centers, and most states are still searching for ways to properly blend various administrative funding streams and coordinate staff responsibilities across programs.

Starting in late 2000, several areas of the country began to experience a deterioration in labor market conditions. This has placed additional unanticipated burdens on staff in one-stop centers during the transition to full WIA operations. The ideas presented in this book for targeting services and improving tools for frontline staff offer a means to achieve and maintain a high level of program effectiveness during periods of high demand for employment services.

The W.E. Upjohn Institute for Employment Research is working closely with the U.S. Department of Labor and the states of Georgia and Washington to pilot test FDSS tools in selected one-stop centers. To help other states develop FDSS features we plan to provide documentation of the pilot(s) and, possibly, a technical assistance guide. With sufficient interest from states, a technical assistance training session on the experience of the pilot activities will also be provided.

The Authors

David E. Balducchi is chief of pilots and demonstrations at the Employment and Training Administration's Office of Policy and Research.

Timothy J. Bartik is a senior economist at the W.E. Upjohn Institute for Employment Research.

Jacob Benus is executive director and vice president of IMPAQ International, LLC, Baltimore, Maryland.

Mark C. Berger is the William B. Sturgill professor of economics and director of the Center for Business and Economic Research at the University of Kentucky.

Dexter Chu is a developer at Infusion Development Corporation, New York, New York.

Terry Colpitts is the chief of continuous evaluation within Evaluation and Data Development of Human Resource Development Canada.

Paul T. Decker is a senior economist at Mathematica Policy Research, Inc.

Kelly DeRango is a research fellow at the W.E. Upjohn Institute for Employment Research.

Ketherine Dickinson is president of Social Policy Research Associates, Menlo Park, California.

Randall W. Eberts is executive director of the W.E. Upjohn Institute for Employment Research.

Jim Finch is deputy director of Workforce Information and Payment Services for the state of Utah.

397

Lloyd E. Fleming is the director of the Office of Workforce Security at the Atlanta Regional Office of ETA.

Wayne S. Gordon is a lead manpower analyst for the Employment and Training Administration of the U.S. Department of Labor.

John Heinberg is a research team leader for the Employment and Training Administration's Office of Workforce Security.

Harold Henson is acting evaluation manager of EI programs Human Resource Development Canada.

Richard A. Hobbie is the unemployment insurance director for the National Association of State Workforce Agencies (formerly ICESA).

Kevin Hollenbeck is a senior economist at the W.E. Upjohn Institute for Employment Research.

Louis S. Jacobson is manager of labor studies at Westat, Inc.

Al Jaloviar is deputy administrator of the UI Division of the Department of Workforce Development for the state of Wisconsin.

Marisa L. Kelso was a consultant to the U.S. Department of Labor when her chapter was written. She is currently a senior manager for Novartis Pharmaceuticals Corporation.

Daniel H. Klepinger is an economist and senior research scientist at Battelle Memorial Institute's Centers for Public Health Research and Evaluation.

Suzanne D. Kreutzer is a senior social scientist at Social Policy Research Associates in Menlo Park, California.

Robert J. LaLonde is a professor at the Harris Graduate School of Public Policy Studies at the University of Chicago.

Jon C. Messenger is a senior research officer in the Conditions of Work Branch at the International Labour Office in Geneva, Switzerland.

Chuck O. Middlebrooks was deputy executive director of unemployment insurance for the South Carolina Employment Security Commission when his chapter was written. He is now retired and a consultant.

Walter Nicholson is a professor of economics at Amherst College in Amherst, Massachusetts.

Donald Oellerich is the deputy chief economist in the Office of the Assistant Secretary for Planning and Evaluation, U.S. Department of Health and Human Services.

Christopher J. O'Leary is a senior economist at the W.E. Upjohn Institute for Employment Research and a member of the National Academy of Social Insurance.

Rob Olsen is an economist with Mathematica Policy Research, Inc.

Helen N. Parker is assistant commissioner for employment services at the Georgia Department of Labor.

Marc Perrett is workforce partnership liaison for the Oregon Employment Department.

Carolyn Peterson-Vaccaro is executive deputy director, New York State Governor's Office, Division for Women.

Anu Rangarajan is associate director of research and a senior economist at Mathematica Policy Research, Inc.

Arun S. Roy is chief of employment insurance policy evaluation at Human Resource Development Canada.

Peter Z. Schochet is a senior economist with Mathematica Policy Research, Inc.

Jeffrey A. Smith is an associate professor of economics at the University of Maryland.

Daniel G. Sullivan is economic adviser and vice president in the Economic Research Department of the Federal Reserve Bank of Chicago.

Wayne Vroman is an economist at the Urban Institute.

Stephen A. Wandner is director of research and demonstration for the Employment and Training Administration of the United States Department of Labor.

Jennifer L. Warlick is an associate professor in the Department of Economics at the University of Notre Dame.

Jack Weidenbach is director of the Workforce Wage Assistance Branch of the Minnesota Department of Economic Security.

Ging Wong is director of policy capacity in the Privy Council Office of the government of Canada.

"Targeting Employment Services"
Conference Attendees

Rod Anderson
W.E. Upjohn Institute for Employment Research
Kalamazoo, Michigan

Margo Arcanin
U.S. Department of Labor/ETA
San Francisco, California

John Beverly
U.S. Employment Service, U.S. Department of Labor
Washington, D.C.

Janet Bloomfield
Michigan Works!
Lansing, Michigan

David Dombrosky
Cuyahoga Work and Training
Cleveland, Ohio

George Erickcek
W.E. Upjohn Institute for Employment Research
Kalamazoo, Michigan

Barbara Flaherty
Employment Security Department
Olympia, Washington

Scott Gibbons
Unemployment Insurance Service, U.S. Department of Labor
Washington, D.C.

Chuck Hartfiel
Minnesota Department of Economic Security
St. Paul, Minnesota

Jim Hegman
Minnesota Department of Economic Security
St. Paul, Minnesota

H. Allan Hunt
W.E. Upjohn Institute for Employment Research
Kalamazoo, Michigan

Eric Johnson
Workforce Investment Act Transition Team, U.S. Department of Labor
Washington, D.C.

Carole Kitti
Office of Management & Budget
Washington, D.C.

Ken Kline
W.E. Upjohn Institute for Employment Research
Kalamazoo, Michigan

Roger LaBonte
Calhoun Intermediate School District
Marshall, Michigan

Gerardo Lara
U.S. Department of Labor
Chicago, Illinois

Susana LaRiccia
Cuyahoga Work & Training
Cleveland, Ohio

Ann Lordeman
Library of Congress, Congressional Research Service
Washington, D.C.

Daniel P. McMillen
Tulane University
New Orleans, Louisiana

Mike Miller
Unemployment Insurance Service, U.S. Department of Labor
Washington, D.C.

Richard Muller
U.S. Department of Labor/ETA
Washington, D.C.

Lyle Neumann
Department of Commerce and Community Affairs
Springfield, Illinois

Brenda Njiwaji
MDCD—Employment Service Agency
Detroit, Michigan

Edward Retka
Minnesota Department of Economic Security
St. Paul, Minnesota

James Rohn
Cuyahoga Work and Training
Cleveland, Ohio

Kathy Sweeney
Minnesota Department of Economic Security
St. Paul, Minnesota

Teri VanHoomissen
Minnesota Department of Economic Security
St. Paul, Minnesota

James Vollman
ALMIS, U.S. Department of Labor
Washington, D.C.

Robert P. Welsh
Ohio Bureau of Employment Services
Columbus, Ohio

Tom West
Michigan Employment Security Agency
Lansing, Michigan

Jack Wheatley
Michigan Unemployment Agency
Detroit, Michigan

Diane Wood
U.S. Department of Labor
Washington, D.C. 20210

Stephen A. Woodbury
W.E. Upjohn Institute for Employment Research
Kalamazoo, Michigan

Richard Wyrwa
W.E. Upjohn Institute for Employment Research
Kalamazoo, Michigan

Cited Author Index

The italic letters *f*, *n*, and *t* following a page number indicate that the cited name is within a figure, note, or table, respectively, on that page.

Subject Index

The italic letters *f*, *n*, and *t* following a page number indicate that the cited name is within a figure, note, or table, respectively, on that page.

About the Institute

The W.E. Upjohn Institute for Employment Research is a nonprofit research organization devoted to finding and promoting solutions to employment-related problems at the national, state, and local levels. It is an activity of the W.E. Upjohn Unemployment Trustee Corporation, which was established in 1932 to administer a fund set aside by the late Dr. W.E. Upjohn, founder of The Upjohn Company, to seek ways to counteract the loss of employment income during economic downturns.

The Institute is funded largely by income from the W.E. Upjohn Unemployment Trust, supplemented by outside grants, contracts, and sales of publications. Activities of the Institute comprise the following elements: 1) a research program conducted by a resident staff of professional social scientists; 2) a competitive grant program, which expands and complements the internal research program by providing financial support to researchers outside the Institute; 3) a publications program, which provides the major vehicle for disseminating the research of staff and grantees, as well as other selected works in the field; and 4) an Employment Management Services division, which manages most of the publicly funded employment and training programs in the local area.

The broad objectives of the Institute's research, grant, and publication programs are to 1) promote scholarship and experimentation on issues of public and private employment and unemployment policy, and 2) make knowledge and scholarship relevant and useful to policymakers in their pursuit of solutions to employment and unemployment problems.

Current areas of concentration for these programs include causes, consequences, and measures to alleviate unemployment; social insurance and income maintenance programs; compensation; workforce quality; work arrangements; family labor issues; labor-management relations; and regional economic development and local labor markets.